Where is the Fear of GOD?

Losing the Treasure of the Lord

by
Charles von Hammerstein

More Abundant Life
San Jose, California

WHERE is the Fear of GOD?
Losing the Treasure of the Lord
by Charles von Hammerstein

Published by:
More Abundant Life
Post Office Box 24526
San Jose, CA 95154 USA
www.MoreAbundantLife.com

All rights reserved. This book or parts thereof may not be reproduced in any form, stored in a retrieval system, or transmitted in any form by any means — electronic, mechanical, photocopy, recording, or otherwise — without prior written permission from the author, except for the inclusion of brief quotations in a review.

All scripture references are proudly and with great assurance of the truth taken from the King James Bible (KJB) — the finest and most accurate translation available anywhere, bar none. Its accuracy and fidelity to the original manuscripts is without compare among any modern version and can easily be proven to be so. "Where the word of a king *is, there is* power" (Ecc 8:4).

Copyright © 2010 by Charles von Hammerstein.
First Printing 2010

Publisher's Cataloging-in-Publication
(Provided by Quality Books, Inc.)

von Hammerstein, Charles.
Where is the Fear of God?. Losing the Treasure of the Lord /
by Charles von Hammerstein.
p. cm.
Includes bibliographical references and index.
Library of Congress Control Number: 2009913447
Soft Cover ISBN: 0-9760302-3-2 / 978-0-9760302-3-2
Hard Cover ISBN: 0-9760302-4-1 / 978-0-9760302-4-9
1. God (Christianity)—Worship and love. 2. Fear of God—Christianity.
3. Fear of God—Biblical teaching. 4. Judgment of God.
I. Title. II. Title: Losing the Treasure of the Lord.

BV4817.V665 2010   248.4   QBI09-3686

Printed in the United States of America

Selah

And fear not them which kill the body,
but are not able to kill the soul:

but rather fear him which is able to destroy both soul and body in hell.
fear him which is able to destroy both soul and body in hell. Mt 10:28

And his mercy is on them that fear him
from generation to generation. Lk 1:50

O that there were such an heart in them,
that they would fear me,

and keep all my commandments always,
that it might be well with them,
and with their children for ever! Dt 5:29

Table of Contents

Dedicatory:	To Awaken the Church	10
Chapter 1.	Why We Forsake the Fear of the LORD	20
Chapter 2.	Cheap Imitations and Artificial Substitutes	40
Chapter 3.	Feigned Faith, Forgotten Name, False Profession	62
Chapter 4.	The Fear of GOD, The Singular Issue of the Heart	82
Chapter 5.	Toward a More Godly, Faithful, and Perfect Heart	100
Chapter 6.	Broken Fellowship from the Loss of God's Fear	122
Chapter 7.	Holiness, Righteousness, & Faithfulness to God	144
Chapter 8.	The Root of Worship and Fruit of Giving	168
Chapter 9.	The Way of Brokenness and God's Fear	190
Chapter 10.	The Testings of the Fear of the LORD	214
Chapter 11.	Warning Signs of Losing God's Fear	230
Appendix I.	Definition of Some Biblical Terms	254
Appendix II.	The Fear of God and Unbelievers	272
Appendix III.	The Scriptures on Fearing God	294
Content Index:	Finding A Specific Topic	308
Thanksgiving:	The Fruit of Our Labors	316
An Epilogue:	A Spirit of Supplanting	318
Resources:	Table for the Hungry	330

Tables

Table 2-1	The Characteristics of Samarianism	54
Table 2-2	The Counterfeiting of What is Real	61
Table 5-1	How His Fear Changes our Heart	120
Table 6-1	Servants of God who were Feared	141
Table 10-1	Testings of the Fear of the LORD	215
Table 11-1	Signs of Losing the Fear of God	231
Table 11-2	Those who Lack the Fear of God	241

Format notes:

1. In quotations where clarifying notes or pronoun changes have been needed these are always enclosed in square brackets to signal the reader. <u>Underlining</u> and **bolding** of certain words have been added for emphasis to help the reader know what is being drawn from the scripture. Where the KJB uses *italics* or small caps (e.g. LORD) these have been preserved.

2. The definitions for certain Hebrew and Greek words have been included for clarity or amplification. These are always taken from the Strong's definition of Hebrew and Greek words,[1] except where noted for English definitions. When the Strong's definition is for a phrase or a longer definition they are enclosed in single quotes ('this is an example'). Where Strong's uses italics in the definition these have usually been preserved. When the Strong's number is supplied it is either Hnnnn or Gnnnn, where H is for Hebrew words & G is for Greek.

3. Outside of quotes, italics are sometimes used to emphasis certain words.

---

[1] Strong, James, <u>Strong's Exhaustive Concordance</u>, Compact Edition, Grand Rapids, Michigan, Baker Book House, 1984.

Abundant Blessings

This book uncovers why we lose the precious gift of the fear of God, which the Spirit plants in every one of our hearts as soon as we are born again. This book is the second of a two-part set on discovering "Where is the Fear of GOD?" We cannot look at the fear of God and not touch so many other areas of our heart and life in Christ. As a result there are found an abundant supply of blessings on many different subjects that many would not even consider when thinking about the fear of God. Hence, let me enumerate a few of them so that you may refer to this book when needed. In these pages we will specially discuss:

- The banner of brokenness
- The heart of integrity & friendship
- A detailed list of beguiling counterfeits
- How the fear of God changes how we worship
- Why we need not be ashamed of the name of Jesus
- Heart surgeries the fear of God needs to perform on us
- Warnings on losing God's fear from Good Kings Gone Bad
- How to prevent the Pharisee spirit from taking root in our heart
- The foundation of being correctable in our relationship with the Lord
- Unveiling the religion of the Samarians that exists in Christianity today

The previous book, <u>Where is the Fear of GOD? Finding the Treasure of the Lord</u>,[2] uncovers the hidden balance of grace, the strength to overcome besetting sins, and the source of intimacy that we so often long for from our heavenly Father. It particularly covers the following areas:

- Understanding the work of the Spirit of God through the Candlestick
- The Fear of God is the doorway to mercy and the way of peace
- Revealing the Salt of the Covenant: the Fear of the LORD
- Renewing ourselves with the washing of repentance
- Learn the hidden wisdom that defeats the enemy
- Why Satan hates the fear of God so much
- How to be intimate with the Lord GOD
- Should we fear God as our Father?

---

[2] Where a relevant subject is covered in the other book it will be referred to in short as <u>Finding the Treasure of the Lord</u>.

Dedicatory: To Awaken the Church
The Darkness of the Days
"For, behold, the darkness shall cover the earth, and gross darkness the people: but the LORD shall arise upon thee, and his glory shall be seen upon thee." Isa 60:2

We are living in the greatest hour of darkness the world has ever known. Wickedness is increasing in an explosive manner. All the prophecies of Jesus have come to pass with chilling accuracy (Mt 24:7+): wars and rumors of wars, nation rising against nation and kingdom against kingdom, famines, pestilences, and earthquakes all in diverse places. Many are being offended by the truth and are betraying one another. Many are forsaking the things of God and are speaking evil of those who truly stand for the kingdom of God, and are hating one another. Many false prophets are arising in the church, and are deceiving many with smooth words. False Christ's and false prophets have appeared who show great signs and wonders and deceive God's elect. Iniquity is abounding and the love of many is waxing cold. Many are not enduring the persecution, affliction, and tribulation that come with truly following Jesus Christ. Many are not enduring sound doctrine, but after their own desires are they accumulating teachers for themselves who will teach them what they want to hear. "And they shall turn away *their* ears from the truth, and shall be turned unto fables." 2Tim 4:3-4

> Yet, in complete blindness to all that is taking place in the spiritual realm, much of the church is perfecting the Laodicean spirit. They are neither cold, nor hot ...

The most grievous of all these things is the apostasy from truth that is sweeping the church. So many are falling from the faith that is founded on sound doctrine. True faith comes by hearing and hearing the word of God. Yet, there is a faith of the Christian masses that bears little resemblance to biblical faith. James had to warn his fellow believers in his day of erring from truth.

> Do not err, my beloved brethren. Brethren, if any of you do err from the truth, and one convert him; Let him know, that he which converteth the sinner from the error of his way shall save a soul from death, and shall hide a multitude of sins.[3] Jam 1:16, 5:19

The word 'err' in the Greek means 'to *roam* (from safety, truth, or virtue)'. As the last days increase in darkness and wickedness I have seen more and more beloved brethren "being led away with the error of the wicked" and fall from their own stedfastness (2Pe 3:17). Yet, in complete blindness to all that is taking place in the spiritual realm, much of the church is perfecting the Laodicean spirit. They are neither cold, nor hot, but are lukewarm – they offend no one at all. They are neither too cold to some, not too hot to others. They are filled with easy compromise, in order to offend no one at all. The true Jesus, on the other hand, was made "a stone of stumbling, and a rock of offence, *even to them* which stumble at the word" (1Pe 2:7-8).

Today you cannot tell the lost from the found. They all dress alike, speak alike, pursue the same goals, watch the same programs, and go to all the same places, yet the saved are not called to be the same as the world. The saved are called to be "an holy nation, a peculiar people" (1Pe 2:9). They are not to blend in with the nation they live in. They are called as a peculiar people to be holy (i.e. set apart) and to have such a uniqueness or 'peculiarity' that they can rightly be called a nation or a people of their own. That is how very different the people of God are to be from those of this world. Ask yourself, "Does this describe me? Does it describe my church?"

---

[3] Note who James calls the sinner: the beloved brethren who are erring from the truth!

How can we do as the world does or worse yet pattern the church after the passing fads and fashions of this dying and corrupt world, when we are exhorted to be "strangers and pilgrims, [*who*] abstain from fleshly lusts, which war against the soul" (1Pe 2:11)? Are we even warring any more against the lusts and desires of this world, or have we succumbed to them? We are no longer to live "the rest of [*our*] time in the flesh to the lusts of men, but to the will of God." 1Pe 4:2 The old life we once had of living for the will of men and for the lusts of men should be long past, now that we are God's holy children. "For the time past of *our* life may suffice us to have wrought the will of the Gentiles, when we walked in lasciviousness, lusts, excess of wine, revellings, banquetings, and abominable idolatries" (1Pe 4:3).

The seeker-sensitive movement seeks to remove the offense of the gospel so that the world is able to easily mingle in our midst – with a comfortableness that sadly betrays how much they are still living just like them. The seeker-sensitive movement is destroying the true church as disciples are wooed from the foundation of sound doctrine into an easy-believism that caters to the desires of the flesh and soul. "Ye therefore, beloved, seeing ye know *these things* before, beware lest ye also, being led away with the error of the wicked, fall from your own stedfastness." 2Pe 3:17

> Is this the church's greatest hour as so many proclaim?
> Or is this the collapse of truth and the wholesale
> forsaking of sound doctrine?

On the contrary, the world ought to be surprised and testify how different and holily we live. "Wherein they think it strange that ye run not with *them* to the same excess of riot, speaking evil of *you*" (1Pe 4:4). People should think it *strange* that we do not live like them! Is this your heart, friend? Was this not the apostolic example left for us? "Ye *are* witnesses, and God *also,* how holily and justly and unblameably we behaved ourselves among you that believe" (1Th 2:10). How many that throng to the seeker-sensitive mega-churches are being instructed by sound doctrine to come out from among the heathen and not touch their ways? Consider Paul's exhortation to the Corinthians to come out from the world and be separate, and ask yourself this. Are the seeker-sensitive movement and the mega-church atmosphere more representative of Paul's spirit or of the Corinthian cosmopolitan spirit?

> Be ye not unequally yoked together with unbelievers: for what fellowship hath righteousness with unrighteousness? and what communion hath light with darkness? And what concord hath Christ with Belial? or what part hath he that believeth with an infidel? And what agreement hath the temple of God with idols? for ye are the temple of the living God; as God hath said, I will dwell in them, and walk in *them;* and I will be their God, and they shall be my people.

Dedicatory – To Awaken the Church

> Wherefore <u>come out from among them</u>, and <u>be ye separate</u>, saith the Lord, and <u>touch not the unclean</u> *thing;* and I will receive you, And will be a Father unto you, and ye shall be my sons and daughters, saith the Lord Almighty. Having therefore these promises, dearly beloved, let us cleanse ourselves from all filthiness of the flesh and spirit, perfecting holiness in the fear of God. 2Co 6:14-7:1

We are commanded to be perfected in holiness in the fear of God. Therefore we must ask, "Where is the fear of God? Where are the men who are teaching it? Are we really being perfected or matured in the true fear of God that causes us to come out from every unclean thing and to be God's holy, separated children?" That is the root of what we have lost in our modern popular Christianity. We have forsaken pleasing God, for pleasing people. We are seeing the richest believers in church history in America, yet poverty embraces the world, and Jesus would say that the American church is destitute and poor. The American church says, "I am rich" and "I am increased with goods, and have need of nothing", yet as Jesus says, thou "knowest not that thou art wretched, and miserable, and poor, and blind, and naked" (Rev 3:17).

Where are God's Called Out and Separated People?

"But ye are a chosen generation, a royal priesthood, an holy nation, a peculiar people; that ye should shew forth the praises of him who hath called you out of darkness into his marvellous light:" 1Pe 2:9

Is this the church's greatest hour as so many proclaim? Or is this the collapse of truth and the wholesale forsaking of sound doctrine? So many believe this is the church's greatest hour and point to the incredible success of the mega-churches, drawing their tens of thousands. On top of all this and despite all the facts to the contrary, so many of those who try to hold to conservative Biblical doctrine still believe it is impossible to fall away. Truly, Satan is having his way in the church, deceiving both the liberal nad the conservative, and no one is taking warning from the scriptures about the times we are in. Paul was NOT speaking of the world when he wrote this warning by the Spirit; he was speaking of the church,

> This know also, that in the last days perilous times shall come. For men shall be lovers of their own selves, covetous, boasters, proud, blasphemers, disobedient to parents, unthankful, unholy, Without natural affection, trucebreakers, false accusers, incontinent, fierce, despisers of those that are good, Traitors, heady, highminded, lovers of pleasures more than lovers of God; Having a form of godliness, but denying the power thereof: from such turn away. For of this sort are they which creep into houses, and lead captive silly women laden with sins, led away with divers lusts, Ever learning, and never able to come to the knowledge of the truth. 2Tim 3:1-7

Where is the Fear of GOD? Losing the Treasure of the Lord

The world has always been corrupt, but God cannot endure when his people become his enemy because they love what is evil. (See Isa 63:9-10.) God's people will be trucebreakers; they will not keep the covenant of peace which they have received. God's people will become traitors, even as Jesus warned this was one of the signs of his coming. "And then shall many be offended, and shall <u>betray</u> one another, and shall hate one another." Mt 24:10 Remember, the born again saint does not have friends who are unsaved, and Jesus said, "And ye shall be betrayed both by parents, and brethren, and kinsfolks, and <u>friends</u>; and *some* of you shall they cause to be put to death." Lk 21:16

> **WARNING**: The lost have always been lovers of their own selves, covetous, boasters, proud, blasphemers, disobedient to parents, unthankful, unholy. That would be no revelation from the Spirit at all. No, what the Spirit reveals *expressly* for the last days is that God's own people will fulfill these things! God's own people would begin to love their own pleasures rather than pleasing the true and living God. Religion would become another convenience item. This is why the judgment draws nigh, because of the corruption of the sons of God.

This is the hour of apostasy that we are in. The church is ever learning, but never coming to the knowledge of the truth. Remember what is truth? Jesus said, "I am ... the truth" (Jn 14:6) and, "Sanctify them through thy truth: thy word is truth." Jn 17:17 Where is the sanctifying of the people of God today? The church has become "lovers of their own selves" and "lovers of pleasures <u>more than</u> lovers of God". Notice it does not say lovers of pleasures *rather* than lovers of God, but lovers of pleasures <u>more than</u> lovers of God. The warning of the Spirit is that people will still "love God". It's just that they will love what **they** love more!

God's people "have forsaken [God] the fountain of living waters, *and* hewed them out cisterns, broken cisterns, that can hold no water" (Jer 2:13). Is it any wonder that they should have "a form of godliness" but deny the power thereof? What we love most will most affect us and most shape us. If we love God more than all, then the power of godliness will shape us into his image, but if we love our ways, our desires, our thoughts, or our pleasures more than him who gave us life, then we will be misshapen by the idols we serve, and the power of God will be denied in our life.

Paul warns of this falling away again and again in his letters and it is always related to departing from the faith and betraying the Lord. "Let no man deceive you by any means: for *that day shall not come*, except there come <u>a falling away first</u>, and that man of sin be revealed, the son of perdition" (2Th 2:3). Men have their libraries of books about "the son of perdition" being the coming antichrist "who opposeth and exalteth himself above all that is called God, or that is worshipped; so that he as God sitteth in the temple of God, shewing himself that he is God." 2Th 2:4 Now there is a real beast, a real false prophet, and a specific antichrist that is coming, as revealed in Revelation. But we too often focus on them to the exclusion of what will precede their coming.

False Prophets shall Flourish

There will be many false prophets, and increasingly so, as the age draws to a close. Jesus warned us that one of the signs of the end of the age would be the arising of many false prophets who would come and deceive God's people. "And <u>many</u> false prophets shall rise, and shall deceive many." Mt 24:11 And look how they come. They will 'arise' – speaking of their great popularity. They will be loved of all men. But Jesus is not concerned about the false prophets of other religions. They have always been around. No, Jesus is concerned primarily about warning us of those who will look like sheep!

Remember, he said, "Beware of false prophets, which come to you <u>in sheep's clothing</u>, but inwardly they are ravening wolves." Mt 7:15 They will appear as good Christians (i.e. as sheep). They will rise in popularity, and all men will speak well of them – for this is the mark of a false prophet (Lk 6:26)! "Beloved, believe not every spirit, but try the spirits whether they are of God: because many false prophets are gone out into the world." 1Jn 4:1

Men Living as Brute Beasts

The Bible speaks of those in the church who will forsake the Spirit and will follow after their own desires. They will be self-willed, presumptuous, and walk after fleshly desires. They will despise authority and accountability to the truth of the Word. What they know they will know naturally and not spiritually. There will be many walking as beasts and increasingly so as the age draws to a close.

> But chiefly them that walk after the flesh in the lust of uncleanness, and despise government. Presumptuous *are they*, selfwilled, they are not afraid to speak evil of dignities. But these, as natural <u>brute beasts</u>, made to be taken and destroyed, speak evil of the things that they understand not; and shall utterly perish in their own corruption 2Pe 2:10,12

> But these speak evil of those things which they know not: but what they know naturally, as <u>brute beasts</u>, in those things they corrupt themselves. Jude 1:10

Paul dealt with such men many a time and had to warn his sons in the faith of them. "One of themselves, *even* a prophet of their own, said, The Cretians *are* alway liars, <u>evil beasts</u>, slow bellies." Tit 1:12 Most think Paul is referring to wild animals when he tells the Corinthians of his dangers and speaks of having to fight with beasts at Ephesus (1Co 15:32). But Ephesus was a civilized metropolis where there were no wild animals. It is unlikely he is referring to anything but carnal believers who refused to submit to the truth. Such men like

"Alexander the coppersmith [*who*] did me much evil: the Lord reward him according to his works." 2Tim 4:14 Paul had to contend with their lower or beastly nature. Strong's definition of 'beasts' bears this out: '(figurative) to *encounter* (furious men)'.

The Anti-Christ Explosion

There will also be many antichrists and increasingly so as the age draws to a close. Jesus warned us as the first sign of the end of the age of such antichrists.

> Take heed that no man deceive you. For many shall come in my name, saying, I am Christ; and shall deceive many. For there shall arise false Christs, and false prophets, and shall shew great signs and wonders; insomuch that, if *it were* possible, they shall <u>deceive the very elect</u>. Mt 24:4-5,24

When Jesus says those who will come will say "I am Christ", he is not saying as so many suppose that they will claim to be Christ, for the disciples of Jesus Christ would never need to be warned about being deceived by such outright lies. No, the subtlety of Satan's work of deception is that he will send wolves in sheep's clothing (Ac 20:29, Mt 7:15). He will plant tares amidst the wheat (Mt 13:25-27). He will manifest false signs and lying wonders (2Th 2:9) – whatever has the outward appearance of light but is inward corruption. "And no marvel; for Satan himself is transformed into an angel of light. Therefore *it is* no great thing if his ministers also be transformed as the ministers of righteousness; whose end shall be according to their works." 2Co 11:14-15

These antichrists or imposters are those who in their own life will say "Jesus is the Christ", but will walk contrary to him and teach what is contrary to his Word. Many of God's people are being deceived in this day and hour by those claiming "Jesus is the Christ" (i.e. that they are Christians) but who spew out false doctrine. This is what Paul spoke of to warn Titus. "They profess that they know God; but in works they deny *him*, being abominable, and disobedient, and unto every good work reprobate." Tit 1:16 John the beloved speaks much of these antichrists. He said we would know that it is the last time by the many antichrists that come as deceivers (1Jn 2:18, 2Jn 1:7).

John defines for us who these antichrists are. They are those who confess not that Jesus Christ is come in the flesh (1Jn 4:3, 2Jn 1:7), meaning they will deny that we must walk as Jesus walked, by crucifying our flesh and denying ungodliness a place in our life. "He that saith he abideth in him <u>ought</u> himself also so to walk, even as he walked." 1Jn 2:6 Now the word 'ought' means 'to owe, to *be under obligation*, to have a duty'. We have a duty and an obligation, a debt of love, that if we claim to live in Jesus (i.e. if we claim to be saved and made alive through the new birth), then we must walk even as Jesus walked.

We cannot say (except for his payment for our sins) that, "O that was for Jesus. I don't need to do that." Yet, this is exactly what the antichrist spirit does. It rejects that Jesus is come in the flesh and that we must walk as he walked. Antichrists are liars and deceivers who will deny the Father and the Son (1Jn 2:22). What does it mean to deny the Father and the Son? Surely some will openly contradict or hiddenly reject or deny the doctrine of the trinity, but this is not John's first concern. His first concern here is that they will deny and reject the Father and the Son their authority to judge. This is their authority as God and as King to rule our lives by the Word. If their authority is denied, there can be no fear of God.

Sons of Perdition

In each case (the beast, the false prophet, and the antichrist), we note two things. First, before the final embodiment of each comes, there will be many who come. Second, these are false brethren who appear as ministers of righteousness but are actually ministers of unrighteousness, which are tares among the wheat. Is not this then what Paul is primarily warning the Thessalonians of concerning "the son of perdition"? By John's definition an antichrist is anyone who claims to be in Jesus but does not walk as Jesus walked – thus, by their lifestyle, denying that Jesus came to enable us to walk in holiness and righteousness here on the earth in the flesh. These are those who oppose and exalt themselves "above all that is called God, or that is worshipped; so that [they] as God [sit] in the temple of God, shewing [themselves] that [they are] God." 2Th 2:4

> The scripture is crystal clear on this: a great falling away must take place in the church before the Lord's return. Some of the elect shall deny the faith

So many today look for a natural temple to be rebuilt, but **WE** are the temple of God. "Know ye not that ye are the temple of God, and *that* the Spirit of God dwelleth in you?" 1Co 3:16 The sons of perdition are people who have been born again, become the temple of God by being indwelt with the Holy Spirit, but who in their life begin to deny the lordship of Jesus by which they were saved. They begin following the Lord and through faithfulness even receive authority from the Lord to do his works, like Judas and Hymenaeus. But they begin, like them, to have their own motives, their own way of looking at things, their own goals and purposes, and they betray the Lord. It all begins by rejecting Jesus' lordship and beginning to follow our own way of thinking. In doing so, the sons of perdition oppose God by refusing his Word. They exalt themselves again as lord of their own lives, being their own authority. As such they show themselves to be god of their own life, or as Paul put it, "so that he as God sitteth in the temple of God, shewing himself that he is God." Friend, who makes the decisions in your life indicates who is God of your life.

True apostles and holy prophets who build the foundation of the church will always be hated, despised, and not well loved, because they will contend with beasts in the church. They will expose the antichrist spirit that is operating in the lives of believers! This is the constant warning of all the apostles, from Paul, to John, to James, to Peter, even to Jude, to warn the brethren to hold to the truth, to "continue thou in the things which thou hast learned and hast been assured of" (2Tim 3:14). The scripture is crystal clear on this: a great falling away must take place in the church before the Lord's return. And in that falling away some of the elect shall deny the faith they once had.

> Now the Spirit speaketh expressly, that in the latter times some shall depart from the faith, giving heed to seducing spirits, and doctrines of devils; Speaking lies in hypocrisy; having their conscience seared with a hot iron 1Tim 4:1-2

The Call to Return

"All the rivers run into the sea; yet the sea is not full; unto the place from whence the rivers come, thither they return again." Ecc 1:7

The fear of the LORD is our call to return to the Lord himself, not for what we can get, but because he *is* the beginning, the source of all we hope for and desire. The fear of God is that instinctual driving force, that call of our spiritual nature beckoning us all from seeking after our ways to return to him. When we were first birthed into the kingdom of God we were born into the pure freshwaters of the word of God. We were birthed in the river of life. "And he shewed me a pure river of water of life, clear as crystal, proceeding out of the throne of God and of the Lamb." Rev 22:1

But so many of us leave that narrow and tribulation-filled way in seeking after more spacious and seemingly peaceful places. The sea is an enticing place where the mere expanse of its openness and freedom can be intoxicating – once we lose our fear! All waters continually flow toward the deep abyss of the sea. We find ourselves migrating slowly to its broad expanse only to find that the purity and freshness of the stream is lost, traded for the cloudy salinity of the waters that cover the earth. Many never make it back to the purity of the streams that flow from the mountain snows, yet it is the calling in every heart to return and find that most needful part. David said, *"If* I ... dwell in the uttermost parts of the sea; Even there shall thy hand lead me, and thy right hand shall hold me." Ps 139:9-10

But where does his right hand lead us? Back to that confined and narrow place from which we began, only to labor upstream hundreds of miles all against the currents of mighty waters. For what, to arrive beaten and battered having suffered the loss of all things? Yes, "for the excellency of the knowledge of Christ Jesus my Lord: for whom I have suffered the loss of all things" (Php 3:8)! We will indeed suffer the loss of all things in order to return to the purity of the waters that issue forth from the throne of his authority. "For thus saith the LORD, Behold, I will extend peace to her like <u>a river</u>" (Isa 66:12). The peace that he extends to each of us is not a peaceful river, but a peace that can only be found as we fight our embattled way back up that river. To return to these pure waters is to labor to return to the door of salvation – the Lordship of Jesus Christ. "Let us <u>labour</u> therefore to enter into that rest, lest any man fall after the same example of unbelief." Heb 4:11 True faith will cause us to labor to draw near to God. It will cause us to diligently seek him (Heb 11:6).

We all must return to the subjection of the Lamb that sits upon the throne. We are saved by making Jesus Lord of our life, yet it is too easy to drift from this narrow gate into the place where we choose our own way again, where he is effectively no longer Lord of our life, but we are. In that case, we may believe, but we no longer follow; we are adrift. We will have to fight against the flood of our own desires, as well as those of others. We will have to swim against the many deep, dark, and murky waters of the traditions and commandments of men. We must hear his call to return to him, for deep calls unto deep (Ps 42:7). This is the way to return to the purity of the Word. We must return to the waters that flow from the throne of the Lamb that was slain, but is alive. We must return to the word of God that issues out from his authority. Our return to the spawning grounds will be a journey where death is constantly set before us, and the fear of losing **our** life in the pursuit of his holiness must be willingly cast aside. It is back we must go to "the streams whereof shall make glad the city of God" (Ps 46:4).

We will find that we were birthed in the spirit of the fear of the LORD and it is to that holy place that we must return – the beginning of the Lord's work in us. Have you ever wondered why the very eyes of our beloved Lord are by the rivers of waters? "His eyes *are* as *the eyes* of doves <u>by the rivers of waters</u>, washed with milk, *and* fitly set." Song 5:12 Because he is waiting for us to return there. He has made "a way in the sea, and a path in the mighty waters" (Isa 43:16). Let us return and recapture the fear of the LORD, which has been lost.

And the Spirit and the bride say, Come.
And let him that heareth say, Come.
And let him that is athirst come.
And whosoever will,
let him take the
water of life freely. Rev 22:17

Chapter 1. Why We Forsake the Fear of the LORD
Losing our Heart to Serve God
"but he forsaketh the fear of the Almighty." Job 6:14

We start our new life in Christ with the spirit of the fear of the LORD, but we do not always keep what we have. As a man may have "cast away the law of the LORD of hosts, and despised the word of the Holy One of Israel" (Isa 5:24), so a man may do with the fear of God. Let us look at how the fear of God is cast away. We have record in the scriptures of those who had God's fear but lost it. Job in his discouragement looked for mercy and strength from his friends. He said, "To him that is afflicted pity *should be shewed* from his friend" (Job 6:14), but what he got instead was the false doctrine of the faith movement

1 – Why We Forsake the Fear of the LORD

that we have today: "Job, your sickness and troubles are because of sin in your life, your negative confessions, and your lack of faith."

Though many problems in our life *are* because of our sin or because we do not trust God and obey him, some problems have nothing to do what we have done or not done. As is evidenced in Job's case, they may in fact be the *result* of our trust in God and walking in righteousness with him. Job was falsely accused, judged, and condemned by those who were his God-believing friends! In doing so, Job says they had forsaken or let go of the fear of the Almighty (Job 6:14). God has left a record for us of those who forsook his fear among the kings of Judah. This nearly always occurred after God had prospered them. Through the magnitude of the victories into which he alone had led them, they allowed pride and self-importance to replace their fear of God.

Warnings from Good Kings Gone Bad

*"And now, Israel, what doth the LORD thy God require of thee,
but to fear the LORD thy God, to walk in all his ways, and to love him,
and to serve the LORD thy God with all thy heart and with all thy soul" Dt 10:12*

We may ask, "What do the kings of Israel or Judah have to do with me? I am certainly not a king, nor of Judah." But you are, dear saint! He "hath made us kings and priests unto God and his Father; to him *be* glory and dominion for ever and ever. Amen." Rev 1:6 Again it is written, thou "hast made us unto our God kings and priests: and we shall reign on the earth." Rev 5:10 He has specifically called us to be kings unto our God. Therefore we must lay hold of the fear of God to keep our heart steadfast in our service to him. We must receive the warnings from the kings who have gone before us. Moreover, we follow the lion of the tribe of Judah (Rev 5:5), and we ourselves through the new covenant are made "the righteousness of God in him." 2Co 5:21 So we also are lions, for "the righteous are bold as a lion." Pr 28:1 Judah means 'praise', so if any people are the lions of Judah (i.e. the kings of praise), it is those of the new covenant who have so much to give praise for. We should take special warning from whatever tripped up and ensnared these kings.

If there was one thing that the LORD required of his people it was to fear him (Dt 10:12). This was even before walking in his ways, loving him, or serving him with all their heart and soul. This shows us the centrality of the fear of God and why God requires this first of his people. It is the fear of God which opens the door to walk in his ways, and to love him by walking in those ways, and to serve him in our love. Therefore, the fear of the LORD is the key. If we lose the fear of God, we will lose our heart and soul to walk in his ways, and to love him, and to serve him with everything we have.

Consider the following kings of Judah. These were not evil kings (initially), but good kings who God clearly moved on their behalf and who clearly trusted in the LORD. Later, they each lost their fear of God and fell away from him. Now God is no respecter of persons. If he judged them for losing their fear of God (even though they were his chosen kings), he must certainly also judge us (as his chosen kings) for losing the gift of the fear of God. Each has a different area of failure by which they lost their fear of God. Each will be instructive for us to take warning.

> Now all these things happened unto them for ensamples: and they are written for our admonition, upon whom the ends of the world are come. Wherefore let him that thinketh he standeth take heed lest he fall. 1Co 10:11-12

The Dangers of Losing God's Purpose
"That he may withdraw man from his purpose, and hide pride from man." Job 33:17

David was a man after God's own heart (1Sam 13:14). This was a man that was better than Saul (1Sam 15:28), a man that God was looking for (Ps 89:20). He is repeatedly called the servant of the Lord.[4] God said of him, "I have found David the son of Jesse, a man after mine own heart, which shall fulfil all my will." Ac 13:22 God gave to him the revelation of the Temple (which his son Solomon built), but it was in the heart of David to build a dwelling place for God. And when he could not build it, because he had set his affection for the house of his God, he set apart his gold and silver for the building of it (1Ch 29:3). His love for God cannot be matched by anyone in the Old Testament.

God delivered David time and time again from Saul who tried to kill him, not to mention also the Philistines and many other foreign armies. God miraculously delivered him from the giant Goliath, with but a sling. God delivered him from the rebellion of his own son, Absalom. He was the most humble of all the kings. He was the one most willing to repent. He was the greatest worshipper of God of all time. He was the one to whom God made the promise that one would sit on his throne for ever (1K 2:45, 9:5). He was the standard that all the kings of Judah were compared against.[5]

BUT David lost his fear of God most dramatically on two separate occasions. The first occurs when he was being pursued by King Saul and fearing for his life. David had trusted completely in God, and God had delivered him multiple times, but he was growing weary of running. "And David arose, and fled that day for fear of Saul, and went to Achish the king of Gath." 1Sam 21:10

---

[4] My servant David: 1Sam 23:10, 25:39, 2Sam 3:18, 7:5,8,20,26, 24:10, 1K 3:6, 8:24-26,66, 11:13,34-38, 14:8, 2K 8:19, 1Ch 17:4,7,18,24, 21:8, 2Ch 6:15-17,42, Ps 18:1, 36:1, 78:70, 89:3,20, 144:10, Jer 33:21-22,26, Eze 34:23-24, 37:24-25, Lk 1:69, Ac 4:25.

[5] "if thou wilt walk before me, as David thy father walked" (2Ch 7:17).

1 – Why We Forsake the Fear of the LORD

David left the promised land and the place of God's protection for a refuge of his own making. The fear of man pushed out the fear of God in David's life. He walked out of the fire and into the frying pan, so to speak. The Philistines would have loved to be able to get their hands on David and to kill him for 'slaying ten thousands' (of Philistines). This was why when later he was delivered miraculously from the clutches of the servants of the king of Gath he would write a psalm in commemoration of how he had lost his fear of God.

> I sought the LORD, and he heard me, and delivered me from <u>all my fears</u>. Ps 34:4

> The angel of the LORD encampeth round about them that <u>fear him</u>, and delivereth them. Ps 34:7

> O <u>fear the LORD</u>, ye his saints: for *there is* no want to them that <u>fear him</u>. Ps 34:9

> Come, ye children, hearken unto me: I will teach you <u>the fear of the LORD</u>. Ps 34:11

Thus, through God's deliverance, mercy, and forgiveness the fear of God was restored in David's life. We can rejoice with him in that, for there is hope also for us. Now he joyfully wanted to teach others the fear of God. He could now continually pray "Teach me thy way, O LORD; I will walk in thy truth: unite my heart to fear thy name." Ps 86:11 And he could sing in 'A Song of degrees':

> If thou, LORD, shouldest mark iniquities, O Lord, who shall stand? But *there is* forgiveness with thee, that thou mayest be feared. I wait for the LORD, my soul doth wait, and in his word do I hope. Ps 130:3-5

BUT the fear of God would be lost a second significant time in David's life. In being delivered from the power of evil men and those who abused authority, in having peace on all sides and his kingdom being established before God, in his idleness as he now surveyed the glory of what God had done through him, his heart was enticed to take another man's wife. He now forsook the fear of God and even covered his adultery by killing his own faithful soldier Uriah, Bath-sheba's husband, who was one of David's 30 mighty men (2Sam 23:24-39). The very act of jealousy of King Saul trying to put David to death, but which David had escaped by God's mercies, David now perpetrated on his own faithful servant Uriah. The hypocrisy was monumental.[6]

---

[6] In fact it was through this amazing hypocrisy that Nathan the prophet was able to catch David in the greatness of his transgression. For when Nathan tells David of the poor man who was unjustly robbed by the rich man, "David's anger was greatly kindled against the man; and he said to Nathan, As the LORD liveth, the man that hath done this *thing* shall surely die [*thus condemning himself*]: And he shall restore the lamb fourfold, because he did this thing, and because <u>he had no pity</u>." 2Sam 12:5-6 Clearly the poor man of Nathan's story was none other than Uriah the Hittite.

Where is the Fear of GOD? Losing the Treasure of the Lord

The effect is still felt today of David's sin.[7] Nathan said, "by this deed thou hast given great occasion to the enemies of the LORD to blaspheme" (2Sam 12:14a). This was a violation of all that God had done in David's life. This is why when Nathan the prophet came to rebuke David, he spoke for God saying,

> And I gave thee thy master's house, and thy master's wives into thy bosom, and gave thee the house of Israel and of Judah; and if *that had been* too little, I would moreover have given unto thee such and such things. 2Sam 12:8

From David's life we learn several sober warnings. First and most importantly is that any one can fall. "Wherefore let him that thinketh he standeth take heed lest he fall." 1Co 10:12 Secondly, we observe that the depth of one's worshipping of God is not sufficient of itself to keep one from great hypocrisy. Thus, from his own deep personal failure David could cry out,

> Who can understand *his* errors? cleanse thou me from secret *faults*. Keep back thy servant also from presumptuous *sins;* let them not have dominion over me: then shall I be upright, and I shall be innocent from the great transgression. Ps 19:12-13

This was why David said, "But as for me, I will come *into* thy house in the multitude of thy mercy: *and* <u>in thy fear</u> will I worship toward thy holy temple." Ps 5:7 Worship must be coupled with the fear of God. So David exhorts those "that fear the Lord, praise him" (Ps 22:23).

Third we learn that the fear of God must be continually maintained. And then when we lose it, we may do the very things we our self condemn and despise. We see this most clearly in David's instructions on learning the fear of God. Every one of his exhortations is active. Immediately after saying he will teach it to us (Ps 34:11), he says "Keep thy tongue from evil, and thy lips from speaking guile. Depart from evil, and do good; seek peace, and pursue it." Ps 34:13-14 Idleness is a dangerous thing, and we cannot allow it as good soldiers of Jesus Christ, lest we get distracted from keeping watch.

David stands as our first witness of the devastating and shameful effects of losing the fear of the Lord. But also David is the very one who gives us great hope, for he recaptures the fear of God, not once but twice, and is then used to teach others of God's fear. May we as partakers of the kingdom of David, of which Christ as the son of David is the head, learn from our forerunner.

---

[7] I have had men actually tell me they had no respect for a God who could forgive such a man as David for the wickedness of this act.

1 – Why We Forsake the Fear of the LORD

The Dangers of Blessings

"Better is little with the fear of the LORD than great treasure and trouble therewith." Pr 15:16

Solomon was beloved of his God (2Sam 12:24-25, Neh 13:26) and the LORD appeared unto him twice (1K 11:9). When asked for what he desired, he pleased God by not asking for himself long life, nor riches, nor for the life of his enemies, but for wisdom, knowledge and an understanding heart to judge God's people (1K 3:5-15).[8] As a result, God made him wiser than all men. Initially, "Solomon loved the LORD, walking in the statutes of David his father" (1K 3:3). Solomon even built the permanent temple of God and dedicated it by prayer and sacrifice (1K 5-8)!

BUT in the glory of God's blessings his heart was enticed by the very blessings which God gave him. God had specifically given charges to the kings of Israel what they were *not* to do, and as Solomon's heart began to drift from his singular heart of serving God's people, he lost his fear of God and broke every one of God's prohibitions to the kings! The king was not to multiply horses, nor was he to cause God's people to return to Egypt to get such horses, yet both were done (Dt 17:16 → 1K 10:28-29). The king was not to greatly multiply unto himself silver and gold, yet Solomon did exactly this – receiving 666 talents of gold a year (Dt 17:17 → 1K 10:14), so much so, that silver "was nothing accounted of the days of Solomon" (1K 10:21, 27).

> **WARNING**: It cannot be accidental that it was exactly 666 talents of gold a year, when 666 is the mark or *character* of the beast (Rev 13:17-18), which has to do with the ability to buy and sell (i.e. to trade as Solomon was doing) in order to increase in riches! The love of money is the root of all evil (1Tim 6:10). Gold is its primary symbol, for this is the most precious substance known to man.
>
> Covetousness is one of the greatest enemies of the fear of God and of the servant of the Lord.[9] Many a servant, once faithful to please their Lord, has forsaken their duty for earthly gain. This is the mark of the beast: seeking after filthy lucre. This is why God's first requirement for service was always that they hated covetousness (Ex 18:21, 1Tim 3:3), and why it was judged so harshly in the New Testament church with Ananias and Sapphira (Ac 5).

But this was not all of Solomon's transgressions. The king was not to multiply wives to himself "that his heart turn not away", yet Solomon did this to the extreme (Dt 17:17 → 1K 10:28-29), having 700 wives and 300 concubines (1K

---

[8] Solomon in his early days truly had the fear of God. Isn't it amazing that everything he asked for springs from the fear of God!

[9] We shall see this in the chapter entitled "Warning Signs of Losing God's Fear".

11:1-4). He loved many strange women, and when he was old, they indeed turned his heart away after their gods. As a result, he worshipped foreign gods and did not keep what the LORD had commanded (1K 11:1-11, Neh 13:26). So through his disobedience to God's warnings, he lost his fear of God.

> For Solomon went after Ashtoreth the goddess of the Zidonians, and after Milcom the abomination of the Ammonites. And Solomon did evil in the sight of the LORD, and went not fully after the LORD, as *did* David his father. Then did Solomon build an high place for Chemosh, the abomination of Moab, in the hill that *is* before Jerusalem, and for Molech, the abomination of the children of Ammon. And likewise did he for all his strange wives, which burnt incense and sacrificed unto their gods. And the LORD was angry with Solomon, because his heart was turned from the LORD God of Israel, which had appeared unto him twice 1K 11:5-9

Because of these things the kingdom was rent from him (1K 11:11), and his sons paid the price. God had also commanded the king to have his own copy of the scriptures so that he may have it with him to read all the days of his life.

> And it shall be with him, and he shall read therein all the days of his life: that he may learn to fear the LORD his God, to keep all the words of this law and these statutes, to do them: That his heart be not lifted up above his brethren, and that he turn not aside from the commandment, *to* the right hand, or *to* the left: to the end that he may prolong *his* days in his kingdom, he, and his children, in the midst of Israel. Dt 17:19-20

The whole purpose of having his own copy of the word of God and reading it daily was to learn to fear the LORD. Notice the fear of God was for a twofold purpose: (1) to keep the king obedient to the word of God, and (2) to keep him humble so that his heart did not get lifted up above his brethren. We have no record of Solomon daily reading the word of God, but by his actions we know he could not have fulfilled this command to daily be in the word of God, for he *did* turn aside from God's commands, to the right and to the left, and his heart *was* lifted up above his brethren.

Herein is a fearful thing, and why we must with all diligence keep our own heart (Pr 4:23). Here was a man who "spake three thousand proverbs: and his songs were a thousand and five." 1K 4:32 By the Spirit of God he wrote three books of the Bible: Proverbs, Ecclesiastes, and the Song of Solomon. He was wiser than all men (1K 4:31), and he taught us *much* about the fear of God.[10] Yet with all his wisdom he still lost the beginning of wisdom, the fear of God, as he was led away by his own lusts and desires!

---

[10] Look at how much Solomon taught about the fear of the LORD (over 30x!): Pr 1:7,29; 2:5; 3:7; 8:13; 9:10; 10:27; 13:13; 14:2,16,26-27; 15:16,33; 16:6; 19:23; 20:2; 22:4; 23:17; 24:21; 28:14; 29:25; 31:30; Ecc 3:14; 5:7; 7:18; 8:12-13; 12:13.

Solomon stands as our first warning. A man may know and possess the fear of God, but he must continually choose it, or he will surely lose it. He stands as a warning to us how easily we may seek the things of God in our life and even receive them, but in our blessings we may forsake the fear that once was ours in great measure.

> A man may know and possess the fear of God, but he must continually choose it, or he will surely lose it.

From Solomon's life we learn an invaluable lesson. The lack of the fear of God is not the result of ignorance. Let us not for a moment think that a man does not fear God because he does not know of it, or because of the lack of the knowledge of God. No! Even the primitive tribesman who knows nothing of the Bible, nothing of the true God, and who has never heard the true Gospel, even he knows to fear God. The fear of God is innate in every ancient culture. It is by nature of how God created us, written into our conscience. It is modern, cultured man who puts away the fear of God, trading it for other things.

Notice what Solomon himself tells us of this. "For that they hated knowledge, and did not choose the fear of the LORD." Pr 1:29 It is not that men lack knowledge, but that the knowledge they already had they hated. This word 'hated' means to make a personal enemy or foe. Scripture alerts us that every man has the basic knowledge of God in him, "for God hath shewed *it* unto them." Rom 1:19 But men deliberately, willfully choose not to fear God, because they do not want to be under his authority – and with true authority there *must* be fear. This is why even Jesus Christ, "the Son of the Father" (2Jn 1:3), but also a man set under authority (Lk 7:8), feared God, the ultimate authority (Heb 5:7). Men do not fear God today, because they *choose not* to hear Him!

Solomon stands as a warning to us also in that God gave him the key in his own hands how to stay in the fear of the LORD: read the word of God all the days of one's life. But he let the incredible riches of the word of God slip from his heart, as earthly riches took its place. May we as kings and priests unto our God and Father remember this. It is by reading and heeding the word of God that we will keep our heart in the things of God and not stray from him who ought to be feared.

The Dangers of Ungodly Relationships

"Be not deceived: evil communications corrupt good manners." 1Co 15:33

Concerning **Jehoshaphat**, it is written,

> And the LORD was with Jehoshaphat, because he walked in the first ways of his father David, and sought not unto Baalim; But sought to

the LORD God of his father, and walked in his commandments, and <u>not after the doings of Israel</u>. Therefore the LORD stablished the kingdom in his hand; ... And his heart was lifted up in the ways of the LORD: moreover he took away the high places and groves out of Judah. 2Ch 17:3-6

Jehoshaphat did *"that which* was right in the sight of the LORD." 2Ch 20:32 The LORD said unto him, "there are good things found in thee, in that thou hast taken away the groves out of the land, and hast prepared thine heart to seek God." 2Ch 19:3 He also removed the remnant of the sodomites out of the land (1K 22:46). In his third year he sent his princes to teach in the cities of Judah, and they had the book of the law of the LORD with them. They went throughout all the cities of Judah teaching the word of God (2Ch 17:3-10). He did this not once, but twice: "and he went out <u>again</u> through the people from Beersheba to mount Ephraim, and <u>brought them back unto the LORD God</u> of their fathers." 2Ch 19:3-4 Imagine, Jehoshaphat's actions were such that they inspired even the kingdoms round about Judah to fear the LORD (2Ch 17:10)! These things must have pleased the LORD very much to see the king with such a concern in his heart, not only to be right himself with the LORD, but also to bring the people back to the LORD.

BUT he made peace with the most wicked king of Israel: Ahab (1K 22:44)! "Now Jehoshaphat had riches and honour in abundance, and joined affinity with Ahab." 2Ch 18:1 (Amazing this compromise again occurs in the midst of great riches and honor.) This phrase 'join affinity' means 'to *give* (a daughter or son) *away* in marriage'.[11] This joined the godly house of Jehoshaphat with the ungodly house of Ahab and Jezebel. Jehoshaphat told Ahab, "I *am* as thou *art*, and my people as thy people; and *we will be* with thee in the war." 2Ch 18:3 This was a very foolish thing to do, which Jehoshaphat was soon to learn.

He nearly lost his life in battle because of doing this. God says that Jehoshaphat helped the ungodly, and loved them that hated the LORD. Therefore, was <u>wrath upon him from before the LORD</u> (2Ch 19:2). Sadly, Jehoshaphat did not learn his lesson and again tried to make peace agreements with the ungodly, and again faced tragedy.

> And **after this** did Jehoshaphat join himself with Ahaziah king of Israel, who did very wickedly: And he joined himself with him to make ships to go to Tarshish: ... Then Eliezer ... prophesied against Jehoshaphat, saying, Because thou hast joined thyself with Ahaziah, <u>the LORD hath broken thy works</u>. And the ships were broken, that they were not able to go to Tarshish. 2Ch 20:35-37

---

[11] This was done by Jehoshaphat's son Jehoram who was given in marriage to Athaliah, the **daughter** of Jezebel, worshipper of Baal and of the groves, and wife of Ahab.

1 – Why We Forsake the Fear of the LORD

> **WARNING**: The grief that came from this joining lasted years. As a result of this compromise with the wicked, <u>neither</u> Jehoshaphat's son, nor his grandson served the LORD, and instead they walked in *all* the ways of Ahab (the very one whom God despised)! Once Jehoram died, this wicked woman Athaliah slew all but one of the royal seed of Jehoshaphat! Take warning, friend, "Be not deceived: evil communications corrupt good manners." 1Co 15:33 The cost for this compromise lasted several generations and claimed the lives of many!
>
> Jehoshaphat's heart is often reflected today in modern ministers. There is a great push for unity. How many pastors or leaders of churches, among whom God was beginning to show them his kingdom, have done just like Jehoshaphat? In their efforts to join hands or join affinity with other pastors to bring about Christian unity, it is all too easy to put away doctrinal differences and so compromise the truth. For the sake of truth we *cannot* compromise, rather, we are called to suffer for righteousness sake (1Pe 3:14). In such cases of unbiblical unity, God will always lift the anointing of his Spirit and can only judge such compromise by 'breaking our works' (1K 22:48).[12]

Jehoshaphat is an example of those who violate the Lord's first requirement of discipleship: "If any *man* come to me, and hate not his father, and mother, and wife, and children, and brethren, and sisters, yea, and his own life also, he cannot be my disciple." Lk 14:26 Jehoshaphat allowed ungodly, natural relationships to jeopardize his life, his family, and his works. So many today lose the fear of God because they put family concerns and natural friendships[13] <u>before</u> the Lord's concerns and his requirement to come out from among the unclean, to be separate, and to touch them not. Yet God promises, if we will do this, and cleanse ourselves from all filthiness of both flesh and spirit, we will perfect holiness in the fear of God (2Co 6:14-7:1)!

The Dangers of Pride: Not Being Under Godly Oversight

"Where no counsel is, the people fall: …
Without counsel purposes are disappointed" Pr 11:14, 15:22

Jehoash (who is also known as Joash) became king when he was but seven years old. "Joash did *that which was* right in the sight of the LORD all the days of

---

[12] Certainly, God wants to bring together men in the kingdom of God who will put aside their titles and their ministries, and truly work together for the sake of Jesus Christ. But the foundation of truth in sound doctrine MUST be the basis of that unity or else it is none other than the unity of Babel to produce something God must destroy.

[13] To Jehoshaphat, joining with Ahab must have seemed like a spiritual joining since this was a cooperative 'reuniting' of the northern tribes of Israel with the southern tribes of Judah – all of which at one time had been united under David.

Jehoiada the priest [*who instructed him*]." 2Ch 24:2 [2K 12:2] Joash also repaired the house of the LORD (V4). **BUT** after the death of Jehoiada the priest, then ...

> came the princes of Judah, and made obeisance to the king. Then the king <u>hearkened unto them</u>. And they left the house of the LORD God of their fathers, and served groves and idols: and wrath came upon Judah and Jerusalem for this their trespass. 2Ch 24:17-18

Joash lost the fear of God and his relationship with him because he listened to ungodly counsel. In doing so, both he and the people forsook the LORD! Though God's wrath was aroused, yet God did not cut him off right away. Instead, God sent prophets to bring them back to the LORD. Because Joash was not willing to listen to the prophets who were sent to him to warn him, then God gave the people up unto destruction. Joash even put to death Zechariah the son of Jehoiada the priest. "Thus Joash the king remembered not the kindness which Jehoiada his father had done to him, but slew his son. And when he died, he said, The LORD look upon *it*, and require *it*." 2Ch 24:22

The LORD did look upon this and did require it, for destruction came upon him. "For the army of the Syrians came with a small company of men, and the LORD delivered a very great host into their hand, <u>because they had forsaken the LORD God</u> of their fathers. So they executed judgment against Joash." 2Ch 24:24 He was left in "great diseases" and his own servants conspired against him and killed him on his own bed (v25)! Here was a man who served God as long as he had godly oversight, but without it he forsook the fear of the LORD. Joash stands as a warning to us not to forget the good words and works which true men of God have sown into us, and not to forsake God's fear by listening to worldly men.

The Dangers of Pride: Rejecting Correction

> Because I have called, and ye refused; I have stretched out my hand, and no man regarded; But ye have set at nought all my counsel, and would none of my reproof: For that they hated knowledge, and did not choose the fear of the LORD: They would none of my counsel: they despised all my reproof. Pr 1:24-25,29-30

Asa "did *that which was* good and right in the eyes of the LORD his God: For he took away the altars of the strange *gods*, and the high places, and brake down the images, and cut down the groves: And commanded Judah to seek the LORD God of their fathers, and to do the law and the commandment. Also he took away out of all the cities of Judah the high places and the images", and he sought the LORD God (2Ch 14:2-7). "Asa's heart was <u>perfect with the LORD all his days</u>." 1K 15:14 In the 15th year of his reign "they entered into a covenant to seek the LORD God of their fathers with all their heart and with all their soul" (2Ch 15:12).

1 – Why We Forsake the Fear of the LORD

Asa showed himself a true disciple, loving God more than his own family, for he even removed his mother from being queen because she had made an idol in a grove (2Ch 15:16). He purged his heart, his home, and his country: "he took away the sodomites out of the land, and removed all the idols that his fathers had made." 1K 15:12 Imagine the godly boldness of such a king today, to so turn back the tide of wickedness by ridding the land of sodomy!

BUT in the 36th year of his reign he did foolishly and relied on the king of Syria, and not on the LORD (2Ch 16:7-9). When corrected by a man of God for it, instead of repenting, "Asa was wroth with the seer, and put him in a prison house; for *he was* in a rage with him because of this *thing*. And Asa oppressed *some* of the people the same time." 2Ch 16:10 Three years later without repentance, in the 39th year of his reign, he "was diseased in his feet, until his disease *was* exceeding *great*: yet in his disease he sought not to the LORD, but to the physicians." 2Ch 16:12 Two years later his time of repentance ran out and he died a bitter and angry man. Here was a man who, though he trusted in God for great deliverances, began to rely on man and when reproved by a man of God for it, he in anger refused to repent and died with a hardened heart. Asa stands as an example to us of one who feared and obeyed God for over 35 years, but because of losing his ability to receive correction, he lost his fear of God. When he lost his fear of God, he lost everything. His life is a warning also to all leaders who will not receive godly correction.

The Dangers of Pride: The Idolatry of Our Heart
"Pride goeth before destruction, and an haughty spirit before a fall." Pr 16:18

Amaziah "did *that which was* right in the sight of the LORD, but not with a perfect heart." 2Ch 25:2 He hired 100,000 mighty men of valour out of Israel for 100 talents of silver. He was rebuked for this, but he accepted this correction (2Ch 25:6). This was commendable, but it revealed he was beginning to leave the LORD and to trust in the strength of man. Sadly, Amaziah's greatest test came upon the heels of victory.

> **Now it came to pass**, after that Amaziah was come from the slaughter of the Edomites, that he brought the gods of the children of Seir, and set them up *to be* his gods, and bowed down himself before them, and burned incense unto them. Wherefore <u>the anger of the LORD was kindled against Amaziah</u>, and he sent unto him a prophet, which said unto him, Why hast thou sought after the gods of the people, which could not deliver their own people out of thine hand? And it came to pass, as he talked with him, that *the king* said unto him, Art thou made of the king's counsel? forbear; why shouldest thou be smitten? Then the prophet forbare, and said, I know that <u>God hath determined to destroy thee</u>, because thou hast done this, and hast not hearkened unto **my counsel**. 2Ch 25:14-16

Because of his victory, his heart became proud, and Amaziah would not hear God's counsel. Then Amaziah tried to go up against Israel and was warned again, but refused to listen.

> Thou sayest, Lo, thou hast smitten the Edomites; and <u>thine heart lifteth thee up to boast</u>: abide now at home; why shouldest thou meddle to *thine* hurt, that thou shouldest fall, *even* thou, and Judah with thee? But <u>Amaziah would not hear</u>; for it *came* of God, that he might deliver them into the hand *of their enemies*, because they sought after the gods of Edom. ... And Judah was put to the worse before Israel, and they fled every man to his tent. 2Ch 25:19-22

His life, similar to Joash's, ends in the death of conspiracy (2Ch 25:27). Here was a man whom pride and its ensuing idolatry caused him to forsake the fear of God, and thereby to follow other gods and to lose everything. Amaziah stands as a warning of the danger of pride, especially resulting from victory.

The Dangers of Pride: The Carelessness of Security

"The LORD of hosts hath purposed it, to stain the pride of all glory, and to bring into contempt all the honourable of the earth." Isa 23:9

Hezekiah "did *that which was* right in the sight of the LORD, according to all that David his father had done. He in the first year of his reign, in the first month, opened the doors of the house of the LORD, and repaired them." 2Ch 29:2-3 Hezekiah urged the Levites to sanctify themselves and to sanctify the house of the LORD God by carrying forth the filthiness out of the holy place (v5). He not only cleansed the house of God, but also cleansed the land, as well as the hearts of the people. He removed the high places, and broke the images, and cut down the groves, and even broke in pieces the brazen serpent from Moses (2K 18:4)!

> **WARNING**: God gave the brazen serpent as a sign to the people so that he might teach them spiritually about the Messiah. The deliverer to come would become sin for them and be crucified to remove the sting of death to heal them – if they would but look unto him. But just like today, God has given us the cross so that by it we may glory "in the cross of our Lord Jesus Christ, by whom the world is crucified unto me, and I unto the world." Gal 6:14 Yet so many use the cross merely as jewelry and decoration and do not crucify the world in their life, or worse, as a religious symbol which they will set in their churches and around their necks, and it becomes as much a piece of idolatry as the brazen serpent of old! O that we would again see true men of God who would arise and break in pieces such idols in God's sight.

Hezekiah cleaved to the LORD, and kept his commandments, and did not depart from following after God. It is written of him, "he trusted in the LORD

1 – Why We Forsake the Fear of the LORD

God of Israel; so that after him was none like him among all the kings of Judah, nor *any* that were before him." 2K 18:5 The LORD was with him, and he prospered wherever he went (vv6-7). He also restored the Passover celebration like it had not been done since Solomon (2Ch 30:19,26).

> Hezekiah ... wrought *that which was* good and right and truth before the LORD his God. And in every work that he began in the service of the house of God, and in the law, and in the commandments, to seek his God, he did *it* with all his heart, and prospered. 2Ch 31:20-21

BUT the scripture says he did not render again according to the benefit which was done unto him (i.e. of being healed of his sickness). His heart became lifted up, and therefore there was wrath upon him, and upon Judah and Jerusalem. Yet Hezekiah humbled himself for the pride of his heart, both he and the inhabitants of Jerusalem, so that the wrath of the LORD came not upon them in the days of Hezekiah. Yet in the business of the ambassadors of the princes of Babylon, who sent unto him to enquire of the wonder that was done in the land, God left him, to try him, that he might know all that was in his heart (2Ch 32:24-31). Hezekiah hearkened to the king of Babylon and showed his messengers *all* the things that were in his house and in all his dominion. God was angry with Hezekiah for this (2K 20:12-19).

Here was a man whose heart was lifted up by what God did for him, and he literally opened the door to the enemy. As a result, his children lost everything and were captured and killed by the enemy. Hezekiah stands as a warning to those who would boast of what they have *because* of the LORD, but in so doing would lose their watchfulness, inviting the enemy in. He also is a warning to us in not bringing forth the full fruits of repentance after God has specially spared us with his abundant mercy.

The Dangers of Pride: Going Beyond our Measure of Rule

> But we will not boast of things without *our* measure, but according to the measure of the rule which God hath distributed to us, ... For we stretch not ourselves beyond *our measure*, ... Not boasting of things without *our* measure 2Co 10:13-15

Azariah or ***Uzziah*** "did *that which was* right in the sight of the LORD, according to all that his father Amaziah did. And he sought God in the days of Zechariah ... and as long as he sought the LORD, God made him to prosper." 2Ch 26:4-5 God helped him against the Philistines, and against the Arabians, and his name spread abroad even unto Egypt. He strengthened himself exceedingly (2Ch 26:6-8). "And his name spread far abroad; for he was marvellously helped, <u>till he was strong</u>.

BUT when he was strong, <u>his heart was lifted up to *his* destruction</u>: for he transgressed against the LORD his God, and went into the temple of the LORD to burn incense upon the altar of incense [*which did not pertain unto him*]." 2Ch 26:15-16 When he was withstood by the priests,

> Then Uzziah was wroth, ... and while he was wroth with the priests, the leprosy even rose up in his forehead before the priests in the house of the LORD, from beside the incense altar. ... and they thrust him out from thence; yea, himself hasted also to go out, because the LORD had smitten him. 2Ch 26:19-20

Therefore Uzziah the king was a leper to the day of his death and had to dwell in a leper's house, and "he was cut off from the house of the LORD" (2Ch 26:21). Here was a man whom his strength deceived him, and he went beyond his measure of rule, thinking nothing of doing that which only the priests were allowed to do. In the very middle of his worshipping of God, he was cut off from God's presence! As a result, he lived the rest of his life in defeat as an outcast being a leper – cast out from the house of the LORD. O how important it is through the fear of the LORD to know the bounds of our habitation and the measure of our rule,[14] which we have from him who called us. Uzziah stands as a warning to all who would forget "to do justly, and to love mercy, and to walk humbly with thy God" (Mic 6:8).

Another Tragic Example of Exceeding their Measure of Rule

Josiah did that which was right in the sight of the LORD, and walked in the ways of King David. Josiah turned neither to the right hand, nor to the left. In the 8th year of his reign, he began to seek after the LORD. In the 12th year he began to purge Judah and Jerusalem from the high places, the groves, the carved images, and the molten images. Josiah did so much to cleanse the land (2K 23:5-11). He put down the idolatrous priests.

Under his rule, the people broke down the altars of Baalim and cleansed not only Judah and Jerusalem, but also in the cities of Manasseh, Ephraim, Simeon, and even unto Naphtali. He cut down all the idols throughout all Israel. In the 18th year of his reign, he repaired and cleansed the house of the LORD (2Ch 34:2-8,30-33). He brought out the grove from the house of the LORD and burned it and stamped it to powder. He destroyed the houses of the sodomites. He defiled the high places and Topheth (in the valley of Ben Hinnom) so that no one could make his son or daughter "pass through the fire to Molech". He also took away the horses that the kings of Judah had given to the sun, at the entrance of the house of the LORD, and burned the chariots of the sun.

---

[14] Measure of rule is another teaching so lacking among ministers of the gospel today. Few indeed even know what is the measure of their rule much less how not to go beyond it. Whatever a man does beyond his measure of rule is unclean in the eyes of God and will be reproved. This teaching is very much needed today, yet so often rejected by those who are strong and whose hearts are lifted up.

When the word of the LORD was discovered, his heart was tender, and he humbled himself before God, and even tore his clothes and wept before God (2Ch 34:27). Then he went into the house of the LORD and he read in the ears of all the people all the words of the book of the covenant. He made a covenant before the LORD, to walk after the LORD, to keep his commandments, his testimonies, and his statutes, with all his heart, and with all his soul, and to perform the words of the covenant which are written in the scriptures. He caused all that were present in Jerusalem and Benjamin to agree to it. He took away all the abominations out of all the countries that pertained to the children of Israel, and made all that were present in Israel to serve the LORD. In all his days he and the people departed not from following the LORD, the God of their fathers.

Josiah put away the workers with familiar spirits, the wizards, the images, the idols, and all the abominations that were spied in the land of Judah and in Jerusalem so that he might perform the words of the law. The scripture says, "And like unto him was there no king before him, that turned to the LORD with all his heart, and with all his soul, and with all his might, according to all the law of Moses; neither after him arose there *any* like him." 2K 23:25 We cannot find a more dedicated king to the LORD. He even excelled David in zeal for God!

BUT after all this, when Josiah had prepared the temple, Necho king of Egypt came up to fight against Charchemish by Euphrates: and Josiah went out against him. The king of Egypt sent ambassadors to him, saying, "What have I to do with thee, thou king of Judah? I come not against thee this day, but against the house wherewith I have war: for God commanded me to make haste: forbear thee from meddling with God, who is with me, that he destroy thee not." But Josiah would not turn his face from him. He disguised himself, so that he might fight with him, and he hearkened not unto the words of Necho, which the Bible says were from the mouth of God. So good Josiah came to fight in the valley of Megiddo and he died there (2Ch 35:20-24). Here was a man who did not listen to warning and meddled with an issue not his. He did not know his measure of rule and so lost his life senselessly for it. Josiah stands as a warning to us of being rash and meddling in issues God has not asked us to. He stands as a warning also of the penalty of walking in the pride of presumption – a life cut short.

Conclusions on Warnings from the Kings of Judah

*"There is a way which seemeth right unto a man,
but the end thereof are the ways of death." Pr 14:12*

We have seen nine kings of Judah who lost their fear of God. They are a historical warning to each of us, for the scripture is not written in vain. Let us then fear the LORD and be exceedingly careful not to misplace it or worse yet to cast it aside. Each of these kings feared, loved, and served God walking in his commandments but each lost the fear of God either temporarily or permanently. Their reasons differed: the fear of man, money and goods, the love of women, neglect of the Word, trusting in the strength of man (whether in others or in themselves), refusing correction from those who speak the word of God, forming relationships with the ungodly, listening to ungodly counsel, and going beyond their measure of rule. But their fall was all the same tragic.

We have seen the destruction and the wrath that came upon them and the loss of God's protection. Let us keep forefront in our eyes that it is indeed a fearful thing to fall into the hands of the living God (Heb 10:31). Let us keep the fear of God before our faces, as it is written (Ex 20:20). Let us beware the blessings and successes that at times attend the fear of the LORD, for Satan would have our eyes on the blessings and not on faithfully serving our God in the fear of the LORD – whatever may come or go.

The Requirement of the Kingdom: Willing to Change

We may easily understand how those kings fell away from the fear of God who sought after money, possessions, glory, or women, *or* those who began to trust in their own strength or in the strength of others, *or* who foolishly turned to other gods. But can we understand those who did not do these things and still lost their fear of God? What of those who though they loved God, no longer received correction from the word of God? How can we guard against these things? How does a servant of God's heart turn from serving and loving the Lord to a place where they despise his correction? It is easy for so many to condemn the actions of one whom has walked away from God, and then to judge the heart that they never loved God in the first place. Yet, we have clearly seen in these kings those who truly were in covenant relationship with the LORD, who knew him and walked with him and received his gifts and even his Spirit, some of whom completely walked away from God.

If we are going to recapture the fear of God in our life, then we must be willing to change, to repent from our ways and to return to the source of the fear of God, which is God himself. The fear of God is not a natural fear. It is a spiritual fear. We know the natural mind will not be able to comprehend the things of the spirit. There is no way we can understand and obtain the spiritual fear of God with a natural understanding or approach. The natural mind and our natural way of thinking will repeatedly be a stumbling block to truly walking by faith in the kingdom of God. So we see one day Jesus healed the man on the mat who was let down through the roof. He asked those listening one question, and they were left with a disturbing contradiction in their natural minds.

> Whether is easier, to say, Thy sins be forgiven thee; or to say, Rise up and walk? ... And they were all amazed, and they glorified God, and were filled with fear, saying, We have seen strange things to day. Lk 5:23,26

1 – Why We Forsake the Fear of the LORD

The Paradoxes of the Kingdom

From their way of thinking they had seen a paradox. This is the literal translation of the word 'strange' from the Greek: *paradoxos* (G3861), meaning '*contrary to expectation* (a "*paradox*")'. Only God could forgive sins, yet here was a man forgiving another man's sins and God was clearly honoring this by the sign of the miraculous healing. They couldn't understand it from where they were standing. The kingdom of God is full of such paradoxes from man's perspective. The scriptures clearly teach: Jesus is fully God, yet fully man; God is one God, but there are three persons in that one, each of them being an individual, yet each of them is fully God; God declares his foreknowledge and predestination,[15] but also man's inviolable free will. As servants of God we are called both to judge and not to judge,[16] and we are both to rest in our salvation and to work it out.

This is why the servant of God cannot judge according to the appearance of things as religious men do, but must judge the inward heart according to the word of God (Jn 7:24). We are warned not to look naturally at things, but spiritually. "Do ye look on things after the outward appearance?" (2Co 10:7), Paul warns. If we are to be led of the Spirit, we cannot judge by the sight of our eyes, nor reprove after the hearing of our ears. But the Spirit will lead us to judge even as it led Jesus to judge, for this is what the Spirit of the LORD that rested upon him came to do (Isa 11:3): to bring forth godly judgment. And this is the very same Spirit which he has given to all those that are born again.

We shall see several kingdom paradoxes along the way. We shall see that we are to serve the Lord with fear AND we are to serve the Lord without fear. We

---

[15] The mystery of these two seemingly contradictory viewpoints has birthed untold extreme and unbalanced teachings which contradict the whole of scripture. We can certainly not deal with that here, but be assured predestination cannot contradict or violate man's complete free will to choose or to reject. This is essential to the message of the gospel, which commands all men everywhere to repent and to choose whom they will serve – that should at least be clear from a simple reading of the scriptures.

A common misconception of the term 'predestinated' will be unveiled later as we look at God's requirement for holiness in the life of the believer in the chapter entitled "Holiness, Righteousness, & Faithfulness to God". Also see the definition of 'Predestinated to be Conformed' in the appendix entitled "Definition of Some Biblical Terms".

[16] So Jesus said, "Judge not, and ye shall not be judged: condemn not, and ye shall not be condemned: forgive, and ye shall be forgiven" (Lk 6:37), but he <u>also</u> said, "judge righteous judgment." Jn 7:24 This latter is a command that we must also fulfill. Similarly, Paul instructs us to do both: "Therefore judge nothing before the time, until the Lord come" (1Co 4:5), "but he that is spiritual judgeth all things" (1Co 2:15).

Some may think by Jesus' words in Luke 6:37 that if we do not judge a particular sin, then we will not be judged for that sin, but nothing could be farther from the truth. We shall all be judged (Rom 14:10, 1Co 14:24, 2Co 5:10, Jude 1:15). It is a matter of *how* we judge that will determine *how* we shall be judged (Jam 2:13, 5:9).

Where is the Fear of GOD? Losing the Treasure of the Lord

are to walk in the fear of God AND in the comfort of the Holy Ghost. We are to fear God in approaching him and we are to fear not in approaching him. These are contradictions to the natural mind, but perfectly balanced companions in the realm of the spirit.

> Above all else, if the heart is not pierced through, darkness acknowledged, and the word of the Lord not humbly submitted to, then we both have failed.

A Spiritual Perspective

It should be clear, then, that we cannot search the scriptures and come to a true understanding of the fear of the LORD from a mental understanding. Too many read the Bible but only their head is engaged, not their spirit. The fear of the LORD must cut away the crust and callousness of our heart and awaken in us a conscience that can be easily pricked. Only then can our spirit man arise to discern spiritual truth and come to spiritual understanding and wisdom. The LORD's challenge to us all is to choose his fear by hearkening to his counsel and receiving his reproofs (Pr 1:29-30).

> **WARNING**: Great care must be taken then in learning the fear of the LORD, both from the side of the teacher, concerning how he rightly brings forth the balance of the word of God, and from the side of the student, concerning how he hears the scriptures and as a disciple of the Lord Jesus does them. So learning the fear of the LORD will be like threading a needle. It will be easy to miss the whole point and end up with nothing, unless there is great care, patience, perseverance, steadiness, and preparation of heart to pursue it. Above all else, if the heart is not pierced through, darkness acknowledged, and the word of the Lord not humbly submitted to, then we both have failed. As one can learn nothing about the great subjects of Love or even Prayer by merely reading a book, so it is with the Fear of the LORD. The heart must be involved, along with a determination – a purposing of spirit – to follow after that which the Lord is showing. It is all too easy to be a satisfied hearer, rejoicing in what revelations we have received vicariously, but never walk in it. As we learn of the fear of God, "Let us walk by the same rule, let us mind the same thing." Php 3:16

Consider this, we only truly *know* what we put into practice in our life. No man knows how to ride a bicycle until after he has learned how to keep it in balance. No one knows the word of God unless they are willing to put it into practice by walking out its truths. Jesus confirmed this for us, "If any man will <u>do his will</u>, <u>he shall know</u> of the doctrine, whether it be of God, or *whether* I speak of myself." Jn 7:17 It is when we are content with learning only, that we are most hardened to the *purpose* of truth. So Jesus warned us, "If therefore the light that is in thee be darkness, how great *is* that darkness!" Mt 6:23

We may think we have light in us because we know the truth, but God says it is darkness if we say and do not. O how great is that darkness when we think it is light! It becomes the very essence of the spirit of the Pharisees. If there be no doing of what we think we know, then we are not really blessed – we only think we are blessed, and we are indeed deceived. Then, even that which we think we have will be taken from us (Mt 25:28-29). This is the caution and spiritual attentiveness that we must have whenever we approach the issues of the word of God, but especially this issue of the fear of God, for we shall see many counterfeits.

We have seen several examples of how we can lose the fear of God in our life. We may cast aside God's fear by not showing pity on the afflicted. We may lose God's fear through covetousness as well as the abundance of possessions. We forsake the fear of the LORD when we exalt ourselves over another. The fear of God cannot remain in us, if we forsake or are careless in our approach toward reading the word of God for ourselves. If we form friendships with the ungodly, especially our own family who are not following the Lord, then the fear of God has been lost in our heart. If we reject godly oversight, counsel, and correction from spiritual overseers in our life, then we are putting away our fear of God. If the pride of one's accomplishments overtakes us, then the fear of God will not be found in us. The devil, our adversary, will immediately take advantage of our loss of God's fear and seek to replace it with a host of counterfeits. Let us next look at the false fear of God – Satan's counterfeit fear.

Chapter 2. Cheap Imitations and Artificial Substitutes
Unveiling the False Fear of God
"their fear toward me is taught by the precept of men" Isa 29:13

As with everything good and perfect that God does, there is also a false. There is a true fear of God that pleases him and on the other side, it is clear from scripture that there is a fear of God that is unacceptable and repugnant to him – one which is sown by the enemy while men sleep, one which is not of the Spirit of God. Herein lays a danger, for the devil is an expert at producing imitations of the true, which have no power to effect the change that our heavenly Father is looking for in our lives.

2 – Cheap Imitations and Artificial Substitutes

The enemy has counterfeited everything from God.[17] Satan is the master counterfeiter, and he knows exactly where to bring his counterfeits – amongst God's people. Christianity is full of false ministries and false ministers, false teachers and false prophets, false signs and false wonders, false visions and false dreams. So many worship God today, "Howbeit in <u>vain</u> do they worship [God], teaching *for* doctrines the commandments of men." Mk 7:7 And on top of all that, there are so many false versions of scripture available, and they keep increasing.[18] So we should not be surprised there is also a false fear of God that is taught. As it is written,

> Wherefore the Lord said, Forasmuch as this people draw near *me* with their mouth, and with their lips do honour me, but have removed their heart far from me, and <u>their fear toward me is taught by the precept of men</u> Isa 29:13

Get this deep in your understanding: the false fear of God is <u>taught</u> by the precept of man. This means millions of Christians are weekly taught the false fear of God in churches across your nation, and it produces no real change in their lives. The false fear of god is taught by the precept or *command* of men. The Pharisees taught such a fear, and false teachers and preachers still teach it today. It is in knowledge only and produces no change in the heart because the heart is far from God. So God exhorts us "neither fear ye <u>their fear</u>, nor be afraid." Isa 8:12 From God's perspective what is taught today as the 'fear of God' is not really the fear of God at all, which is why God calls it "their fear" in both Isaiah 8:12 and 29:13, yet of the true fear of God, he repeatedly calls it "my fear":

> if I *be* a master, where *is* <u>my fear</u>? saith the LORD of hosts unto you Mal 1:6

> but I will put <u>my fear</u> in their hearts, that they shall not depart from me. Jer 32:40

> know therefore and see that *it is* an evil *thing* and bitter, that thou hast forsaken the LORD thy God, and that <u>my fear</u> *is* not in thee, saith the Lord GOD of hosts. Jer 2:19

Why does he say "their fear" is not "my fear"? Because they were not *changing* to grow in obedience to his word. As he declares elsewhere, "Because they have no <u>changes</u>, therefore they fear not God." Ps 55:19 Without a manifested change in our thinking and our actions, God says we do not in truth fear him. In Isaiah 29:13 we saw how God's people may have a 'fear toward God' but their hearts have been removed far from him. Notice how the false fear of God allows one's actions to be far from where one's heart is. This is the devastating reality. We may have a fear of God that God himself says we do **not** fear him.

---

[17] See the Table "The Counterfeiting of What is Real" at the end of this chapter.

[18] See the definition of 'The Bible' in the appendix entitled "Definition of Some Biblical Terms" in the book <u>Finding the Treasure of the Lord</u>.

The Fruits of the False Fear of God
The False Fear of God Produces No Change

The first and most apparent deficiency of the false fear of God is it does not **change** us. This should be no surprise at all, for how can it change us when our heart is able to be far from him even as we are worshipping him? This lack of change is manifested in continued disobedience. The false fear of God enables people not to deal with obedience to the word or the command of God, and to think they can still love God without obeying him. Yet Jesus told his own apostles the night he was betrayed, "**If** ye love me, keep my commandments. ... **If** a man love me, he will keep my words" (Jn 14:15,23). Let us be warned: continued disobedience in an area is a tell-tale sign that we have lost the fear of God in that area and that it must be recaptured.

True change can only be manifested when the heart is truly changed. This is the first fruit of salvation, for we were given a new heart (a heart of flesh) and our old heart (the stony heart) was removed (Eze 36:26). This is why God calls us a new creation (2Co 5:17), because of this new heart we have received. Thus, our heart must be changed if there is to be genuine change in our life. Any change that takes place without the heart being changed is merely an external covering that will eventually wear out. It takes tremendous force of will to maintain external change. Eventually the hypocrisy of it will wear through our resolve. We will grow exceedingly weary, until we finally cast it aside and return to our old way. So many in twelve step programs appear to be changed, but eventually they return to their addiction because of the lack of an inward change.

> Let us be warned: continued disobedience in an area is a tell-tale sign that we have lost the fear of God in that area and that it must be recaptured.

The False Fear of God Produces Hypocrisy and Pride

This separation of heart from actions and the inability to see oneself in the light of God's evaluation leads us invariably to the second greatest deficiency and bad fruit of the false fear of God: **zealous hypocrisy**. Hypocrisy cannot be avoided in this situation, because of the separation of the heart from the actions. Hypocrisy is birthed through the deception of thinking we are actually worshipping God in a way that pleases him, when, in fact, we are unwilling to look at our own disobedience.

In addition to hypocrisy, **pride** cannot be far behind, because whenever we think we are pleasing God when we are not, then we are thinking more highly of ourselves than we ought. This produces the worst hypocrisy of all. Notice in

2 – Cheap Imitations and Artificial Substitutes

Isaiah 29:13 that these were worshippers *and* ministers of God. He was in their songs and on their lips. They represented the Lord and taught of him, but he was not near in their hearts. They outwardly honored him, but inwardly ignored him! So we see the hypocrisy of the outward actions versus the reality of the inward heart.

The false fear of God and hypocrisy are not only friends they are brethren. They descend from one other, and thus so easily produce one another. Think on this: there is a false fear of God that people have today in which they will draw near to God with their mouths in prayer, they will praise him and honor him with their songs, they will regularly attend church services, yet in all this their heart will be removed far from him. This is truly a fearful thing, for when one speaks of the need for the fear of God, they already know they have it. And they do have it, of a sort, but they have the *wrong one*!

In this way the false fear of God actually births spiritual pride. Unlike the true fear of God, this false fear utterly fails to remove the **haughtiness** and **arrogance** that lies dormant in every man's heart. It blinds us both from whence we came and what still lies in the darkness of our own heart (Ps 40:2, Rom 7:14-24). So the LORD must remind his people, "Hearken to me, ye that follow after righteousness, ye that seek the LORD: look unto the rock *whence* ye are hewn, and to the hole of the pit *whence* ye are digged." Isa 51:1 If we are not continually having our sin and iniquities revealed by the light of God's truth shining in the dark places of our heart, then we will surely increase in the smugness of self-righteousness that is hypocrisy.

We Forget What Our Sinful Nature is Like

Through the fear of God taught by the precept of man, pride, arrogance, haughtiness, and high-mindedness actually grow stronger. The false fear of God will build and strengthen in our hearts an overweening pride. Overweening pride is the pride that takes pride in itself. So often we forget where we have come from and the depth of the wickedness and iniquity that we walked in prior to being saved. But worse, we forget that *any* of us can so easily revert back to our old life after being saved. The scriptures are full of such examples of those who turned back from following the Lord to go back to the old.[19]

---

[19] Some of those who went back to their old life: King Saul, God's anointed, departed from the LORD through his continued disobedience (1Sam 15:11) and his consulting with a familiar spirit when he had put them all away (1Sam 28:3,7); the Exodus people many times in heart went back to Egypt (Ps 78:8-11,40-42,56-57, Ac 7:37-39); the people in Jeremiah's day turned back to the sins of their fathers (Jer 11:9-10, 32:32-34); Demas loved this present world and forsook his calling & thereby the Lord (2Tim 4:10); all of Asia turned their backs on Paul, the servant and messenger of God (2Tim 1:15, 4:16); and many of Jesus' disciples walked with him no more (Jn 6:66).

If we do not think we can fall from our stedfastness or from grace as God says we can (2Pe 3:17, Gal 5:4), then hypocrisy must inevitably overtake our life and the fear of God will be far from us. "Wherefore let him that thinketh he standeth take heed lest he fall." 1Co 10:12 God's word does not speak in vain (i.e. to no purpose). If we don't take heed to the state of our heart, we will fall.

The Spirit of the LORD must continually reprove us of sin and expose it inside us. We often think of the Spirit's ministry of reproving sin being primarily for the world – which clearly it is. As Jesus said, "when he [*the Comforter*] is come, he will reprove the world of sin, and of righteousness, and of judgment" (Jn 16:8). When we were of the world this is how the Spirit brought us to Jesus, by convicting us of our sin, revealing our lack of righteousness, and impressing on us the certain judgment we were under. But this ministry of the Spirit of truth is to never cease in our life! "Behold, thou desirest truth in the inward parts: and in the hidden *part* thou shalt make me to know wisdom." Ps 51:6

It is because of the sinful nature into which we were born (Ps 51:5) that the Spirit of truth has a continual work to do in order to bring the light of truth into our innermost parts. We know God does not continually remind us of past sins that we have confessed, for he has cleansed us of them. He has cast all our sins behind his back (Isa 38:17). "As far as the east is from the west, *so* far hath he removed our transgressions from us." Ps 103:12 But he *does* regularly remind us of the sinfulness of our own heart (Ps 51:3), what is beginning to take root, so that we may take warning and not be foolish by not being sober, vigilant, and watchful, or by thinking we could not again do such things. Let us be watchful of our heart, for it is there that the battle to keep the fear of God alive is waged.

Comparing the True Fear of God with the False
"did he not fear the LORD, and besought the LORD" Jer 26:19

The true fear of God will cut to a man's heart and expose his evil and selfish desires, giving no place for arrogance and pride to hide. It will continually crush our pride as our sins, iniquities, and failures become more and more visible to us. The true fear of God will cause conviction of sin, a seeking after God, and a repentant heart. Hear what the elders proclaimed,

> Did Hezekiah king of Judah … [*persecute, despise, and kill the servant of God?*] did he not fear the LORD, and besought the LORD, and the LORD repented him of the evil which he had pronounced against them? Jer 26:19

The true fear of the LORD will cause us to seek him and, if we give place to it, to repent of our actions, but the false fear of God produces none of these fruits. It is this painful 'revelation knowledge' of our shortcomings, which the true fear of the LORD brings about, that prevents the mold of hypocrisy from forming. The false fear of God will cause us to think we are someone else,

2 – Cheap Imitations and Artificial Substitutes

someone better than we truly are. The true fear of God keeps us from this self-deception of high-mindedness. "For if a man think himself to be something, when he is nothing, he deceiveth himself." Gal 6:3 Without the painful, regular revelation of truth, which shows us our own sins, we will most assuredly begin to convince ourselves that we are someone in the Lord, when we are nothing. We must not think more highly of ourselves than we ought to think (Rom 12:3). Jesus in fact, contrary to the self-esteem doctrine that is promulgated in "growing" churches today, taught us that after we have done everything commanded us of the Master that we ought to consider ourselves only "unprofitable servants" who have but "done that which was our duty to do." Lk 17:10

> **WARNING**: How can people teach (supposedly from the scriptures) self-esteem when Jesus himself said, "Take my yoke upon you, and learn of me; for I am <u>meek and lowly</u> [i.e. *humiliated*] in heart" (Mt 11:29). Jesus taught us to be humiliated in heart, that is, to have a low self-esteem. He taught us to deny our self, not to affirm it. He taught us to hate our self, not to love our self.[20] Jesus knows we already love our self – that is the problem. Hear the truth, "For no man <u>ever yet</u> hated his own flesh; but nourisheth and cherisheth it" (Eph 5:29). Jesus did *not*, as so many falsely claim today, teach us to love our self and to esteem ourselves highly in him. Rather, we are taught to esteem others, and that *not* because of who they are. We are taught to esteem others for what they have done! "And to esteem them very highly in love <u>for their work's sake</u>." 1Th 5:13 Everyone by nature already loves them self. Jesus took this as a fact[21] and so did Paul (Rom 13:9) and James (Jam 2:8).

Because the true fear of God always exposes our heart, it will require our hearts to draw near to the Lord in acknowledgment of the truth. As our hearts begin to draw near to the Lord in spirit and in truth, instead of being so vocal before him, often we begin to see a holy silence settle over us. We immediately begin when the true fear of God settles on our heart to lose the foolish playfulness that so often marks modern "worship". In the holy place there are no "jam" sessions for the Lord. The world is shut out and its ways must depart when the Holy One dwells among his people. Solomon warns us when we go to the house of God, let us be more ready to *listen* than to talk. We ought to:

> be more ready to hear, than to give the sacrifice of fools …. Be not rash with thy mouth, and let not thine heart be hasty to utter *any* thing before God: for God *is* in heaven, and thou upon earth: therefore let thy words be few. … a fool's voice *is known* by multitude of words. Ecc 5:1-3

---

[20] Deny ourselves: Mt 16:24, Mk 8:34, Lk 9:23. Hate ourselves: Lk 14:26, Jn 12:25.

[21] Jesus shows we already love ourselves: Mt 19:19, 22:39, Mk 12:31.

And what does Solomon finish this whole section on speaking rashly before God and the making of vows with? "For in …many words *there are* also *divers* vanities: but fear thou God." Ecc 5:7 The true fear of God will often cause us to shut our mouth before God and before his messenger. With the true fear of God we know we have no excuse for our disobedience. Therefore, we will not accuse another, when we are the one who has disobeyed Almighty God. Notice Job has little to say once God himself shows up (Job 42:1-6). This was a sign of his true heart of repentance and of humbling himself before the LORD. As David says to God concerning his sin with Bathsheba, "Against thee, thee only, have I sinned, and done *this* evil in thy sight: that thou mightest be justified when thou speakest, *and* be clear when thou judgest." Ps 51:4 Before the true fear of God is working in us, we are more concerned with justifying ourselves in the sight of others than with seeing God be justified.

God can only be justified, and his judgments proven to be right when we acknowledge that we have sinned against him. We cannot blame someone else for getting us to disobey the LORD and to sin against him. That is exactly what Adam and Eve did from the beginning. They both hid from God (Gen 3:8). Eve blamed the devil (Gen 3:13) and Adam blamed God (Gen 3:12). But like them, we are the one that he is dealing with. We cannot blame the devil, our family, the pressures of life, or any circumstance for any sin we have committed. To do so is to call God a liar. "If we say that we have not sinned, we make him a liar, and his word is not in us." 1Jn 1:10 Thus, the true fear of God always must lead us back to truth and reveal our own actions and deeds from God's eyes, not our own. It is so easy for a person to say, "O, I know what I have done wrong", when in fact they have no idea, from God's perspective, of what they have truly transgressed.

The Beginning of the False Fear of God: A Guilty Conscience

"I heard thy voice in the garden, and I was afraid, because I was naked; and I hid myself." Gen 3:10

So how does the false fear of God so pervasively infect us? The false fear of God arises from the heart of a guilty conscience that would hide from the living God (as we have seen with Adam and Eve). Thus, it does not prepare the heart to stand before God. It is birthed from the fear of *consequences*, not original actions. The false fear of God came into the creation at the very beginning as a result of the fall. When Adam and Eve first disobeyed God's commandment, then and there out of their fallen nature was birthed the false fear of God, which is to hide ourselves from authority. Listen as our first father, Adam, reveals why he feared God:

> And they heard the voice of the LORD God walking in the garden in the cool of the day: and Adam and his wife hid themselves from the

2 – Cheap Imitations and Artificial Substitutes

> presence of the LORD God amongst the trees of the garden. And the LORD God called unto Adam, and said unto him, Where *art* thou? And he said, I heard thy voice in the garden, and I was afraid, because I *was* naked; and I hid myself. Gen 3:8-10

Notice how they were not afraid because of what they had done or that they had disobeyed the LORD, but they were afraid because they were *naked*. The coming of the LORD reminded them of their changed condition, their unacceptable state, but not their disobedience.[22] Thus, God's questioning to both of them focuses on bringing to the forefront of their thoughts what they had done, for it was not even in their thinking. Unto the man the LORD God said,

> "Hast thou eaten of the tree, whereof I commanded thee that thou shouldest not eat?" Gen 3:11 "And the Lord God said unto the woman, What *is* this *that* thou hast done?" Gen 3:13

God had to deliberately remind them of their disobedience so that they would understand why he was going to have to bring the severity of the judgments in the curses upon them. God, here, is doing the very work of the Holy Spirit for them. He is reproving and convicting them of sin, judgment, and righteousness (Jn 16:8-11). They were ready to excuse themselves and to accuse others, even as the scripture shows is in all of our hearts. Even though they did not have the Law, yet they were a law unto themselves, "which shew the work of the law written in their hearts, their conscience also bearing witness, and *their* thoughts the mean while accusing or else excusing one another" (Rom 2:15). Though they were brought face to face with their sin, they were not willing to come to repentance through the acknowledgment of the truth (2Tim 2:25).

How often our fear of God is of this sort. This false fear of God is a carnal fear and not a spiritual fear. It profits nothing at all. It is an enemy to both us and to God. It is to be most hated. It will always drive us further away from God and keep us from being reconciled both to one another and to God – even as we see it did in the garden. So it was the *consequence* that brought about Adam and Eve's carnal fear, and not the *significance* of their disobedience, which would have produced a spiritual fear leading to repentance.

Substituting Sacrifice for Obedience

We need to look more at what is this carnal or fallen fear of God, which enables us to believe we are actually pleasing God and honoring him in our worship and our speaking, when in fact, our heart is far from him. What is it that reveals that our heart is far from the very one that we claim we are worshipping and giving thanks to? If our worship does not reveal what our heart is set on, then how can we know **what** our heart is set on?

---

[22] Are we not warned in Revelation that the Lord's second coming shall be similarly received by so many on the earth?!

We can know by what we most treasure! "For where your treasure is, there will your heart be also." Mt 6:21 If our greatest concern and thought is for the Lord, then what he asks of us will be our delight, not our burden. So the false fear of God arises from the vain hope of believing that what we do for God will please him when we have not done what he has asked for. It is substituting *sacrifice* (i.e. what we want to give to God) for *obedience* (i.e. what God asked us to give to him). It is thus "will worship" (Col 2:23). This can only bring forth his disapproval, rejection, and anger. This substitution occurs many times in scripture from King Saul and his half-hearted obedience, to Nadab and Abihu and their strange fire, to much of what is done in the name of God today that has no solid foundation in the scriptures.

Substituting Man's Wisdom for the Wisdom of God

The false fear of God will not only cause us to substitute our sacrifices of what we would give to God, for the obedience he demands, it will also cause us to rely on our own wisdom, rather than the eternal wisdom of God. Thus, not only our works get substituted for his works, but our way and the 'wisdom' of it gets substituted for his way and wisdom. All of this is because of the false fear of God. The wisdom of man, which is the wisdom of this world, is the greatest stumbling block to the kingdom of God today, just as it was in Jesus' day. Even Jesus was not able to break through the hardness of heart that guards those with the false fear of God, who worship in vain.

> *Ye* hypocrites, well did Esaias prophesy of you, saying, This people draweth nigh unto me with their mouth, and honoureth me with *their* lips; but their heart is far from me. But in vain they do worship me, teaching *for* doctrines the commandments of men. Mt 15:7-9

Why is so much of our modern worship vain or useless from God's perspective? It teaches the commandments of men and forsakes the commandment of God. The doctrines of men, especially from well-known preachers, sadly have more weight than the scriptures by which all things are to be tested and proved. Rare is the Christian today that will truly build their life only off of "what saith the scriptures" and not what saith 'great men'. We live again in the subtlety and deception of the days of the doctors and scribes![23]

---

[23] I am continually amazed as a man of God, when someone through the word of God is challenged on what they believe, how often they resort to what they have read or heard others say and NOT to what saith the scriptures. Where are the noble Bereans today? Why will men *not* do as true men of old did and 'reason out of the scriptures' (Ac 17:2)? To which of the scribes or doctors of the Law did Jesus, the apostles, or any of the writers of the New Testament ever refer to or use as their authority? None. Even Paul (though raised under a doctor of the Law) refused to base his doctrine off of what men said, but always went back to God's word. Remember, only "the word of the Lord endureth forever." 1Pe 1:25

2 – Cheap Imitations and Artificial Substitutes

> Why is so much of our modern worship vain or useless from God's perspective? It teaches the commandments of men and forsakes the commandment of God.

God says the false fear of God comes from the precepts or commands of men. If the fear of God is reduced to a set of rules and laws effecting outward behavior, but not radically provoking and stripping the heart, then the lips will honor God, but the heart will be far from him. Thus, the fear of God taught by the precept of men does nothing to convert the wicked heart that each and every one of us has. By nature we are fallen creatures who love the world and the ways of the world. We despise the things of God and have each gone our own way (Isa 53:6). Even after salvation, without proper discipleship, without the renewing of our mind by the washing with the water of the word, and without learning how to deny ourselves as Jesus taught, we will still continue to follow our own desires and do what we believe to be right.

In our search to recapture the fear of the LORD we will need to be set free in many areas and return to the foundation of the word of God. We will have to cover many different parts of our walk with the Lord. This is because the fear of the LORD will touch every part of our heart. The greatest difficulty all of us have in understanding God's fear is it has no comparison with our experience or comprehension of natural fears. It is a spiritual fear, not a natural fear, and we cannot comprehend it naturally – though so many try to.[24]

Remember, the kingdom of God is a spiritual kingdom, which must be spiritually discerned. The kingdom will turn our way of thinking upside down, for God's ways and thinking are completely contrary to man's ways and thinking. Jesus had to correct even the thinking of his closest followers many times.

> **WARNING**: Just know, disciples are not instantly made perfect and are very much in a process of growth and transformation from the old into the new. Many times it is not until we begin to change and to leave the old that the old now becomes exposed even more in our lives. This should not be a cause for despair and quitting, but of assurance that the Lord is indeed working on us and that the process of change has already begun. The old things we sometimes do not even know dwell within us must be raised to the surface and exposed, so that they might be acknowledged, repented of, and healed by the Word.

---

[24] This is why so many confuse the true fear of God with reverence, claiming that the fear of God is merely 'an awe, a deep respect of God', and that it is not in fact what it claims to be and that is 'fear'. The scripture shows the fear of God on the contrary is something completely different than reverence. It is a genuine fear and trembling.

The more one walks with God in the true fear of God the more one will acknowledge and know of a certainty in their own heart the truth of what the Bible says, "their inward part is very wickedness" (Ps 5:9). Yet, "Behold, thou desirest truth in the inward parts: and in the hidden *part* thou shalt make me to know wisdom." Ps 51:6 And remember what wisdom is, "Behold, the fear of the Lord, that *is* wisdom" (Job 28:28). In order to cleanse our inward parts of wickedness and to put truth there instead, God must make us to know the fear of the LORD for "the fear of the LORD *is* the instruction of wisdom" (Pr 15:33). This is why the fear of the LORD is the hidden wisdom of God.[25]

The true fear of God will cause our hearts to draw near to God. But the fear of God that comes from the precept or command of men causes our heart to subtly draw away from the LORD. Our lips still honor him and our mouth still praises and prays to him, but our heart becomes far from him, because truth is not in our inward parts. This is one way you can measure whether you are learning the true fear of God or just what is taught by the precept of men. Is your heart becoming softer, your conscience more sensitive? Is your openness to being corrected by God through brethren and earthly authorities increasing? Are you more dependent on the local house of God and the fellowship of the saints? If any of these is not growing, then you are learning only the counterfeit fear of God, and you, like Adam and Eve, are hiding from God behind the apron of a guilty conscience.

The False Fear Found in False Worship

"But in vain they do worship me, teaching for doctrines the commandments of men." Mt 15:9

The development of the false fear of God can be most clearly seen in the development of the religion of Samaria, which I will call 'Samarianism'. In Samarianism we will see a fear of God taught by the precept of men. Years later Jesus would speak to the woman of Samaria and would reprove them of ignorant worship. "Ye worship ye know not what" (Jn 4:22), he said. The Samaritans were worshipping God, but they did not even **know whom** they were worshipping! That is amazing, but all too often repeated even to this very day! Let us examine both the roots and the fruits of this religious belief. We will see that it produces a fear of God that freely allowed doing things displease God.

Samaria was a place of mixing the things of God with the unholy practices of other religions. It was a place full of idolatry and harlotry.[26] It was full of worship and religion, but of which Jesus himself said they were **not** true wor-

---

[25] For more on the hidden wisdom of God see "An Epilogue: Enduring Fear of God" in the book <u>Finding the Treasure of the Lord</u>.

[26] Idolatry and harlotry: Hos 7:1-4 & 8:5-6, Eze 23.

2 – Cheap Imitations and Artificial Substitutes

shippers, for they did not worship in spirit <u>and</u> in truth (Jn 4:23-24). The Samaritans of Jesus' day began hundreds of years before when the king of Assyria took Israel captive because of their compromise and idolatry. The Assyrian king transported them into his homeland and brought in strangers or foreigners in their place (2K 17:23-24). What is amazing, even in the details here, is that Israel in the Hebrew means *'those who prevail* or *rule with God'*. Yet, who were 'those who prevail or rule with God' taken captive by? By the king of Assyria, and Assyria means *'successful* or *prosperous'*.

What did this king of prosperity do to the people of God who should have been prevailing or overcoming with God? The king of prosperity brought them into captivity, removed them from the true covenant place they should have been abiding in, and mixed them with strangers and aliens who did not know their ways and were full of their own idolatrous practices. If people could only see today how this same process has happened in so many parts of Christianity, especially in America, from the faith teachers, to the seeker-sensitive movement, to the very operation of the mega-churches. It is all too relevant today. Samarianism is alive and well in America. Let us look at these foreigners (2K 17):

> So <u>they feared the LORD</u>, **and** made unto themselves of the lowest of them priests of the high places, which sacrificed for them in the houses of the high places. <u>They feared the LORD</u>, **and** served their own gods, after the manner of the nations whom they carried away from thence. **Unto this day they do after the former manners**: they fear not the LORD, neither do they after their statutes, or after their ordinances, or after the law and commandment which the LORD commanded the children of Jacob, whom he named Israel; With whom the LORD had made a covenant, and charged them saying,
>
>> Ye shall not fear other gods, nor bow yourselves to them, nor serve them, nor sacrifice to them: But the LORD, who brought you up out of the land of Egypt with great power and a stretched out arm, him shall ye fear, and him shall ye worship, and to him shall ye do sacrifice.
>>
>> And the statutes, and the ordinances, and the law, and the commandment, which he wrote for you, ye shall observe to do for evermore; and ye shall not fear other gods. And the covenant that I have made with you ye shall not forget; neither shall ye fear other gods. But the LORD your God ye shall fear; and he shall deliver you out of the hand of all your enemies.
>
> Howbeit they did not hearken, but they did **after their former manner**. So these nations <u>feared the LORD</u>, **and** served their graven images, both their children, and their children's children: as did their fathers, **so do they unto this day**. 2K 17:32-41

Exposing Samarianism

Remember, everything that is written is written for our admonition that we should not fall in the same example of disobedience. "Now these things were our examples, to the intent we should not lust after evil things, as they also lusted. Now all these things happened unto them for ensamples: and they are written for our admonition, upon whom the ends of the world are come." 1Co 10:6,11 Note this sober warning that God places in his word, "<u>Unto this day</u> they do after the former manners … so do they <u>unto this day</u>" (2K 17:34,41).

The word of God is eternal. It does not pass away and it does not speak in vain When scripture records it is so even "unto this day", then we must know there is a spiritual law at work that causes this to continue throughout man's generations. In this case, a spiritual disobedience resulting in the false worship of Samarianism will be in every generation of sinful man.[27] Of course, this way of mixture had continued all the way down to Jesus' day as well. The Samaritans of his day had their own way of worshipping God (Jn 4:20), yet Jesus declares to the Samaritan women, "Ye worship ye know not what" (Jn 4:22). I pray that we can see that this vain worship is alive and well even unto this very day.

> When the scripture records it is so even unto this day, then we must know there is a spiritual law at work that causes this to continue throughout man's generations.

Let's summarize what we see about the formation of Samarianism (2K 17):

1. v25: in the beginning, they had no fear of God before their eyes - Rom 3:16-18
2. v28: their fear toward God was taught by the precept of man - Isa 29:13
3. v29: they refused to forsake their idols, making their own gods - Rom 1:22-23
4. v32: a form of godliness, but denied the power - 2Tim 3:5 [2K 22:17, 23:5]
5. v33: they learned the ways of the heathen around them - Jer 10:2
6. v34: they mixed the word of God with their own traditions [also vv40-41]

These foreigners mixed the holy things of God with heathen, idolatrous practices. Sadly, the exact same thing is done today in Christianity, which is why we do what we do at Christmas and Easter when the New Testament church

---

[27] It is not coincidental that the 10 northern tribes of Israel, which all fell away into idolatry, were soon ruled out of the very city of Samaria! Their kings from Omri and Ahab (1K 16:28-32, 18:2, 21:17-18, 22:10) were ruled out of Samaria. This not only possessed Omri's line, which ended with the sons of Ahab, Ahaziah, & Jehoram (2K 1:2-3, 3:1, 6:19-20), but also the entire line of Jehu and all his generations. These also all ruled out of the chief city of Samaria: Jehoahaz, Joash/Jehoash, Jeroboam II, Zachariah, Shallum (2K 10:1,17,35-36, 13:1,6, 13:9-13, 14:14-16,23-23, 15:8,13-17,23-27, 17:1-6, …).

2 – Cheap Imitations and Artificial Substitutes

never held such practices. In verses 32-33 & 41 of 2Kings 17 we see in each case they **added** to what God had asked:

1. "they feared the LORD **&** made unto themselves … priests of the high places"
2. "They feared the LORD, **&** served their own gods"
3. "So these nations feared the LORD, **&** served their graven images"

We can so clearly see the process of substituting their own sacrifices for the obedience which God had commanded. Each time they added something that God neither asked for, nor accepted. The only thing we are called to add to the fear of God is obedience to God's commandments. "Let us hear the conclusion of the whole matter: Fear God, **and** keep his commandments: for this is the whole duty of man." Ecc 12:13 They feared the LORD but not with purity or with their whole heart, for in their heart were still worldly ways. They still held onto what they knew and where they had come from. Remember, to them the ways which they had been raised in and had known were NOT idolatry from their point of view – but these old ways *were* idolatrous from God's point of view. So it is today.[28]

We must hold up everything to the light of scripture to see if it is idolatry from God's perspective, not ours. The fear that allows us to still have our high places (when they all need to be torn down) is not the true fear of the LORD, which will cause us to detest all idolatry. The fear that allows us to still serve our own gods or "god as we conceive him to be" (when there is only one God whom we are to serve) is not the true fear of the LORD, which will bring us into intimacy with him. The fear that allows us to still serve our graven images (i.e. the ideals and plans that we have for our life) – when there is only one way, one life, and one truth that we are to follow after – is not the true fear of the LORD, which enables us to depart from iniquity and to hate evil.

Remember, the false fear of God always leads people away from the true God and back into idolatry and vain worship. So what did Samarianism turn into? Through the process of being given over to their own ways for over 400 silent years between the Old and New Testaments (where no prophetic voice brought forth the word of the LORD to bring correction), we see them in the New Testament as their own religious order, worshipping God where they wanted and how they wanted. Though they were despised of the Jews, they were still considered separate from the Gentiles (Mt 10:5)! Let us see the spiritual law or principles that work among them. They were a very unique people:

---

[28] How few Christians indeed can acknowledge or see that the very things done in churches during Christmas and Easter are full of pagan idolatry and have their roots, not in Biblical practices, but in heathen practices. Thus, in God's eyes they are idolatrous practices and the whole of them ought to be forsaken, not preserved as traditions.

Table 2-1   The Characteristics of Samarianism

1. full of <u>good works</u>, like the good Samaritan (Lk 10:33),
2. full of <u>personal permissibility</u>, like the adulterous woman at the well (i.e. 'you worship how you want & we'll worship how we want', Jn 4:20),
3. full of <u>ignorant worship</u>: wasn't according to the truth (Jn 4:22, Ac 17:23),
4. full of <u>easy-believism</u>: knew Jesus *not* as Lord, only as Saviour (Jn 4:39-42),[29]
5. full of those who <u>buy & sell the things of God</u> (Ac 8:13-22, 2Pe 2:3, Pr 23:23),
6. full of <u>divination & enchantments</u>: sold themselves to do evil (2K 17:17),
7. full of those who make themselves out to be <u>some great one</u> (Ac 8:9-13),
8. full of those who <u>bewitch</u> the people by their <u>sorceries</u> (Ac 8:9-13),
9. full of <u>false prophets</u> who cause God's people to err (Jer 23:13),
10. full of <u>heathen practices and idolatry</u> (2K 17:8,12).

The Mixture and Merchandizing of Christianity

How sad that all of these elements in different measures are present in modern day Christianity. Jesus is worshipped and exalted as Saviour, but denied his place as Lord – first, of his people and second, of his church. The end result of mixing the fear of God with our ways and the ways of the world will always be these ten fruits! There is a tolerance, independence, and permissibility in today's Christianity that was never known in previous generations of those who followed Christ Jesus. There is an easy-believism and an ignorant worship, and the overflowing of every kind of tradition and doctrine of men. When is the last time you heard a Christian radio talk show host interviewing another Christian bring correction to their doctrinal error? When is the last time you heard a Christian TV host when talking with someone with Catholic beliefs warn them of the idolatry in that religion and the judgment to come against it for violating the scriptures and that they <u>must</u> be born again or face eternal damnation? Probably never.[30]

---

[29] Notice how they recognize Jesus as "the Saviour of the world", yet they do not recognize nor submit to him as Lord. Later when the demands of the cross of discipleship come, notice how Jesus is *not* received (Lk 9:51-62)! This *is* the religious spirit of our day, that at first rejoices to hear the kingdom of God, because it is new to their ear, and they hear and see the life that is in it, but when the demands to live a crucified life by carrying the cross is made known, they want nothing more to do with it.

[30] It is a sad commentary on both sides that Catholic doctrine routinely over many, many years has falsely condemned Bible-believing Christians for not holding to their Catholic heathen, idolatrous, and anti-scriptural practices, yet supposedly Bible-believing Christians today will bring forth no such true warning from God's Word that awaits all such idolaters!

2 – Cheap Imitations and Artificial Substitutes

You may think, "But Christianity does not buy and sell the things of God!" O, really? Why then are we warned as children of God in the book of Proverbs NOT to sell the truth (Pr 23:23)? What then is the modern merchandising of the gospel that has taken place, which so many hail: from Christian music and its conforming to the world, to Christian books and the appeal to the masses, to the putting away of sound doctrine, and the silencing of the cutting edge of truth in the Church? Christianity is more concerned today with not offending new-comers, than offending sinners with the stumbling block of the gospel, so that they may learn by conviction to stop offending a holy God! But then, who talks about a holy and terrible God any more?

Remember, it was by the multitude of Lucifer's merchandise that he was filled with violence and sinned and fell from God's glory (Eze 28:16). He tries to ensnare so many in Christianity today so that they may similarly fall from grace and become profane. So Peter warns us in the last days of false prophets and false teachers who will *deny* "the Lord that bought them", secretly bringing in damnable heresies. "And through covetousness shall they with feigned words make merchandise of you: whose judgment now of a long time lingereth not, and their damnation slumbereth not." 2Pe 2:3

We are in the last days, and we have everything that Samarianism had. We have false prophets who speak in the name of the Lord. We have heathen, worldly practices in the church. There is idol worship – reflected in Christian stardom and ministers who are known better than the books of the Bible. There are ministries and ministers who have sold themselves to do what they think is good, but which God calls evil. They parade themselves before God's people as some great ones and who bewitch them by their sorceries. And indeed, we have so many who truly do not know *what* they are worshipping. In summary, the scriptures say of those who once were the children of God but became the Samarians:

> And they rejected his statutes, and his covenant that he made with their fathers, and his testimonies which he testified against them; and they followed vanity, and became vain, and went after the heathen that *were* round about them, *concerning* whom the LORD had charged them, that they should not do like them. 2K 17:15

If we are to recapture the fear of God, we must seriously examine ourselves and our churches to see whether we are in the faith (i.e. in sound doctrine) and are set apart from the world. We must prove our own selves and know our own selves by the word of God (2Co 13:5). We must put our selves to the tests of discipleship, servanthood, humility, and obedience that Jesus puts all who would follow him to. We must line up our life with the word of God to see if it is *his* word and nothing else, or whether compromise and idolatry have entered in. Is the word of God truly our standard, or do we live with our traditions just like the Samarians and the Pharisees? Have we followed after vanity and become vain, by going after the heathen that are around about us? Do we *do* like the nation that we live in – when God has said that we "should <u>not</u> do like them" (2K 17:15)?

> **WARNING**: God's judgment against the Samarians is one of desolation and emptiness, resulting from being judged by the sword of the word of God (Hos 13:16). It is only after God's kingdom (his rule and reign over us) is preached and received that people are set free from the powerful delusion of Samarianism and the false fear of God. Notice how once those of Samaria received the word of the Lord (Ac 8:25), they now learned <u>how to walk</u> in the true fear of God. "Then had the churches rest throughout all Judaea and Galilee and <u>Samaria</u>, and were edified; and walking in the fear of the Lord, and in the comfort of the Holy Ghost, were multiplied." Ac 9:31 This is the importance of God's kingdom coming into our life. Without it, recapturing the fear of God in our heart will be impossible. The kingdom of God, which brings back God's rule, must be established in our hearts if we are ever to taste of the true fear of God.

God has always desired a people who would come out from the world and not touch its uncleanness. The world will always leave its spot and stain upon us, as long as we fellowship with it or desire any of its ways.

> Wherefore come out from among them, and be ye separate, saith the Lord, and touch not the unclean *thing*; and I will receive you, And will be a Father unto you, and ye shall be my sons and daughters, saith the Lord Almighty. 2Co 6:17-18

> Flee out of the midst of Babylon, and deliver every man his soul: be not cut off in her iniquity; for this *is* the time of the LORD's vengeance; he will render unto her a recompence. Jer 51:6

So we have been called out of the world to be disciples of the Lord to follow him and not to be entangled in the affairs of this world (2Tim 2:4). He is still looking for a people that he can make into a holy, spotless bride, without blemish.[31] Let us learn to become that chaste virgin who is "prepared as a bride adorned for her husband." Rev 21:2

The False Fear of God that has No Obedience

"If thou wilt not <u>observe</u> to do all the words of this law that are written in this book, that thou mayest fear this glorious and fearful name, THE LORD THY GOD" Dt 28:58

---

[31] Once we are saved, the Lord Jesus still must *prepare* us as a chaste virgin to be purified, to remove the blemishes and spots, by continually washing us with the word of God as we submit to him in obedience by denying ungodliness and worldly lusts (Eph 5:25-27, 2Co 11:2, Tit 2:11-14). There is much in our thinking that must be changed by our repeated submission to his truth.

2 – Cheap Imitations and Artificial Substitutes

Without hearing the word of God regularly there will be no enduring fear of God in the life of the believer. Without the Word we grow daily in self-dependence and a deceiving self-confidence that first came into Lucifer himself. He was gifted with divine wisdom and a host of other graces, yet he lost that most important grace, the grace of the fear of God, and so he was deceived. So it may happen to any man, for as Bunyan says in his book <u>The Fear of God</u>, "There is a faith and hope of mercy, that may deceive a man, because they are alone, and not attended with those companions that accompany salvation." [32]

Remember, the companion that we received at salvation: the fear of God. We must not forsake this holy helpmate of grace. In the book <u>Finding the Treasure of the Lord</u> we saw the most important companion of faith and hope is the fear of God. If it is missing, it calls into jeopardy all of grace's work. It is the fear of the LORD that arises from the word of God that is clean and enduring and that continually produces conviction of sin and presents afresh the glory of God before us to keep us humble and thankful. Yet at the same time we must remember, it is not just hearing the word of God that will produce the fear of God. We must add obedience unto what we hear. "If thou wilt not <u>observe</u> to do all the words of this law that are written in this book, that thou <u>mayest fear</u> this glorious and fearful name, THE LORD THY GOD" (Dt 28:58). Thus it is clear that 'observing to do all the words of this law that are written in this book' [i.e. the book of the Bible] will enable us to 'fear this glorious and fearful name, THE LORD THY GOD'.[33]

> There is a faith and hope that may deceive a man because they are alone, and not attended with those companions that accompany salvation.

As God spared the servants of Pharaoh who feared the word of the LORD and obeyed (Ex 9:20), so there is a blessing unto all who will fear him and obey him today. We may fear him and not obey, without a blessing from God. We may obey him and not fear him, without a blessing from God. But if we fear and obey, he is pleased. The two must go together. Because Levi feared God "and was afraid before my name" **and** obeyed God, therefore God gave him his covenant of life and peace (Mal 2:5). Thus, our daily study of the scriptures and our personal submission to the truths of scripture are paramount to maintaining and growing the clean and enduring fear of the LORD.

---

[32] "The Fear of God" by John Bunyan, The Religious Tract Society, London, UK, 1679 (reprinted 1839), p. 96-97.

[33] See the chapter entitled 'Feigned Faith, Forgotten Name, False Profession' under the section "The Feari of God & the Fear of His Name" for warnings on the wrong way to fear God's holy name.

Wherefore now **let** the fear of the LORD be upon you; <u>take heed and do it</u>: for *there is* no iniquity with the LORD our God, nor respect of persons, nor taking of gifts. 2Ch 19:7

Deceiving & Being Deceived

"But evil men and seducers shall wax worse and worse, deceiving, and being deceived." 2Tim 3:13

Both God and his servants wonder where is the fear of God in people's hearts, especially in the people of God. According to the prophecy of the New Covenant (Jer 32:40), the fear of God is birthed in us by the Holy Spirit as soon as we receive salvation. So we also ought to seriously wonder where is the fear of God in our heart? Is is still there growing or has it been lost or forsaken? If therefore it is absent, it is because either we have willingly laid it aside through an evil conscience, or it has been stolen from us by false teachings and traditions of religious men. This then is the great crime worked against the precious saint of God. He is falsely taught and persuaded that the fear of the LORD is not for today or *worse* that it is something different than what God's word says it is – saying it is but a reverence or a deep respect and awe of God.

The Fearful Day of the LORD

Such teachings have extracted from the heart of God's holy seed that which the Spirit of God has sown in them to prepare them for the Lord's coming. Remember, "for the day of the LORD *is* great and very terrible; and who can abide it?" Joel 2:11 The coming of the Lord is repeatedly known as the great and the terrible or dreadful day of the LORD.[34] Many times Christians have the idea that it will be a great day for the saved, but a terrible day for the lost. But this is not at all the meaning of these words, nor is it in agreement with the rest of the references to the day of the LORD. 'Terrible' (or 'dreadful' as in the case of Malachi 4:5) in Hebrew means 'to *fear*; morally to *revere*; causatively to *frighten*', and 'great' does not mean 'fantastic and wonderful', but rather 'high and mighty'. The day of the Lord will be a fearful day – even for the saved. Remember, the Bible says, "<u>who</u> can abide it?"

So many have the idea that the day of the Lord will be a great party for the Christian, a day of great rejoicing, and much light, a day to be longed for and desired, yet the Bible paints a very different picture. The day of the Lord will be a day of great darkness, not light. There will be no partying on that day, and there will be sorrow, not joy, especially for those who *desire* the day of the LORD. Listen to God's stunning words,

---

[34] The terrible day of the Lord: Joel 2:31, Mal 4:5, Ac 2:20.

2 – Cheap Imitations and Artificial Substitutes

> Woe unto you <u>that desire</u> the day of the LORD! to what end *is* it for you? the day of the LORD *is* <u>darkness</u>, and not light. *Shall* not the day of the LORD *be* <u>darkness</u>, and not light? even <u>very dark</u>, and no brightness in it? Am 5:18,20 (also Isa 13:9-10, Joel 2:31)

The Bible does not say *rejoice* for that day. Rather it says, "Howl ye; for the day of the LORD *is* at hand; it shall come as a destruction from the Almighty." Isa 13:6 It does not say dance, and skip, and shout for that day. It says, "Blow ye the trumpet in Zion, and sound an <u>alarm</u> in my holy mountain: let all the inhabitants of the land <u>tremble</u>: for the day of the LORD cometh, for *it is* nigh at hand" (Joel 2:1). It says, "Behold, the day of the LORD cometh, <u>cruel</u> both with <u>wrath</u> and <u>fierce anger</u>, to lay the land desolate" (Isa 13:9). It is the day of the *vengeance* of the Lord GOD of hosts (Jer 46:10) and "as a <u>destruction</u> from the Almighty shall it come." Joel 1:15

Did you hear that? Those in God's holy mountain, which is the Church, ought to be trembling and be in alarm when they think of the day of the Lord! Thus, Paul says, "For we must all appear before the judgment seat of Christ; that every one may receive the things *done* in *his* body, according to that he hath done, whether *it be* good or bad." 2Co 5:10 That day shall come as a thief in the night, suddenly (1Th 5:2, 2Pe 3:10) upon all who are not soberly waiting and watching! We must daily through the fear of God prepare for that day.

> So many have the idea that the day of the Lord will be a great party for the Christian, a day of great rejoicing, and much light, a day to be longed for and desired, yet the Bible paints a very different picture.

We live in a truly grievous day when the Lord is near to returning, yet his people are caught up in the affairs of this life and are not living soberly. Because we have lost the fear of God, we have also lost soberness, for only the fear of God will keep us sober. Because we have lost soberness, therefore we have lost our spiritual watchfulness. Yet, this is exactly how we are called to wait for the fearful day of the Lord: with watchfulness and soberness. "But the end of all things is at hand: be ye therefore <u>sober</u>, and <u>watch</u> unto prayer." 1Pe 4:7 We are called as saints of God *not* to be surprised by the day of the Lord, nor to be caught unawares. In relationship to that day, Paul warns, "Therefore let us not sleep, **as *do* others**; but let us <u>watch</u> and be <u>sober</u>." 1Th 5:6

Even in Paul's day some of the church was already sleeping and not watching or being sober, for he says "as *do* others" (1Th 5:6). Thus, he instructed Titus to teach every one to be sober or *circumspect*, from the aged men, to the old women likewise, to the young women, and to the young men (Tit 2:1-6). The importance of soberness can be seen not only that all age groups were to be taught it, but also that it was the first thing to be taught them.[35]

This word 'sober' comes from the word which means 'to *abstain* from wine (*keep sober*), i.e. (figurative) *be discreet*'. But the word itself includes more than that, for it means 'to be *circumspect*'. One may drink no alcohol at all, and yet not be circumspect or watchful in their spiritual life. Our soberness and watchfulness must be that we don't fall into the wiles of the devil, which are to bring us into bondage through worldliness and doing things like the world. Jesus continually taught his disciples to watch (especially in regard to his coming), yet how often they did not watch!

> Watch therefore, for ye know neither the day nor the hour wherein the Son of man cometh. Mt 25:13 (also Mt 24:42, Mk 13:33-35)
>
> Watch ye therefore, and pray always, that ye may be accounted worthy to escape all these things that shall come to pass, and to stand before the Son of man. Lk 21:36
>
> And what I say unto you I say unto **all**, Watch. Mk 13:37

Jesus spoke to his disciples that they *must* watch and pray always to escape the things that were to come to pass. How far we are with our rapture mentality (with our "I'm outta' here" attitude) from such a spirit of watchfulness and taking warning. How are the saints of God being properly prepared for such a sobering day without the fear of God to make them watchful in spirit? It cannot be done. We can only be prepared with soberness for his coming **with** the fear of the Lord working deeply in our heart. Without it, so many are deceived and being deceived, thinking that they are already ready, when they are woefully unprepared for that great and terrible day.

---

[35] Consider this, to be sober is the *first* instruction given to the aged men (Tit 2:2). It is the *first* instruction given to the young women (Tit 2:4), and it is the *only* instruction given to young men (Tit 2:6)!

2 – Cheap Imitations and Artificial Substitutes

Table 2-2   The Counterfeiting of What is Real

Item[36]	True/Good	False/Evil
way	Jn 14:6, Ac 9:2, 16:17, 19:9,23, 22:4, 24:14,22	Ps 119:104,128
spirit	Neh 9:20, Ps 143:10	2Co 11:4
gospel	Gal 2:5,14, Eph 1:13, Col 1:5	2Co 11:4
God/gods	Jn 17:3, 1Jn 5:20, Jer 10:10, 2Ch 15:3, 2Co 1:18, 1Th 1:9	Gal 4:8, Jer 2:11, 5:7, 16:20, 19:26
Christ/christs	1Jn 5:20, Jn 17:3	Mt 24:24, 2Co 11:4
apostles, prophets, & teachers	Eph 4:11-15, 3:5, 2:20, 1Co 12:28	2Co 11:13; Mt 7:15, 24:11,24, Ac 13:6, 1Jn 4:1; 2Pe 2:1
ministers, ministries	Eph 6:21, Col 4:7, 1:7; 1Tim 4:6, 1Pe 4:10	2Co 11:15, Lk 16:1-8
congregation(s)	Ps 68:10, 74:2,4	Ps 26:5, Nu 14:27,35
worship(pers)	Jn 4:23	Mt 15:9/Mk 7:7
brethren	Php 4:3; Gen 42:19,33-34	2Co 11:26, Gal 2:4
heart	Heb 10:22	deceived: Isa 44:20, Ob 1:3, Ro 16:18, Jam 1:26
riches	Lk 16:11	Mt 13:22/Mk 4:19
light	Jn 1:9, Isa 42:16	Isa 5:20, Mt 6:23/Lk 11:35
grace	1Pe 5:12	Jude 1:4
vine	Jn 15:1-4	Jer 2:21, Hos 10:1, Dt 32:32
fruit	Jn 15:16, Lk 8:15	Mt 7:17-18, 12:33
visions, dreams	Ac 2:17, 9:10, 10:17, 16:9, 18:9, 26:19	Jer 14:14, 23:32, Zec 10:2, Jude 1:8
miracles, wonders, signs, gifts	Ac 2:22,43, 4:30, 5:12, 6:8, 14:3, 15:12, Rom 12:6, 15:19, 1Co 12:4, 2Co 12:12, Heb 2:4	2Th 2:9-12, Mt 24:24/Mk 13:22, Rev 13:11-13, Pr 25:14
witness, testimony	Jn 21:24, 2Co 6:8, Tit 1:13, 3Jn 1:12, Rev 3:14, Pr 14:25, 1K 22:16	Ps 27:12, Pr 6:19, Mt 26:59-60, Ac 6:13, Dt 19:18 [2Tim 3:3, Tit 2:3]
saying, proverb, words, report	1Tim 3:1, Jn 4:37, 2Pe 2:22, Rev 19:9, 21:5, 22:6, 1K 10:6	Gen 37:2, Nu 13:32, 14:37, Neh 6:13, 2Co 6:8
doctrine/teachings	Pr 4:2, 1Tim 1:10, 4:6, 2Tim 4:3-4, Tit 1:9, 2:1,7	Mk 7:7, Eph 4:14, Col 2:22, 1Tim 1:3, 4:1, Heb 13:9
holiness	Eph 4:24	Ac 3:12
versions of scripture	Ps 119:160, 2Sam 7:28	2Co 2:17, 2Co 4:2, Mal 2:6-8

---

[36] We also see a true *tabernacle* (Heb 8:2, 9:24), therefore there must be a false one also. In addition, there are other examples, such as true *laws* & *judgments* (Neh 9:13, Eze 18:8, Zec 7:9, Jn 8:16, Rev 16:7, 19:2, Ps 19:9), as well as false (Dan 7:25, Isa 24:5).

More Abundant Life

Chapter 3. Feigned Faith, Forgotten Name, False Profession
Further Unveiling the False Fear of God
"their fear toward me is taught by the precept of men" Isa 29:13

In these last days we are going to and fro, increasing in knowledge, and many hunger for spiritual experiences, yet at the same time we are often not growing in intimacy with each other or with the Lord. Let us consider the glory of the LORD for a moment in relationship to fearing him. The glory of the LORD will surprisingly be one of the things that draws us nearer to God to have intimacy with him. Not only is the LORD himself to be feared, but also the things concerning him are to be feared as well. We are to fear:

- his goodness (Hos 3:5, Jer 33:9),
- his great & mighty works (2K 17:36),
- his glory (Ps 102:15, Isa 59:19, 2:10,19,21).

God's glory is manifested among several ways, one of which is by the glory of his name. Thus, the scriptures proclaim that we should not only fear God, but we should also fear his name. The love and admiration of God's name cannot be given justice here, even if we took a whole chapter (much less part of

3 – Feigned Faith, Forgotten Name, False Profession

one). O the volumes of praise that belong to our awesome God for his marvelous name! "Who shall not fear thee, O Lord, and glorify thy name? for *thou* only *art* holy" (Rev 15:4). Yet it would be remiss indeed to not touch upon this vital point, for the understanding and proper knowledge of his name will allow us to know the LORD in a more intimate way and to recapture the fear of God.

The Fear of God & the Fear of His Name
"that all people of the earth may <u>know thy name</u>,
<u>to fear thee</u>, as do thy people Israel" 1K 8:43

The fear of God's name is recorded in scripture over and over again. Men may mock fearing God's name, but it has always been holy – far more holy than man ever realizes. Notice even in Revelation 15:4 that the glory of God's name is rooted in his holiness. For this purpose, God had to make his third commandment evidently clear that if we take his name in vain we are worthy of death: "for the LORD will <u>not hold him guiltless</u> that taketh his name in vain." Ex 20:7 Men may try to hide God's name and think this is how we fear his name.[37] But just as we have seen that we are to fear God and to trust in him, so it is with his name. "Who *is* among you that feareth the LORD ... let him <u>trust in the name</u> of the LORD, and stay upon his God." Isa 50:10

> **WARNING**: We are to fear God's name *and* to trust in his name. The fear of his name is not some way of avoiding saying it, anymore than the true fear of God is fleeing or hiding from God. Fearing God will draw us closer to him, if we fear him in truth and not in hypocrisy. So fearing God's name will cause us to speak his name <u>more often</u>, not less often! Fearing God's name has nothing to do with NOT speaking his holy name and calling him by some other title. That is what men think, but God says to fear his name is to <u>obey him</u>. "If thou wilt not <u>observe to do</u> all the words of this law that are written in this book, **that thou mayest fear** this glorious and fearful name, THE LORD THY GOD" (Dt 28:58).

Fearing the glorious and fearful name "THE LORD THY GOD" comes about as we observe to do the word of God. That is the true servant's heart: to do his master's will – not for selfish gain, but because he is our master. This is reflected in Nehemiah's prayer. "O LORD, I beseech thee, let now thine ear be attentive to the prayer of thy servant, and to the prayer of <u>thy servants,</u> who

---

[37] A large portion of this chapter is dedicated to exposing the false doctrine of referring to God as "G-d" and in English to Yeshua or Joshua or some other non-Biblical variant, rather than the revealed and preserved name of Jesus. This is of great importance because the fear of God and the fear of his name are intimately linked. If we do not rightly fear his name, we cannot fear him.

Where is the Fear of GOD? Losing the Treasure of the Lord

desire to fear thy name" (Neh 1:11). Note in it how servants desire to fear the name of their Lord. This word 'desire' means 'to be *pleased* with, to delight in'.

For servants of the LORD, the fearing of God's name is their desire and delight. So the fear of God's name becomes its own reward. We are to love his name and so honor it that we fear his name. Men may mock fearing God, but there is truly a reward for those who will fear his name. God promises both the healing of unrighteousness and growth in maturity to those who will fear his name. "But unto you that fear my name shall the Sun of righteousness arise with healing in his wings; and ye shall go forth, and grow up as calves of the stall." Mal 4:2 For us to grow up and produce fruitful labor (as an oxen unto our master) we need to fear his name. To be healed from our unrighteous ways we need to fear his name. One day at the end of time there will be a reward for those who fear his name, may we be patient and faithful to wait for it. Truly, we need to learn to fear God *and* his name.

> And the nations were angry, and thy wrath is come, and the time of the dead, that they should be judged, and that thou shouldest give reward unto thy servants the prophets, and to the saints, and them that fear thy name, small and great; Rev 11:18

WARNING: Seeing that spiritual maturity and spiritual healing from unrighteousness both come from learning to fear the name of God, what does it mean when we have a generation of youth who are being taught about a 'rad Jesus and calling him "JC" or "my homeboy"? It truly reveals how we have lost the fear of God, for his name is no longer holy on our lips. It shows that those who are teaching and instructing such youth truly have no fear of God, no real spiritual maturity in God's eyes, and they have not been healed from the unrighteousness of their own worldly ways!

Knowing and using the name of God should produce the fear of God in us as we see the power of the Almighty and grow in understanding of his ways. We see David came in the name of the LORD. "Then said David to the Philistine, Thou comest to me with a sword, and with a spear, and with a shield: but I come to thee in the name of the LORD of hosts" (1Sam 17:45). We ought, like Jesus, like David, like the prophets of old, and like the disciples themselves, come to people in the name of God declaring unto them the truth. This was Peter and John's example, repeatedly.[38] This was passed on to the disciples (Ac 4:30). Philip, when he went to Samaria, preached the name of Jesus Christ (Ac 8:12). He did not hide it or change it, but declared it plainly. Paul was even bolder to speak in the name of Jesus. Of Paul it is spoken that "he had preached **boldly** at Damascus in the name of Jesus." Ac 9:27 While Paul was in Jerusalem "he spake **boldly** in the name of the Lord Jesus, and disputed against the

---

[38] They repeatedly spoke in Jesus' name: Ac 3:6,16, 4:10,17-19, 5:28-29,40-41, 10:43,48.

3 – Feigned Faith, Forgotten Name, False Profession

Grecians: but they went about to slay him." Ac 9:29 Paul was not willing to be silent about the name of Jesus, even if it cost him his life. Neither can we be silent about the name of Jesus.

Oftentimes the very beginning of the fear of God in a person's life begins simply with learning to know the name of God. The greatness of God's name is able to inspire us not only to worship him with thanksgiving, praise, and adoration, but also to fear him. This is because the name of God carries and illustrates both his character, his honor, and his authority. Both in the Hebrew and the Greek the word for 'name' carries this tri-fold purpose.

> The primary word for 'name' in the Old Testament is *shem* (H8034) which means 'an appellation, as a mark or memorial of individuality; by implication <u>honor, authority, character</u>.' It comes from a root which carries 'the idea of definite and conspicuous position.'

Thus, God's name is the mark and the memorial of his individuality and uniqueness. His name reveals a portion[39] of his honor, his authority, and his character. The New Testament usage for 'name' is very similar. The primary word for 'name' there is *onoma* which means 'a "name" (literally or figuratively) (<u>authority, character</u>)'. Thus, both Old Testament and New, from cover to cover the Bible maintains that within God's very name is represented his authority and his character. This is why the revelation of the nature of God comes to us when we learn his holy and awesome name! Without his name we lose a portion of our understanding the awesomeness of his greatness.

God's name is so representative of his very person and his authority that to take his name in vain was to face death by stoning (Lev 24:11-23). God held men, women, and children directly accountable for not properly honoring his name. "Thou shalt not take the name of the LORD thy God in vain: for the LORD will not hold *him* guiltless that taketh his name in vain." Dt 5:11 Thus, the name of God and the fear of the LORD go hand in hand, because both are used by God to bring us into the understanding of his holiness. Solomon's prayer of dedication of the temple that he built unto God was that when the stranger would come and offer prayer and his prayer would be heard, it would be for this reason: "that all people of the earth may <u>know thy name</u>, to fear thee, as *do* thy people Israel" (1Kings 8:43/2Ch 6:33). The fear of the LORD was manifest in the people of Israel *because* they knew the name of God and called upon him when they had need and not upon any other god. The knowledge of God's name is vital to fearing him. If we would recapture the fear of God, then we must also recapture the knowledge of his name. This is the importance of knowing the name of God.

---

[39] This is of course why he has so many names, so that he may reveal the incredible fulness of who he is.

We must come to learn the name of the LORD, if we are to have the proper fear of him. Many today think that the name of God is lost and not preserved, since they believe it was not spoken by the Israelites – supposedly because they did not want to use it in vain and so be guilty of an eternal sin. Though this is indeed what religious men, like the Pharisees did, yet those who knew God and followed him wholeheartedly did not decline from using God's name. The scripture shows God's servants who were in true covenant with him did not hide God's name, but with great joy declared it.

A False Fear of God: Not Saying God's Name

"Thou shalt fear the LORD thy God; him shalt thou serve, and to him shalt thou cleave, and swear by his name." Dt 10:20

When the scripture speaks of fearing the name of God it does NOT mean the false mystical fear of not pronouncing or writing God's name. That is just the latest wind of doctrine that has affected the religious and falsely pious. Calling the LORD thy GOD "G-d" in speech or in writing is anti-scriptural. It is just another form of strange fire – something God never asked for or commanded. In fact, "G-d" is not God at all. He was never known by such a name by those who knew him. Search the scriptures. You will find no such name. It is some new, strange god which our forefathers in the faith never knew. Nowhere in scripture or by the followers of the true Lord are such practices done or encouraged. Why do people do this today? They do this in order, supposedly, that the name of God not be blasphemed or taken in vain. Yet if they would know the truth, they would find it is not by unbelievers that the name of God is shamed and blasphemed, but it is by the life and actions of his own people.[40]

> Thou that makest thy boast of the law, through breaking the law dishonourest thou God? For <u>the name of God is blasphemed among the Gentiles through you</u>, as it is written. Rom 2:23-24

> And when they entered unto the heathen, whither they went, <u>they profaned my holy name</u>, when they said to them, These *are* the people of the LORD, and are gone forth out of his land. But I had pity for mine holy name, <u>which the house of Israel had profaned among the heathen, whither they went</u>. Therefore say unto the house of Israel, Thus saith the Lord GOD; I do not *this* for your sakes, O house of Israel, but for mine holy name's sake, <u>which ye have profaned among the heathen</u>, whither ye went. And I will sanctify my great name, <u>which was profaned among the heathen, which ye have profaned in the midst of them</u>; and the heathen shall know that I *am* the LORD, saith the Lord GOD, when I shall be sanctified in you before their eyes. Eze 36:20-23

---

[40] God's name is blasphemed by the disobedience of his people: Jer 23:10-11, Eze 22:26-27, 1Tim 6:1.

3 – Feigned Faith, Forgotten Name, False Profession

What glory is there when we hide the name of God?[41] How is the Lord magnified when we do *not* use the name of Jesus, but only Christ or God? This is exactly what people do today. So many speak of Christ and God, but they rarely use the name of Jesus. Why? Because there are many Christs and many gods. There is little offense when one speaks of Christ or God. But there is only one Jesus and he is the stumblingblock; that is where offense comes. Greatness is given to God when his name is published, when it is written out! "Because I will publish the name of the LORD: ascribe ye greatness unto our God." Dt 32:3 The word 'publish' means 'to *call* out to (i.e. properly *address* by name)'. God is magnified and glorified when he is properly addressed by his name, when it is called out and not hidden. Think of all those who are hiding God's name by writing or publishing "G-d". How does *that* acribe greatness unto our God?

God, in fact, had to raise up men, set them on high in their kingdoms, and grant them world-conquering power in order to gain even part of the glory that was due his holy and awesome name when he took these men and their kingdoms down. Through the destruction of Pharaoh, God brought glory to his name. "For the scripture saith unto Pharaoh, Even for this same purpose have I raised thee up, that I might shew my power in thee, and that <u>my name might be declared throughout all the earth</u>." Rom 9:17 Did you hear that? God used the whole situation of the entire destruction of Egypt and the toppling of the mighty Pharaoh for one purpose: that his **name** might be DECLARED throughout ALL the earth.

God is not interested in hiding his name from mankind! On the contrary, he wants his name to be declared, 'to be *heralded thoroughly*' to all mankind. Solomon in dedicating the house of God says "that all people of the earth may <u>know thy name</u>, to fear thee" (1K 8:43). Note how the knowledge of God's name brings about the fear of God. God is not trying to hide his name from the people of the earth as religious men of today would have us do. He has always been trying to do just the opposite, to declare his name to all people. We bring shame by *not* declaring his name, but we bring glory to his name by declaring it in truth and in righteousness. Let us walk in integrity and proclaim his name, and we will see those come from afar to investigate the name of our God.

> Who *are* ye? and from whence come ye? And they said unto him, From a very far country thy servants are come **because** <u>of the name of the LORD thy God</u>: for we have heard the fame of him, and all that he did in Egypt, Jos 9:9

---

[41] When we compare the record of the testimony God has left us, God has magnified his son Jesus by using his name more often than his titles. We see Jesus used 977 times, but Christ by itself (i.e. without Jesus) only 293 times and even Lord by itself (i.e. without Jesus) in the New Testament 531 times. [Note: Some of these uses also refer to the Father.] The personal name of Jesus is clearly given preeminence, even over all his titles.

Where is the Fear of GOD? Losing the Treasure of the Lord

So the queen of Sheba "heard of the fame of Solomon <u>concerning the name of the LORD</u>" (1K 10:1). Hear again King Solomon, "that all people of the earth may <u>know thy name</u>, to fear thee" (1K 8:43). Men always put things in reverse order from what God has set. Men think that if we fear God we should conceal his name from unbelievers. God says make it known so that they may fear. Throughout the scripture the LORD is not keeping his name secret, rather he is telling it to them that love him, so that they may tell others: "and this *is* his name whereby he shall be called, THE LORD OUR RIGHTEOUSNESS." Jer 23:6 When the Son of God was to be born into this earth it was prophesied more than 700 years before his birth what his name would be (Isa 9:6)! While he was not yet in his mother's womb the angel came and spoke to her what his name should be (Mt 1:21,25)! Let us know and treasure and speak of his wonderful name.

O the foolishness of men who would try to "protect" the name of God and keep it 'holy' by not speaking it, yet by their own actions they profane it, making it *unholy*. These are the traditions and the hypocrisies of the Pharisees that have added to the word and distorted it to keep their own control and authority. God is not interested in reviving the Gnostic myths of secret words of power or secret names of God. This is the lie that John the beloved fought already in the first century. Let us not ignorantly return to that which he exposed and condemned. The name of God is the treasure that God has given to them that know and love him.

> The secret of the LORD *is* with them that fear him; and he will shew them his covenant.[42] Ps 25:14
>
> Some *trust* in chariots, and some in horses: but we will <u>remember</u>[43] the name of the LORD our God. Ps 20:7

If we trust in the LORD, we will remember his name as we make mention of it. Let his name always be sweet upon our lips. God revealed his name to Abraham and to Moses and to all those who had intimate encounters with him. Notice how God declared his name unto Moses, not as a secret or as something to be hidden, but as a *reward* of his faithfulness, something that with great joy Moses should in turn declare unto the people.

> And he said, I will make all my goodness pass before thee, and I will <u>proclaim the name of the LORD</u> before thee; … And the LORD descended in the cloud, and stood with him there, and <u>proclaimed the name of the LORD</u>. And the LORD passed by before him, and <u>proclaimed</u>, The LORD, The LORD God, merciful and gracious, longsuffering, and abundant in goodness and truth Ex 33:19, 34:5-6

---

[42] Remember, his name *is* his covenant with us.

[43] The word 'remember' here means 'to *remember*, by implication to <u>mention</u>'.

The Revelation of God's Name

"And I appeared unto Abraham, unto Isaac, and unto Jacob, by the name of God Almighty, but by my name JEHOVAH was I not known to them." Ex 6:3

God is continually revealing, not hiding his name. Moses did not hide the name of God from the people. He did not write 'G-d'. No, he made it plain and wrote it down for all to see. He says, "Because I will <u>publish</u> the name of the LORD: ascribe ye greatness unto our God." Dt 32:3 Did Moses keep this name secret? No, he told all of Israel the name of the LORD! As it was proclaimed or 'called out' to him, so he proclaimed it and published it to God's people.

> **WARNING**: Do not let people twist the word of God and say that "the LORD" is not God's name. The scripture is perfectly clear, "The LORD **is** his name" (Am 5:8)! All the great saints of old "called upon the name of the LORD".[44] That means they didn't keep his name hidden or secret, rather they used it openly whenever they prayed or called out for God's help. His promise to us is, if we call upon his name, he will hear us (Zec 13:9).

Can we think of anything so foreign to scripture itself as *not* writing or pronouncing the name of God? God has always been in the process of revealing, not concealing his great name. God revealed himself and his name to Abraham, yet more to Moses, more to David, and to the prophets, and still more even to us of the new covenant who have come to know the name of the Lord as Jesus. Think of what we're losing when we refuse using God's name. John the beloved wrote, "But I trust I shall shortly see thee, and we shall speak face to face. Peace *be* to thee. *Our* friends salute thee. Greet the <u>friends by name</u>." 3Jn 1:14

> "Greet the <u>friends by name</u>." 3Jn 1:14
> Intimacy demands a name. Those who do not know
> the name of God, do not know God personally.

Thus, if we do not know a person's name, or equivalently, if we do not greet them "by name", then we are not truly friends. **Intimacy demands a name**. The more the Old Testament saints knew God, the more they knew of his name. Those who do not know the name of God, do not know God per-

---

[44] Seth's seed called on the name of the LORD (Gen 4:26). Abram called on the name of the LORD (Gen 12:8, 13:4, 21:33). Isaac called on the name of the LORD (Gen 26:25). Moses, Aaron, & Samuel all called on the name of the LORD (Ps 99:6). David called on the name of the LORD (1Ch 16:7-10, Ps 105:1, 116:4,13,17). Elijah called on the name of the LORD (1K 18:24). Jeremiah called on the name of the LORD (Lam 3:55). We also are to call on the name of the Lord (Ac 2:21 & Rom 10:13).

sonally. There is no true intimacy without the knowing of one's name. The same can be said of our relationship with the Lord. If we do not use his name when greeting him, then it truly bewrays the fact that we are not the friends of God as Abraham was, and that we have no real intimacy with God.

But What is His Name?

The question that comes up (especially in regard to our English Bible) is, "Do we have the actual name of God recorded for us in the scripture?" Certainly there are many descriptive names based on his positions and titles which he holds, but these we would not call his actual name. He has in fact, though, given us his personal name. So God himself instructs us, "And I appeared unto Abraham, unto Isaac, and unto Jacob, by *the name of* God Almighty, but by my name **JEHOVAH** was I not known to them." Ex 6:3 Thus, he once went by the name God Almighty, but now he has revealed a deeper, a more intimate name: "JEHOVAH".[45]

Contrary to what some say today, JEHOVAH *is* his personal divinely inspired name. Why does God instruct us that his name is literally JEHOVAH? "That *men* may know that thou, whose name alone *is* JEHOVAH, *art* the most high over all the earth." Ps 83:18 Hear what the scripture says, his name is JEHOVAH. Even as we know our master's full name as "our Lord Jesus Christ"[46] or "Jesus Christ our Lord" (1Co 1:2), so we also know him on a first name basis as "Jesus".[47] So, we have the Father's shortened and more personal name once recorded for us. It is "JAH". "Sing unto God, sing praises to his name: extol him that rideth upon the heavens by his name **JAH**, and rejoice before him."[48] Ps 68:4

The Reason for Revealing His Wondrous Name

God has revealed his name not so that we may hide it, but so that we may meditate on it. So we see that those "that feared the LORD, thought upon his name." Mal 3:16 If we did not have the revelation of his name preserved for us intact and without error, then we could not think on his name today, nor would we have an inerrant, preserved word of God. The name of the LORD is so integrated into our very walk of faith with him that it is the very door of salvation.

---

[45] Every time "JEHOVAH" appears by itself it is always in small caps (Ex 6:3, Ps 83:18, Isa 12:2, 26:4). Only when it is combined with another modifier is it normal capitalization, such as in Jehovah-jireh, Jehovah-nissi, & Jehovah-shalom (Gen 22:4, Ex 17:15, Jdg 6:24).

[46] See Ac 15:26, 1Co 1:10, 5:4, Eph 5:20, 2Th 1:12, 3:6.

[47] The name of the Lord is Jesus: Mt 1:21,25, Lk 1:31, 2:21.

[48] It is not coincidental that this intimate name of God, JAH, is recorded only once for us and that, that one time, it is in the context of rejoicing before him.

3 – Feigned Faith, Forgotten Name, False Profession

By calling on the name of the LORD, we receive salvation[49] and the process of coming to know God by faith begins.

As we call upon his name to obtain mercy and find grace to help in time of need, we come to know the power of his name and the fear of God increases within us. The priests of old from Moses, Aaron, and his sons, had the fear of God's name. The fear of God and the fear of his name are to go together. Even unto the end times we see there are a people whom God will reward "that fear thy name" (Rev 11:18). Where is the fear of God's name today (Mal 2:5)? We have lost the fearfulness of God's great name. Where is the fear of God today? "Who shall not fear thee, O Lord, and glorify thy name?" Rev 15:4 When we truly fear God, we will glorify God's name, not hide it.

> The fear of God always involves the fear of his name.
> It is impossible to fear God and *not* to fear his name.

God gave the covenant of a natural priesthood to the tribe of Levi for his stand on the word of God. Those Levites, according to the command of God, were willing to put obedience to God before even their own family and, per his command, slay those who had forsaken God. As a result, God chose them out to be his peculiar and royal priesthood. In the spiritual realm today, God has chosen us in Christ to be his peculiar and royal priesthood (1Pe 2:9,5). IF we likewise would fulfill the requirements of discipleship to follow our chief shepherd Jesus, as they followed their shepherd Moses, we *must* be willing to love him more than any other, especially our own friends and family. This is why Jesus said in the first requirement of discipleship, "If any *man* come to me, and hate not his father, and mother, and wife, and children, and brethren, and sisters, yea, and his own life also, he cannot be my disciple." Lk 14:26

The covenant of the priesthood that God gave unto Levi of life and peace was because of the fear that he feared God with *and* because he feared God's name (Mal 2:5). The fear of God always involves the fear of his name. It is impossible to fear God and *not* to fear his name. Note how immediately Malachi goes from asking where is God's fear to them that despise or *disesteem* God's name. "… if I *be* a master, where *is* my fear? saith the LORD of hosts unto you, O priests, that despise my name. And ye say, Wherein have we despised thy name?" Mal 1:6 It was after Joshua's generation passed away that "there arose another generation after them, which knew not the LORD" (Judges 2:10). It seems there has been an age-old problem of not declaring his name and his works to the next generation! May we not be of that spirit of unfaithfulness, but

---

[49] Whosoever shall call on the name of the Lord shall be saved: Ac 2:21; Rom 10:13; Ps 116:13.

may we publish his name and make it known to all the earth so that people may ascribe greatness unto our God.

Let us look at God's fearful and glorious name (Dt 28:58). Think of this, the <u>fearful</u> name "THE LORD THY GOD".[50] How many of us know the fearfulness, the frightfulness of God's name? This should immediately reveal how far what we have been taught in Christianity is from what the apostles and prophets must have taught. When we hear the phrase "the LORD thy God" we think of security and comfort, but the Bible says we need to come to know the fearfulness of the LORD thy God![51] God's people ought to have a great fear of his name, because his name represents his authority. God's protection is extended to them that do. "But unto you that fear my name shall the Sun of righteousness arise with healing in his wings; and ye shall go forth, and grow up as calves of the stall." Mal 4:2

The Purity of the Name of Jesus

For those who speak English, changing the precious name of Jesus to Yeshua or Joshua or some other Jewish variant flies in the face of the preservation of God's word. "Remove not the ancient landmark, which thy fathers have set." Pr 22:28 We must know and believe that God has preserved the scriptures and has produced a translation of those scriptures which is inerrant (i.e. without error). Remember, God gave the Old Testament in Hebrew and the New Testament in Greek, but he gave us the Bible in these last days in English. He promised that he would give a pure language, "For then will I turn to the people a <u>pure language</u>, that they may all call upon the name of the LORD, to serve him with one consent." Zep 3:9

No one can argue the overwhelming effect that the King James Bible has had over any other translation. All the great revivals occurred under its influence. Why? "Where the word of a king *is, there is* power" (Ecc 8:4). There is a profound significance that people often do not give serious thought to concerning the King James Bible. It was the only translation ever mandated by a king, thus it alone is called the Authorized Version. Out of all the names of the kings that it could have been, in God's sovereign power it was King James.

After one is born again, the first two books a new believer should read are the gospel of John and the epistle of 1John to get a foundation in what it is to be born again. But the very next book a new believer ought to read and to study well is the book of James, which deals all with the character that God wants to

---

[50] The capitals are *not* added by me, but are in the King James translation, clearly for emphasis.

[51] The scripture declares that even among the heathen God's name is to be dreadful: "for I *am* a great King, saith the LORD of hosts, and my name *is* dreadful among the heathen." Mal 1:14

3 – Feigned Faith, Forgotten Name, False Profession

develop in a believer's life and how to keep hypocrisy out. James is the book of godly character, which is what the Lord desires every one of his children to grow up into. Can we doubt then why God ordained that, of all the names of the kings that it could have been, it was exactly this: King James! This is the power and strength of the King James Bible that through the purity of the translation and the pure language that God gave it in, it produces godly character, just like the epistle of the same name, the epistle of James.

Can we now come in and say that God was wrong in giving us the name 'Jesus' in English? No, for no greater scholarship by true believers has ever been done before or since the King James Bible. These were first and foremost men that held to the unwavering truth and preservation of the scriptures (that all the modern translations reject). Hence, they did not go to unsound sources to try to 'find' the word of God. Though they compared other sources to ensure the soundness of their translation, yet their one *source* for God's word was the original Hebrew text and the original Greek text. They rejected the false and impure sources and did not trust in such works as the Septuagint[52] and the Codex Vaticanus[53] in which they saw the corruptions of men's views and opinions. Therefore as it is written,

> Be it known unto you all, and to all the people of Israel, that by <u>the name of Jesus Christ</u> of Nazareth, …. Neither is there salvation in any other: for there is none other name under heaven given among men, whereby we must be saved. Ac 4:10,12

I wonder of such people who want to change the name of the Lord Jesus and to put away the name of God, what will they do when God fulfills his holy word? The Bible says that "we will call upon thy name" when he has quickened us or made us alive (Ps 80:18). If we are born again today and made alive by the breath of the Holy Spirit, then by the scriptures "we will call upon thy name" today. It was Pharisees like Saul, speaking prior to his salvation, who said, "I verily thought with myself, that I ought to do <u>many things contrary to the name of Jesus</u> of Nazareth." Ac 26:9 This is the same religious spirit that works in the hearts of men who truly need to have an encounter with Jesus of Nazareth. We ought not to do anything contrary, against, or *antagonistic* to the name of Jesus.

For His Name's Sake

And what of all the scriptures that speak of suffering for his name's sake? Who can suffer for 'G-d' or 'Yeshua'? Persecution in the book of Acts came

---

[52] The Septuagint is the Greek translation of the Old Testament along with the New Testament in Greek. According to many witnesses over the ages, including the King James translators, it was a very poor translation of the Hebrew text.

[53] This is Rome's corrupted manuscript with many editorial changes and missing portions of scripture.

upon those that called upon the name of the Lord,[54] not on those that hid it, or did not confess it. Peter encourages us, "If ye be reproached <u>for the name of Christ</u>, happy *are ye;* for the spirit of glory and of God resteth upon you: on their part he is evil spoken of, but on your part he is glorified." 1Pe 4:14 Thus, when we are reproached for using the name of the Lord, we should be happy, for on our part he is being glorified. But how can we *possibly* suffer for his name's sake if we never <u>speak his name</u>?

> **<u>WARNING</u>**: We live in a world today of people pleasers, who would not offend, yet Paul said if we seek to please men, then we CANNOT be the servant of Christ (Gal 1:10). I would challenge all who say they are messianic Jews but refrain from using the name of Jesus because it offends fellow Jews and is a stumbling block unto them and therefore they would rather use a neutral, non-offensive name such as Joshua, or Yeshua. It is for those *very* reasons that God would have you NOT use those names, but use the name that does offend.
>
> Remember, Jesus *knew* that the Jews would be extremely offended if he spoke of eating his flesh and drinking his blood, and this is *why* he specifically said this, because he *knew* it would offend (Jn 6:51-57)! He wanted to find out, who truly would follow him, not for what they could get, but for whom he was. Jesus made no apology for offending people with truth (Jn 6:60-61, Mt 15:12-14). If people are offended when we speak the word of God and it testifies that the name of the Lord is Jesus, then Jesus would say "Let them alone: they be blind leaders of the blind. And if the blind lead the blind, both shall fall into the ditch." Mt 15:14 But let him who knows the name of the Lord proclaim it.

Have we forgotten who Jesus is? He *is* the stumblingblock! He *is* the stone which the builders rejected. IF a man cannot bear to hear the name of Jesus, then so would God have it, and we do violence against the kingdom of God by trying to lessen the offense of his name. Consider, how do we honor the saints who went before us who put their lives in jeopardy for the very name of Jesus?! Judas and Silas were men who "hazarded their lives <u>for the name of our Lord Jesus Christ</u>." Ac 15:26

How can our Lord, or such witnesses in heaven, think highly of those who deny his name today or the name of his Father, for the sake of supposedly reaching the lost, when men are recorded with honor in the scriptures for counting themselves blessed to suffer and die for the name of the Lord?! Paul was ready wherever he went to die **"for the name of the Lord Jesus"** (Ac 21:13). Are you willing, as those before you, to die for the name of Jesus? Is the name of Jesus as precious to you as it was to those who truly knew him?

---

[54] Persecution in the name of Jesus: Ac 4:7,10,17-19, 5:28-29,40-41, 9:14,21.

3 – Feigned Faith, Forgotten Name, False Profession

And what of those who do *not* call upon the name of the LORD? What does the scripture say of them? "Pour out thy fury upon the heathen that know thee not, **AND** upon the families that <u>call not on thy name</u>" (Jer 10:25, also Ps 79:6). Did you hear that? God mentions two separate groups of people who will face his judgment. First, God mentions those who do not know him, then he mentions those who evidently do know him, but who do not call upon or use his name! God likens those who do *not* call on his name to be in the same state as he does the heathen, that is, they are still lost and under the judgment of God, being children of disobedience and children of wrath.

I pray on the contrary you will have the heart as a true follower of the Lord, even as David, who did not hide the name of God but said, "I will <u>declare thy name</u> unto my brethren" (Ps 22:22). I pray you will follow in the footsteps of Jesus who said, "And <u>I have declared</u> unto them thy name, <u>and will declare *it*</u>: that the love wherewith thou hast loved me may be in them, and I in them." Jn 17:26 When one is truly saved they will not hide the name of God, rather they will proclaim it with joy and honor, that the same love we have in our heart for the Lord may also be in others. Hear what the saints declare,

> I will take the cup of salvation, and <u>call upon the name of the LORD</u>.[55] Ps 116:13

> quicken us [i.e. *make us alive*], and we will <u>call on thy name</u>. Ps 80:18

> Therefore with joy shall ye draw water out of the wells of salvation. And in that day[56] shall ye say, Praise the LORD, <u>call upon his name</u>, declare his doings among the people, make mention that his name is exalted. Isa 12:3-4

Those who are truly saved *will* call upon the name of the LORD and *will* make mention of it! "And it shall come to pass, *that* whosoever shall call on the name of the LORD shall be saved."[57] This is how salvation came in the New Testament, by calling on the name of the Lord: "wash away thy sins, <u>calling on the name of the Lord</u>." Ac 22:16 In fact, the Bible defines the saints (i.e. those who are sanctified in Christ Jesus) as those "that in every place <u>call upon the name of Jesus Christ our Lord</u>, both theirs and ours" (1Co 1:2). Isn't that amazing? Rather than hiding the name of Jesus, those who are true saints will call upon the name of Jesus "in every place". Do not let Jewish fables and commandments of men turn you from the truth (Tit 1:14).

---

[55] The word 'call upon' here means 'to *address* by name'! This same word is also used in the next two passages.

[56] That is, when you have drawn water out of the wells of salvation through the new birth.

[57] We must call on the name of the Lord for salvation: Ac 2:21 / Rom 10:13 / Joel 2:32.

The Counterfeit Fear of God: A Feigned Faith

"out of a pure heart, and of a good conscience, and of faith unfeigned: From which some having swerved have turned aside" 1Tim 3:5-6

Let us now look at the opposite extreme. Consider those who use the name of the Lord in vain. Many have a feigned faith today. They may even use the name of Jesus, but their 'faith' is really *'speaking* or *acting under* a false part'. It is merely *pretending*. When an actor assumes a part and then begins to believe that they are in fact that part – that is a feigned faith – for they in fact know they are not that person. Feigned faith is hoping that something is one way, when in reality it is known in the heart to be otherwise. Jesus said, "For many shall come in my name, saying, I am Christ; and shall deceive many." Mt 24:5 This is the day and hour we are in, where many claim to be of the Lord, but are not:

> Not every one that saith unto me, Lord, Lord, shall enter into the kingdom of heaven; but he that doeth the will of my Father which is in heaven. Many will say to me in that day, Lord, Lord, have we not prophesied in thy name? and in thy name have cast out devils? and in thy name done many wonderful works? And then will I profess unto them, I never knew you: depart from me, ye that work iniquity. Mt 7:21-23

WARNING: Men, without the fear of God, will try anything if they think it will work, even if they don't fully believe in it. So we have record in the scriptures of the seven sons of Sceva who used the name of Jesus as a 'charm' or a word of power, because they had seen it work in a man of God's life. But they themselves were unwilling to walk as men of God, laying down their lives for the sake of the truth. This form of hypocrisy or play-acting occurs all too often in Christianity as young ministers try to copy the flair and flamboyance that they see in those whom they believe to be "successful" ministers of the gospel, and error begets error, and the blind lead the blind.

At its root a feigned faith is willing self-deception. So how can such hypocrisy last? Only by an evil conscience. Remember again, "the end of the commandment is charity out of a pure heart, and *of* a good conscience, and *of* faith unfeigned: From which some having swerved have turned aside" (1Tim 3:5-6). A good conscience will always produce an unfeigned, a sincere, and a genuine faith. But an evil conscience will contrariwise lead to a feigned faith. It is our conscience that convicts us of sin (Jn 8:9, Heb 10:2), for it witnesses to us (Ro 2:15), it testifies to us (2Co 1:12), and it manifests to us the truth (2Co 5:11). This it does, when we are born again, all through the Holy Ghost. "I say the truth in Christ, I lie not, my conscience also bearing me witness in the Holy Ghost" (Rom 9:1).

3 – Feigned Faith, Forgotten Name, False Profession

> When someone who claims to be a Christian can have
> a casual attitude toward sin or more accurately toward
> the word of God which reproves their sin,
> then you know they have an evil conscience.

It is our conscience which instructs us to be subject to authority, especially the Lord's authority which is directly manifested through his Word. "Wherefore *ye* must needs be subject, not only for wrath, but also <u>for conscience sake</u>." Rom 13:5 'Be subject' here is also translated 'to be under obedience' (1Co 14:34) and 'obedient' (Tit 2:5,9). Our conscience impresses on us that we must be obedient to the Lord. Thus, when someone who claims to be a Christian can have a casual attitude toward sin or more accurately toward the word of God, which reproves their sin, then you know they have an evil conscience. They have chosen to reject the conviction of the Holy Ghost and have decided to willfully do what they want. They have rejected the Lord's control and right to be master of their life and in truth have departed from the faith.

When one lives too long in this state, resisting the Holy Spirit, the conscience will become seared. Like a pot left on the stove without being stirred, the sauce must burn. Once a man's conscience has been seared, he will *always* speak lies in hypocrisy. Sadly, such professing Christians are not uncommon in the church. All of this testifies again as to why the fear of God must be recaptured by the church of Jesus Christ.

> Now the Spirit speaketh expressly, that in the latter times some shall <u>depart from the faith</u>, giving heed to seducing spirits, and doctrines of devils; <u>Speaking lies in hypocrisy</u>; **having their conscience seared with a hot iron**; 1Tim 4:1-2

This is the spirit that will increase in these last days: the spirit of hypocrisy, which speaks lies because of having a seared conscience. This is what makes modern day preachers and teachers so dangerous when they put away concerning faith a good conscience. If their life is being lived in willful compromise to God's holy standards, then doctrines of demons and lies will be intermixed with what they teach.

> **WARNING**: How rarely do we consider our actions in the light of how it affects others. The New Testament resounds with the examples of those who have been set forth as an example to us that we may follow their faith. In particularly, we see Jesus (Jn 13:15, 1Pe 2:21), Paul (Php 3:17, 2Th 3:7-9), and the elders (Heb 13:7, 1Pe 5:3), each of whom had the fear of God and whose faith grew out of that fear! We tend to over-emphasize faith and ignore that which caused true faith to spring up – the fear of God.

This is why God calls his servants to be without compromise in their lives, for they are called to be the example. Timothy was exhorted, "but be thou an example of the believers, in word, in conversation, in charity, in spirit, in faith, in purity." 1Tim 4:12 The deacons were to be "holding the mystery of the faith in a pure conscience." 1Tim 3:9 If we have a hope of redemption, then we also must purify ourselves in preparation for his coming. "And every man that hath this hope in him purifieth himself, even as he is pure." 1Jn 3:3

We are not saying servants of God at times will not falter, stumble, and sin – for all men fall short of the glory of God. No man is perfect, except the Lord himself. We are all compassed with infirmity or moral *frailty* (Heb 5:1-2). No, what we are speaking about is the unwillingness to be corrected and to be subject to the Lord and to the Word of his power (Heb 1:3). We are speaking of those who deny the Lord's right to rule their life (2Pe 2:1 & Jude 1:4) by ignoring or willfully contradicting God's word and refusing his messengers. We are speaking of those who, though they *say* they follow and serve the Lord, by their actions and deeds deny him. As Paul warned Titus, "They profess that they know God; but in works they deny *him*" (Tit 1:16). Paul warns that the word that such false professors will bring forth will "eat as a canker" (2Tim 2:17). It will slowly corrupt the pure influence of the word of God and bring in pain, harm, and spiritual infection. Notice how Paul in 2Timothy 2:16-17 goes immediately from these teachers who have departed from the faith into <u>us</u> needing to purge ourselves from iniquity.

> But shun profane *and* vain babblings: for they will increase unto more ungodliness. And <u>their word will eat as doth a canker</u>: of whom is Hymenaeus and Philetus; Who concerning the truth have erred, saying that the resurrection is past already; and overthrow the faith of some.
>
> Nevertheless the foundation of God standeth sure, having this seal, The Lord knoweth them that are his. And, Let every one that nameth the name of Christ depart from iniquity. But in a great house there are not only vessels of gold and of silver, but also of wood and of earth; and some to honour, and some to dishonour.
>
> If a man therefore purge himself from these, he shall be a vessel unto honour, sanctified, and meet for the master's use, *and* prepared unto every good work. Flee also youthful lusts: but follow righteousness, faith, charity, peace, with them that call on the Lord out of a pure heart. 2Tim 2:16-22

The False Fear of God that is Taught

*"but have removed their heart far from me,
and their fear toward me is taught by the precept of men"* Isa 29:13

3 – Feigned Faith, Forgotten Name, False Profession

'Learning the fear of God' is mentioned over and over again in the scripture. When we are properly taught the word of God, and we receive it with a pure heart and keep it with a good conscience, it will surely produce the fear of the LORD. This is one sure way for us to know if we are being taught the purity of God's word, or whether we are being taught the watered down mixture of men's views and opinions. If we are being taught the purity of God's word, unmixed with man's religion, we will learn to fear God, and that fear will produce conviction for change (Ps 55:19).

But what of those teachers who are unwilling to walk in the fear of God, those who have no real fear of God, those who abuse the grace of God? How may we learn the fear of God from them? This brings us to a great danger, for there is a fear toward God that is taught by the precept or *command* of men and which does not produce the grace of God in balance.

> Wherefore the Lord said, Forasmuch as this people draw near *me* with their mouth, and with their lips do honour me, but have removed their heart far from me, and their fear toward me is taught by the precept of men: Isa 29:13

For some who teach the fear of the LORD, it is but a precept or a command to give to the sheep. It is not a working principle in their life, nor one they regularly choose. Hence, it is not the fountain of life God has meant it to be. So there is a fear of God that is taught by the precept of man that is a false fear of God – an imitation of empty religion.

What does this counterfeit fear of God produce? The very opposite of the true fear of God. The true fear of God that originates from God strips away hypocrisy, but we read of the fear of God that originates from men that it produces a people who draw near to God with their mouth, and their lips honor him, but they have removed their heart far from him (Isa 29:13). This is similar to the Samarians who were taught to fear the LORD by the precept of men,[58] and yet in their superstitious fear of God they still served their own gods!

> one of the priests whom they had carried away from Samaria came and dwelt in Bethel, and taught them how they should fear the LORD. <u>They feared the LORD, and served their own gods</u>, after the manner of the nations whom they carried away from thence. 2K 17:28,33

Many a Christian today has a fear of God similar to the Samarians who "feared the LORD, **and** served their own gods, after the manner of the nations". You say how so? Whenever we do things in our life as born again Christians

---

[58] Remember, *all* the priests whom had been carried away from Samaria had lost their true fear of God, in that they had departed from the Lord in their heart through an evil conscience. This is the judgment that was against them from all the prophets who warned them (i.e. Isaiah, Micah, Jeremiah, Hosea, …). Hence, their teaching of God's fear could only be from the precept of man and not from the living reality in their life.

because the culture around us does it, when its roots are in paganism, then we are doing "after the manner of the nations" around us and God is angered. He warns us, "Thus saith the LORD, Learn not the way of the heathen" (Jer 10:2).

How then may we learn the fear of God from men with these very real dangers? How can we learn the fear of God from men, but *not* learn it from men, but of God from whom it truly comes? Clearly, we must learn the fear of God, and the LORD will use men of God to teach it to us. But we must be careful (1) *how* we learn and (2) *who* is doing the teaching. Firstly, we must allow the word of God to be our light that guides us down the narrow way, our weight and rule by which all things are measured.

> **WARNING**: We must learn God's fear with our heart engaged and willing to change and not merely our mind. Secondly, we must learn from true men of God who have gone through much brokenness[59] and are after God's own heart (1Sam 13:14). This is that narrow way that we must pass through.

> Enter ye in at the strait [*narrow*][60] gate: for wide *is* the gate, and broad *is* the way, that leadeth to destruction, and many there be which go in thereat: Because strait [*narrow*] *is* the gate, and narrow [*crowded*: afflicted, troubled] *is* the way, which leadeth unto life, and few there be that find it. Mt 7:13-14

God's Restoration of His Fear

The narrow gate we must pass through is crowded, and to pass through it will bring forth both affliction and troubles. On the one side, it is clear from scripture that we are to be taught the fear of God, and that that teaching comes through anointed and appointed men of God by the word of God. On the other side we see the true fear of God is very, very rare today. Yet God is always faithful to raise up humble, broken servants like Moses to teach the people what the LORD expects of them and how to have the fear of God (Dt 31:12-13). This continues even today. Whenever God wants to remove his people from mixture and the ways of the world, he will raise up a man who will teach his people the fear of the LORD.

---

[59] The brokenness of the vessel: Ps 31:12, 34:18, 38:8, 51:8,17, 69:20.

[60] The Old English word 'strait' is not our present day English word 'straight' (with the silent 'gh'). Our present day word 'straight' means 'without bend or curve', whereas the Old English word 'strait' (without the 'gh') means '*narrow* (from obstacles *standing* close about)'. Both words are used in the scripture. 'Straight' (with the silent 'gh') is used in reference to John's ministry to "Make straight the way of the Lord" (Mt 3:3/Mk 1:3/Lk 3:4-5/Jn 1:23).

3 – Feigned Faith, Forgotten Name, False Profession

Every time God's people went into bondage, this pattern was repeated as God led his people out of the world and back into his divine purposes. After the deportation and then the subsequent return from bondage, there was a whole new breed of people who needed to learn the fear of God. So God raised up a priest whom he sent unto them to teach them how they should fear the LORD (2K 17:28). So when God was establishing the kingdom of God here on earth through the reign of David, God used David to teach the people the fear of the LORD. "Come, ye children, hearken unto me: I will teach you the fear of the LORD." Ps 34:11 Remember, Jesus was the son of David[61] and his kingdom was typified and foreshadowed by David's. Jesus was the fulfillment of the promise made to David that he would have a seed that would sit on his throne and rule for ever.[62] Jesus, as the true king of the kingdom of God, also taught the fear of the LORD (Lk 12:5).

So if we would be brought out of the bondage of the world, we must learn the fear of God, and we must learn it from men. The authority and transforming power of it will *not* come from the command or precept of men, but from the word of God to which we must hearken and obey. As we learn the fear of God we must not learn the precepts of men. What we learn we must know, believe, and receive it as it is in truth the word of God, not the word of any man (1Th 2:13).

So we have covered the false fear of God and its fruit. We have seen that the true fear of God is coupled with the fear of God's name, and that the fear of God's name is not the avoidance of using his name, but rather living a life that glorifies and honors him, while joyfully proclaiming his name. We then looked at the feigned faith that works in many because of putting away the true fear of God. Lastly, we saw the perils of learning the fear of God, when both the false fear of God and the true are both taught. But we can be assured that God will always raise up holy men which will teach the pure fear of God. Let us now go on to learn the deep work the fear of the Lord must do on our heart.

Let us draw near with a true heart in full assurance of faith,
having our hearts sprinkled from an evil conscience,
and our bodies washed with pure water.
Hebrews 10:22

---

[61] Jesus, the Son of David: Mt 1:1,20, 9:27, 12:23, 15:22, 20:30-31, 21:9,15, 22:42.

[62] 1Ch 17:11-14, 2Ch 6:16/Jer 33:17, 2Ch 7:18, Ps 89:27-29 → Lk 1:32

Chapter 4. The Fear of GOD, The Singular Issue of the Heart
The Heart Surgery We All Need

"O that there were such an heart in them, that they would fear me" Lev 25:17

When the new covenant of grace and fear is established in our heart as God has always intended, it will have a profound effect upon our heart. The fear of God will cause us to have a completely new heart. Let us examine the effect of the fear of God upon our heart. The fear of God has its beginning, as we have seen, in the Spirit of God dwelling in us through the new birth. He is after all "the spirit ... of the fear of the LORD." Isa 11:2 He is the source of the clean and enduring fear of God.

But the fear of God also has a foundational root in our will. Though the fear of God is both a gift and a grace of the Spirit of God, it is something we must respond to and live out. Its growth and maintenance requires our continual choice. You must daily "choose the fear of the LORD" (Pr 1:29). You must again and again "<u>let</u> him *be* your fear, and <u>let</u> him *be* your dread." Isa 8:13 We must allow the gift of the fear of God to do its appointed work in us. Even as we can resist and frustrate the grace of God, so also the fear of God can be resisted, frustrated, and finally rejected. "Wherefore now <u>let</u> the fear of the LORD

4 – The Fear of GOD, The Singular Issue of the Heart

be upon you; <u>take heed and do *it*</u>: for *there is* no iniquity with the LORD our God, nor respect of persons, nor taking of gifts." 2Ch 19:7 Both of these scriptures talk about 'letting' or allowing the fear of God to be in our heart. We must seek it, choose it, grow up in it, and guard it so that we don't depart from it. We have also seen that our growth in the fear of God may be extracted and even shipwrecked by several reefs: false doctrine, continued disobedience, accusing others and excusing ourselves, varied kinds of pride, and hypocrisy.

> **WARNING**: We must not confuse the *work* of the fear of the LORD and the obedience it produces with man-made or man-initiated works. The fear of the LORD is in no way related to religious dead works. In fact, the fear of the LORD exposes and reproves such hypocrisy and blindness! The fear of the LORD will greatly affect how we think and what we do, producing good fruit.
>
> The true fear of the LORD is continually exposing the plague of our own heart (IK 8:38-43). Though it is a choice on our side (just like salvation), its source is of the Spirit of God (Isa 11:2), not of man. Our part is to choose it, desire it, seek after it, and to walk in it. But it is not only what we do on our side, there is also a corresponding response on the part of the LORD when he sees our desire for the fear of God. God himself sees and rewards our desire to possess and grow in the fear of God.

The Root: Our Heart

Because the fear of God so involves our will, we must look at our heart, for our choices come from our heart. We do that which we most want to do at the time. This is the sinfulness of sin. To experience the true fear of God we must have our heart dealt with, for it is there, in the recesses of our heart, where our will still maintains tight control. We cannot learn the fear of God without having the issues of our heart exposed. This is why few desire the fear of God today, especially once they find out what it will cost. It is not a quick fix. The true fear of God cannot reside in our mind or only our thoughts. It must dwell within our heart. Remember, God's eternal desire for his people, "O that there were <u>such an heart in them</u>, that they would <u>fear me</u>, and keep all my commandments <u>always</u>, that it might be well with them, and with their children <u>for ever</u>!" Dt 5:29 It is in the innermost parts of our heart where we must fear God. It must be in truth and not in word only. This is the new covenant that God promised to make with his people: he would put his fear in our hearts.

> And I will give them **one heart**, and one way, <u>that they may fear me</u> for ever, for the good of them, and of their children after them: And I will make an everlasting covenant with them, that I will not turn away from them, to do them good; but I will put <u>my fear</u> **in their hearts**, that they shall not depart from me. Jer 32:39-40

> We cannot learn the fear of God without having the issues of our heart exposed. This is why few desire the fear of God today, especially once they find out what it will cost.

God warned that there would be people who would abort this process – those who would honor him with their lips, but their hearts would be far from him. And why would this happen? Because they "have removed their heart far from [God], and their fear toward [God] is taught by the precept of men" (Isa 29:13). The process of having the true fear of God planted and growing in our heart is aborted whenever we refuse to allow God to do the heart surgery he must do on every one of our hearts.

The scripture reveals that we often are double-hearted,[63] trying to serve God and ourselves. This is what discipleship and the fear of God are to remove from us so that we might be brought into the singleness that is in Christ. It is not coincidental that singleness of heart does not exist in the scripture apart from the fear of God,[64] for only his fear can make our heart truly single. If the LORD is to make one heart out of our double heart, then he first must cut out and remove much. This is why the fear of the LORD is **the** issue of our heart.

A New Heart Through the Fear of the LORD
"A new heart also will I give you" Eze 36:26

Through the new birth we get a new heart, a new spirit, AND we get God's spirit put within us. Ezekiel prophesied of the new heart and new spirit that God through the new covenant would give us.[65]

> A <u>new heart</u> also will I give you, and a <u>new spirit</u> will I put within you: and I will take away the stony heart out of your flesh, and I will give you an heart of flesh. And I will put my spirit within you, and cause you to walk in my statutes, and ye shall keep my judgments, and do *them*. Eze 36:26-27

The new heart is a heart that has been cleansed through the perfect sacrifice of the Son, so that it is purged from the conscience of sins (Heb 10:2,22). The new spirit is a resurrected spirit that is raised in newness of life (Rom 7:6) in us through the new birth.

---

[63] Double-hearted: Ps 12:2, 1Ch 12:33, 1K 18:21.

[64] Every time singleness of heart is mentioned in the scripture so is the fear of God (Ac 2:43,46, Eph 6:5, Col 3:22)!

[65] Many times this passage in Ezekiel is misread and people think that the "new spirit" is the same as "my spirit", but this is clearly not the case, for each is preceded with the conjunction 'and', showing each is a separate thing that God will give us.

4 – The Fear of GOD, The Singular Issue of the Heart

We were dead in transgressions and sins (Eph 2:1,5), but that death was not a natural death, or even a soulish death, for we were very much alive both in body and in soul. No, that death was a spiritual death (Rom 8:10-11, 1Pe 4:6). Our spirit was dead to the things of God, so that we were cut off from the life that is in him. Thus, our *spirit* is what needed to be resurrected and have new life brought into it. Once we are a new creation, through the new birth with a new heart and a new spirit, now the Spirit of God may dwell in us – for we no longer stink of death. Now we are made alive from the dead (Rom 6:13). Now God's Spirit may speak or bear witness to us through our 're-born' spirit (Rom 8:16).

But for what purpose are these things done for us through the new birth? For the very purpose that Ezekiel prophesied, so that we would walk in God's statutes and keep his judgments and do them. This is exactly what we saw Jeremiah prophesied concerning the new covenant. It was given so that we may fear God for ever. The Spirit of God is given to us not just so that we could know the truth, but so that we can *do* the truth. This is the Holy Spirit's tri-fold purpose in our life.

1. First, his Spirit is given to us to get us to **know the truth**, for he is the Spirit of truth (Jn 14:17, 15:26, 16:13, 1Jn 4:6, 5:6). He will guide us into all truth (Jn 16:13). He will teach us all things and bring all things to our remembrance that Jesus has said to us (Jn 14:26). He will bear witness of the truth and reprove men of sin, righteousness, and judgment (Jn 16:8). And he will testify of Jesus and glorfy Jesus, the truth (Jn 15:26 & 16:14).

2. Second, his Spirit is given to us to **keep his judgments** (i.e. his divine law). This keeping of God's law is first and foremost the hedging about, the guarding and protecting of the word of God in our heart so that it is not stolen.[66] It is having our loins girt about with *the truth* (Eph 6:14).

3. Third, he is given to us to **move us to do the word of God**, not to be hearers only. "For it is God [the Holy Spirit] which worketh in you both to will and to do of *his* good pleasure." Php 2:13 So we have received the power to **be** witnesses of Jesus (Ac 1:8) by the life of the Spirit as we learn to submit and obey the Father's will.[67] This is *the life* of the Spirit that brings forth fruit unto God. The Spirit is given to help us **walk in God's statutes** or ordinances – his prescribed pattern of discipleship. He helps us to be under God's authority as we walk in Jesus' footsteps and follow him who is *the way*.

---

[66] We can thank God for the Spirit's help in this area, for Jesus said of the Spirit, "he shall teach you all things, and bring all things to your remembrance, whatsoever I have said unto you." Jn 14:26

[67] This is even as Jesus did. The life he lived as our example was not in his own power or strength. He was declared to be the Son of God by the power of the Spirit (Lk 4:14, Ac 10:38, Rom 1:4). Even so his servants are to be made known by the same power of the Spirit (Rom 15:19, 1Th 1:5).

This is God's great plan. He re-created us so that we would be "his workmanship, created in Christ Jesus unto good works, which God hath before ordained that we <u>should walk in them</u>." Eph 2:10 Let us look at how the fear of God sculpts and molds our heart into God's workmanship so that we may walk in the works that he has prepared for us. God desires his fear to produce in us a faithful and perfect heart. This is the goal, the fruit that he is looking for.

We are God's workmanship, and it is our heart that he wants to make into his re-creative masterpiece. As a master he paints the palette of our heart using the oil-based colors of the manifold grace of God (1Pe 4:10). But what is his brush? It is the fear of God. He does this through his instruction, conviction, correction, and training. Through his chastenings and reproofs the word of life becomes real to us as the fear of God is awakened in our hearts. Now we begin walking faithfully before him in the fear of God fulfilling the good works he has before ordained for us.

Obtaining a Soft and Humble Heart

*"O LORD, why hast thou made us to err from thy ways,
and hardened our heart from thy fear?" Isa 63:17*

The fear of God will cause our heart to draw near to him with a true heart. But when we do not have the fear of God, we err from God's ways and our heart becomes hardened. "O LORD, why hast thou made us to err from thy ways, *and* <u>hardened</u> our heart from thy fear?" Isa 63:17 An erring heart is a hardened heart.[68] It is impossible to walk in darkness or to depart from truth for any length of time and not have the heart hardened toward both God and his word. Let us consider the hardening of the heart that surrounds losing the fear of God. There are two kinds of hardened heart that we need to be healed of.

The first kind of hardened heart is the **unfeeling** heart. The word 'hardened' in Isaiah 63:17 means 'to be (or make) *unfeeling*'. When God causes us to err from his ways, our heart gets hardened from his fear. The hardening of our heart from his fear causes it to be *rendered insensitive*. So many today have an unfeeling or insensitive heart toward the fear of God. They have no feeling at all toward it because it is not even in their thinking.

Note that the prophet says 'our heart is hardened from God's fear'. Thus, we see that the removal of God's fear is related to the hardening of our heart. "Happy is the man that feareth alway: but he that hardeneth his heart shall fall into mischief." Pr 28:14 Hardening one's heart is put in direct opposition to having the fear of God. He that does not continue in the fear of God is one who is allowing his heart to be hardened against God. When Pharaoh refused to fear God, he thus was at the same time both hardening his own heart and hav-

---

[68] We often forget this when speaking to someone who has fallen away from the truth.

4 – The Fear of God, The Singular Issue of the Heart

ing his heart hardened by God.[69] The heart which is lacking the fear of God or where is little fear of God is a heart which is getting continually harder. Such a heart that lacks the fear of God is continually reproved before God.[70] If we now harden our heart against such reproof and refuse to desire God's fear, then it will end in destruction. "He, that being often reproved hardeneth his neck, shall suddenly be destroyed, and that without remedy." Pr 29:1

Contrariwise, a heart that fears God is spiritually a soft heart. A sensitive heart toward the fear of God must be restored, if the fear of the LORD is to be recaptured and the heart reclaimed for God. Since this hardening of the heart comes from erring or departing from God's ways, the way back is clearly to return in repentance to his ways. Only as we turn back again to the ways of the Almighty can our heart's insensitivity be removed and the fear of God return.

The second kind of hardened heart that must be removed is the **callousness** or toughness that builds up. The scripture shows the fear of God is put in direct opposition to hardening the heart, and that trouble always follows the heart that becomes hardened. "Happy *is* the man that feareth alway: but he that hardeneth his heart shall fall into mischief." Pr 28:14 The word 'hardeneth' here means 'to *be dense*, i.e. tough or *severe*'. Those that fear God are those that are continually softening their heart toward him and cultivating a willing response to his voice.

This is the beginning of the wonderful fruit of God's fear and the precious effect it has on our heart. The true fear of God will cause us to have a soft heart that is sensitive to his voice, a teachable heart to hearken to his word, a humble heart that will follow his lead, a correctable heart that is willing to change its direction, and a servant's heart that is desirous to give to the LORD. This is why we so need the fear of God. We cannot do away with it.

We can know how we are faring in our growth or shrinkage of the fear of God by whether our heart is growing harder or softer in our Christian duties of pursuing the Lord: in the reading and studying of the word of God, in regular prayer, in serving the Lord, in choosing to deny our own desires in order to take care of the need of others, and even in our response to the tribulations of life – sickness, lack, misunderstanding, contentions, rejections, persecutions, and loss. This is how God proves the genuineness and the depth of our fear, for the fear of God initially brings affliction, not blessing. Through these testings God ensures that our fear of him is sincere and not self-seeking. The blessings of the fear of God, which are many, come in time as we faithfully endure the many testings of the fear of God.

---

[69] See how many times the scripture speaks of Pharaoh's heart being hardened: Ex 4:21, 7:3,13-14,22, 8:15,19,32, 9:7,12,34-10:1,20,27, 11:10, 14:4,8, 1Sam 6:6.

[70] We are reproved if we do not have the fear of God: Neh 5:9, Jer 2:19, 5:22.

Where is the Fear of GOD? Losing the Treasure of the Lord

Breaking the Grip of Pride

One evil that is especially deadly to the fear of God is that of pride. When pride enters our heart it corrupts the fear of God and turns it into the false fear of God that works in knowledge only, but not in power. We may find ourselves thinking we love God's commandments, but we have deceived ourselves when we have no intention of doing them. Remember, the true fear of God will cause us to hate pride and arrogancy (Pr 8:13).

The scriptures show the fear of God is put in direct opposition to being wise or proud of heart. "Men do therefore fear him: he respecteth not any *that are* wise of heart." Job 37:24 Those who think they are wise of heart will not fear God, for they have their own way of seeing and doing things. If we are wise in our own eyes, we will not depart from the evil that is working in our heart – for pride and arrogancy themselves are the greatest of evils. Thus, we are warned in the wisdom of Proverbs, "Be not wise in thine own eyes: fear the LORD, and <u>depart from evil</u>. A wise *man* feareth, and <u>departeth from evil</u>: but the fool rageth, and is confident." Pr 3:7, 14:16 In God's eyes, the fool is confident and rages or fights against God's wisdom. Thus, the fool will not depart from evil, whereas the wise man fears God and does depart from evil.[71]

Once Lucifer lost his fear of God, he found a 'freedom' to say all that he wanted to do. His independence proved his undoing and led him into rebellion. Thus, he was alienated from God and cast forth out of heaven. The LORD of heaven cannot receive those who lack his fear, but those who have it he is near. The fear of God is the secret to his presence by escaping our selfish pride. God resists the proud, but he gives grace to the humble. When we draw near to him by humbling ourselves, then he will draw near to us (Jam 4:6,8).

The removal of pride through the fear of the LORD is one of the most profound fruits affecting so many other parts of the believer's life. God's solution to our pride and the spirit of boasting and comparing and judging of others is the fear of God (Pr 28:13-14). Notice the verse right before Proverbs 28:14, on fearing God and not having a hardened heart, has to do with confessing our sin! Clearly, fearing God is manifested by not hardening our heart when we sin, but quickly confessing and forsaking it. This is exactly the same context that Paul warns the Romans of in his letter to them. His exhortation to them to escape the highmindedness of the Roman way of thinking is to embrace the fear of God (in particular the fear of God's judgments). So he says, "Well; because of unbelief they were broken off, and thou standest by faith. Be not highminded, but fear." Ro 11:20

---

[71] The beginning of wisdom is the fear of the LORD, as we have heard many times. Therefore, that person who fears not God *must* be both proud of heart *and* still be full of their own wisdom, not God's.

4 – The Fear of GOD, The Singular Issue of the Heart

This is how the fear of God keeps us from a hardened heart, by leading us right away to repentance unto the acknowledging of the truth. Paul gives us the New Testament command, "Boast not … Be not highminded, but <u>fear</u>" (Rom 11:18,20). The pride of life afflicts all of us. It is our first heart, the fallen nature, which is in us all. It is this grip of pride that would cover all we do and cause our thinking to be rooted in self. This is what we must be sheltered from: the pride of man that is in each of us. So the psalmist praises God for his great shelter from the pride of man that God specially provides for those who fear him.

> *Oh* how great *is* thy goodness, which thou hast laid up <u>for them that fear thee</u>; *which* thou hast wrought for them that trust in thee before the sons of men! Thou shalt <u>hide them</u> in the secret of thy presence <u>from the pride of man</u>: thou shalt keep them secretly in a pavilion from the strife of tongues. Ps 31:19-20

WARNING: That the 'self' is the same as our soul is easily seen in scripture, but that it was not so in the beginning and never intended to be this way by God, is what is so often missed. When man was first made, God breathed into him the breath of life that formed the spirit of the man. Then the man became a "living soul" (Gen 2:7). But remember his spirit preceded his soul. The man's soul had its direct *dependency* on both the spirit and the body. It was not an independent entity. It was a living soul (apart from sin), but its life came from the spirit of the man, which came directly from the Spirit of God.

Once sin came, death and corruption came with it.[72] So now apart from Christ, we are dead in trespasses and sins (Eph 2:1). We know Adam and Eve's soul didn't die, but their spirit did. Thus, we all became spiritually dead, for we all have been reproduced in their image and likeness now. This is why we **must** be born again in spirit (Jn 3:5-8) and be given a new spirit.[73] As a result of being dead in spirit, our soul became one and the same with our 'self'. For example, 'I' in Lamentations 3:24 is the Hebrew word for soul; so is 'himself' and 'yourselves' in many scriptures.[74] So we see the soul in the Old Testament is so often translated 'self', 'me', 'you', 'us', or a variant of it, but <u>never</u> in the New!

Only the secret of his presence can hide us or keep us from the pride that is naturally in every man. The secret of God's presence is reserved for those who fear him. As it is written, "The secret [i.e. the *intimacy*] of the LORD *is* with them that fear him" (Ps 25:14). This is the great goodness that God has laid up for those who fear him: the secret of his presence. The fear of the LORD, then, is the secret to God's presence *and* the secret to escaping the pride of man.

---

[72] Rom 5:12, 2Pe 1:4, 2:19

[73] Eze 11:19, 18:31, 36:26

[74] The soul as 'himself': Am 2:14-15, 6:8, Job 32:2, 18:4, Jer 51:14. The soul as 'yourselves': Jer 37:9, 17:21, Dt 4:15, Jos 23:11.

Where is the Fear of GOD? Losing the Treasure of the Lord

Obtaining a Humble Heart

The fear of the LORD and humility are often linked together. "The fear of the LORD *is* the instruction of wisdom; and before honour *is* humility." Pr 15:33 "By humility *and* the fear of the LORD *are* riches, and honour, and life." Pr 22:4 Similarly, the lack of the fear of God is always equated with the pride of our heart. "They are <u>not humbled</u> *even* unto this day, <u>neither have they feared</u>, nor walked in my law, nor in my statutes, that I set before you and before your fathers." Jer 44:10 "Men do therefore fear him: he respecteth not any *that are* wise of heart." Job 37:23-24

Pride itself is one of the major devices the enemy uses against God's people and their leaders. It is the root of what caused Lucifer to fall and to become the very adversary of God, and it is now the essence of what drives his purpose. Let no one think that the pride that Satan insidiously works to plant in our being is only outward and brash. Lucifer himself was an angel. Angels are described in the Bible as ministering spirits sent forth to *serve* (Heb 1:14). Thus, Lucifer's fall in pride was a spiritual one involving spiritual pride. Pride has many masks, but the worst is that which is self-justifying. Often this masquerades behind a cloak of being spiritual. This takes place whenever we take pride in what we believe we are 'justified' to take pride in. This kind of spiritual pride then has a firm footing based on a false belief (i.e. in the way we see an issue). This is what makes such pride exceedingly difficult to be removed, because it hides beneath supposed 'self-evident' or privately revealed 'truth'.

We must choose not to be wise in our own eyes in order to have the true fear of God and humility of mind (Pr 3:7). So it is written, "The fear of the LORD *is* to hate evil: <u>pride</u>, and <u>arrogancy</u>, and the evil way, and the froward mouth, do I hate. Counsel *is* mine, and sound wisdom: **I** *am* understanding; **I** have strength." Pr 8:13-14 To have the fear of God we must hate pride and arrogancy – first and primarily that which lies within our own heart and mind. Notice how God takes us from hating evil, pride, and arrogancy and immediately declares that counsel and sound wisdom are <u>his</u>, not ours, that <u>he is</u> understanding and <u>he has</u> strength, not we ourselves!

This is the message of the fear of the LORD – a removal of our self-sufficiency (i.e. our counsel, wisdom, understanding, and strength) and a dependency on him whom we ought to fear. Thus, the prayer of David is "Put them in fear, O LORD: *that* the nations may know themselves *to be but* men. Selah." Ps 9:20 The fear of the LORD is a gift from God enabling us to begin to see who God is for *who* he is, and then to also see who we are in comparison to God. Even in our greatest and most triumphing day we are still "but men. [Stop and think about it]." Only the fear of God can convince us and continually remind us of that. No wonder we need it before our very eyes (Rom 3:18), so that we may continually see it.

4 – The Fear of GOD, The Singular Issue of the Heart

As the fear of the LORD grows in us so will our hatred of evil, pride, arrogancy, and the froward mouth. The fear of the LORD is one of the Spirit's primary tools for bringing us to a place of repentance, so that we through the Spirit begin to see and think like the LORD and to desire what he desires. Thus, the fear of the LORD will fashion our desires. We so need this in a world driven by the desires of the flesh, the desires of the eyes, and the prideful desires of life. Through the fear of the LORD, we come to know that counsel and sound wisdom does not lie within us, but is God's, and that understanding is in him (Col 2:3). When God gave instructions on how to preserve the life of the king, God specifically gave instructions that he was to daily seek wisdom and understanding from the LORD by reading the word of God.

> And it shall be with him, and he shall read therein all the days of his life: that he may <u>learn to fear the LORD his God</u>, to keep all the words of this law and these statutes, to do them: **That his heart be not lifted up above his brethren**, and that he turn not aside from the commandment, *to* the right hand, or *to* the left: to the end that he may prolong *his* days in his kingdom, he, and his children, in the midst of Israel. Dt 17:19-20

Searching for knowledge, understanding, and wisdom from the word of God on a daily basis would cause the king to learn to fear the LORD, something every leader truly needs. That fear of God, through a pure conscience, would in turn keep his heart from being lifted up above his brethren. This is all too applicable to us today, for we are spiritual kings and priests before our God and Father (Rev 1:6, 5:10), and are so often caught up in vainglory and esteeming ourselves better than others (cp. Php 2:3).

Without the fear of God, a man or woman will grow in pride and be lifted up in their own eyes above their brethren, especially if they are being fed the philosophies of men. This is exactly what has happened in denominational religion. Leaders raised in Bible Colleges are nurtured on the teachings of men, and filled with the knowledge that puffs up. They are filled with the religious orders of the kingdoms of men: hierarchies of bishops,[75] reverends, priests, and synods. Men lifted up above the brethren. It is none other than the Nicolaitan spirit of the Pharisees which God greatly hates (Rev 2:15). If ever there were a day when the fear of God and the humility that comes by it was needed, it is today.

---

[75] 'Bishop' and 'Pastor' (as well as 'Apostle', 'Prophet', and 'Evangelist') are greatly misused today as titles for the exaltation of men as clergy above the people. They were never meant by God to be titles that precede men's names – the record of scripture proves that. For an explanation of this see the definition of Bishops in the appendix entitled "Definition of Some Biblical Terms".

Fearing God with a Single Heart

"Servants, obey in all things your masters ...
in singleness of heart, fearing God" Col 3:22

As we have seen already, the promise of the new covenant was that God would give us one heart and one way so that we may fear him (Jer 32:38-40). If our heart becomes divided it will prevent us from properly being able to fear God. It is impossible to have a true fear of God if our heart is divided. Our fear of God must be in singleness of heart. This is why (as we have seen) every time in the scripture singleness of heart is mentioned it is always mentioned in connection with fearing God: "in singleness of heart, fearing God" (Col 3:22) and "with fear and trembling, in singleness of your heart, as unto Christ" (Eph 6:5).

It is impossible to have the fear of God without our heart being made single. If we still long for any of the old life, any of that which we have been delivered from, then we will end up as Lot's wife who looked back, desiring the natural comforts of life, and we will lose the fear of the LORD. We will lose the respect for his word and his command to be a holy and separate people. The fear of God causes us not to look back. It has a way of uniting our thoughts, our desires, and our heart on the will of God, what he sets before us. The fear of God becomes our lens to stay focused on our Lord and King. We begin to delight ourselves in him and not in substitutes.

When we see a divided heart within us, we must cry out for the fear of God to be restored, because we know in that area we do not have it. We must find where we have lost it and why, and we must seek it with all our heart. Only through the fear of God can our heart become united.[76] Such is the cry of David in prayer, "Teach me thy way, O LORD; I will walk in thy truth: <u>unite my heart to fear thy name</u>." Ps 86:11 Did you hear that? We do not fear his name, because our heart is *not* united – it is divided, it is double, it is not one, but two hearts that desire competing things, and that will keep us from fearing God.

A continually divided heart will waver back and forth and will eventually grow weak in its commitment to the Lord. A divided heart will, thus, become a hardened heart – a heart that becomes dull of hearing God's voice – because it is continually wavering back and forth between the will of God and its own will. In this, the divided heart, which is the heart that has lost its fear of God, will always err from God's ways. So the prophet cries out, "O LORD, why hast thou made us to **err from thy ways**, *and* hardened our heart from thy fear?" Isa 63:17 God reproves us, declaring that it is because of our own wickedness and our

---

[76] You can find out more about uniting our heart in the fear of God in the chapter entitled "Recapturing the Purity of the Fear of the LORD" in the section 'Uniting Our Heart through the Word to Fear the LORD' in the book <u>Finding the Treasure of the Lord</u>.

4 – The Fear of God, The Singular Issue of the Heart

backslidings "that thou hast forsaken the LORD thy God, and that my fear *is* not in thee, saith the Lord GOD of hosts." Jer 2:19

Our desires MUST die, and must be replaced with the single, solitary desire to please our heavenly Father even as Jesus' heart and mind were set. It is the desire for other things that will extinguish the clean and enduring fire of the fear of God that is to burn in our bosom. Jesus said, "the lusts of other things entering in, choke the word, and it becometh unfruitful." Mk 4:19 Can you see now, in a clearer light, the focus of Philippians 2?

> ^{5}Let this mind be in you, which was also in Christ Jesus: ^{8}... he humbled himself, and became obedient unto death, even the death of the cross. ^{12}Wherefore, my beloved, as ye have always obeyed, not as in my presence only, but now much more in my absence, work out your own salvation with fear and trembling. ^{13}For it is God which worketh in you both to will and to do of *his* good pleasure. Php 2:5,8,12-13

A Pure Heart: Conscious of His Presence

"serve him with a perfect heart and a willing mind:
for the LORD searcheth all hearts, and
understandeth all the imaginations of the thoughts" 1Ch 28:9

Pride, selfishness, independence, and a host of other impurities all lodge in our hearts. We have much that God's Spirit is continually working on to purge from us. The fear of God not only prepares our heart for the LORD and for his work, it also will purify it. The fear of God is the consciousness of his presence. When we have the fear of God we are astutely aware that the LORD is not only overseeing and watching our actions, but is in fact the inspector and observer of the innermost thoughts of our heart.

> Thus, we fear God because we are **sure** he sees and knows our heart. This is the awesomeness of God's presence, from which we cannot hide.

God knows our hearts all too well, and for this reason we ought to fear him all the days of our life (1K 8:39-40). Thus, we fear God because we are **sure** he sees and knows our heart. In Noah's day it was recorded, "And God saw ... *that* every imagination of the thoughts of [man's] heart *was* only evil continually." Gen 6:5 Notice, it does not say he *knew*, rather it says he continually *saw* every imagination of the thoughts of man's heart![77] This is the awesomeness of God's presence, from which we cannot hide.[78]

> For he looketh to the ends of the earth, *and* <u>seeth</u> under the whole heaven Job 28:24
>
> The eyes of the LORD *are* in every place, <u>beholding</u> the evil and the good. Pr 15:3
>
> the LORD <u>looketh</u> on the heart 1Sam 16:7
>
> Neither is there any creature that is not manifest <u>in his sight</u>: but all things *are* naked and opened unto <u>the eyes of him</u> with whom we have to do. Heb 4:13

This is the unsearchable greatness of the Almighty God (Ps 145:3) that we need to come to know. Our God sees the innermost parts of every one of our hearts. The LORD searches all hearts and understands ALL the imaginations of the thoughts of every single person on earth! Because of this, David says to his son Solomon that he should therefore know God and serve him with a perfect heart and a willing mind (1Ch 28:9).

If we would know him, we must know he sees the secret thoughts of our mind and the innermost parts of our heart – both the thoughts *and* the intents. They are both as billboards to him. Nothing is hid from his sight. If we could have deeply planted in our consciousness, the consciousness of God's presence, then the fear of the LORD would actively keep us serving the LORD with a perfect heart and a willing mind. Remember, in Exodus 20 it was the nearness of God's presence and his awesomeness, and his great power and incredible glory that caused the fear of God to be before them and to keep them from sinning.

So often we spend so much time knowing about *issues* in the word of God, rather than knowing the GOD of the scriptures. Remember what Jesus reproved the Pharisees for in their study of the scriptures. "Search the scriptures; for in them ye think ye have eternal life: and they are they which <u>testify of me</u>." Jn 5:39 They were reading the scriptures along with many other books, but they were not coming to know the author of the scriptures. If we would take the time to truly know him as he is, and not as men say he is, then, like David, it would be easy to "serve him with a perfect heart and a willing mind."

The fear of God has a preserving effect on us, because we have a present awareness that we are his creation and his possession, no longer our own. The fear of God helps us to avoid the corruption and ungodly longing that comes from envying the lost. When we find our satisfaction in him, nothing else will

---

[77] Certainly God knows the thoughts of man (1K 8:39, Ac 1:24), but he does not *just* know them by his omniscience, he also knows them by *seeing* what is in our heart.

[78] There is no place anyone can hide from him, not even death can hide us from him: Job 34:22, Ps 139:12.

4 – The Fear of GOD, The Singular Issue of the Heart

satisfy. Thus, "Happy *is* the man that feareth alway" (Pr 28:14). No longer will we look to the false happiness and the temporal pleasures of sinners. "Let not thine heart envy sinners: but *be thou* in the fear of the LORD all the day long." Pr 23:17 The fear of the LORD is envy's cure. The fear of God will keep us from desiring what sinners have and to be content with our portion in the Lord. In removing ungodly desires and wants from our heart that stem from the ways of the world, our heart begins to become single in the Lord through the fear of God (Col 3:22, Eph 6:5), and it can then rest content in him.

An Enlarged Heart:
To Run the Way of His Commandments
"Then thou shalt see, and flow together,
and thine heart shall fear, and be enlarged;" Isa 60:5

Once our heart is single and united on his purposes, God, through his fear, will begin to enlarge our heart. Why must our heart be enlarged? Because it is too small, too self-centered, too narrow in scope to be greatly used of God. The fear of God helps expand our heart so that God has more to work with. To those Jews which had just believed on Jesus (Jn 8:30-31) he declared to them that they were still bound up and enslaved in their ways. This is the state of all new believers. Though they are forgiven, they are as infants still attached to the ways of the world in many areas, both in their desires and in their thinking. "Now I say, *That* the heir, as long as he is a child, differeth nothing from a servant, though he be lord of all; … Even so we, when we were children, were in bondage under the elements of the world" (Gal 4:1,3). Therefore, Jesus instructed these new believers that to be made free they needed to become disciples: "Then said Jesus to those Jews which believed on him, If ye continue in my word, *then* are ye my disciples indeed; And ye shall know the truth, and the truth shall make you free." Jn 8:31-32

Sadly, this verse has been taken out of context so many times it is hard for Christians to hear it correctly. This verse does not say what everyone believes it to say, namely, that by simply knowing the truth "the truth shall make you free." NO! Knowledge of the truth sets no one free, *unless* they have a heart to submit to it and live by it (i.e. unless they are willing to continue in it as a true disciple as Jesus commanded). Consider the very Jews Jesus was speaking to. They knew the truth. They had the sacred scriptures. Knowing the truth wasn't the problem. The problem was they were not learning to obey what they knew, but instead they were relying on what men said. So Jesus could say they didn't *know* the truth because they were not prepared to do *only* the Word. Even though they were children of Abraham (i.e. those in covenant relationship with God), they sought to kill Jesus, the very word of God, because his word had no place in them (Jn 8:37). The word of the Lord was not able to pass or enter into their hearts, because they did exactly what Christianity does today: they had their own interpretation of it based on their own traditions and the commentaries of what men say, which made the word of God of none effect (Mt 15:3-6). They had the word, but they did not do the word because of their traditions. And why did their traditions rule them, rather than the word of God? Because they had lost their fear of God.[79]

Understanding True Liberty: The Door of Discipleship

This is why we so need Jesus' discipleship pattern to be in the church – to train us to pattern our life only after the word of God, and *not* the traditions of men or what we know. Jesus brought in the kingdom of God, God's rule and reign over the hearts of men, by the authority of the word that commands us to follow him as disciples. So Jesus' call to men, over and over again, was to follow him. If we will let the apostolic word cut to our heart to bring change, then we will become disciples, not of men, but of Jesus Christ.[80] Disciples will know the truth and be made free. This is why many in Christianity may have knowledge of the scriptures, but they are not free and have no revelation into the kingdom of God, because they are not being discipled according to Jesus' pattern.

Freedom has been so misunderstood in America in these last days that she now thinks that it is being able to do whatever you want. Yet experience proves painfully otherwise. When we do whatever we want, we quickly become enslaved by our pleasures and by sin. True freedom is not the ability to do what we want. It is the ability to do what is right. We were created by God to serve, and we will end up serving something, whether it is the Lord or a host of other substitutes, which he calls idols. Thus, Jesus said in rebuke to Satan's temptation to worship him, "it is written, Thou shalt worship the Lord thy God, and <u>him only shalt thou serve</u>." Mt 4:10/Lk 4:8 This is why making Jesus Lord of our life is the door of salvation, which is to lead to a lifelong pursuit of worshipping God and serving only the Lord. Nearly everyone *says* they want to be free, but who will become a slave to the Lord so that they might be free indeed? That is the call of scripture: to love God with all our heart.

> Fear not: ye have done all this wickedness: yet turn not aside from following the LORD, but serve the LORD with all your heart; … Only fear the LORD, and serve him in truth with all your heart: for consider how great *things* he hath done for you. 1Sam 12:20,24

---

[79] Remember, we have already looked at this. The remainder of these verses in Matthew 15 (namely verses 7-9) go on to quote Isaiah 29:13, which show that they had a false fear of God taught them by the precept of men.

[80] Remember, Jesus is <u>the</u> apostle (Heb 3:1) and all the apostles learned to speak and do was what Jesus had commanded them (Mt 11:1, 28:19-20, Ac 1:1-2, 2Pe 3:2 →Mt 21:6).

4 – The Fear of God, The Singular Issue of the Heart

We Must Serve to be Free

This is why we must count the cost on how much do we truly value freedom. Jesus said we must count the cost, if we would follow him (Lk 14:28). Are we willing, as our spiritual forefathers were, to forsake our lesser freedoms in order to obtain the greatest freedom? It is a paradox of the kingdom, but to be free we must serve. Paul reveals the danger of doing our own will. "For, brethren, ye have been called unto liberty; only *use* not liberty for an occasion to the flesh, but by love serve one another." Gal 5:13 Liberty is often "an occasion to the flesh". Liberty brings with it the snare of being 'a *starting*-point or an *opportunity*' for our sinful flesh. If we would remain free and not be entangled again in the yoke of bondage to the flesh, we must use our freedom in Christ, not to serve ourselves, but to serve one another in love.

If we are free indeed, then we must maintain and guard that freedom by serving others in love. Service to others is what safeguards our liberty. So Peter confirms, "As free, and not using *your* liberty for a cloke of maliciousness, but as the servants of God." 1Pe 2:16 So that we can more clearly see the juxtaposition of simultaneously being free and being servants of God, listen just to the beginning and ending of this verse again: "As free, … but as the servants of God." We can only remain free in the Lord when we are serving him and others in the love of God. This is the only freedom that can be kept. All other liberties will degrade into some form of bondage.

Making Room for the New

God cannot enlarge our heart without demolishing the old, so that he might make room for the new. If we would have our heart enlarged, we must allow him to make room there. The cost, if we would have the Lord rebuild our life according to his pattern, is we must allow him to first demolish all that is of the old and all that is not squared up in divine order on the foundation of the doctrine of Christ (Heb 6:1). As the Lord does his reconstruction on our heart, he will tear out the old, rip up all veneer, cut out all hidden rot and falsity, and establish a new foundation with structural members of strength within us. This he does for the purpose of enlarging our heart to make it more like his own.

If we will continually choose the fear of God, it will continue to make our heart single on his purpose. We must not forget, that though we so often have *our* purposes for our life, what matters most is *his* purpose for our life. This singleness of purpose will produce a greater desire to follow the Lord in all ways and will lead us to the inescapable path of discipleship. As discipleship takes place he teaches us his ways and how to obey. This is followed by servanthood where the Lord teaches us his heart and how to faithfully serve him with joy.

Thus, the fear of God opens the door for our heart to be enlarged toward the Lord and toward his purposes so that we desire even more to serve him.

Where is the Fear of GOD? Losing the Treasure of the Lord

Notice how when we begin to see all that God has done for us, it draws us together with him and in turn causes our heart to fear him. "[1] Then thou shalt see, and [2] flow together, and [3] thine heart shall fear, and [4] be enlarged" (Isa 60:5). This is a beautiful verse, which links discipleship and gaining the knowledge of the truth through it ("[1] Then thou shalt see") with the unity of being of one heart and one mind ("and [2] flow together"). This unity is produced by the fear of God growing even further in us ("and [3] thine heart shall fear"), and finally the enlarging of our heart ("thine heart shalt … [4] be enlarged").

> Natural fear makes the heart shrink & shrivel, but the fear of God makes our heart '*broaden*, make room, and open wide'.

Once the fear of God comes and the eyes of our understanding are opened, it brings with it an enlarging of our heart. Natural fear makes the heart shrink and shrivel, but the fear of God makes our heart '*broaden*, make room, and open wide'. In the last days when men's hearts are failing them for (natural) fears and so many hearts are being hardened, we truly need this enlarging of our heart through the fear of God. Our hearts need to be broadened and room made in them in preparation to meet our coming bridegroom, the Lord Jesus Christ.

Will We Endure to the End?
"Behold, we count them happy which endure." James 5:11

God shows throughout history that only a remnant shall be saved; only a remnant shall endure to the end. Consider these remnant examples. Though the call to repentance in Noah's day went out to all the world for 120 years, yet only 8 responded to be saved. Ten lepers were healed, but only one returned to give glory to God and was saved (Lk 17:12-19).[81] Over a million people left Egypt during the Exodus, but only 2 men, Joshua and Caleb, entered the promised land. Jesus fed and healed literally thousands during his ministry, yet only 120 endured to Pentecost!

We could give so many other examples, but the clear point is God will forsake whatever needs to be discarded, or even lost, in order to redeem and find but one. This is proved by the parables of the lost sheep (Lk 15:3-7), the lost coin (Lk 15:8-10), and the lost son (Lk 15:10-32). Search out and seek how many times in the scriptures God speaks, not of the masses being saved, but of

---

[81] Note, 'whole' in v19 is *sozo* [G4982] which means 'saved'.

4 – The Fear of GOD, The Singular Issue of the Heart

only a remnant being saved.[82] Note how Paul says that it is the same even now "at the present time":

> Esaias also crieth concerning Israel, Though the number of the children of Israel be as the sand of the sea, a <u>remnant</u> shall be saved: … **Even so then at this present time also** there is a <u>remnant</u> according to the election of grace. Rom 9:27, 11:5

Many in Jesus' day began to follow the Lord, yet when Jesus began to speak his hard words on what they had to change in their life, many walked away from him from that day. "Many therefore of his disciples, when they had heard *this*, said, This is an hard saying; who can hear it? … From that *time* many of his disciples went back, and walked no more with him." Jn 6:60,66 Notice how the walking away of so many of his disciples happens to take place in John 6:66. Remember, 666 is the number of man, which in turn is the number or character of the beast. The mark or influence of the world (i.e. of the beast) on a person's thinking is that they will hear for a time, but then walk away when the word demands change. Many things we will need to cover will be hard sayings, sayings which put a demand on our heart to be willing to forsake all to follow the Master. It is when God puts his demand upon our life that, if there be no fear of God, we also will walk away and return to empty religion. Thus, the helpmate of discipleship is the fear of God, and it will lead us and teach us how to serve God acceptably.

---

[82] The remnant: 2K 19:4,30-31, 2Ch 30:6, Ezr 9:8,14, Neh 1:3, Isa 1:9 [very small], 10:20-23, 11:11,16, 37:4,31-32, 46:3, Jer 6:9, 15:11, 23:3, 31:7, 40:11,15, 42:2, Eze 6:8, 11:13, 14:22, Joel 2:32, Am 5:15, Mic 2:12, 5:3,7-8, 7:18, Zep 3:13, Hag 1:12,14, Zec 8:6,12, Rev 12:17.

Chapter 5. Toward a More Godly, Faithful, and Perfect Heart
The Finishing of God's Creation

"And he charged them, saying, Thus shall ye do in the fear of the LORD, faithfully, and with a perfect heart." 2Ch 19:9

We have looked at the beginning work that the fear of the LORD will do in our heart if we allow it. We have focused first on the inward changes that must take place and have looked at the new heart, the humble heart, the single heart, the pure heart, the enlarged heart, and the willing heart. Now let us look at how the fear of the LORD affects our heart externally, that is, in how we respond to others. Let us look at how the fear of the LORD changes our heart to faithfully, selflessly live before others.

5 – Toward a More Godly, Faithful, and Perfect Heart

A Selfless, Sacrificial Heart
"Honour all men. Love the brotherhood. Fear God." 1Pe 2:17

Without the fear of God, we remain the self-centered creatures that we have grown up in the natural to be. No one, not even the born again believer will, of their own, deny themselves. Remember, when we are born again we are brand new babes. As brand new babies we must grow up in the things of God (1Pe 2:2). This is particularly done through the process of discipleship, in which we learn how to daily <u>deny ourselves</u>, pick up our cross, and follow him (Lk 9:23). The denial of ourselves is required for all who would follow Jesus. It is not an optional part of our life in Christ. But how does this denial of self become a part of us, and not just we in our natural strength trying to put our old nature to death (which is impossible)? Only through the fear of God. This is why discipleship without the fear of God only produces knowledge that puffs up. Discipleship needs the fear of God as a helpmate so that the way of discipline is properly infused with a heart that is set on fire with the fear of God.

The fear of God has a profound effect on the focus of our hearts. Once our desires are changed and our heart is opened up so that we have a greater capacity to love in truth, and after we begin to desire what the Lord desires, the fear of God, through the Spirit, prepares the way for our heart to be selfless. No longer are we and our concerns the center of our attention. For the fear of the LORD to dwell in us, the LORD must displace every other focus. He alone must be exalted in our heart and his concerns must become supreme. The more our focus is directed unto him, the more he will direct our hearts toward those he cares about. Thus, a trademark of the fear of God is sincere compassion. Fear without love has torment, both for the one who has the fear, as well as those who know such a person, but fear with love has no such torment.

In Psalm 112 we see an expounding of what the man who fears God is like. It begins, "Praise ye the LORD. Blessed *is* the man *that* feareth the LORD, *that* delighteth greatly in his commandments." Ps 112:1 Note how the fear of God cannot be disassociated from God's commandments, which is part of our love toward God. Obadiah, the governor of Ahab's house, was such a man. Obadiah "feared the LORD greatly" (1K 18:3), and his own testimony was, "I thy servant fear the LORD from my youth." 1K 18:12 Look at how his fear of God is evidenced. "For it was *so*, when Jezebel cut off the prophets of the LORD, that Obadiah took an hundred prophets, and hid them by fifty in a cave, and fed them with bread and water." 1K 18:4 Obadiah's selflessness is demonstrated first in that he laid his own life down for the lives of men of God who were in jeopardy from the wicked. Second, it was demonstrated by his compassion to continually take care of their need. Thus, Obadiah was walking in the fruits of the fear of God. This is why Psalm 112:4 details, concerning the man that fears the LORD, that "*he is* gracious, and <u>full of compassion</u>, and righteous."

Where is the Fear of GOD? Losing the Treasure of the Lord

The Proof of our Love: "Love the Brotherhood." 1Pe 2:17

The fear of God will manifest in compassion upon those whom the Lord takes special notice of – like the poor, the needy, the hurting, and the broken. But this God-fearing compassion will begin to be moved in our bowels, first and foremost, to care for the family of faith. So many want to go to the lost, yet have never learned to take care of and to love their own local body of believers. Thus, Paul must warn the church, "But if any provide not for his own, and specially for those of his own house, he hath denied the faith, and is worse than an infidel." 1Tim 5:8 Jesus' first concern with Peter in restoring him after he had denied the Lord three times was to remind him to take care of Jesus' sheep.

> Simon, *son* of Jonas, **lovest thou me** more than these?
> ... He saith unto him, <u>Feed my lambs</u>.
>
> He saith to him again the 2nd time, Simon, *son* of Jonas, **lovest thou me**?
> ... He saith unto him, <u>Feed my sheep</u>.
>
> He saith unto him the third time, Simon, *son* of Jonas, **lovest thou me**?
> ... Jesus saith unto him, <u>Feed my sheep</u>. Jn 21:15-17

As with Peter, it is easy to proclaim our great love for Jesus. But as the Lord did with Peter, so he will prove the genuineness of our love for him. Many times even the thought of proving or testing our love for another offends us. Yet true, deep love is not offended by this, and actually rejoices in being put to the test. So David rejoiced to prove his love for Saul's daughter by bringing the requested 100 Philistine foreskins. In fact, David was pleased, and he went out and brought back *twice* what was asked of him (1Sam 18:26-27).

It is only shallow, self-conceited, self-righteous love that is offended by the challenge to be proved. God is truly our example in this. When man looked around him at the suffering in the world and wondered if God really cared, God did not get angry at our doubt. Rather, he helped us in all of our infirmities (Rom 8:26), so that he might prove to us the great and exceeding depth of his abounding love toward us. "But God <u>commendeth</u> his love toward us, in that, while we were yet sinners, Christ died for us." Rom 5:8 God did not wait for us to come to him. He came unto us and paid the greatest price. He did not watch man, helpless, hopeless, and lost, to find a way on his own. Rather, at great cost he made a way to us, where there was no way: "Himself took our infirmities, and bare *our* sicknesses." Mt 8:17 God is willing to have his love proved, but are we?

The apostles many times had to prove the love of the saints. So James puts his hearers to the test as to whether they have a genuine love or only words.

> If a brother or sister be naked, and destitute of daily food, And one of you say unto them, Depart in peace, be ye warmed and filled; notwithstanding ye give them not those things which are needful to the body; what *doth it* profit? Jam 2:15-16

5 – Toward a More Godly, Faithful, and Perfect Heart

It is far easier to claim that we love God, than to show our love for God by loving his children, the redeemed of the Lord, and especially to do good to them that are of the household of faith. But this was Jesus' test of Peter, as we have seen. If you love me, then take care of my sheep. It was James' test of the church, and so it was John's. So it is the Lord's test of us.

> Hereby perceive we the love *of God*, because he laid down his life for us: and <u>we ought to lay down *our* lives for the brethren</u>. But whoso hath this world's good, and seeth his brother have need, and shutteth up his bowels *of compassion* from him, how dwelleth the love of God in him? My little children, <u>let us not love in word</u>, <u>neither in tongue</u>; but in deed and in truth. 1Jn 3:16-18

> If a man say, I love God, and hateth his brother, is a liar: for <u>he that loveth not his brother</u> whom he hath seen, how can he love God whom he hath not seen? And this commandment have we from him, That he who loveth God <u>love his brother also</u>. 1Jn 4:20-21

Sent Forth to Show His Love

After we have faithfully proved our love for the brethren by serving them in love, then the Lord will lead us to go forth and love those we do not know. He will send us especially to the hurting, the poor, and the lost. Such is the pattern of the New Testament. It was not until the apostles had been faithful as elders to oversee and care for the church in Jerusalem that he led them out to other cities, those of Judea, Galilee, and Samaria (Ac 9:31, 8:14), Lydda, Sharon, and Joppa (Ac 9:32-36), and then finally to the Gentiles in Caesarea (Ac 10).

So we see the same pattern with the Gentile church. Barnabas and Paul taught the disciples there for a whole year until they manifested the character of Christ, and so were called Christians (Ac 11:26). Then the Lord put them to the test, would they take care of the brethren first? Prophets came from Jerusalem and prophesied of the great dearth that should be throughout all the world (Ac 11:28). Did they go to the world, or did they, according to pattern, immediately go to the saints in Jerusalem? "Then the disciples, every man according to his ability, determined to send relief unto <u>the brethren</u> which dwelt in Judaea: Which also they did" (Ac 11:29-30). They were put to the test by God's Spirit. Would they take care of their own family, *before* going to the world? Yes, they first learned to love their own. "Love the brotherhood. Fear God." 1Pe 2:17 They passed the test with flying colors and that is why soon after they returned from their journey to Jerusalem, that they were now released by the Spirit of God to be sent to the Gentilic world (Ac 13:1-4).

If we would reach the world for Jesus, let us first learn to reach our own spiritual family at home. We must learn how first to love one another and take care of our own family. This is true on the macrocosm as it is on the individual level. If we cannot provide for our own family, we are in God's eyes worse than an infidel. "But if any provide not for his own, and specially for those of his own house, he hath denied the faith, and is worse than an infidel." 1Tim 5:8 This is why the requirements for a spiritual leader, the elder, is that he knows how to rule well (i.e. literally 'to *stand before*') his own house, "having his children in subjection with all gravity; (For if a man know not how to rule his own house, how shall he take care of the church of God?)" (1Tim 3:4-5). Similarly, the servant of the church, the deacon, must '*stand before*' their children and their own houses well (1Tim 3:12).

True ministry always begins at home, and then when one is found faithful there, they are released into wider spheres of influence. Thus, how we respond and treat those who know us best, determines our effectiveness and usefulness in ministry. For in truth, ministry is serving people. When we learn to love the brethren we also gain a great assurance in the faith. So, "We <u>know</u> that we have passed from death unto life, <u>because we love the brethren</u>." 1Jn 3:14

Nehemiah is the perfect example of a disciple of the Lord who served God with the fear of God. He learned how to be faithful where he was, desiring nothing for himself. He allowed the LORD to enlarge his heart for God's people so that when he heard of their suffering he emptied himself to see whatever he could do to bring relief. With prayer and fasting he sought God. We have seen how Nehemiah desired to fear God, and this only increased in him.

> Moreover from the time that I was appointed to be their governor in the land of Judah, from the twentieth year even unto the two and thirtieth year of Artaxerxes the king, *that is,* twelve years, I and my brethren <u>have not eaten the bread of the governor</u>.
>
> But the former governors that *had been* before me were chargeable unto the people, and had taken of them bread and wine, beside forty shekels of silver; yea, even their servants bare rule over the people: but <u>so did not I, because of the fear of God</u>. Neh 5:14-15

Nehemiah did not take this course of action because someone told him he ought to do it. He did not do it because he himself thought it was a good idea. It was wholly **because of the fear of God** within him that he was moved to deny himself for the sake of others! We will never come to the selflessness of true servants of God, if we do not add the fear of God to discipleship.

A Preserved Heart: A Heart of Integrity

"And the LORD commanded us to do all these statutes, to fear the LORD our God, for our good always, that he might preserve us alive, as it is at this day." Dt 6:24

The fear of God preserves people's lives, not only the one who has it, but all who will be influenced by them. One man who fears God may save an entire company of people. So it was with Paul. Not only was his life saved by hearkening and trusting in the word of the Lord, but all those that were with him on the ship that heard his word were also saved (Ac 27:21-44). So it was with Levi, because he feared God and was afraid of God's name "he walked with [God] in peace and equity, and <u>did turn many away from iniquity</u>." Mal 2:5-6 The fear of God has a great preserving effect in other's lives. It truly is the covenant of salt[83] which preserves not only our self but others from corruption. It is this fear of God that keeps us from becoming hypocrites, as we have seen, because it continually purges and preserves our heart and conscience from living a lie. The fear of God heals us from the blindness that we all have of not being able to see our own sins and faults.

The scripture testifies that the lost are blinded by the god of this world so that they cannot see the light of the glorious gospel of Christ. Hence, the gospel is hid from them (2Co 4:3-4). Because they are blind, God warns us not to put a stumbling block before them – especially the stumbling block of being disobedient or insubordinate children of God! "Thou shalt not curse the deaf, nor put a stumbling block before the blind, but shalt fear thy God: I *am* the LORD." Lev 19:14 Notice how God instructs us not to put a stumbling block before the blind. How do we avoid doing this? By fearing God. This is why introducing the preceding section in 2Corinthians, Paul begins with the necessity of maintaining a good conscience in the life of those who minister Christ.

> Therefore seeing we have this ministry, as we have received mercy, we faint not; But have renounced the hidden things of dishonesty, not walking in craftiness, nor handling the word of God deceitfully; but by manifestation of the truth commending ourselves to every man's conscience in the sight of God. 2Co 4:1-2

When we do not walk in the fear of God and thus do not maintain a good conscience before him, we are putting a stumbling block before the blind, and God is angered. For this, many of God's children will come under the chastisement of the Lord, even as he has promised. "And that servant, which knew his lord's will, and prepared not *himself*, neither did according to his will, shall be beaten with many *stripes*." Lk 12:47 So Paul exhorts Timothy as an example to others, "Take heed unto thyself, and unto the doctrine; continue in them: for in doing this thou shalt both <u>save thyself, and them that hear thee</u>." 1Tim 4:16

We are called by the apostles for this very reason to be obedient.[84] So Nehemiah warns the remnant of those who were trying to rebuild their faith and their walk with God as they rebuilt the walls around Jerusalem, "It *is* not good that ye do: ought ye not to walk in the fear of our God <u>because</u> of the reproach of the heathen our enemies?" Neh 5:9 Why should we walk obediently before

---

[83] This is described in the section 'The Salt of the Covenant: The Fear of the LORD' in the chapter entitled "The Door of Mercy to All Those who Fear the LORD" in the book <u>Finding the Treasure of the Lord</u>.

[84] The apostolic injunction to be obedient is everywhere: 1Pe 1:14, 4:17, Rom 15:18, 2Co 2:9, Eph 6:1,5, Tit 2:5,9, 3:1, Col 3:20,22, 2Th 1:8, 3:14, Heb 5:9, 13:17.

God in the fear of the LORD? So that reproach does not come upon God because of those unbelievers who observe our life and see open hypocrisy.

A Faithful Heart
"for he was a faithful man, and feared God above many." Neh 7:2

When we see how our life affects others, the fear of God will move us to be faithful. Faithfulness is directly dependent on the fear of God being in our heart. When we lose our fear of God, we will always lose our faithfulness toward God. The fear of God is what keeps our heart serving faithfully. It keeps our heart on the difficult and narrow path of the highway of holiness that we have been commanded to walk on. The fear of God keeps our heart faithful when it would otherwise begin to wander. "That I gave my brother Hanani, and Hananiah the ruler of the palace, charge over Jerusalem: for he *was* a faithful man, and feared God above many." Neh 7:2 Great fear of God produces great faithfulness toward God in our service of him.

> Faithfulness is directly dependent on the fear of God being in our heart. When we lose our fear of God, we will always lose our faithfulness toward God.

David's heart as a servant of God was that he was <u>devoted</u> to the fear of God. "Stablish thy word unto thy servant, who *is devoted* to thy fear." Ps 119:38 No wonder David was able to keep his servant's heart over his lifetime and remain faithful as a servant of God. Many a king who followed after David became puffed up and filled with pride by their position and no longer served the LORD.[85] God is able to establish our hearts and the promise of his word as we remain servants of God who are devoted to his fear. In David's devotion to the fear of God, his cry was that God's word would be established, that it would 'rise up' before him. David was continually singing, speaking, and meditating on the law of the LORD so that his devotion to the fear of God might be satisfied. David truly fulfilled the warning that was given to kings to learn God's fear by continually reading the scriptures (Dt 17:19-20). Let us learn to *"be thou* in the fear of the LORD all the day long." Pr 23:17

The order of what God tells us is very important. Thus, when he records in his word that the fear of God precedes service, which precedes obedience and

---

[85] Remember the section on 'Warnings from Good Kings Gone Bad' in the chapter entitled "Why We Forsake the Fear of the LORD". There it was illustrated how many of the kings of Judah departed from serving God because they lost their fear of him. Even David for a season lost his fear of God, and sinned grievously against God. David paid dearly in suffering over many years for the sins associated with Bathsheba.

5 – Toward a More Godly, Faithful, and Perfect Heart

which keeps us from rebelling against God's commandments, and ends in faithfulness, we must know there is a relationship of *precedence* one to the other. This is the promise:

> If ye will [1] fear the LORD, and [2] serve him, and [3] obey his voice, and [4] not rebel against the commandment of the LORD, then shall both ye and also the king that reigneth over you <u>continue following</u> the LORD your God 1Sam 12:14

We cannot hope to obey his voice and do his will over the long run without fearing him. Faithfulness is being able to "continue following the LORD your God". If we have allowed the fear of God to take hold of our heart, this will be our desire: to follow him wherever he asks us to go.

The Effect of the Fear of God: A Perfect Heart

"Thus shall ye do in the fear of the LORD, faithfully, and with a perfect heart." 2Ch 19:9

The fear of the LORD will produce not only a faithful heart, but also a perfect heart. "And he charged them, saying, Thus shall ye do in the fear of the LORD, faithfully, and with <u>a perfect heart</u>." 2Ch 19:9 Notice the progression in this verse: the fear of the LORD enables us to walk faithfully and with a perfect heart. We need a perfect heart which comes from the fear of the LORD. God's messengers are sent to us for the purpose of perfecting us (i.e. maturing us) in our walk with the Lord.

> Whom we preach, warning every man, and teaching every man in all wisdom; that we may present every man perfect in Christ Jesus: Whereunto I also labour, striving according to his working, which worketh in me mightily. Col 1:28-29

The Bible enjoins that we are to be perfect before God. God sets it before our eyes repeatedly, so that we will not ignore it, nor rationalize it away. This is something we would rather not look at or think about or be reminded of, for it involves exposing all the inward parts of our heart. But God's command to be perfect is inescapable:

> Be ye therefore <u>perfect</u>, even as your Father which is in heaven is perfect. Mt 5:48
>
> Thou shalt be <u>perfect</u> with the LORD thy God. Dt 18:13
>
> Let your heart therefore be <u>perfect</u> with the LORD our God 1K 8:61
>
> I *am* the Almighty God; walk before me, & be thou <u>perfect</u>. Gen 17:1
>
> Finally, brethren, farewell. Be <u>perfect</u> 2Co 13:11

God's demand to be perfect will expose all dishonesty and any compromise, yet this is why we so much need it, and why we must take a good, long look at it. As Jesus warned, "Take heed therefore that the light which is in thee be not darkness." Lk 11:35 Repeatedly, God's condemnation of the kings of Judah who did not follow him was "his heart was not <u>perfect</u> with the LORD his God, as *was* the heart of David his father."[86]

Yet even as we see God's disappointment with the kings who should have served him with a perfect heart, God uses David as the yardstick. God declares that David had a perfect heart toward him. The fact that David fell short and sinned is notorious, yet God still says David's heart was perfect with him. So, though we know this side of heaven we will never be sinless, yet it is clearly possible for our heart to be perfect with the LORD! In fact, God expects it to be so, for he commanded Abraham, our father of faith, to be perfect (Gen 17:1). We can take comfort also that it was not only David who had a perfect heart – as if he were some special exception. On the contrary, besides David there were others who had a perfect heart toward the LORD.

- Though Asa did not do all the LORD asked of him to do, "nevertheless Asa's heart was <u>perfect</u> with the LORD all his days." 1K 15:14
- Hezekiah, in the midst of facing God's judgment for his foolishness, prayed for mercy, "I beseech thee, O LORD, remember now how I have walked before thee in truth and with <u>a perfect heart</u>, and have done *that which is* good in thy sight." 2K 20:3
- The "men of war, that could keep rank" who came to David's side "came with <u>a perfect heart</u> ... to make David king" (1Ch 12:38).
- Of those who gave to the building of the house of God in David's day, it is written, "with <u>perfect heart</u> they offered willingly to the LORD" (1Ch 29:9).
- David's final charge to his son Solomon as well as his prayer for him was that he serve God "with <u>a perfect heart</u> and with a willing mind" (1Ch 28:9, 29:19).
- Similarly, it was Jehoshaphat's charge to the Levites. "And he charged them, saying, Thus shall ye do in the fear of the LORD, faithfully, and with <u>a perfect heart</u>." 2Ch 19:9

It is the LORD's desire for us also. The eyes of the LORD still search "through out the whole earth, to shew himself strong in the behalf of *them* whose heart *is* <u>perfect</u> toward him." 2Ch 16:9 He would have us fear him, so that what we do, we do faithfully and with a perfect heart. Faithfulness and a perfect heart can only be developed in our heart under the careful tutorage of the fear of God.

But let us not mistake a perfect heart with good intentions. Consider the child who, when asked of their parent to do a particular thing (such as to get ready to leave for a special event), does something else 'good' instead (such as clean up their room). No matter how 'good' that other thing was, it will never

---

[86] See 1K 11:4, 15:3 and also 2Ch 25:2.

5 – Toward a More Godly, Faithful, and Perfect Heart

be pleasing enough – for it was not what was asked! Rather than bring forth approval, such good deeds instead must bring forth displeasure and correction from the authority.

So it is with the LORD. He has asked us to prepare our life for the coming of his Son, and if we do anything else in place of this, no matter how good it may be, we can only come under his judgment for being foolish. Remember, this was the condemnation of the five foolish virgins. Though they were virgins in purity, yet they did not prepare for the coming of the bridegroom! If we have not made our self ready as he has commanded, then we will never go with him. Such is the prophetic cry, *"Prepare ye the way of the Lord, make his paths straight."* Mt 3:3 Let us learn the particular obedience that springs forth from the fear of God and makes a perfect heart.

> **WARNING**: What is truly amazing is that we, like Amaziah, can do *"that which was right in the sight of the LORD, but not with a perfect heart."* 2Ch 25:2 Think of that saint! We may do what is right in the sight of God, and yet he still is displeased because we do not do it with a **perfect** heart. Having a perfect heart toward God is not about being good and not doing evil. We often can convince ourselves that because we "haven't done evil" in a particular situation and that we have made a great effort "to be good" that God will be pleased with this. But there is an obedience that does not please God at all. This shows us that God is looking for more than just obedience! He is looking for the obedience that has the fear of God in it. A man may do right, but for the wrong reason, for he may yet still love evil in his heart! Remember, "The fear of the LORD *is* to hate evil: pride, and arrogancy, and the evil way, and the froward mouth, do I hate." Pr 8:13

A Willing Heart: Delighting in the Word of God
"Thy people shall be willing in the day of thy power" Ps 110:3

The true fear of God will cause our heart to be set on the things of God, rather than on our own desires. The fear of God will always cause us to see the word of God in a totally different light, than when we are without it. We will receive the scriptures as they truly are, the very words of God, without error, without compromise, without apology, and without compare. Through the fear of God we properly apprehend the word of God as his law, his promise, his covenant. When we, through the fear of God, begin to receive the word of God as it was originally intended, it begins to be the law of God – binding us to God's purposes and preserving us from destruction. The word of God therefore now also inspires us to fear God.

> Therefore what is bound by the text, is bound, and what is released by the text, is released; also the bond and release are unalterable. This

therefore calleth upon God's people to stand more in fear of the word of God, than of all the terrors of the world.[87]

Consider this: the very first words of God ever written down and handed to the people of God were the ten commandments. They are first recorded in Exodus 20. Immediately after coming down from the mount with the ten commandments written by the very finger of God, it is recorded, "And Moses said unto the people, <u>Fear not</u>: for God is come to prove you, and that <u>his fear</u> may be before your faces, that ye sin not." Ex 20:20

> Hearing God's word with a pure heart ensures and secures our continual fear of God. The fear of God in turn will change our attitude toward God's word so that the authority of his word will be exalted.

The word of God, especially in the form of his commandments, was given to keep us in the fear of God so that it would be before our faces, that we sin not. God reminded the people 40 years later of his exhortation to continue to hear the word of God so that they would always fear him: "the LORD said unto me, Gather me the people together, and I will make them <u>hear my words</u>, that they may <u>learn to fear me</u> all the days that they shall live upon the earth, and *that they may teach their children.*" Dt 4:10

Hearing God's word with a pure heart ensures and secures our continual fear of God. The fear of God in turn will change our attitude toward God's word so that the authority of his word will be exalted. So no one can say they fear God with the fear that God desires, if they do not wholeheartedly love God's word and delight themselves in it. The scripture records that those with a poor and contrite spirit will tremble at God's word, and that God is looking for such a response (Isa 66:2,5). Thus, God promises to destroy those who despise his word, "but he that feareth the commandment shall be rewarded." Pr 13:13

Where once the word of God was a burden, a wearying thing, and a mystery, it now becomes our delight, our strength, and our light. So David, who feared God greatly, witnesses repeatedly of his great delight in the word of God.[88] And so we read, "Praise ye the LORD. Blessed *is* the man *that* feareth the LORD, *that* delighteth greatly in his commandments." Ps 112:1 In fearing God we will delight in God's ways. In delighting in his ways (especially over our ways or the ways of the world), our desire will be to seek first his kingdom and his

---

[87] Bunyan, p. 22.

[88] Psalm 119 alone should convince us of David's true delight in the word of God: Ps 119:16,24,35,47,70,77,92,143,174.

righteousness. We begin to delight ourselves in pleasing the heavenly Father by doing his will.

Delighting to do God's will always follows delighting in his word and having it in our heart. Notice how the psalmist speaks of his delight to do God's will as being the direct result of God's word being in his heart. "I delight to do thy will, O my God: yea, thy law *is* within my heart." Ps 40:8 Thus, the fear of God, which leads us to tremble and to turn to his word, becomes the key to delighting in God and in doing his will. Without his fear we pick and choose whether we want to do his will. This often explains our lack of desire for the word of God. Why would our soul want to *hear* what it does not want to do?

Once the fear of God is strong in our heart, we begin to love both his word, his ways, and his will. A new willingness in our heart will be birthed. Part of this willingness and desire to please him, rather than ourselves, springs from the simple joy that the fear of God produces in us. "**Happy** *is* the man that feareth always" (Pr 28:14). When we truly delight in pleasing God, we will have a great willingness and strength to serve, for the joy of the Lord (that happiness that is found in him) is our strength (Neh 8:10). Thus, it is written of the woman that fears the LORD, "She ... worketh willingly with her hands." Pr 31:13 This word 'willingly' means with '*pleasure* and *desire*'. This is one of the most beautiful outward works that the fear of the LORD produces in us. When the fear of the LORD possesses our heart, we will take pleasure in God's will and desire to serve others.

The Willing Heart is a United Heart

God is looking for a willing heart, a heart that desires what he desires, which can only come in truth from one who has the fear of God working in them. You ask how so? Because it is only the fear of God that will drive out our sinful and selfish desires and cause us to begin to hate what God hates and to love what he loves. "Teach me thy way, O LORD; I will walk in thy truth: unite my heart to fear thy name. I will praise thee, O Lord my God, with all my heart: and I will glorify thy name for evermore." Ps 86:11-12

The word 'unite' here means 'to *be* (or become) *one*'. The fear of the LORD will cause us to hate evil, especially pride, arrogancy, and the evil way. This then enables our heart to be united toward him, for now we begin to delight in what he delights and no longer in the pleasures of sin or of our own desires. The uniting of our heart will cause us to "hate the evil, and love the good, and establish judgment in the gate" (Am 5:15). This unity of heart removes duplicity and double-heartedness from us. There is a renewing and a purifying of our mind that can only come through God's fear. Notice how the psalmist speaks about the perfection of God's commandments before and after, but at the very heart of these revelations is the fear of the LORD.

> The statutes of the LORD *are* right, rejoicing the heart: the commandment of the LORD *is* pure, enlightening the eyes. The <u>fear of the LORD</u> *is* clean, enduring for ever: the judgments of the LORD *are* true *and* righteous altogether. Ps 19:8-9

With a united heart, immediately there begins to form within us one way, one life, one truth (Jer 32:39). There is a singleness that begins to grow within us that causes our eyes to be blind to many things that once captivated our thoughts and desires. "Who *is* blind, but my servant? or deaf, as my messenger *that* I sent? who *is* blind <u>as *he that is* perfect</u>, and blind as the LORD's servant?" Isa 42:19 Once our heart is united, our delight will be his good, pleasing, and perfect will and in his commandments (which are the immediate expression of his will). Then, and only then, will our heart be perfect before God. Then we will be able to do all things with a willingness that pleases him, because now we are delighting ourselves in the will of God and not our own desires. Now we can see why "the LORD taketh pleasure in them that fear him" (Ps 147:11).

WARNING: But some may say, "What we *do* does not please God, for he cannot be pleased by mere man. He is not benefited by our righteousness, or anything we do. What profit does he receive when we make our ways right before him?" People are not alone in such thinking, for Eliphaz said this very thing. "*Is it* any pleasure to the Almighty, that thou art righteous? or *is it* gain *to him* that thou makest thy ways perfect?" Job 22:3

In our continual failures we may be tempted to think this same way. But know and be assured that Eliphaz did not speak for God in this. He was one "that darkeneth counsel by words without knowledge" (Job 38:2). It was to Eliphaz directly that God said, "My wrath is kindled against thee, and against thy two friends: for ye have <u>not spoken of me *the thing that is* right</u>" (Job 42:7). God rebuked Eliphaz for speaking folly.[89] Thus, we must reject Eliphaz' counsel as foolish words and hold fast to the testimony of scripture: "The LORD **taketh pleasure** in them that fear him" (Ps 147:11). Do not let the discouragement or the weariness of your own heart deceive you. Never think that your choices do not matter to God. They are the very issues of life.

Being perfect before God is not about being flawless and never missing him, for we have already mentioned some very imperfect and sinful men whom the scripture declares had a perfect heart toward God. Rather, having a perfect heart, as we are seeing, is about an undivided heart – that we have no other secret loves. It is the removing of idolatry. Having a perfect heart toward God means he and he alone has undivided rule in our heart.

The importance of his rule or lordship cannot be pushed aside. It is impossible to separate a true love for God from a willingness to submit to his unchal-

---

[89] This word 'folly' in verse 8 means '*foolishness*, i.e. (moral) *wickedness*; concretely a *crime*'.

5 – Toward a More Godly, Faithful, and Perfect Heart

lenged authority to direct our life. When we have an unwillingness to receive and honor his authority by submitting to his commandments, then we at the same time have a breakdown in our love for our sacred Husband. Without a perfect heart, eventually we will have a break in our intimacy with God.[90] So we see with Solomon. "For it came to pass, when Solomon was old, *that* his wives <u>turned away his heart</u> after other gods: and his heart was not perfect with the LORD his God, as *was* the heart of David his father." 1K 11:4 Whenever one of God's people did not have a perfect heart toward him, it was always because they began to love something other than the will of God.

We cannot be as the rich young ruler who loved God, yet still loved his possessions, for then our heart is not perfect with God, because it is divided. The love of other things will always keep us from a perfect heart. And the rich man deep in his heart <u>knew</u> that he was not perfect with God, which is why he came to Jesus asking, "What lack I yet?" "Jesus said unto him, If thou <u>wilt be perfect</u>, go *and* sell that thou hast, and give to the poor, and thou shalt have treasure in heaven: and come *and* follow me." Mt 19:21 Jesus challenged the rich young ruler, as he does us all, to be radically single and whole-heartedly devoted to him. Anything in our life that competes with our love for God we ought to violently cut off. This is why, not once, but twice, Jesus spoke of doing radical surgery to cut off what causes us to depart from God (Mt 18:9 & 5:29).

A Heart Made Whole

It is the fear of God and the fear of God alone that enables us to fulfill this seemingly impossible command to be perfect before God. Now the perfect heart that God desires us to have must be complete. This is the life that we are to have in Jesus. "And ye are <u>complete</u> in him" (Col 2:10). We must come to this revelation: our heart can only be complete in him. There is nothing else that can complete it. If we seek for satisfaction or fulfillment or completion outside of the Lord Jesus, we will surely and repeatedly be disappointed. We may find temporary peace and enjoyment in many things which God has given for us to enjoy (1Tim 6:17), but none of them can take the place of our God.

Our heart has been created to only be fulfilled and completed in him. Success cannot make you complete. The abundance of resources or goods cannot make you complete. Marriage cannot make you complete. Children cannot make you complete. Jesus came that we might have life, and that that life would be more abundant (Jn 10:10), but that life as Paul so marvelously shows is "in Christ", "in him", and not in any other person or thing. Our fulfillment can only be found in the life that he gives us to live. The life that Jesus wants to give

---

[90] The word 'perfect' in 2Ch 19:9 means '*complete*, especially *friendly*'. It is translated into English as 'full, whole, made ready, peaceable, quiet'. When our heart is being made perfect through the fear of God it will be made whole, complete, and ready (to do his will).

us is exceeding abundantly above that we can think or imagine, but it can only come when we give up our life and put on his life. "But put ye on the Lord Jesus Christ, and make not provision for the flesh, to *fulfil* the lusts *thereof*." Rom 13:14 Our flesh always restrains the flow of his power and the enjoyment of his life. If we would see the power of his life working unrestricted in us, we must lay down our life and take up his.

Concerning the perfection that God is calling us to, there are two different concepts used for 'perfect' in the Old Testament, which we need to explore. Both of them mean 'to be complete, entire, and whole', but there is an important difference between them that we will see. Though both of them produce a wholeness, we will find a different and important focus of each. The first one focuses on *truth* in the inmost part.[91] The second word focuses on relationship and therefore has to do with *friendship*. Let's look at each of them in turn.[92]

A Perfect Heart of Integrity
"a perfect and an upright man, one that feareth God,
and escheweth evil? and still he holdeth fast his integrity" Job 2:3

The perfect heart of truth in the inmost part deals with a pure conscience and with integrity. This is the heart that moves us to depart from what God hates. To have this perfect heart of integrity we must allow the fear of the LORD to remove all dishonesty and deception. We must renounce or disown all inward dishonesty to the truth. As Paul states, "But [we] have renounced the hidden things of dishonesty, not walking in craftiness, nor handling the word of God deceitfully; but by manifestation of the truth commending ourselves to every man's conscience in the sight of God." 2Co 4:2 The heart of integrity must be rid of deception, for the perfect heart is a heart that is girded with truth. Is this not the essence of what integrity[93] is? Honesty of heart. If there is any falsity in

---

[91] The first type of a perfect heart uses one of the following similar Hebrew words. Each of these comes from the root word 'tamam' (H8552) which means 'to *complete*'.

– tamiym, H8549, *entire* (literal, figurative or moral); also (as noun) *integrity, truth* :- without blemish, complete, full, perfect, sincerely (-ity), sound, without spot, undefiled, upright (-ly), whole. [perfect 18x]

– tam, H8535, *complete*; usually (moral) *pious*; specifically *gentle, dear* :- coupled together, perfect, plain, undefiled, upright. [perfect 9x]

– tom, H8537, *completeness*; usually (moral) *innocence* :- full, integrity, perfect (-ion), simplicity, upright (-ly, -ness), at a venture. [used only 1x]

[92] The second type of a perfect heart will be looked at in depth in the section entitled 'A Perfect Heart of Friendship'.

[93] The most common Hebrew word for integrity in the Old Testament is our root word for 'perfect' (i.e. tom, H8537, e.g.: Gen 20:5-6, 1K 9:4, etc.).

5 – Toward a More Godly, Faithful, and Perfect Heart

our inward man, if any deception or lie, any hypocrisy of living one way but acting another, it is impossible to have a perfect heart toward God or men.

The fear of God will enable us to walk openly before him. It does this by removing the lie that we can live in sin or for our selfish motives and still be walking in fellowship with the LORD. The fear of the LORD prevents this from happening. The fear of God will never allow us to conceal our sin and not repent. This is the inestimable value of the fear of the LORD, and why it is the salt of the covenant which preserves us. It must be recaptured. Without the fear of the LORD the lie and deception of sin, or as Hebrews puts it, "the deceitfulness of sin" (Heb 3:13), remains in us, and will first harden our heart and then cause us to depart from the living God (v12). With the fear of the LORD, we are driven to acknowledge truth and confess our sin before God so that we are cleansed from all unrighteousness. Only then is the work of preparing a perfect heart of integrity begun.

Truth in the Inward Parts

David in his great psalm of repentance reveals, "Behold, thou desirest <u>truth in the inward parts</u>: and in the hidden *part* thou shalt make me to know wisdom." Ps 51:6 This is what God *is pleased* with and *desires*: our inmost thoughts to be filled with truth. What is the truth that God desires to be in our inward parts? But the word of God. As Jesus said of his Father's word, "thy word is truth." Jn 17:17 God desires his truth would be written in our inward parts. How will God make us to know wisdom in the hidden part? By putting his fear there. "Behold, the fear of the Lord, that *is* wisdom" (Job 28:28). God will make known his wisdom in our hidden part through the fear of God.

> The fear of God exposes and reproves our hypocrisy and the falsehood of our inmost thoughts. The fear of God, which leads us to repentance, then enables us to have intimacy with the LORD and to hear his voice.

The fear of God allows us to hear his word so we "receive with meekness the engrafted word, which is able to save [our] souls." Jam 1:21 This is how truth and integrity and a perfect heart are produced and maintained. The fear of God exposes and reproves our hypocrisy and the falsehood of our inmost thoughts. The fear of God, which leads us to repentance, then enables us to have intimacy with the LORD and to hear his voice. The ability to hear his voice, along with the humility to know our own sins and failures, allows us with meekness to receive the engrafted word – the word which is cut into our heart by the 'dividing asunder'.[94]

> For the word of God *is* quick, and powerful, and sharper than any twoedged sword, piercing even to the dividing asunder of soul and spirit, and of the joints and marrow, and *is* a discerner of the thoughts and intents of the heart. Heb 4:12

The word of God as a sword pierces to the dividing asunder of our heart, dividing our soul from our spirit,[95] and so engrafts the truth deep into our heart, IF we will but receive it with meekness. It has been shown earlier that the fear of the LORD produces a soft and humble heart. Thus, the fear of God is the key then, not only to intimacy with the LORD, but also to having the word of God received with humility, so that it can be written on the inward parts of our heart! The fear of the LORD prepares our heart so that the word of truth may be written on its inward parts. The writing of God's word upon our hearts can only be done through the implanting of the fear of God. This in fact *is* the new covenant as we have seen![96] When his law is written in our inward parts it will produce an intimacy with him in being his people and him being our God.

We have been given the Old Testament not only so that we may see the prophecies that were made beforehand of Christ Jesus, but also so that we may see the details of men's lives and God's dealing with them. It is this insight that gives us the clearest pictures of men who walked with God. Look at a beautiful example of this. At the beginning of Joshua's leadership, God miraculously dried up the waters of the Jordan, so that they might cross over into the promised land. Why did God do this? "That all the people of the earth might know the hand of the LORD, that it *is* mighty: <u>that ye might fear the LORD</u> your God for ever." Jos 4:24

God did it for the sake of the heathen so that they might know the power of God's mighty hand, but he also did it for the sake of his people so that they would always fear him! Yet by the end of Joshua's life they had forgotten their fear of the LORD. So Joshua had to exhort them to return to what they once were shown and taught. "Now therefore <u>fear the LORD</u>, and serve him in sincerity and in truth: and put away the gods which your fathers served on the other side of the flood, and in Egypt; and serve ye the LORD." Jos 24:14 The fear of the LORD will produce godly service that will be done in integrity. The fear of the LORD enables us to do whatever we do in "sincerity and in truth".

---

[94] This word 'dividing asunder' is the Greek word *merismos* (G3311).

[95] Though it may not be evident at first glance, by study it can be shown that the soul and the spirit are actually the compartments or inward parts of our heart.

[96] See the chapter entitled "Understanding the New Covenant of Grace & Fear" in the book <u>Finding the Treasure of the Lord</u>.

5 – Toward a More Godly, Faithful, and Perfect Heart

This word 'sincerity' is our word for 'perfect' which we have seen already.[97] Only the fear of God will so affect our heart that it can be made into that perfect heart of integrity.

The Example of Job's Life: A Heart Laid Open

This integrity of heart is most openly displayed in Job's life. The scripture states three separate times that Job was "a perfect and an upright man, <u>one that feareth God</u>, and escheweth evil" (Job 1:1, 1:8, 2:3). It is of such importance that when Job is first introduced to us in the scripture, this is the first thing we are told of him. Twice the LORD himself speaks of it to Satan, as a witness against the devil. This fear of God was what made Job perfect and upright before God and produced his integrity of heart. This in turn produced an intimacy with God, for we see God knew Job intimately and spoke of him very, very highly. God would not cast away or reject Job because of this, for it is written, "Behold, God will not cast away a perfect *man*" (Job 8:20).

God directed Satan to 'consider' (literally 'to *put* his *heart upon*') Job. "And the LORD said unto Satan, Hast thou considered my servant Job, that *there is* none like him in the earth, a perfect and an upright man, one that feareth God, and escheweth evil?" Job 1:8 (also 2:3, 1:1) There is something about Job's life that brought reproof and rebuke to Satan's disobedience, which is why Satan wanted to discredit and destroy him. We should put our heart upon Job and seriously think about his life. His life should cause us, likewise, to desire to be upright and to eschew evil.

The crucial element was that Job feared God. This was the source of Job's perfectness and uprightness. We have already seen that a perfect heart comes from the fear of God. Thus, a perfect and upright man is "one that feareth God". And who is it that escheweth (i.e. departs from) evil? The "one that feareth God". Thus, the core or source of every thing that God boasted of Job to Satan started and had its root with the fear of God! This is the importance of the fear of God and why God takes such pleasure in them that have it. It is also why Satan hates it so much.[98]

A Perfect Heart of Friendship
"Thus shall ye do in the fear of the LORD, faithfully, and with a perfect heart." 2Ch 19:9

---

[97] Namely, tamiym, H8548.

[98] Refer to "An Epilogue: Enduring Fear of God" in the book <u>Finding the Treasure of the Lord</u> to see why Satan so hates the true fear of God.

Let us now look at the second part of having a perfect heart. The perfect heart of friendship focuses on relationship. It comes from words that carry the connotation of being *friendly*.[99] This 'friendly' perfect heart is designed to fulfill our God-created purpose to love God with all our heart, mind, soul, and strength, and to serve him with our whole heart. This is the heart that keeps us from departing from God because we love him. Much like the perfect heart of integrity, the perfect heart of friendship also helps us keep and fulfill God's commandments. This time our obedience is not so much because of the integrity and truth that we would manifest to others externally, but more so because of the genuineness and truth of our friendship and our affection toward God himself. Our desire for intimate friendship propels us to love what he loves.

> Let your heart therefore be perfect [i.e. *friendly*] with the LORD our God, to walk in his statutes, and to keep his commandments, as at this day. 1K 8:61

> And give unto Solomon my son a perfect [i.e. *friendly*] heart, to keep thy commandments, thy testimonies, and thy statutes, and to do all *these things* 1Ch 29:19

This perfect heart of friendship with the LORD we can only obtain in the fear of the LORD. "And he charged them, saying, Thus shall ye do <u>in the fear of the LORD</u>, faithfully, and with a perfect [i.e. *friendly*] heart." 2Ch 19:9 Notice how we are to do our service unto the LORD faithfully and with a friendly heart *in* the fear of the LORD. The key is the fear of the LORD. Only it will enable us to do what we do faithfully and with a perfect heart of friendship.

> God so yearns to find those with a friendly heart toward him
> – those that want to hear what he has to say –
> that he continually searches the whole earth for them.

Having a perfect heart of friendship opens the door to intimate fellowship with the LORD. "Finally, brethren, farewell. Be perfect, … and the God of love and peace <u>shall be with you</u>." 2Co 13:11 Notice how the call to be perfect is followed with God being with us. God is diligently looking for those who will be perfect through the fear of God. "For the eyes of the LORD run to and fro throughout the whole earth, to shew himself strong in the behalf of <u>*them* whose</u>

---

[99] These use one of the following similar Hebrew words.

— shalem, H8003, from 7999 (shalam); *complete* (literal or figurative); especially <u>*friendly*</u> :- full, just, made ready, peaceable, perfect (-ed), quiet, whole.

— shalam, H7999, to *be safe* (in mind, body or estate); figurative to *be* (causative *make*) *completed*; by impl. <u>to *be friendly*</u> :- make amends, (make an) end, finish, full, give again, make good, (re-) pay (again), (make) (to) (be at) peace (-able), that is perfect, perform, (make) prosper (-ous), recompense, render, requite, make restitution, restore, reward.

heart *is* perfect toward him." 2Ch 16:9 God so yearns to find those with a friendly heart toward him – those that want to hear what he has to say – that he continually searches the whole earth for them. It lies within each of us to choose the fear of the LORD. God is asking, "What man *is* he that feareth the LORD?" Ps 25:12 And again, immediately after his call to fear him, he speaks of the intimacy of how the secret of the LORD is with them that fear him (v14).

Conclusions on the Effect of the Fear of the LORD on our Heart

This then is the two-fold effect of a perfect or "whole" heart. The first is to have *truth* in our innermost being so that we walk in openness and integrity. The second is to be *friendly* – to be disposed to promote the good of another. Let us have a perfect and complete heart toward the LORD through the fear of God, so that when he searches all our inmost being, he may find only truth and friendship there. This is where we will find our heart-strength to live for him.

So often this plan is short-circuited (as we have seen with the good kings gone bad). God's works are not done by his servants many times as he would have them to be done. Our heart does not become that perfected workmanship in his hands, so that it is the willing heart, the united heart, the enlarged heart, the servant's heart, the obedient heart, and the faithful heart that he desires. Why? Because the new heart, which we have been given, is not allowed to mature into what he has purposed for us, because we lose the fear of God that his Spirit first brought to us. If we would experience the fulfillment of the new covenant and the purpose of why we were given a new heart, a new spirit, and his Spirit, we MUST recapture the fear of God and have it growing within us.

We have seen what a dramatic effect the fear of God brings about on the heart. The fear of God is truly **the** issue of our heart. We cannot properly apprehend, nor experience the fear of God without opening wide our heart and allowing God to do surgery on it. This is why we cannot afford NOT to be naked and open before him with whom we have to do. Only the word of God when coupled with the fear of God can do this exposing work on the hidden parts of our heart. The word of God is clearly that two-edged sword, which as a scalpel, so pierces and divides asunder the secret places of our heart that even the thoughts of our heart are divided from its intents (Heb 4:12). But we will never see this skilful work be done, if the fear of God is absent. O how great the work that needs to be done on the heart of God's people! We have seen that when our heart is intimately involved in the process of gaining and growing in the fear of God, the fear of God will produce a great harvest.

Table 5-1 How His Fear Changes our Heart

The New Heart:[100]	References (Eze 36:26, Jer 32:38-40)
1. Soft Heart:	Isa 63:17, Pr 28:14
2. Humble Heart:	Job 37:24
3. United Heart:	Ps 86:11, Eph 6:5, Col 3:22
4. Single Heart:	Eph 6:5, Col 3:22
5. Pure Heart:	Ecc 12:13, 1Tim 1:5
6. Enlarged Heart:	Isa 60:5
7. Willing Heart:	Pr 28:14, 1Ch 28:9
8. Obedient Heart:	Dt 13:4, 1Sam 12:14, Col 3:22
9. Servant's Heart:	Dt 10:12, 1Sam 12:14
10. Preserved Heart:	Dt 6:24
11. Faithful Heart:	2Ch 19:9, Neh 7:2
12. Perfect Heart:	2Ch 19:9

> TABLE NOTES: The first 6 effects that the fear of God has upon our heart are discussed in the previous chapter. The remaining are discussed in this chapter, except where noted. Note that the first 5 effects that the fear of God has upon our heart (i.e. softening it, humbling it, uniting it, making it single, and purifying it) are all *compacting* in nature. All of these effectively remove things from our heart that either shouldn't be there or are unnecessary. Thus, they all work to break down a puffed up and rigid heart. These make our heart smaller in the sense of having fewer desires or loves. This is part of God's purification process on our heart where he removes the useless slag and dregs within us. Through this purifying process there is a compacting of our heart for an increase (Eph 4:16).
>
> Once this compacting is accomplished, God is now able to do an *enlarging* work on our heart for him and his perfect will. Hence, we see the last 7 effects of God's fear upon our heart begin to take place. God enlarges our heart by beginning to place his heart, what he cares for, in our single heart. Thus, the enlarged heart soon becomes the *selfless* servant's heart, which is faithful and perfect before him.

---

[100] The first six hearts are all discussed in the previous chapter. The remaining hearts are covered in this chapter, except for two. These two hearts we have reserved for discussion in upcoming chapters, namely the Obedient Heart and the Servant's Heart.

Where is the Fear of GOD? Losing the Treasure of the Lord

Chapter 6. Broken Fellowship from the Loss of God's Fear
The Divorce of the Spirit

"Then they that feared the LORD spake often one to another: and the LORD hearkened, and heard it" Mal 3:16

The fear of God will deeply circumcise our heart if we keep a good conscience. But if the grace of God is not allowed to produce the fear of God and to work in conjunction with it, then the grace of God will be frustrated in our life and will soon be in vain. Let us look at the results of the loss of the fear of God in our heart.

6 – Broken Fellowship from the Loss of God's Fear

The Derailing of the Purpose of God's Deliverances

"But the LORD your God ye shall fear; and he shall deliver you out of the hand of all your enemies." 2K 17:39

The true understanding of God's grace and forgiveness should not lead to carelessness or smug assurance, as it so often does today. Rather, it should lead to the conviction to fear God continually for what he has done to pay the price for our sin and his rightful demand upon our life to command our obedience. "If thou, LORD, shouldest mark iniquities, O Lord, who shall stand? But *there is* forgiveness with thee, <u>that thou mayest be feared</u>." Ps 130:3-4

Forgiveness, if properly understood, will always lead us to the fear of God. The reception of true grace is utterly humbling. We finally see what we are, and we see how ugly it truly is. This detesting revelation produces the fear of God to flee from our sinfulness and to find refuge in the LORD God alone. Grace then, though removing our guilt and condemnation and the remembrance of past sins, ought to <u>increase</u> our hatred of temptation, sin and its utter sinfulness.

> The true understanding of God's grace & forgiveness should not lead to carelessness or smug assurance ... Rather, it should lead to the conviction to fear God continually

Why then does the opposite so often happen? Instead of godly fear and true humility being the offspring of grace, we often find smugness, pride, self-conceit, and complacency. Yet Paul, who understood the grace of God better than any, wrote that God's "grace *which was bestowed* upon me was not in vain." Why? Because he "laboured more abundantly than they all" (1Co 15:10). When teachers teach of God's forgiveness, why does it *not* produce the fear of God? Why instead does the doctrine of grace seem to produce the exact opposite – the lack of fear? According to the Word, this cannot be the case. Therefore, a false balance is being brought forth in contemporary teachings on forgiveness. God has always longed for the day when those he has forgiven would have the fear of God. His goodness to us, despite our unfaithfulness, ought to bring about a deep and lasting fear of God. Rather than take advantage of God's goodness, he expects us to "fear the LORD and his goodness in the latter days." Hos 3:5 This is the new covenant that God would create in our heart.

> And I will cleanse them from all their iniquity, whereby they have sinned against me; and I will pardon all their iniquities, whereby they have sinned, and whereby they have transgressed against me. ... all the nations of the earth, which shall hear **all the good** that I do unto them: and <u>they shall fear and tremble</u> for **all the goodness** and for all the prosperity that I procure unto it. Jer 33:8-9

If we are born again today, saved from the wrath of God through Jesus Christ, then eternal, abundant, continual thankfulness ought to spring from our vessels – unless of course, we have forgotten what we have been forgiven for and delivered from. With great power and an outstretched arm the LORD has brought us out of this world (2K 17:36). We therefore owe him the continual debt of love: to serve him with a sacrificial spirit, to worship him, and to fear him. May we never forget why he has delivered us.

Grace which Denies His Lordship

Yet rarely today are forgiveness and the understanding of the depth of God's forgiveness producing what the scriptures say it should produce: the fear of God. This can only be because the grace of God that is being taught today is *not* the Biblical grace that was taught by the original apostles. Pay close attention to what took place in the early church. In Acts 2 as the grace of God was imparted to these new believers at Pentecost "fear came upon every soul" through the apostles' doctrine (Ac 2:43)! Consider on the other hand what Jude prophesies:

> For there are certain men crept in unawares, who were before of old ordained to this condemnation, ungodly men, turning the grace of our God into lasciviousness, and denying the only Lord God, and our Lord Jesus Christ. Jude 1:4

The scripture is truly being fulfilled today in that men are turning the forgiveness of God into a license to do what they please, to freely and unashamedly sin, and to deny the fear of God that is due the LORD. The word 'denying' in the NT does not so much mean that these men will not believe in God. No, like Hymenaeus and Alexander, they have faith in God, but concerning faith they have put away a good conscience (1Tim 1:19-20). Rather, denying means 'to *contradict*, i.e. *disavow, reject*'. Interestingly, it comes from the root words 'not' + 'to speak'. These men, though they say they believe in Jesus Christ, will not speak of him. Listen carefully to those who supposedly speak in the name of the Lord today, especially on television. You will rarely hear them speak of Jesus, which is the name above all names, and the Father, but they will speak all the time of Christ and God. They are denying the only name by which man can be saved. But beyond that, they will even deny the work Jesus has done and for what purpose it was done. Remember, Jesus did not save us so that we could continue in sin. God forbid the scripture says (Rom 6:1-2,15)!

What does it mean to turn the grace of God into lasciviousness? It means to be 'incontinent, wanton', which in turn mean '*powerless, i.e. without self-control*' and 'to live in pleasure'. Lasciviousness is giving oneself over to one's own will and desires. It is being given over to follow after one's lusts. This is what the grace of God has been turned into by many today.

6 – Broken Fellowship from the Loss of God's Fear

> **WARNING**: This is none other than the doctrine of 'once saved, always saved' – that no matter what we do we will not be cut off. Yet the scripture is quite clear, "Behold therefore the goodness and severity of God: on them which fell, severity; but toward thee, goodness, if thou continue in *his* goodness: <u>otherwise thou also shalt be cut off</u>." Rom 11:22 The once saved always saved doctrine always produces a smugness, a spiritual pride in the hearts of those who embrace it. Yet God says, "God resisteth the proud, and giveth grace to the humble." 1Pe 5:5 So, even by the effect of this doctrine on their own heart, it is clear they are not walking in the true grace of God, for God gives grace to the humble, not to the proud.

God promises that those who are humble will receive the true grace of God (1Pe 5:5). This will be evidenced by their continued humility and the promise of God being fulfilled. When men get proud because of what they believe is their state before God (i.e. that they cannot fall from grace), the grace of God will no longer be given to them as a result. When the grace of God is turned into lasciviousness it produces consciences which are seared, no longer sensitive to the conviction of sin or to boasting of what they think they have – when it is in the very process of being taken from them. They become just like the Pharisees of Jesus' day who were *sure* that they were the children of Abraham, children of the covenant who could not be cut off. But the kingdom of God *was* taken away from them and given to others who would bring forth the fruits thereof (Mt 21:43). God is NOT a respecter of persons; if he did it then, he <u>must</u> do it now, for he does not change.

This brings us right back to why we should fear God, even though he is our Father. As Peter says, "And if ye call on the Father, who without respect of persons judgeth according to every man's work, pass the time of your sojourning *here* <u>in fear</u>" (1Pe 1:17). This word 'pass' in the Greek means 'to *busy* oneself'. Where are the men of God today who truly are teaching God's people to busy themselves in their pilgrimage here on this earth <u>in fear</u>? Instead, today's pop-culture Christianity keeps believers happy, entertained, laughing, and guilt-free. James is surely speaking of our day when he warns, "Ye have lived in pleasure on the earth, and <u>been wanton</u>; ye have nourished your hearts, as in a day of slaughter." Jam 5:5

Few today know the purpose of grace. God's grace does indeed cleanse us and wash us from our sins and bring us into the unfathomable forgiveness of God, but grace does more than that also. The purpose of grace is to teach us to turn away from ungodliness and to teach us to stand. The grace of God is to perfect us, establish us, strengthen us, and settle us (1Pe 5:10). In Peter's closing remark he says, "I have written briefly, exhorting, and testifying that this is the **true** grace of God <u>wherein ye stand</u>." 1Pe 5:12

We need to be taught the true grace of God wherein we are able to stand against compromise and disobedience. The more grace we walk in, the more we should know how to stand and NOT sin. How rarely is this taught. Where is "the grace of God that bringeth salvation ... Teaching us that, denying ungodliness and worldly lusts, we should live soberly, righteously, and godly, in this present world" (Tit 2:11-12)? The true grace of God will teach us to deny ungodliness and worldly lusts. It will teach us to live soberly or moderately and will put an end to lasciviousness and a wanton life-style.

> **WARNING**: Where is the moderation of the Christian life being taught? It has been replaced by a doctrine of covetousness, a doctrine of self-seeking, and getting all we can get from God. Ministries today *use* Jesus to give people what they want, and Jesus is not pleased. The true grace of God will teach us to live righteously, conscious that we are called to live in all good conscience before both God and man, that we are called to live in submission to the Lord who saved us and to live a life of obedience for him who suffered for us. The true grace of God will teach us to live godly, to live like Jesus did, who emptied himself and took on the form of a servant and humbled himself to be obedient unto death (Php 2:7-8). I pray that you are regularly being taught, friend, by your spiritual leaders to humble yourself and to become obedient unto death as your Master was, for we have an obligation "to walk, <u>even as he walked</u>." 1Jn 2:6

Likemindedness
"Fulfil ye my joy, that ye be likeminded" Php 2:2

To walk with God we not only must be cleansed from our iniquities, but as we have seen we must also be agreed with him on what he says is iniquity. We must come to a likemindedness. "Can two walk together, except they be agreed?" Am 3:3 To be in disagreement with the Lord over what he declares to be sinful, when we think it is acceptable or at least excusable, is to have no true intimacy with our heavenly Father, with his Word, or with his Spirit. This is the great need for true repentance in the church. The refusal to change the way we think and the pride of thinking that we have no need to repent can only be removed through the fear of the LORD.

Only his fear working in conjunction with the constant washing of the water of the Word can bring about the likemindedness with the Lord that will produce the intimacy that Jesus had with the Father. God desires to teach us his ways and to help us understand the way he thinks, but by nature and experience, our thoughts are not at all like God's. God says,

> For my thoughts *are* not your thoughts, neither *are* your ways my ways, saith the LORD. For *as* the heavens are higher than the earth, so are my ways higher than your ways, and my thoughts than your thoughts. Isa 55:8-9

6 – Broken Fellowship from the Loss of God's Fear

Our thoughts are not even *close* to God's thoughts. God's ways and thoughts are higher than the heavens are from the earth! This is why Paul had to exhort the saints in Philippi to "Let this mind be in you, which was also in Christ Jesus" (Php 2:5). Similarly, let us be exhorted and convinced to learn how to be likeminded with the Lord through the path of repentance and the restoration of the fear of God. Let us see how this is to work.

The fear of God begins by knowing his forgiveness and now following him. God's great forgiveness ought to lead us to fear him, which in turn ought to lead us to walking in his ways. "Then hear thou from heaven thy dwelling place, and forgive … That they may fear thee, to walk in thy ways " (2Ch 6:30-31). The fear of God then grows as we learn to walk in uprightness before him. "He that walketh in his uprightness feareth the LORD" (Pr 14:2). "Blessed *is* every one that feareth the LORD; that walketh in his ways." Ps 128:1 We must walk with God in the light of the truth of his word in order to have fellowship with him. This intimacy of walking together with the Lord is greater than we can imagine. This word 'agreed' in Amos 3:3 in the Hebrew means 'to *meet* (at a stated time), to *engage* (for marriage)'. This is why it is translated in Exodus 21:8-9 as 'betroth'. God wants us to be so agreed that we are of one mind, that we are *married* to him in our thoughts and actions, that we meet and come together in our way of thinking with him to the place that he has determined.

One of the places God said he desired to meet with us and commune with us was above the mercy seat.[101] This is why we so need to confess our sins to God and to be continually immersed into repentance (i.e. the changing of our way of thinking to agree with God's). If we cannot be agreed with God in our thinking, we can never walk with him. We need to learn to have the mind of Christ in us by putting to death our way of thinking. So we are instructed, "**Let this mind be in you, which was also in Christ Jesus**" (Php 2:5). We must put off the behavior and life of the old man that we all too well know from before we were saved: "put off concerning the former conversation the old man, which is corrupt according to the deceitful lusts; And be renewed in the spirit of your mind" (Eph 4:22-23).

This renewal of our mind is to be in the knowledge of God (Col 3:10). We must wash and cleanse our way of thinking and bring it in line with the truth of scripture. "And be not conformed to this world: but be ye transformed by the renewing of your mind, that ye may prove what is that good, and acceptable, and perfect, will of God." Rom 12:2 Once we can prove or actually '*test* and *approve*' what is God's will, then we will be able to walk together with God in the intimacy that he has always desired for us. Then the transformation of our life will begin afresh so that we become those living holy and acceptable sacrifices unto him that so please him (v1).

---

[101] The scripture uses this same word as in Amos 3:3 for 'agreed' as it does for 'meet' in Ex 25:22, 30:6,36.

> **WARNING**: We are often led to believe that because we are born again, therefore we *have* the mind of Christ. So this whole exhortation of being likeminded with the Lord often falls on deaf ears. We cling to: "For who hath known the mind of the Lord, that he may instruct him? But we have the mind of Christ." 1Co 2:16 Yet the context of 1Corinthians is quite clear. The born again saints in Corinth did NOT have the mind of Christ! Paul and his fellow laborers who were writing had the mind of Christ *for* the Corinthians, but the Corinthians most certainly did not.[102] This is why Paul had to exhort them to "be perfectly joined together in the same mind and in the same judgment" (1Co 1:10) and why he had to exhort them to be reconciled to God (2Co 5:18-20).

Likemindedness is repeatedly mentioned in the New Testament. It brings great joy, not only to God but also to men of God who take oversight over our souls. "Fulfil ye my joy, that ye be likeminded, having the same love, *being* of one accord, of one mind." Php 2:2 (see also Rom 15:5) We are called to "*Be of the same mind* one toward another." Rom 12:16 (see also Php 4:2) Paul exhorts us "by the name of our Lord Jesus Christ, that ye all speak the same thing, and *that* there be no divisions among you; but *that* ye be perfectly joined together in the same mind and in the same judgment." 1Co 1:10 The Corinthians needed to come to the mind of Christ on many issues. This is why Paul wrote two letters to them. In many areas they were still ignorant concerning spirituals (1Co 12:1) and were still thinking carnally, naturally, fleshly (1Co 3:1-3, 2Co 10:4).

To gain the attention of his people, our king Jesus will bring forth his judgments so that his fear will fall upon us. So it was when he judged Ananias and Sapphira in the early church. The result was[103] "great fear came upon all the church, and upon as many as heard these things." Ac 5:11 His fear will cause us to put away our desires and purposes and to be completely focused on his. Only then can we truly become the army of the Lord. This is the unity that the people of God truly need, not one that is based on excitement or even desire, but based on his fear. All who have the fear of God know that they are not in charge, and that Jesus is the Lord and Master, and that we are all under authority. So it is written, "Submitting yourselves one to another in the fear of God." Eph 5:21

---

[102] This can be proved by carefully noting the clear distinction Paul maintains throughout chapter two of the pronouns 'you/ye' and 'we/us', thus distinguishing between the 'we/us' who were writing the epistle and who had the mind of Christ for the Corinthians, versus the 'you/ye', i.e. the Corinthians, who did not have the mind of Christ, and who were carnal, natural, and fleshly. 1Corinthians 3 bears this out as Paul reproves them, letting them know, "And I, brethren, could not speak unto you as unto spiritual, but as unto carnal, *even* as unto babes in Christ." 1Co 3:1

[103] Is it possible that the Lord is giving us a hint in how his own Church is slow in coming to the fear of God? Notice the first time when Ananias was judged there is no mention of fear coming upon the church (v5). It was only after Sapphira was likewise killed that now "great fear came upon all the church".

6 – Broken Fellowship from the Loss of God's Fear

The Problem with the Fear of God's Judgments

"Who knoweth the power of thine anger? even according to thy fear, so is thy wrath. So teach us to number our days, that we may apply our hearts unto wisdom." Ps 90:11-12

The greatest problem with the fear of God's judgment is the desire to not be honest and to not acknowledge the truth concerning our deeds. We cannot expect to be spared from his judgment if we walk away from the light of his truth. God calls us into the light. This is the message of the kingdom of God – it is a call to repentance, a call to acknowledge the truth. "Therefore I will judge you, O house of Israel, every one according to his ways, saith the Lord GOD. Repent, and turn *yourselves* from all your transgressions; so iniquity shall not be your ruin." Eze 18:30 All of us become experts at covering our sin and compromise, but it only leads to ruin.

> And this is the condemnation, that light is come into the world, and men loved darkness rather than light, because their deeds were evil. For every one that doeth evil hateth the light, neither cometh to the light, lest his deeds should be reproved. But he that doeth truth cometh to the light, that his deeds may be made manifest, that they are wrought in God. Jn 3:19-21

This desire to hide from the light of truth is in every one of us, at the core of our fallen nature. So it is written of all of our hearts, "for we have made lies our refuge, and under falsehood have we hid ourselves" (Isa 28:15). Even after we enter into covenant relationship with the LORD, the temptation to not acknowledge truth in the face of authority is very real.[104] If openness and humble repentance characterized the church, then true servants of God who maintain God's order would not be so often evil spoken of and lied about by those of their own congregation!

> **WARNING**: This is why those who bring unverifiable charges against the overseer or elder are to be rebuked *before all* (1Tim 5:19-20) – to bring back the fear of God into the congregation! Those who "despise dominion, and speak evil of dignities" (Jude 1:8) are those who have no fear (Jude 1:12). As Peter succinctly puts it, they "despise government. Presumptuous *are they*, selfwilled, they are <u>not afraid to speak evil of dignities</u>." 2Pe 2:10 God wants us to be *afraid* to speak evil of dignities! He wants the proper fear of authority to be restored to his people,[105] for he knows how it will deliver us from destruction. Thus, he uses public discipline in the church to restore his fear in his people.

---

[104] If this were not the case, the role of the overseer or elder would be easy indeed!

[105] We will look more at the proper fear of authority. See the section entitled 'The Proper Fear of Authority'.

Where is the Fear of GOD? Losing the Treasure of the Lord

Hypocrisy at its core is lying against the truth. This is the killer of the heart of many of God's children, for now the conscience is rendered insensitive. This is what causes many a son in the kingdom of God to rebel and perish, because they will not come to the light of the truth to have the dark places of their heart exposed. They begin to love darkness and to put away a good conscience. This is seen in both testaments. Men who walked as servants of God for a time, but greed, covetousness, and self-serving entered their heart and shipwrecked them from God's calling. Balaam, the prophet of God, was such a man, a man who heard from God and prophesied what God would do, but the time came when, because of his desire for money, honor, and reputation, he could not hear God's warning and correction. Ultimately he perished for it (Jos 13:22). Gehazi was another such man who served Elisha. As a prophet in training, he was one who was learning to hear the voice of God, but covetousness entered his heart, and leprosy was his lot (2K 5:25-27).

We never give thought to what a great loss this is in losing the fear of God. Concerning the loss of the fear of God, Thomas Watson, an English nonconformist Puritan preacher, in his preaching said, "Let this be 'for a lamentation', that the fear of God is so vanished from our world. Why is it almost nowhere to be found? Some fear shame, others fear danger—but where is he who fears God?"[106]

> The question God has repeatedly put to his own people throughout the scripture is, how can they say they love him and submit to his authority, if they will not hearken to the message of correction that he gives to those he sends?

Paul's greatest struggles lay with such men who forsook their holy calling, those who concerning faith put away a good conscience (1Tim 1:19). These were the Hymenaeus' and Alexander's, the Demas' and Philetus' – those who once were brethren and faithful servants of God at Paul's side, but had left Paul, forsaken sound doctrine, and were leading others into destruction in their life by shipwrecking their faith.

What does it mean that, concerning faith, these people were "made shipwreck"? These people were now stranded and spiritually ruined. Their faith was no longer bringing them to their expected destination! They were erring and falling short of heaven, yet they still believed in the Lord. They still thought they were in the way of righteousness, still were assured they were right with God, yet they lived in false hope and in true hypocrisy. Their conscience was seared with a hot iron (1Tim 4:2), and their actions were such that they were "even

---

[106] From the work "Great Gain is Godliness" by Thomas Watson (ca. 1620-1686), from the section entitled 'It is a Christian duty to fear God.'

denying the Lord that bought them" (2Pe 2:1). The question God has repeatedly put to his own people throughout the scripture is, how can they say they love him and submit to his authority, if they will not hearken to the message of correction that he gives to those he sends?

The Remnant of Those who Persevered unto the End

Once the judgments of God fall, God expects that we will be humbled by such things, and in the fear of God we will return to his commandments and his way. When we provoke God's anger and wrath by the work of our hands, when we put away the sound counsel of his word, we, just like the children of Israel in Jeremiah's day, come under his hand of judgment. We are made "a curse and a reproach among all the nations of the earth" (Jer 44:8). When this happens God wants us to recall two things. First, we must come to know the evil we have done and to acknowledge it and repent (Jer 44:10). Second, we must believe he is faithful to forgive us if we cry out to him (Ps 130).

But as is so often the case, when one has hardened his heart so that he does not receive correction from God's word, he will rarely receive it even from God's judgments. But even for one, God will always fulfill this path. His judgments ought to bring us to fear him, but as we see in the writings of the prophets as well as in Revelation itself, because of the stubbornness of man's heart, very often they do not. In these cases, God's hope is that those who remain will yet "hear, and fear".[107] God is not moved by the fact that many perish, nor does he abandon his methods. He is always looking for the few – those who will come down the narrow way of the kingdom, which he has prepared. If even only one is saved through judgment, then God's will is served.

We naturally flee judgment. This flight response is used by God so that we will flee from iniquity. It is the appropriate response to true authority, especially the absolute authority that belongs to God himself. We ought never to lose the fear of God's holy throne of judgment, for it is integral with his rule and his role in our life. But what are we to flee from, and where are we to flee to? These are the most important questions. These are what determine whether the fear of God's judgment works righteousness and nearness or yet more distance. Do we fear being caught or exposed and having to face the penalty of our disobedience? Or do we much more fear "**him** with whom we have to do"? Do we fear both truth and light, and flee from the only thing that can truly deliver us? Do we flee from God and find our own false refuge? Or do we flee instead to the city of refuge which he has provided – the presence of God?

---

[107] Hear and fear: Dt 13:11, 17:13, 19:20, 21:21.

Edification or Exaltation:
a False Peace and Comfort versus the True

"For the idols have spoken vanity, and the diviners have seen a lie, and have told false dreams; they comfort in vain: therefore they went their way as a flock, they were troubled, because there was no shepherd." Zec 10:2

We have a great assurance of God's love throughout the scriptures. His willingness to go the extra mile and to do above and beyond what anyone could think or imagine is unquestionable. He is above reproach. Jonah says, "for I knew that thou *art* a gracious God, and merciful, slow to anger, and of great kindness, and repentest thee of the evil." Jnh 4:2 But does this assurance of love remove all fear of judgment? No. As said before, it is just as a trusting child's relationship with a loving father, yet who still *rightfully* fears their father's displeasure and anger. Does the father lose his authority and his right to judge and to discipline his own children, especially as they grow older, only because he loves them? No. In fact, it is because he loves us that he will chasten us quickly. "He that spareth his rod hateth his son: but he that loveth him chasteneth him betimes [i.e. *quickly*]." Pr 13:24 The early church throughout the book of Acts had the fear of God. It was a consistent teaching of the apostles in their letters. We find this perfect balance recorded for us as the churches matured:

> Then had the churches rest throughout all Judaea and Galilee and Samaria, and were edified; and walking in the fear of the Lord, and in the comfort of the Holy Ghost, were multiplied. Ac 9:31

Thus, the early church learned the secret of being able to acknowledge both his mercy and his judgment. David himself, as a lover of God, says "I will sing of mercy and judgment: unto thee, O LORD, will I sing." Ps 101:1 As they were edified or built up in the things of the Lord, they now walked in his fear. This is the fruit of true apostolic teaching. The doctrine brought forth by the apostles caused disciples of God to walk in the fear of God. Modern Christian teaching produces no fear, yet so many people feel 'edified' by what they are getting. How is this possible, for they are no longer being instructed to walk in the fear of the LORD? Therefore, the edification being taught today cannot be the same as that of the first century. Here is the "edifying" that people are getting:

> For they have healed the hurt of the daughter of my people slightly, saying, Peace, peace; when *there is* no peace. Were they ashamed when they had committed abomination? nay, they were not at all ashamed, neither could they blush Jer 8:11-12

Our lack of the fear of God is the direct result of putting our desire for comfort before our need for conviction!

We are so focused on having our own peace and comfort that we have no time or room for the fear of the LORD, and hence are easily offended and too 'uncomfortable' to be able to receive it. We have so departed and been alienated from the apostolic anointing that the conviction of such men (who turn cities upside down) is no longer received. Our lack of the fear of God is the direct result of putting our desire for comfort before our need for conviction! Notice that the fear of the Lord in the early church <u>preceded</u> the comfort of the Holy Ghost. We have so many wonderful teachers who are doing God's job – before the appointed time. Too often men replace the true inner peace that can only come from the comfort of the Holy Ghost by their doctrines and philosophies and by a false peace. Too often believers have relied on the soothing speeches of those who bring peace to their soul, but at the same time bring in the spirit of error. They do this, rather than finding their comfort in the Holy Ghost.

His Comfort Follows Our Mourning

Remember who the Holy Ghost is: He *is* the Comforter. Only the Holy Ghost can bring the comfort and exhortation that sets our heart in God's peace. Often though, we must be brought to a place of mourning first. "The Spirit of the Lord GOD *is* upon me ... to comfort all that mourn" (Isa 61:1-2). This is why the power of the word that will bring us out of our compromise and into the fear of the LORD is so necessary. We need the apostolic and prophetic mantles again, for they are what stir up the flame of passion and conviction in men's consciences.

The true apostolic and prophetic mantles will cause us to be put in remembrance that God will judge his people. He will chasten our willful and unrepented of disobedience. As Jesus tells the church, "As many as I love, I rebuke and chasten: be zealous therefore, and repent." Rev 3:19 This is the call of the kingdom of God: repentance. Once the dread of judgment is awakened in both the lost sinner and the wandering child of God, then God through the Holy Ghost can bring forth the comfort of love (Php 2:1, 2Co 1:3-4, 2Th 2:16-17).

> **WARNING**: This pricking of the consciences of men is not for political reform, but for moral reform, not externally, but internally. It is the rending of our heart that God is concerned with. No apostle or New Testament prophet was ever seen involved in the politics of this world or in trying to change the laws of the land. Rather, they were trying to bring the hearts of men to repentance and to turn to the Lord with their whole heart.[108]

---

[108] The present Christian Right, who would exhort men to protest and get involved in politics, are none other than the spirit of the Herodians revived. The Herodians were those involved in politics of which Jesus would have nothing to do with, nor would his

As we have seen already, God waits for *us* in order to be gracious unto us and have mercy. He is ever ready, but we must return unto him. Sometimes we make the mistake of wanting to comfort, when it is not time for that. As soon as one leaves the flock, we want to go and comfort them, when the scripture indicates some times our role is to admonish them of their error or to warn them of the way they are headed. Consider this, the prodigal's father <u>did not leave home</u> to go and seek his wayward son, for he knew his son had willfully chosen the way he desired to go. He had to let him eat the cornhusks.

The good shepherd will search for his lost sheep (i.e. when the saint is but young and tender) for they know no better, being inexperienced and innocent, but the compassionate father will not search for his own lost son because he was of age and responsible for making his own decisions.[109] It is our unwillingness to repent and touch not the unclean in these cases, that delays God's mercies and prevents his comforts from coming to us. The true spiritual purpose of our life is then frustrated, just like the prodigal's. Any other comfort than the painful exhortation to repent and acknowledge our error will only bring forth a deceptive, false comfort that will slowly shipwreck us and ultimately kill us.

When another well-meaning brother or sister or even teacher in the Lord brings comfort to us when we are still walking in our own way, they bring a false peace. We will believe all is well, but we are still not directed back to our purpose in the Lord, so we are spiritually still wandering. This accounts for how we may feel happy, but no real progress in growth or maturity is taking place in our life. Thus, the comfort we have received, instead of healing our broken heart, only causes us to be deceived. Twice God says, "They have healed also the hurt *of the daughter* of my people <u>slightly</u>, saying, Peace, peace; when *there is* no peace." Jer 6:14, 8:11

Only after we are brought to repentance does God want his comfort to come and overflow us. Our holy Father would not have us find *any* comfort in our disobedience or backslidden state. He has by skilful purpose ensured through the curse and his judgments, that our sin will plague us and be as pricks in our eyes and thorns in our sides. Instead of peace and rest, in this case, he desires that we would "find no ease ... but the LORD shall give thee there a trembling heart, and failing of eyes, and sorrow of mind" (Dt 28:65).

If his comforts are brought to us before the conviction of sin, then often no alarm and no straightening of our way occurs. We never get back on the nar-

---

servants. For he said, "My kingdom is not of this world: if my kingdom were of this world, **then** would my servants fight" (Jn 18:36).

[109] Both sons in the prodigal story are fully mature sons, for that is what the Greek word means (*huios*, G5207) that is used for 'son' in this passage of scripture. Responsibility comes with age. So the parents of the man born blind said, "he is of age [i.e. *mature*]; ask him: he shall speak for himself." Jn 9:21

row path, and we are still in danger concerning where we are headed. Over and over again the scriptures demonstrate how comfort only came *after* conviction. In Isaiah 51 we see the redeemed of the LORD shall return (i.e. repent) and will come with joy and singing: "they shall obtain gladness and joy; *and* sorrow and mourning shall flee away." Isa 51:11 It is then that we see God reveals himself as the one who comforts them (v12). When we "see eye to eye" with the LORD and are brought again to Zion (i.e. the house of God), that is when the LORD will comfort his people (Isa 52:8-9).

God is angry with us when we are caught in any idolatry, for he is a jealous God. Many times we do not want to hear that, but it is truth. This is the condemnation we feel when we are walking in known sin. As long as we continue turning away in our heart from acknowledging the truth about our sin and repenting of it, we are caught in the snare of the devil, "taken captive at his will." 2Tim 2:26 When we are following our own heart, it is then that the LORD hides himself from us.

> For the iniquity of his covetousness was I wroth, and smote him: I hid me, and was wroth, and he went on frowardly <u>in the way of his heart</u>. I have seen his ways, and will heal him: I will lead him also, and restore comforts unto him and to his mourners. Isa 57:17-18

Not until he can heal us of our idolatry (in this case, covetousness) and our waywardness, can he turn us from our way and lead us back to himself. Only then can he restore comforts unto us, for it is in his presence that true comfort is found! He says, "I will turn their mourning into joy, and will comfort them, and make them rejoice from their sorrow." Jer 31:13 This is why he promises

> to comfort all that mourn [i.e. *lament*]; To appoint unto them that <u>mourn</u> in Zion, to give unto them beauty for ashes, the oil of joy for <u>mourning</u>, the garment of praise for the spirit of <u>heaviness</u>; that they might be called trees of righteousness, the planting of the LORD, that he might be glorified. Isa 61:2-3

His comfort waits for our mourning or lamenting over our sin. This is why in all these verses we see comforting coming to those who mourn. The same is true in the New Testament. "Blessed *are* they that mourn [i.e. *grieve*]: for they shall be comforted." Mt 5:4 This is why we must learn that as we walk through the valley of the shadow of death,[110] in our struggles with sin, it is God's rod (of

---

[110] When we hear of "the shadow of death" we usually think in a limited scope of only being in situations where death seems near physically (such as sickness or warfare). Often in scripture the term is used more in an eternal sense of the underworld (Job 10:20-22, 38:17) or in a spiritual sense of being under sin's bondage (Job 24:16-17, 34:22; Mt 4:16, Lk 1:79). The latter can be seen in the following: "Such as sit in darkness and in <u>the shadow of death</u>, *being* bound in affliction and iron; Because they rebelled against the words of God, and contemned the counsel of the most High: ... He brought them out of darkness and <u>the shadow of death</u>, and brake their bands in sunder." Ps 107:10-11,14

correction) and his staff (of leading) that are to be our comfort (Ps 23:4). As holy men of God we ought to be warning people, lighting a flame of conviction in their conscience, and only *after* the alarm is raised should comfort be poured out to soothe the wounds of their conscience.

Awakening from a False Comfort

Many find a false comfort, a false peace, in hiding from God. This is the example of Jonah, a true covenant disciple, a prophet of God, and a servant of the LORD. Consider his condition. He is running from God in disobedience to what he knows is the revealed will of God. Yet we find him sleeping in the midst of destruction where "there was a mighty tempest in the sea, so that the ship was like to be broken." Jnh 1:4 And where was Jonah? "But Jonah was gone down into the sides of the ship; and he lay, and was fast asleep." Jnh 1:5 O how sweet was Jonah's sleep (or so he thought) as he was in the hold of the ship! But did his peace remain when he was brought face to face with the judgment of God? Did he enjoy the same rest when he was cast into the tempestuous sea and sunk to the ocean floor (Jnh 1:11-15, 2:6)? Was it so comfortable for 3 days in pitch darkness in the putrid digestive juices of the belly of the whale?

Jonah is the type and shadow of the believer who is running from God and following his own desires, rather than the will of God. They will always end up in the miserable state of the prodigal, living with and like the pigs. What is God's call to us when we are trusting in lies, enjoying a false security, and hiding from him? It is to awake and arise, to walk circumspectly and be wise, to redeem the time and understand God's will.

> Wherefore he saith, [1] Awake thou that sleepest, and [2] arise from the dead, and Christ shall give thee light. See then that ye [3] walk circumspectly, not as fools, but as wise, [4] Redeeming the time, because the days are evil. Wherefore be ye not unwise, but [5] understanding what the will of the Lord *is*.[111] Eph 5:14-17

This is why God pursued Jonah *with his judgments*: to restore the proper fear of God. Why would God pursue his children with judgments? Isaiah reveals the secret. "Judgment also will I lay to the line, and righteousness to the plummet: and the hail shall sweep away the refuge of lies, and the waters shall overflow the hiding place." Isa 28:17 It is through God's judgments and the righteousness of them that, like hail destroying crops, so God's anger against us is able to sweep away 'the refuge of lies' that we trust in. God's anger burned in this way against his servants, like Jonah and Moses and you and I, to help us all see, what we *cannot* see.

---

[111] Eph 5:14 is quoting from Jonah 1:6 when the shipmaster came to Jonah to wake the 'man of God' from his slumber and prayerlessness – for he was about to perish for his lack of spiritual watchfulness.

6 – Broken Fellowship from the Loss of God's Fear

> **WARNING**: It is a sad commentary on the human heart. But when we are running from God, when we are refusing correction, our heart will always take refuge in lies. What is this "refuge of lies" that God must, with his pelting hail of judgment, sweep away (Isa 28:17)? It is trusting in God's goodness to *overlook* our disobedience, and then continuing to find our own rest, relaxation, and enjoyment in going our own way. It is finding a 'hiding place', a false security, in doing what we want to do – all the while we are denying his lordship and ignoring his commandments.

Sometimes we are blind in an area of our life, so that like Jonah, we cannot see it the way God does. In this case because we are running from God we need a great storm, an expression of God's anger and displeasure, which puts our life in jeopardy, to awaken us from our spiritual slumber and slothfulness. If we could but be more dedicated to truth in our own heart, we might be spared such things. So let us renounce "the hidden things of dishonesty, not walking in craftiness, nor handling the word of God deceitfully" so that the truth might be manifested in us and our conscience be commended and approved in the sight of God (2Co 4:2). The fear of God's judgment should cause us, if we truly know God,[112] to flee *to* the light so that we can be healed of the numbing, but deadly, cancer of enjoying sin, which slowly destroys us.

The Proper Fear of Authority

"So Samuel called unto the LORD; ... and all the people greatly feared the LORD and Samuel." 1Sam 12:18

Another issue that must be rightly balanced is that the fear of God strips away the fear of man, but at the same time establishes and increases the respect for authority (or we could equally say the **fear** of authority). Even a cursory searching of the scriptures concerning the fear of the LORD shows repeatedly the fear of the LORD is put in direct juxtaposition against the fear of man. The fear of the LORD is repeatedly seen to drive out the fear of man.[113]

Yet this does not mean that we are <u>not</u> to fear authority. No, the Bible says, "Render therefore to all their dues: tribute to whom tribute *is due;* custom to whom custom; <u>fear to whom fear</u>; honour to whom honour. Owe no man anything" (Rom 13:7-8). We are clearly called to render what is due to each person who is in authority, and to some fear is due them. This is a difficult subject to approach because of the abuse of authority through men who say they are of God, but have never been broken on the anvil of discipleship. Thus, this is of great importance and cannot be avoided. Rendering fear unto those in authority

---

[112] As we come to know the LORD we come to know that it is impossible to truly flee from him (Ps 139:7-11).
[113] See in particularly: Mt 10:26,28,31, Ps 118:4-6.

is not difficult to understand, so much as it is difficult to keep from misunderstanding and from abuse.

God maintains in his kingdom a strict line of authority which is not to be broken, but when carnal men or men that lose their fear of God come to know this, they may do untold damage to the lives of many innocent sheep. But the beauty of authority as God has established it he will not put away because of the evil of men. The same could be said of God's wonderful grace. Though it has been abused by many, even turning the grace of God into lasciviousness (Jude 1:4), to their own destruction, yet salvation is still, and will always be, by grace through faith. He will not put it aside for all the abuse of carnal men. So it is with his authority. He will not dispense with it, nor put it aside, and therefore neither can we. We must come to him even in salvation acknowledging his authority through our confession of him as our Lord. No matter how you have been hurt by authority, it is still and will always be the will of your heavenly Father to bring you into and safely under his authority.

Many, because of their great hurts and abuses which they have wrongfully suffered (although sometimes rightfully) will finally acknowledge that they must trust God's authority and allow him to have the rule. But they come to an equally damaging view point, which is to somehow mysteriously allow God to have all authority, yet at the same time refuse any man of God to have any authority. This cannot be, for God clearly grants his authority to his servants. To better understand this, let us first look at the principle of representation. God holds in high esteem his faithful servants and with great jealously at times comes to their defense. Though, as we discussed already, the fear of God will remove the fear of man, by that we do not mean that it will remove the rightful fear of leaders that God grants them. To understand this we must look at David who represented in his life the kingdom of God on earth.

David was a man who trusted God deeply, yet in that trust he was repeatedly hurt. You may say, "How so?" The wounds of David's heart by the persecution of men who abused authority are poured out as a continual trail of sorrow across the pages of the Psalms. Those which are most precious to us now in our trials and despairs came at great cost to the servant of God who only wanted to please the LORD. Brokenness was the manner of David's life for many years as he submitted his life and his heart under the hammer of God's afflictions. Though we are unwilling to look at it and to rejoice in it, it was the Saul's, the Doeg's, the foolish Nabal's who caused so much sorrow and heartache to David that in reality were the hammer that God used to shape David's heart so preciously. Thank the Lord that God did not hesitate to allow and to send these troubles into David's life, nor ours, and thank him again that David did not shrink back, nor become bitter through all of these sore trials.

> The LORD hath <u>chastened me sore</u>: but he hath not given me over unto death. Ps 118:18

6 – Broken Fellowship from the Loss of God's Fear

> *Thou,* which hast shewed me <u>great and sore troubles</u>, shalt quicken me again, and shalt bring me up again from the depths of the earth. Ps 71:20

David never hated men, never despised them, never blamed them, never held unforgiveness in his heart against them. David never let the intensity of his sore and his great troubles make him bitter. Rather he allowed these experiences to drive him into deeper intimacy with the LORD through brokenness. Brokenness was the key to keeping him from bitterness. The banner of the fear of the LORD was displayed boldly in David's life – he would not touch the anointed of the LORD. Look at how many times this issue arose of not doing evil or speaking evil against an authority, even when the authority *was* evil and self-serving.

(1) And he said unto his men, The LORD forbid that I should do this thing unto <u>my master, the LORD'S anointed</u>, to stretch forth mine hand against him, seeing <u>he is the anointed of the LORD</u>. 1Sam 24:6

(2) Behold, this day thine eyes have seen how that the LORD had delivered thee to day into mine hand in the cave: and *some* bade *me* kill thee: but *mine eye* spared thee; and I said, I will not put forth mine hand against <u>my lord</u>; <u>for he *is* the LORD's anointed</u>. 1Sam 24:10

(3) And David said to Abishai, Destroy him not: for who can stretch forth his hand against <u>the LORD'S anointed</u>, and be guiltless? The LORD forbid that I should stretch forth mine hand against <u>the LORD'S anointed</u>: ... let us go. 1Sam 26:9,11

(4) This thing *is* not good that thou hast done. *As* the LORD liveth, ye *are* worthy to die, because ye have not kept <u>your master, the LORD'S anointed</u>. 1Sam 26:16

(5) The LORD render to every man his righteousness and his faithfulness: for the LORD delivered thee into *my* hand to day, but I would not stretch forth mine hand against <u>the LORD'S anointed</u>. 1Sam 26:23

(6) And David said unto him, How wast thou not afraid to stretch forth thine hand to destroy <u>the LORD'S anointed</u>? And David said unto him, Thy blood *be* upon thy head; for thy mouth hath testified against thee, saying, I have slain the LORD'S anointed. 2Sam 1:14,16

David learned what each child of God must learn if they would grow up into the head, which is Jesus Christ, the son of David. We must learn to be broken and contrite in spirit. We must learn in our hurt and pain never to strike out at authority or to take matters in our own hands. It is for the LORD to set up and for the LORD to take down. If we speak evil of authority, then we follow the child of rebellion, Absalom, and we follow after the father of rebellion, Satan. The scripture is full of such warnings to not allow bitterness to defile us or to despise authority. This is why it is not coincidence that immediately after exhorting Titus to "rebuke with all authority" Paul must warn Titus to not allow anyone to despise him. "These things speak, and exhort, and rebuke with all authority. Let no man despise thee." Tit 2:15 This is the natural response of man when rebuked with authority: they despise it.

> God shows us that to fear him *is* to obey the voice of his servant, for this is what the true fear of God always produces: submission to authority.

We can never grow up into the head, if we only allow God to have authority, but refuse to submit ourselves to the authorities which God himself establishes here on earth. There are some, because of the authority of their position, that God says we <u>owe</u> them fear. What kind of fear do we owe them? The word fear here is the Greek word (5401) *phobos* which means '*alarm* or *fright*'. It is where we get all our English words "phobia" from. If they hold a position of authority (which is clearly the context of Romans 13), then we must render them the fear due their office.

There has never been room in the kingdom of God for those who take authority lightly or who challenge it. Rebellion has been judged and condemned by God even before man was ever created. Rebellion was removed from God's presence forever, when Lucifer in rebellion to God was cast from heaven. Let us be assured of this, there are no, nor shall there ever be, rebels in heaven. We must take warning in this and be humbled. We have no right to challenge authority – not even Satan himself. It is never allowed in the sight of God to ridicule or to name-call or to mock even the vilest man of authority, nor the demons, nor Satan himself.

> Thou shalt not revile the gods, nor curse the ruler of thy people. Ex 22:28 I wist not, brethren, that he was the high priest: for it is written, Thou shalt not speak evil of the ruler of thy people. Ac 23:5

It has nothing to do with their character, their personal life, their failings, or even their wickedness. It has to do with the office they occupy by God's appointment. We have two New Testament warnings by two different apostles that we ought not to bring railing accusations against dignitaries. Let us heed their warning.

> But chiefly them that walk after the flesh in the lust of uncleanness, and <u>despise government</u>. Presumptuous *are they*, selfwilled, <u>they are not afraid to speak evil of dignities</u>. Whereas angels, which are greater in power and might, <u>bring not railing accusation against them</u> before the Lord. 2Pe 2:10-11

6 – Broken Fellowship from the Loss of God's Fear

> Likewise also these *filthy* dreamers defile the flesh, <u>despise dominion</u>, and <u>speak evil of dignities</u>. Yet Michael the archangel, when contending with the devil he disputed about the body of Moses, <u>durst not bring against him a railing accusation</u>, but said, The Lord rebuke thee. Jude 1:8-9

Thus, God expects us not only to fear him, but also to fear the authorities which he has established – both in the natural realm, as far as natural rulers and administrators, as well as in the spiritual realm, spiritual overseers and administrators. This is why we are specially commanded to fear the king, in addition to fearing the LORD. "My son, fear thou the LORD <u>and</u> the king" (Pr 24:21). We also see specific examples of God's servants who were to be feared. Holy men of God, because of the authority they walked, in were feared. Let us look at some of these leaders of God's people whom God's covenant people feared.

Table 6-1   Servants of God who were Feared

1. <u>Moses</u> (Ex 14:31):
   And Israel saw that great work which the LORD did upon the Egyptians: and <u>the people feared</u> the LORD, and believed the LORD, and <u>his servant Moses</u>.

2. <u>Joshua</u> (Jos 4:14):
   On that day the LORD magnified Joshua in the sight of all Israel; and they <u>feared him, as they feared Moses</u>, all the days of his life.

3. <u>Samuel</u> (1Sam 12:18 & 16:4):
   So Samuel called unto the LORD; and the LORD sent thunder and rain that day: and all the people <u>greatly feared</u> the LORD and <u>Samuel</u>.
   And Samuel did that which the LORD spake, and came to Bethlehem. And the elders of the town <u>trembled at his coming</u>, and said, Comest thou peaceably?

4. <u>John the Baptist</u> (Mk 6:20):
   For Herod <u>feared John, knowing that he was a just man and an holy</u>

In addition to these we don't have time to tell of men like Elijah and Elisha who were feared of the people when they saw God working through them. Without any argument, even though it may not be specifically mentioned with many other leaders, clearly they also must have been feared, for "The God of Israel said, the Rock of Israel spake to me, He that ruleth over men *must be* just, ruling in <u>the fear of God</u>." 2Sam 23:3 When a man rules in the fear of God, the man will not only have it, but will bring forth the fear of God in the people. So it is in the New Covenant also. Jesus feared God, and he was rightfully received with fear (Mk 5:15, 10:32, Mt 27:54). Paul feared God and so did his sons in the faith, Timothy and Titus, for so he taught them (1Tim 5:20). This same fear of God was finally brought to the Corinthians through Titus, after they were brought to repentance with godly sorrow (2Co 7:10). We read that Titus was received with fear. "And his inward affection is more abundant toward you, whilst he remembereth the obedience of you all, how <u>with fear and trembling ye received him</u>." 2Co 7:15 Men of God who are sent with a message from God are to be received with fear and trembling.

Notice how their 'obedience to God' was a result of 'the fear of God' they had in receiving men who were 'sent of God' – even when that man was only in representation! Titus was but Paul's messenger, but the Corinthians received him as they would receive their father in the faith. Why would God want us to fear those who represent him? Is it because they will do us evil, if we do not believe them? No. The LORD wants to test us to see if we will truly submit to his authority, by seeing if we have ears to hear his words being spoken through an earthly, fallible, but anointed messenger.

This way the Lord can know if we truly obey in heart or just in letter and with eye service (Eph 6:6). "Servants, obey in all things *your* masters according to the flesh; not with eyeservice, as menpleasers; but in singleness of heart, <u>fearing God</u>" (Col 3:22). Isn't it amazing what we have already learned! This one verse in Colossians 3:22 joins so many aspects of the fear of the LORD. We see the fear of God producing a **singleness of heart** that leads us to **obey** those in **authority** over us. The fear of men-of-God must result in obeying their word as if they brought to us the very words of God.

> For this cause also thank we God without ceasing, because, when ye received the word of God which ye heard of us, ye received *it* <u>not as the word of men, but as it is in truth, the word of God</u>, which effectually worketh also in you that believe. 1Th 2:13

God shows us that to fear him *is* to obey the voice of his servant, for this is what the true fear of God always produces: submission to authority. "Who *is* among you <u>that feareth the LORD, that obeyeth the voice of his servant</u>, that walketh *in* darkness, and hath no light? let him trust in the name of the LORD, and stay upon his God." Isa 50:10 Why must we obey God's servants as if he himself has spoken through them? Because the scriptural pattern is that true servants of God **do** bring forth God's message to us, both through wise counsel and through warnings. "Whom we preach, <u>warning</u> every man, and teaching every man in all wisdom; that we may present every man perfect in Christ Jesus" (Col 1:28). When warning is brought from the word of God concerning something that grieves the heart of God, his people are called to hear the servant as if God was speaking to them directly. This is the fear of God that has truly been lost in these last days of uncorrectability.

6 – Broken Fellowship from the Loss of God's Fear

Chapter 7. Holiness, Righteousness, & Faithfulness to God
Pleasing Him in Our Walk

"Having therefore these promises, dearly beloved, let us cleanse ourselves from all filthiness of the flesh and spirit, perfecting holiness in the fear of God." 2Co 7:1

Called to be Holy, Called to be Different
"for thou art an holy people unto the LORD thy God, and the LORD hath chosen thee to be a peculiar people unto himself, above all the nations that are upon the earth." Dt 14:2

In the last days the prophecy of scripture warns us that men shall be increasingly unholy (2Tim 3:2). We are seeing this come to pass as never before – especially within the church. The lack of holiness in the church is why there is no fear of God today. The lack of holiness is why there is so little real testimony for the Lord and so little lasting fruit. It is why the church in many areas looks and acts just like the world, and why character in leadership is at an all time low. It is why there is so much activity in churches, but so little intimacy with God, such shallow knowledge of who the living God is, and so little effectual, fervent prayer. Be not deceived, if we truly fear the LORD there are things he expects of

7 – Holiness, Righteousness, & Faithfulness to God

us that we must change in. We cannot be like the world and please God, for we have been called out of darkness and into his light. Our calling is to show forth his light of his life. Peter says we have been chosen so that we "should shew forth the praises of him who hath called [us] out of darkness into his marvellous light" (1Pe 2:9).

When we were lost, the scripture says that we were *darkness*, but now in Christ we are light in him. As the light of the world (Mt 5:14), we are to have no fellowship with darkness (2Co 6:14). We are not to walk in darkness (Jn 8:12), nor to abide in it (Jn 12:46), nor to be like it. We are now called as children of light, not to blend in with the world, but in fact to reprove the unfruitful works of darkness. "For ye were sometimes <u>darkness</u>, but now *are ye* light in the Lord: walk as children of light: And have no fellowship with the unfruitful works of <u>darkness</u>, but rather reprove *them.* " Eph 5:8,11

We are called to be his *peculiar* people.[114] Because we are chosen by God, we are, thereby, called to be a peculiar people. "For the LORD hath chosen Jacob unto himself, *and* Israel for his peculiar treasure." Ps 135:4 This word 'peculiar' in the Hebrew carries a unique meaning. It is a treasure of unusual value which is '*shut* up or locked away', so that it can be kept safe. God is saying that as his people, we are a treasure of great value to him; we are as a precious gem, which he would keep us set apart for his purposes, and not the world's.

That means we ought to be different from the world, not the same. The world in general ought to hate and despise the obedient Christian because this is what the world does to all who truly follow Jesus. As Jesus said, "If ye were of the world, the world would love his own: but because ye are **not** of the world, but I have chosen you out of the world, <u>therefore the world hateth you</u>." Jn 15:19 When our life begins to reprove the unfruitful works of darkness, then indeed we will be hated just like Jesus was. "Remember the word that I said unto you, The servant is not greater than his lord. If they have persecuted me, they will also persecute you" (Jn 15:20) – *if* we walk as he walked.

In the New Testament 'peculiar' means '*being beyond* usual, i.e. *special* (one's own)'. Thus, it carries with it both the meaning of being unique and different as well as the significance of belonging to someone. Our peculiarity or uniqueness is that we belong to God as his holy people (1Pe 2:9). To be God's peculiar people, he had to "redeem us from all iniquity, and purify [*us*] unto himself" (Tit 2:14). Titus 2:14 shows us it is by purifying us to be his holy people that we become his peculiar people, a people set apart and dedicated to him. We are chosen to be different and unusual. But what is our difference? Our difference, from those who are not his people, is that we allow him to continue to purify our lives for his purposes, not only in position as he has already done, but also in practice.

---

[114] Called out to be a peculiar people: Ex 19:5; Dt 14:2, 26:18; Ps 135:4; Tit 2:14; 1Pe 2:9

Where is the Fear of GOD? Losing the Treasure of the Lord

> **WARNING**: As a man of God who knows the scriptures, I am continually shocked by those who are given airtime on well-known Christian television and radio programs who proclaim that we can "glorify" God by our individuality, when by that they mean we can look like the world and act like the world, yet speak of Jesus! Everything the Bible ever teaches us is that we are called to come out from among the unclean, to be separate in how we live, act, and speak, and to touch not the unclean things which they do (2Co 6:17-7:1).
>
> So many today want to *attract* people to the Lord through entertainment and using worldliness (i.e. being like the world) which Jesus never did. We have forgotten who Jesus is: "For such an high priest became us, *who is* holy, harmless, undefiled [i.e. not soiled or tainted], separate from sinners" (Heb 7:26). Though he reached out to sinners, yet he did not live carnally like them or talk ungodly like them, nor did his disciples. Jesus was not in any way worldly in his manner of speech or life. He didn't have tattoos or earrings or as so many think long hair (1Co 11:14). Let us be like Elisha, who by the way he lived and spoke, people knew he was a holy man. As the woman of Shunem said of him, "Behold now, I perceive that this *is* an **holy man** of God, which passeth by us continually." 2K 4:9

Holiness and the Fear of God

We are chosen as his people to *be* a holy people, because he is first and foremost holy. If we are of his seed, then he requires us to bear the fruit of his nature. It is his holiness and the fact that we are his children that is to drive us to walk in his holiness. "But as he which hath called you is holy, so be ye holy in all manner of conversation; Because it is written, Be ye holy; for I am holy." 1Pe 1:15-16 Without holiness we can have no intimacy with God. If we do not follow after or *pursue* holiness, "no man shall see the Lord" (Heb 12:14). The LORD is a holy God, and he dwells in the holy place (Isa 57:15), so we cannot have intimacy with him without holiness. David prescribes that if we would dwell with God on his holy hill, we must be holy in our behavior and actions (Ps 15). This is what is so distressing about the general state of the church: that there is so little holiness.

The fear of God and God's holiness are inexorably intertwined. It is God's extreme holiness that moves us to fear him so greatly, and it is his fear that keeps us walking in holiness before him. Holiness begets holiness through the fear of the Lord. If we have little understanding of God's holiness, we will have little fear of him. Likewise, if we have little fear of God, then we will have no personal holiness. It is because we do not understand that he only is holy (Rev

15:4), that we do not fear him.[115] His holiness demands our fear. So those who overcame the beast cry out, "Who shall not fear thee, O Lord, and glorify thy name? for *thou* only *art* holy" (Rev 15:4). Those who gain the victory over the beast are those who overcome the world in their life through their fear of God.

> It is because we do not understand that he <u>only</u> is holy …
> that we do not fear him. His holiness demands our fear.

Clearly, this was their secret of overcoming the beast, that they knew and understood that God only is holy. God's holiness made them fear him, and their fear of God caused them to depart from iniquity and so overcome the beast. Holiness is being set apart and sanctified for God's purposes. Personal holiness can only take place in our life, as with these overcomers, when we fear God. The fear of God enables us to walk in holiness so that we overcome the world, and we gain the victory over the beast (and the beastly nature). God's holiness is therefore the key to our fear of God. If God is not holy before our eyes, then we will not fear him. So many do not fear God for this very reason, because they have no concept of his exceeding holiness.

Holy Men of God as an Example

Let us consider an earthly example. John the Baptist was a humble, obedient servant of God. He continually refused the accolades and praises of men. When he was asked if he was the Christ, he openly confessed, "I am not the Christ." Jn 1:20 When he was asked if he was Elijah or the prophet, he answered, "No." Jn 1:21 What did he say of himself? "He said, I *am* the voice of one crying in the wilderness, Make straight the way of the Lord, as said the prophet Esaias." Jn 1:22-23 He was but a voice, one who was willing to continually decrease so that Jesus could continually increase (Jn 3:30). He was truly a holy man who sought not the praises of men. What was sinful man's response to John's holiness? **To fear John.** "For Herod feared John, <u>knowing that he was a just man and an holy</u>" (Mk 6:20). Consider this, if an earthly ruler such as Herod, who feared none of his subjects, feared John because he was a holy man, do we *not* think that we ought to fear God whose holiness far exceeds that of a mere man?!

If we will come to know God's glorious holiness, we will indeed fear him. Moses and all the Exodus people beheld God's awesome holiness and his mighty wonders, and they had the fear of God before their faces. God miraculously delivered his people from the Egyptian army by parting the Red Sea and

---

[115] This we have discussed briefly concerning our understanding of God being our father and whether we should fear him or not. As Peter declares for us, it is *because* we call on our heavenly Father who judges impartially that we therefore fear him (1Pe 1:17).

bringing God's people safely across on dry land, while making it muddy for Pharaoh's chariots. Much like those who overcome the beast in the last days, Moses and the people sang this song unto God when they overcame the Egyptians: "Who *is* like unto thee, O LORD, among the gods? who *is* like thee, <u>glorious in holiness</u>, **fearful *in* praises**, doing wonders?" Ex 15:11

God's holiness will always cause our worship of him to be given in fear. So the psalmist says, "O worship the LORD in the beauty of <u>holiness</u>: **fear** before him, all the earth." Ps 96:9 Because there is no one like God, because he is glorious in his holiness, therefore even in our praises of him we are to fear him. So David echoes the same fearfulness in worshipping God, "in thy fear will I worship toward thy holy temple." Ps 5:7 This is his exceeding greatness, that he is fearful even in his praises.

The Effect of God's Fear: Holiness
"perfecting holiness in the fear of God." 2Co 7:1

The effect of the fear of God can be immediately seen in a person's life. The essence of the fear of God is seen in the depth of our submission to authority. Our subjection to authority (or our lack thereof) can be seen immediately by those who are under authority, both in the natural realm and in the spiritual realm. Even the lost can tell if we are truly under God's authority or not. This is why shame is brought to the name of the LORD by those who openly confess his name, when it is obvious they still run their own life, make their own decisions, and do what benefits them most.

We have already seen how the effect of the fear of God produces intimacy with the LORD and with his ordained leaders. The effect of the fear of God is to be pleasing to him (Ps 147:11). We have seen how the fear of God brings about a perfect heart and enables us to be easily led by him. All of these things work to produce a holiness in our lives that God receives with great joy. Because of the profound work that the fear of God does in us, it can easily be discerned by the spiritual man whether it is present or absent in another. The lack of the fear of God is very apparent, not only to God, but also to men who walk with God. So Abraham perceived when he went down to Egypt that there was no fear of God in that place (Gen 20:11).

We have promise after promise of blessing given to those who will walk in the fear of God.[116] The fear of the LORD is the door to mercy, salvation, protection, deliverance, a whole heart, answered prayer, approval from God, intimacy with the Lord, fellowship with the saints, being led of the Holy Ghost, faithfulness, obedience, wisdom, worship, blessing, service, and giving. "Having there-

---

[116] See the chapter "The Inestimable Treasure of God's Fear" in the book <u>Finding the Treasure of the Lord</u>.

7 – Holiness, Righteousness, & Faithfulness to God

fore these promises, dearly beloved, let us cleanse ourselves from all filthiness of the flesh and spirit, perfecting holiness in the fear of God." 2Co 7:1

The prospect of inheriting God's promises should drive us to practical holiness, a holiness which we walk out by responding in willing submission and obedience to his commandments. We have an imputed holiness which is by faith, as soon as we are saved. The new man of salvation was created in true holiness. Yet we must continually put on that new man: "that ye put on the new man, which after God is created in righteousness and <u>true holiness</u>." Eph 4:24 We cannot think that holiness has its beginning or its root in us. No, its root and beginning is in the Lord and how he has re-created us through the new birth. Peter testifies openly of this. "And when Peter saw *it*, he answered unto the people, Ye men of Israel, why marvel ye at this? or why look ye so earnestly on us, <u>as though by our own power or holiness</u> we had made this man to walk?" Ac 3:12 We have not power or holiness that works the works of God. It is his power and his holiness that works in us. *Nevertheless*, the scripture declares we must learn to walk in holiness and sanctification.

> That every one of you should know how to possess his vessel in <u>sanctification</u> and honour; For God hath not called us unto uncleanness, but unto <u>holiness</u>. He therefore that despiseth, despiseth not man, but God, who hath also given unto us his <u>holy</u> Spirit. 1Th 4:4,7-8

God has called us unto holiness, and we need to follow after it, to *pursue* it. We are urged to follow after holiness (Heb 12:14). That means regarding holiness and how we live, there is something yet to fulfill, something yet to attain to in our life, something still to pursue. We are to grow up into a separation from sinful ways and thoughts and keeping ourselves unspotted from the ways of this world. "Neither be partaker of other men's sins: keep thyself pure." 1Tim 5:22 "Pure religion and undefiled before God and the Father is this … to keep himself unspotted from the world." Jam 1:27 We are the "elect … through sanctification of the Spirit, unto obedience" (1Pe 1:2). The Holy Spirit is trying to lead us unto the "obedience to the faith" (Rom 1:5, 16:26). To better understand how practical holiness is to be in our life let us use God's teaching to women on this issue. We know spiritually we are the bride of Christ, so what a woman of God is instructed to do naturally, so all believers are to do spiritually unto their true and first husband, the Lord Jesus Christ. The aged or mature woman of God is to "*be* in behaviour as <u>becometh</u> holiness" (Tit 2:3).

How does the mature woman come to this place of holy behavior? By faith alone? No, it requires faith's chaperone or governess, the fear of God. These mature women must begin as young women (in their childbearing days) to "continue in faith and charity and holiness with sobriety." 1Tim 2:15 This word 'continue' (*meno*, Greek 3306) means 'to *stay* (in a given place, state, relation or expectancy)' and is the word so often translated in the New Testament 'abide'. Thus, they must abide in faith and continue in it, but it must be coupled or joined with other things, such as charity, holiness, and the fear of God. Peter instructs women of God that their chaste or holy behavior must be *coupled* with fear (1Pe 3:2). Holiness and the behavior that becomes it can only be produced in our life through the fear of God.

So many preach a powerless gospel that implies there is nothing we need to attain to, nothing we need to grow up into. Yet Paul himself was following after the Lord in order to attain 'perfection'.[117] There were things Paul had already attained to in his life and that some of the Philippians as well had matured into, yet there were still many things remaining.

> If by any means <u>I might attain</u> unto the resurrection of the dead. **Not as though I had already attained**, either were already perfect: but I <u>follow after</u>, if that I may apprehend that for which also I am apprehended of Christ Jesus. Nevertheless, whereto <u>we have already attained</u>, let us walk by the same rule, let us mind the same thing. Php 3:11-12,16

One of the things we are to attain to is a greater knowledge of God and his ways. "A wise *man* will hear, and will increase learning; and a man of understanding shall attain unto wise counsels" (Pr 1:5). We are to grow up in our understanding of the Lord and not be childish in how we approach him and know him (1Co 14:20). Paul encouraged Timothy as a minister of the gospel not to forget that he had attained in his life to the words of faith and of good doctrine. "If thou put the brethren in remembrance of these things, thou shalt be a good minister of Jesus Christ, nourished up in the words of faith and of good doctrine, whereunto thou hast attained." 1Tim 4:6 So we must also grow in holiness toward the LORD.

Fleeing Riotous Living

If we are born again, then we have passed from condemnation to acceptance, from judgment to mercy. "Verily, verily, I say unto you, <u>he that heareth my word</u>, and believeth on him that sent me, hath everlasting life, and shall not come into condemnation; but is passed from death unto life." Jn 5:24 But let us not return to the way of disobedience where we do not hearken to his voice, as we did when we were lost. The promise of escaping his condemnation is predicated on hearing his word. If we will no longer hear his word, we cannot expect to escape his condemnation any more than Lucifer who refused God's ordained will. We are no longer children of wrath, nor children of disobedience as we once were by nature (Eph 2:3). Only let us not return to the vomit of living in the world and like the world, doing our own thing (2Pe 2:20-22).

---

[117] Note, *not* perfection in an absolute sense, but in terms of maturity. The word 'perfect' in Php 3:11 means 'to become *complete*, i.e. (figurative) *consummate* (in character)'.

We will all fall short, but we dare not journey into a far country, and there waste our substance with riotous living (Lk 15:13), and think that we are safe. No, we are perishing there! Riotous living is not allowed in God's house. This word 'riotous' is an interesting one in the Greek. It is *asotos* (G811) and comes from its sister word *asotia* (G810). *Asotos* is the adjective 'riotous' and *asotia* is the noun 'riot'. That is how close they are related. So when we look at the definition of *asotia* we will understand *asotos* also. *Asotia* is a compound word coming from '*a*' (i.e. not) + *sozo* (i.e. saved). Thus, *asotia* is literally 'not saved' and properly means *unsavedness*. Besides being translated as 'riot', *asotia* is also translated as 'excess'. Thus, when any child of God lives in excess or riot (i.e. wildly), they are living like the unsaved and not like a child of God! Let us not live like the world or be friends with the world, lest we be judged with the world.

> **WARNING**: So many desire the heavenly Father's mercy and forgiveness as demonstrated so lavishly in taking back the prodigal son, but at the same time they would refuse to accept the Father's true judgment that when we live in sin we are dead, no matter who we are. "Behold therefore the goodness and severity of God: on them which fell, severity; but toward thee, goodness, if thou continue in *his* goodness: otherwise thou also shalt be cut off." Rom 11:22 We must take God for who he is. We cannot take only the parts we like. Judgment and mercy are both with him (Isa 16:5; 30:18), and we cannot forget that we are betrothed to the LORD in both judgment and in mercies (Hos 2:19).

Even the prodigal son had to come to know this in his own heart, before he could decide to go home and return to his father (Lk 15:17-18). Let us take warning and beware of the father's own judgment concerning this state that his son was in, for it clearly represents the heavenly Father's judgment. He says, not once but twice, "this my son was dead, and is **alive again**; he was lost, and is found." Lk 15:24 (also v32) If we return to a sinful life and do not come out from among the world and be separate from it, as he has commanded us to (2Co 6:17-18), then our heavenly Father considers us as those who are both dead and lost!

Holy, Blameless, and in Love

Let us not become as many of God's people throughout the ages who became a disobedient and stiff necked people, uncircumcised in heart and ears, and rebellious against their Father.[118] We are children of God by faith in Christ Jesus (Gal 3:26-27), but we are called to be "as obedient children, not fashioning [ourselves] according to the former lusts in [our] ignorance" (1Pe 1:14). When

---

[118] Only a small sampling of the hundreds of references in the scriptures of God's people hardening their hearts against him and against his ways: 2K 17:6-20, Neh 9:16-17,26-31, Isa 1:2-4, Jer 7:23-28, 17:23, 19:14-15, Eze 3:4-7, Ac 7:51-53, Dt 31:27-29.

we were lost, we were ignorant of God's command to be holy and obedient. But now that we are saved we are no longer ignorant. We know we must depart from iniquity as his children (2Tim 2:19). We are accepted in the beloved (Eph 1:6), but we also are chosen that "we <u>should be</u> holy and without blame before him in love" (Eph 1:4). So we have a requirement to be holy and without blame and in love, and all these are <u>our</u> responsibility! It is <u>our</u> part to love the LORD our God with all our heart, soul, mind, and strength. Seventeen times we are given the specific command to "love the LORD".[119] It is <u>our</u> part to walk in holiness. So, so many scriptures admonish us on this, but let us just take Peter's.

> But as he which hath called you is holy, so <u>be ye holy</u> in all manner of conversation [i.e. *behavior*]; Because it is written, <u>Be ye holy</u>; for I am holy. 1Pe 1:15-16

It is <u>our</u> part also to walk blameless before God.[120] Paul exhorts us in our life to "do all things without murmurings and disputings" (Php 2:14), so that we may be blameless sons of God, who are without rebuke (v15). In light of the world's fiery destruction to come and the promise that we look forward to of a new heavens and a new earth, Peter exhorts us to be prepared for the coming of the Lord by being blameless before God. "Wherefore, beloved, seeing that ye look for such things, be diligent that ye may be found of him in peace, without spot, and blameless."[121] 2Pe 3:14

The Promise of Sonship Demands Holiness

"Wherefore come out from among them, and be ye separate, saith the Lord, and touch not the unclean thing; and I will receive you, And will be a Father unto you, and ye shall be my sons and daughters, saith the Lord Almighty." 2Co 6:17-18

Paul exhorts us to "cleanse ourselves from all filthiness of the flesh and spirit" (2Co 7:1). Many evangelical teachers have no concept that there can be a filthiness or uncleanness in our spirit after we are born again and cleansed by his blood. But Paul says to born again saints that they needed to cleanse themselves from certain practices and relationships which were defiling them, not only in the flesh, but also in spirit. What is the filthiness that Paul is talking about?

---

[119] These are all specifically the command to "love the Lord": Dt 6:5, 11:1,13,22, 13:3, 19:9, 30:6,16,20; Jos 22:5, 23:11; Ps 31:23, 97:10, 116:1; Mt 22:37; Mk 12:30; Lk 10:27.

[120] Jesus was blameless, of course (Mt 3:15, 17:27), but so was Paul (2Co 6:3). It is a requirement for both a bishop (i.e. an elder) and a deacon to be blameless (Tit 1:5-7, 1Tim 3:2,10). Widowers also were to be blameless (1Tim 5:5-7). John the Baptist's parents, as a priestly family before God, lived blamelessly (Lk 1:6).

[121] 2Peter 3:14 does *not* say "be found in him … blameless". It says "be found of him … blameless". He will do the inspection when he comes to see **if** he finds us blameless.

7 – Holiness, Righteousness, & Faithfulness to God

First, it is fellowship or 'joinings' with unbelievers, which the Bible calls being unequally yoked together. This is in 2Co 6:14-15a. Paul then turns the corner and speaks of a different set of compromising relationships. Notice how the first three comparisons (righteousness with unrighteousness, light with darkness, Christ with Belial) are all joined with the conjunction AND. But then, in introducing the new set of comparisons (he that believeth with an infidel, the temple of God with idols), the conjunction is **OR**.[122]

> Be ye not unequally yoked together with unbelievers: for what fellowship hath righteousness with unrighteousness? and what communion hath light with darkness? And what concord hath Christ with Belial? **OR** what part hath he that believeth with an infidel? And what agreement hath the temple of God with idols? for ye are the temple of the living God; as God hath said, I will dwell in them, and walk in *them;* and I will be their God, and they shall be my people. Wherefore come out from among them, and be ye separate, saith the Lord, and touch not the unclean *thing;* and I will receive you, And will be a Father unto you, and ye shall be my sons & daughters, saith the Lord Almighty. 2Co 6:14-18

Now contrary to Strong's definition, an infidel is *not* 'one *without* Christian *faith* (specially a *heathen*)'. These infidels are in fact believers who are unfaithful to the Lord. The Greek word for infidel is *apistos* and comes from the root *a* which means 'not' and *pistos* which means 'trustworthy or faithful'. It does not come from the word 'peitho', which is to believe. The infidel is not one who does not believe, rather he is one who is unfaithful to his belief.

WARNING: Strong's definitions are a great help many times. We ought to hold them in high regard, especially for his work's sake, which is one of great diligence and monumental effort (especially concerning it was done before computers)! Many Christians owe him a debt of thanksgiving for his faithful and tedious labors. But his works, as any work of man, are not perfect, nor are his definitions equal in weight to the scripture. When the Biblical usage of the words contradicts Strong's definition or when his own understanding of certain Biblical insight is lacking, we must be willing to discard his definitions and hold fast to what is revealed by our study of the word of God.[123]

This is where we get the English word 'infidelity'. Infidelity is not unbelief. It is a violation of one's own faith or trust. It is unfaithfulness. An unmarried man and woman who have intimacy outside of marriage are not showing infidelity. They are showing immorality. Only a spouse, who has a sacred trust of

---

[122] For emphasis, I have capitalized and emboldened the change in conjunction from 'and' to 'or' so that the shift in comparisons is readily seen in 2Corinthians 6:14-18.

[123] Examples of this are his definitions of soul and spirit, which mix the two and do not properly separate them, even though scripture says they can be definitively divided.

marriage to be faithful to their married partner, can show infidelity. This is confirmed by the only other use of the word infidel in the scripture. "But if any provide not for his own, and specially for those of his own house, he hath <u>denied the faith</u>, and is worse than an infidel." 1Tim 5:8 In this verse, 'infidel' is the same word 'apistos'. The infidel is one who has denied (i.e. 'to *disavow, reject, abnegate*') the faith they once followed. When Paul wants to show what a shame it is for a believer to not take care of his own family, he compares them to what is *most* shameful – not an unbeliever, but one who, as a believer, has turned their back on the things of God they once knew and followed! They have denied the faith they once held fast.

Paul speaks about two types of corrupting relationships, one which makes us filthy in the flesh, the other in spirit. Can you see that so much clearer now? Fellowshipping or joining in commitments with the lost will make you filthy in the flesh for <u>they are flesh</u>. They have no living spirit; they are dead spiritually, so they cannot defile your spirit. They can only defile your *flesh*. They have never been cleansed from the filth of the flesh. As Paul states, they are those who are unrighteousness, darkness, and wickedness. This is why their head is Belial, whose name means 'wickedness'.[124]

On the other hand there is a defiling of our *spirit* that comes from fellowshipping with those who <u>have a spirit</u>, but are walking contrary to God's commandments. Fellowshipping or joining in commitments with the backslidden, those who have departed from the faith, will make us filthy in our spirit. These have been born again and been given a new spirit, but have allowed their spirit to become defiled again by following after the idolatry of their own will. They have returned to the vomit from which they were delivered. "But it is happened unto them according to the true proverb, The dog *is* turned to his own vomit again; and the sow that was washed to her wallowing in the mire." 2Pe 2:22

The infidels are those who have left their first love (Rev 2:4) and have allowed other loves to come into their heart. Thus, Paul speaks of them in connection with idols, for when a believer's heart turns away from the Lord, idolatry always enters in. No wonder Paul says, "Wherefore, my dearly beloved, <u>flee</u> from idolatry." 1Co 10:14 Remember, idolatry is NOT just the external praying to man-made idols of stone, wood, or precious metals. Other religions do these things. The inward idolatry is that which is most deadly in the Christian believer. It is desiring and serving something other than the Lord. This is the subtlety of spiritual idolatry. Therefore, the scripture says "covetousness, which is idolatry" (Col 3:5). Idolatry is that which our heart becomes set upon.

---

[124] 'Belial' means wickedness and is translated in the OT both 'wicked' (Nah 1:11,15; Dt 15:9; Job 34:18; Ps 101:3) and 'ungodly' (2Sam 22:5; Ps 18:4; Pr 16:27, 19:28).

7 – Holiness, Righteousness, & Faithfulness to God

Come Out and Touch Not the Unclean

When Paul says "touch not the unclean", what is he referring to? In context, the unclean are two groups of people. The first group are those who have never been cleansed (i.e. the lost). The second group are those who have returned to the pig sty (i.e. the backslider and the infidel). These are those whom we must learn to come out from and to touch them not. To touch in 2Co 6:14 means 'to *attach* oneself to, i.e. to *touch* (in many implied relations)'. We must not attach ourselves (in relationship) to them that are unclean. Our only relationship to them is to exhort them to be cleansed through repentance unto restoration – either unto salvation in the first case or unto restoration in the second.

This is why we have been given the ministry of reconciliation (2Co 5:18-19). Note carefully when Paul speaks of this ministry, though it may be obvious that it is to bring the lost to the Lord Jesus, the primary ones to whom he says we are to bring to reconciliation is brethren! "Now then we are ambassadors for Christ, as though God did beseech *you* by us: we pray *you* in Christ's stead, be ye reconciled to God." 2Co 5:20 It was the Corinthians, born again believers, who needed to be reconciled to God! Paul was beseeching them for this purpose.

So what are these promises, in particular, that Paul says should motivate us to "cleanse ourselves from all filthiness of the flesh and spirit, perfecting holiness in the fear of God" (2Co 7:1)? They are the promises of sonship and intimacy with the heavenly Father. If we will cleanse ourselves from all filthiness of the flesh and spirit by not attaching ourselves in relationships with the lost and the infidels, if we will touch not the unclean things of immorality and idolatry, then God promises to receive us and to be a Father unto us, and we, like never before, will experience what it is to be his sons and daughters. This is the sure and promised intimacy that results from living in holiness with the Lord. Remember, holiness requires sanctification, and sanctification is 'to be set apart for holy purposes'. When we live our life unto God and not unto our own desires or conveniences, then his holy purposes begin to be established. We find ourselves in his hands.[125]

In order to perfect holiness in the fear of God, we must allow the fear of God to move us to set apart our hearts and lives from all uncleanness and compromise. God, of course, absolutely forbids his children to fellowship with, to be friends with, or to love the world – that much ought to be clear from the scriptures.

> Ye adulterers and adulteresses, know ye not that the friendship of the world is enmity with God? whosoever therefore will be a friend of the world is the enemy of God. Jam 4:4

---

[125] This is the place that the Shulamite so desired in intimacy to be, in his hands (Song 2:6, 5:4,14, 8:3).

Where is the Fear of GOD? Losing the Treasure of the Lord

> Love not the world, neither the things *that are* in the world. If any man love the world, the love of the Father is not in him. 1Jn 2:15

Breaking Fellowship with Willfully Disobedient Brethren

Many Churches are not even being taught that they cannot be friends with the world. But so many more Christians and even Christian leaders do not see the apostolic pattern, that whenever another brother or sister in the Lord walks deliberately contrary to the word of God and refuses correction, then we are to have no fellowship with them. The Bible commands us not even to sit down and eat with them. Does God command this because he hates such people and will have nothing to do with them? No, but he would bring them to shame by our obedience to not keep company with them. In this way they are to be warned to repent. Do we obey God's command to separate ourselves from willfully disobedient believers because we think we are better than they or because we despise them? God forbid. Rather, we fear God — seriously considering the end of such willful disobedience, which will result in death and eternal separation if one continues in this way. We love the errant believer enough as our own family to know that it is only through following God's prescribed pattern of discipline that the rebellious can be restored.

> Know ye not that the unrighteous shall not inherit the kingdom of God? <u>Be not deceived</u>: neither fornicators, nor idolaters, nor adulterers, nor effeminate, nor abusers of themselves with mankind, Nor thieves, nor covetous, nor drunkards, nor revilers, nor extortioners, shall inherit the kingdom of God. 1Co 6:9-10

Again, why do we separate from the disobedient believer? To warn them of the end of disobedience, which is spiritual death (Jam 1:15). Those who live as the lost will be judged with the lost and will share in the penalty of their sins, which is eternal separation. We must not keep company with ANY man that is called a brother but who lives in open sin. The "doctrine which is according to godliness" (1Tim 6:3) is that we must come out from among the unclean and touch them not.

Any man who rejects this doctrine, Paul instructs us to withdraw ourselves from them *also* — for they will be the next one taken down by the enemy! We are to warn those who walk in darkness, or who teach false doctrine, and avoid them (Rom 16:17, Tit 3:9). If they do not repent of their false teaching after two admonitions, we are called to <u>reject</u> them (Tit 3:10-11). This is the importance and necessity of both doctrinal purity and practical purity. Consider the wisdom of God in the following verses which warn obedient believers to depart and separate from disobedient and disorderly believers.

> But now I have written unto you <u>not to keep company</u>, if any man that is called **a brother** be a fornicator, or covetous, or an idolater, or a railer, or a drunkard, or an extortioner; with such an one <u>no not to</u>

7 – Holiness, Righteousness, & Faithfulness to God

eat. But them that are without God judgeth. Therefore <u>put away from among yourselves</u> that wicked person. 1Co 5:11,13

<u>I have not sat with</u> vain persons, neither will I go in with dissemblers. I have hated the congregation of evildoers; and <u>will not sit with</u> the wicked. Ps 26:4-5

If any man teach otherwise, and consent not to wholesome words, *even* the words of our Lord Jesus Christ, and to the doctrine which is according to godliness; He is proud, knowing nothing, but doting about questions and strifes of words, whereof cometh envy, strife, railings, evil surmisings, Perverse disputings of men of corrupt minds, and destitute of the truth, supposing that gain is godliness: <u>from such withdraw thyself</u>. 1Tim 6:3-5

This know also, that in the last days perilous times shall come. For men shall be lovers of their own selves, covetous, boasters, proud, blasphemers, disobedient to parents, unthankful, unholy, Without natural affection, trucebreakers, false accusers, incontinent, fierce, despisers of those that are good, Traitors, heady, highminded, lovers of pleasures more than lovers of God; Having a form of godliness, but denying the power thereof: <u>from such turn away</u>. 2Tim 3:1-5

Now we command you, brethren, in the name of our Lord Jesus Christ, that ye <u>withdraw yourselves</u> from every **brother** that walketh disorderly, and not after the tradition which he received of us. And if any man obey not our word by this epistle, note that man, and <u>have no company with him</u>, that he may be ashamed. Yet count *him* not as an enemy, but admonish *him* as a brother. 2Th 3:6,14-15

And if he shall neglect to hear them, tell *it* unto the church: but if he neglect to hear the church, <u>let him be unto thee as an heathen man and a publican</u>. Mt 18:17

Now I beseech you, brethren, <u>mark them</u> which cause divisions and offences contrary to the doctrine which ye have learned; <u>and avoid them</u>. Rom 16:17

And <u>have no fellowship</u> with the unfruitful works of darkness, but rather reprove *them*. Eph 5:11

WARNING: Over and over again I have seen those who explain away these godly warnings and continue to fellowship with the defiled of heart are the *first* to likewise fall into the same error and straying. Those who reject the wisdom of God's counsel will become defiled by those who are defiled. Their heart will then become cold to the things of the Spirit. Why? Because the Spirit must correct this error, and when anyone has deliberately violated the word of God they have turned a deaf ear to the first ministry of the Spirit. Hence, they no longer are able to hear the true voice of the Spirit that would lead them back to truth.

Where is the Fear of GOD? Losing the Treasure of the Lord

When a defilement springs up in one, the scripture promises *many* will be defiled (Heb 12:15-16). This is why God would have us come out from among the unclean and touch them not. Those who choose friendship and relationship over obedience to the word of God are the first to die spiritually and to wander in their life. It is only the fear of God that enables people to forsake even their best friendships to pay the price to continue following the Lord. Jesus said it very plainly, and we will all be put to the test on this: "If any *man* come to me, and hate not his father, and mother, and wife, and children, and brethren, and sisters, yea, and his own life also, he cannot be my disciple." Lk 14:26

Following the Lord is Forsaking All

If we are not willing to lose all for his sake and to leave behind the closest of friends, then Jesus said we are not worthy to be his disciple, nor are we worthy to receive the kingdom of God! If we fail this test, we cannot follow him, so says our Lord and Master.[126] Many walk away from Jesus over this singular issue: natural and familial relationships versus spiritual obedience to the words of the Master. This is the beginning of holiness. Only this allows the intimacy of being able to experience the Father's heart as sons and daughters. If we love any one more than the commands of our heavenly Father, then we have allowed our heart to be separated from him already.

> So many say they seek to know the intimacy of the Father's heart, yet are unwilling to pay the price to put him first.

So many say they seek to know the intimacy of the Father's heart, yet are unwilling to pay the price to put him first. Think on this. Even the father of faith, Abraham whom we are to "walk in the steps of that faith of our father Abraham" (Rom 4:12), was put to the ultimate test in this very area. Would he forsake even his beloved son for obedience to the Lord? Do we think that we can enjoy Abraham's intimacy as the friend of God without following in his footsteps? Holiness and the cost of holiness – i.e., forsaking all to follow him – produces intimacy with the LORD. Contrariwise, the compromise of unholiness produces separation. "But your iniquities have separated between you and your God, and your sins have hid *his* face from you, that he will not hear." Isa 59:2

I pray we see from this, that the fear of the LORD is the key to an intimate walk with God. "The secret of the LORD *is* with them that fear him; and he will shew them his covenant." Ps 25:14 "He hath given meat [i.e. *spiritual sustenance*] unto them that fear him" Ps 111:5 If we desire to experience the depth of our sonship with the Father, then we must be willing in the fear of God to perfect

---

[126] Not worthy of Jesus: Mt 10:37-38, 22:8.

holiness by coming out from among and being separate from and not touching the unclean (2Co 6:17). To obtain this intimacy with the LORD and the spiritual meat that he desires to feed us with, we must come out from among both the lost and the infidel. We must be separate and touch not the unclean. Then, he will receive us and make his habitation in our heart, for then our heart will be a sanctified and prepared place for him.

A Good Spirit: Departing from Evil
We must depart from evil and do good (Ps 34:14a)

We must perfect holiness in the fear of God. There is no other way that we will ever be able to keep walking with him. This is why God speaks of making a highway of holiness that we are to walk with him in. "And an highway shall be there, and a way, and it shall be called The way of holiness; the unclean shall not pass over it" (Isa 35:8). Let us look at how to perfect holiness. 'Perfecting' in 2Co 7:1 means 'to *fulfill further* (or *completely*), i.e. *execute*'. We know we have an imputed holiness which we have as a free gift that was given us as a result of salvation. But Paul is exhorting us to fulfill completely or to execute that holiness we have received by faith.

We cannot 'make' ourselves holy, but we must every day, because of who he has called us to be, *choose* to be holy and to separate ourselves unto God for his purposes. There is a holiness that we all need to grow up into in the Lord, which is part of the maturing process. This holiness is to depart from evil. How do we depart from evil? We must depart from evil through the fear of the LORD. This appears to be the first fruit of the fear of the LORD, for it is mentioned 5 times (the number of grace).

> A wise *man* feareth, and departeth from evil Pr 14:16
>   and by the fear of the LORD *men* depart from evil. Pr 16:6
>
> Be not wise in thine own eyes: fear the LORD,
>   and depart from evil. Pr 3:7
>
> The fear of the LORD *is* a fountain of life,
>   to depart from the snares of death. Pr 14:27
>
> Behold, the fear of the Lord, that *is* wisdom;
>   and to depart from evil *is* understanding. Job 28:28

'Depart from' in each of these verses means 'to *turn* off'. We must turn off evil in this generation and turn away from it. If there was ever a more appropriate verb to describe today what we must do to depart from evil, it is this: turn it off. The radio and the music of the world, even Christian music, which emulates the world today, just needs to be *turned* off, so that you may depart from the uncleanness of the world. God will protect you from its influences, if you take a stand against it. When we willingly allow corruption to be heard, then we enter into temptation, and it will influence us, for music affects our spirit.

Where is the Fear of GOD? Losing the Treasure of the Lord

> If there was ever a more appropriate verb to describe today what we must do to depart from evil, it is this: turn it off.

The television also needs to be *turned* off, for it is the world embodied. TV is driven by the lust of the flesh, the lust of the eyes, and the pride of life. Just watch the commercials and this will be proven. TV fosters everything that the humble servant of God is to depart from: covetousness, greed, excessive desire, being busy about many things, the external appearance, pride, and the glory of man – not to mention all the wickedness that unregenerate man glories in, the works of the flesh. TV is filled with adultery, fornication, uncleanness, lasciviousness, idolatry, witchcraft, hatred, variance, emulations, wrath, strife, seditions, heresies, envyings, murders, drunkenness, revellings, and such like" (Gal 5:19-21).

Why? Because these gratify the flesh. TV dulls our spiritual senses, lessens our godly desires, and eliminates our time for prayer. It easily can consume far more time than the study of the word of God, by which Jesus said a man must live (Mt 4:4/Lk 4:4). If we would be diligent to regularly turn off these sources of ungodliness and replace them with godly exercise, such as prayer and meditating on the word of God and serving others, we would immediately see a great increase in holiness in our walk with the Lord.

'Depart from' (in the preceding verses on the fear of the LORD) is also translated 'eschew'.[127] In English 'eschew' means 'to avoid, to shun, to flee from, <u>to stay away from deliberately</u>, to stay clear of.' The fear of the LORD working in us will nag at us to avoid and to deliberately stay away from evil and any appearance of it. The fear of the LORD is a spiritual compass that continually points away from sin and compromise and directs our attention toward our first love, Jesus Christ. Remember, "by the fear of the LORD *men* depart from evil." Pr 16:6

Time and time again we see men departed from evil by the fear of the LORD. How does the fear of the LORD cause us to depart from evil and stay far from it? There are two parts. First is departing from it, and second is staying far from it. First, the fear of the LORD enables us to depart from temptation when we do find it in our heart, because we consider the LORD God and his dread. We consider who it is who has spoken. It is his greatness and the power of his judgment as King of kings that curbs our appetite for going our own way.

> But know that the LORD hath set apart him that is godly for himself: the LORD will hear when I call unto him. Stand in awe, and sin not: commune with your own heart upon your bed, and be still. Selah. Ps 4:3-4

---

[127] As in Job 1:1, 1:8, and 2:3.

7 – Holiness, Righteousness, & Faithfulness to God

This word 'awe' in the Hebrew means 'to *quiver* (with any violent emotion, especially anger or fear)'. We will 'sin not' when we learn to stand before God waiting for his voice with the quivering of fear, knowing that he hears when we call and will speak to us. We must 'Selah', stop and think about the fact that he has set us apart for himself. We are no longer our own. This will produce the awe, the trembling of sinning not.

When we are liable to temptation, when we know we are weak and susceptible, when things in our heart are not as they should be, we need to keep a guard upon our heart. This guard is the fear of the LORD. It is how we are to guard our heart. "Let not thine heart envy sinners: but *be thou* in the fear of the LORD all the day long. For surely there is an end; and thine expectation shall not be cut off." Pr 23:17-18 While undergoing temptation we often think it will never end. But hear what the scripture says, "surely there is an end"! If we will abide in the fear of the LORD, then we will not succumb to temptation. This is how Jesus overcame. It is how we must overcome. "Who in the days of his flesh, when he had offered up prayers and supplications with strong crying and tears unto him that was able to save him from death, and was heard in that he feared" (Heb 5:7).

The fear of God keeps us from temptation by changing our heart and the desires of it. Many things are no longer temptations, once we hate them and despise them. It is far easier to say no to that which we have a strong disliking for, than it is to deny what which we inwardly crave and desire. This is why we must recapture the fear of the LORD in our hearts, if we would become overcomers. Our faith must be rooted in God's judgments and not our own desires. The Corinthians had many worldly and selfish desires, but notice how once sorrow of a godly sort came, immediately fear was restored and the first fruits of fear were a godly vehement desire and zeal.

> For behold this selfsame thing, that ye sorrowed after a godly sort, what carefulness it wrought in you, yea, *what* clearing of yourselves, yea, *what* indignation, yea, *what* **fear**, yea, *what* <u>vehement desire</u>, yea, *what* <u>zeal</u>, yea, *what* revenge! In all *things* ye have approved yourselves to be clear in this matter. 2Co 7:11

Let our desire be to fear his name, as those in Nehemiah's day (Neh 1:11), so that we may rebuild the walls of self-control and holiness, and thereby restore the honor to the church of Jesus Christ. It is by our lives that we dishonor Jesus; it is by the holiness of the fear of God in departing from iniquity that we will be as a bride adorned in glory. "Then thou shalt see, and flow together, and thine heart shall fear, and be enlarged" (Isa 60:5). The fear of God both enlarges our heart, makes it single (Eph 6:5, Col 3:22), and makes it one with his (Ps 86:11). Until room is made in our heart, we do not have room for God's desires. Our heart is too small. Until our heart is made single, we cannot follow after God's desires, for we still have our own.

Where is the Fear of GOD? Losing the Treasure of the Lord

This is why our heart must not only be enlarged, and made single, it must be united with his. Our heart is brought into unity in the fear of God so that we not only desire what he desires, but there is no competition in our heart for him. This is part of our intimacy with the LORD, that we are one in thought and desire with him through his fear. This is the work of his fear: to keep us near him, by keeping us from departing from him (Jer 32:40) and far from evil.

Notice in the scriptures what we saw concerning departing from evil: "Be not wise in thine own eyes: fear the LORD, and depart from evil." Pr 3:7 The fear of the LORD must begin by removing the natural pride and independence we all have. We must first know we cannot do it on our own. We must have God's wisdom, counsel, and commandments to know what we ought to do. Without the fear of the LORD we are all too ready to follow our own way and to argue and dispute with men of God and even with the LORD himself, but when the fear of God comes alive within us, we will now listen with a willing and obedient heart. We become more ready to hear than to speak.

> Keep thy foot when thou goest to the house of God, and be <u>more ready to hear</u>, than to give the sacrifice of fools: for they consider not that they do evil. <u>Be not rash with thy mouth</u>, and let not thine heart <u>be hasty to utter *any* thing before God</u>: for God *is* in heaven, and thou upon earth: therefore <u>let thy words be few</u>. For in the multitude of dreams and <u>many words</u> *there are* also *divers* vanities: but **fear thou God**. Ecc 5:1-2,7

The Work of a Good Conscience to Keep us in the Fear of God

This is the beauty of the fear of the LORD and keeping a good conscience – that they keep us from departing from the LORD. God has set up the fear of God in our heart so that as long as we maintain a good conscience, we will not forsake him. God has promised, "And I will make an everlasting covenant with them, that I will not turn away from them, to do them good; but I will put my <u>fear in their hearts, that they shall not depart from me</u>." Jer 32:40 But what if we should lose the fear of God, what then? God has given us a conscience to reprove us, to turn us from our way, and to remind us of his holiness. If we will maintain a good conscience, it will ultimately lead us back to the fear of God.

> Thine own wickedness shall correct thee, and thy backslidings shall reprove thee: know therefore and see that *it is* an evil *thing* and bitter, that thou hast forsaken the LORD thy God, and that <u>my fear *is* not in thee</u>, saith the Lord GOD of hosts. Jer 2:19

When we reject the fear of God directly, or we put it away by choosing to love evil instead of hating it, then we lose the precious gift of the fear of God. God not only tells us that the fear of God is what enables us to depart from evil, but he even tells us that the fear of God is the very hating of evil. "The fear of the LORD *is* to hate evil: pride, and arrogancy, and the evil way, and the fro-

7 – Holiness, Righteousness, & Faithfulness to God

ward mouth, do I hate." Pr 8:13 So many times we are unable to depart from iniquity because we still love it. The fear of God is the cure. The fear of God will cause us to hate evil so that we may then depart from it. Thus, the fear of God will by its nature cause us to hate what God hates: evil, the evil way, pride, arrogancy, and the froward (i.e. *'perverse* or *fraudulent'*) mouth. Notice in Job 1:1 and 8 how the words 'feareth God' are sandwiched between 'a perfect and upright man' and 'one that ... escheweth [i.e. *turneth* away from] evil'. The fear of God produces an *outward* uprightness and an *inward* hating of evil by which we turn away from evil.

WARNING: The conscience itself will begin to show us the wickedness of not having the fear of God in our heart, where it belongs. This sometimes is the confusion and the condemnation that people go through because of their conscience. Their conscience continues to bear witness to their heart that they have forsaken the LORD, because they do not have the fear of the LORD. Their mind, on the other hand, because of false teachings about the fear of God, tells them there is no reason to be condemned. Because so few are taught correctly about the fear of God, no one sees the reason for such seemingly baseless condemnation. The individual confesses all known sin, yet still they feel the weight of their conscience testifying to them that they are not right with God. Hence, after a while, they are made to understand by teachers, counselors, and friends – all of whom may not know the fear of God – that their condemnation is from the devil and needs to be rebuked and resisted.

Departing from Iniquity

Because the fear of God is to hate evil, this is why the fear of God cannot co-exist with evil. In the fear of God we will depart from evil,[128] or evil if it is allowed to find a place in our heart will cause us to depart from the fear of God. They are enemies of one another. Notice how the fear of God is likened to delighting in God's commandments. Behold, "Blessed *is* the man *that* feareth the LORD, *that* delighteth greatly in his commandments." Ps 112:1 Thus, it was written of Jesus who knew the fear of God better than any of us, "Then said I, Lo, I come: in the volume of the book *it is* written of me, I delight to do thy will, O my God: yea, thy law *is* within my heart." Ps 40:7-8

If we have lost our delight and joy in the word of God
or in doing what he has commanded us,
we will soon lose our fear of God.

---

[128] Departing from evil through the fear of God: Pr 3:7, 14:16, 14:27, 16:6, Job 28:28.

Where is the Fear of GOD? Losing the Treasure of the Lord

If we have lost our delight and joy in the word of God or in doing what he has commanded us, we will soon lose our fear of God. The fear of God and the delighting in truth cannot be long separated. If you delight in his word, you will grow in his fear. If you find his word a burden, then the fear of God will depart. Let us now look at another way the fear of God helps us depart from evil.

We depart from God by sinning. The fear of God is designed by its very nature to keep us from departing from God in this way. "Fear not: for God is come to prove you, and that **his fear** may be before your faces, that ye sin not." Ex 20:20 This is why the arrogant man and the religious man will always hate the fear of God, because they have never encountered or experienced it. They have no dread that issues from the presence of God that is before their face that restrains their lusts. Notice where the fear of God was: it was before their faces. The fear of God is designed to 'get in our face'! It is to remain immediately before our eyes. Once we have experienced it, we cannot deny its impact. Because the fear of the Lord was designed to be in our face, we will see things very differently when we have it. The fear of God will cause us to "stand in awe, and sin not: commune with your own heart upon your bed, and be still. Selah." Ps 4:4 May the fear of God be ever before our faces, so that we sin not against our holy God.

The fear of the LORD opens the door of our heart to be able to receive instruction from the LORD. In this way the fear of the LORD enables us to depart from evil and stay far from it, because we are able to receive his instruction. The intimacy we have only through the fear of the LORD is a key element in this. When we are intimate with someone their words mean so much more. It is easier to hear correction and instruction when we are intimate friends. Notice also how we have seen God links the fear of the LORD with humility (Pr 3:7). The fear of God humbles us by magnifying the LORD and his wisdom. With the fear of God it is easier to acknowledge his greatness and our utter dependence upon him. This is how the fear of the LORD enables us to receive instruction. In fact God himself is sure of this effect. "I said, Surely thou wilt fear me, thou wilt receive instruction" (Zep 3:7).

God knows if we fear him that we will surely receive his instruction. This is why we see the beautiful promise, which we have mentioned several times already, "The secret of the LORD *is* with them that fear him; and he will shew them his covenant." Ps 25:14 Through the fear of the LORD we come to understand his covenant and the things which he has kept secret from the wise and prudent. As we grow and mature in the Lord through the fear of God, he is able to give us spiritual meat by which we may grow strong (Ps 111:5). When we have the fear of God working in us, then the word of God will become rich, succulent meat for our hungry spirit and not just milk to keep us alive. It is that sustenance that will make us faithful.

7 – Holiness, Righteousness, & Faithfulness to God

Fighting the Good Fight of Faithfulness

"If ye will fear the LORD, and serve him, and obey his voice, and not rebel against the commandment of the LORD, then shall both ye and also the king that reigneth over you <u>continue following</u> the LORD your God" 1Sam 12:14

The fear of the LORD will produce a faithful spirit in us enabling us to continue to follow the LORD. The fear of God will keep our feet, hands, thoughts, and heart rooted on God's purpose in our serving of the Master. This faithful spirit will keep us in two important and inseparable ways. As we have been observing, it will keep us <u>departing from</u> sin (Ex 20:20, 2Tim 2:19) and <u>from departing</u> from our King (Heb 3:10-12). Without both we cannot long remain with the Lord. We will be as those sown among the thorns which grew up, but became choked by the weeds,

> such as hear the word, And the cares of this world, and the deceitfulness of riches, and the lusts of other things entering in, choke the word, and it becometh unfruitful. Mk 4:18-19

In fact, God has put his fear in our heart as the fulfillment of the promise of the new covenant so that we would not *depart* from him.[129] "And I will make an everlasting covenant with them, ... but I will put my fear in their hearts, <u>that they shall not depart from me</u>." Jer 32:40 Many today turn this promise completely around and make it not a covenant of faithfulness dependent on our fearing God, but rather a license of promiscuity. God is not saying that the new covenant is such that we *will* not depart from him. Yet that is what men teach.

We must not deny the Word itself, which clearly states that in the last days men *will* depart from the faith and *will* turn away from sound doctrine and *will* perish. If any one will look around with their own eyes with Bible in hand and measure things by "what saith the scriptures", they will find that men everywhere are departing from the faith – in the name of God! "Now the Spirit speaketh expressly, that in the latter times <u>some shall depart from the faith</u>, giving heed to seducing spirits, and doctrines of devils" (1Tim 4:1).

> The fear of God will keep our feet, hands, thoughts, and heart rooted on God's purpose in our serving of the Master.

Today so many false teachers and prophets are proclaiming in the last days great revivals, where millions will come to Christ. But we must ask to what Christ are they coming? Certainly not Jesus, the Christ of the Bible, who

---

[129] See the chapter entitled "Understanding the New Covenant of Grace & Fear" in the book <u>Finding the Treasure of the Lord</u>.

prophesied exactly the opposite, namely, that the masses would fall away and perish, and only a *few* would find the narrow way to salvation!

> Enter ye in at the strait gate: for wide *is* the gate, and broad *is* the way, that leadeth to destruction, and many there be which go in thereat: Because strait *is* the gate, and narrow *is* the way, which leadeth unto life, and few there be that find it. Mt 7:13

Jesus himself was questioned on whether there will only be a few saved – for even in his day people thought the masses would come to salvation. And what was his response? Was it, "Rejoice, for many shall be saved"? Listen to *his* words and compare them to what men say today who are building their own ministries.

> Then said one unto him, Lord, are there few that be saved? And he said unto them, Strive to enter in at the strait [i.e. *narrow*] gate: for many, I say unto you, will seek to enter in, and shall not be able. Lk 13:23-24

Did you hear that? He said *many* would strive to enter in, but would *not* be able. Jesus said that if we would enter in, we **must strive**. We must '*struggle*, literally to *compete* for a prize, figuratively to *contend* with an adversary, or to *endeavor* to accomplish something'. Jesus never preached an easy believism salvation. With so little fear of God today is it any wonder there is so little faithfulness among those who call upon the name of the Lord.

7 – Holiness, Righteousness, & Faithfulness to God

Chapter 8. The Root of Worship and Fruit of Giving
Preparing for Acceptable Worship

"Who is like unto thee, O LORD, among the gods? who is like thee, glorious in holiness, fearful in praises, doing wonders?" Ex 15:11

The Marriage of Fear & Obedience: Producing a True Heart of Service

"Serve the LORD with fear, and rejoice with trembling" Ps 2:11

If we are to understand the true fear of God we cannot divorce it from obedience. Obedience is the other leg of the fear of God. The fear of God cannot stand without a purpose and commitment to be obedient. The fear of the LORD will move us to take action in agreement with the word of God. Without the word of God [i.e. knowing what to obey] and obedience,[130] the true fear of God cannot continue to grow in us.

Serving, Obeying, and Fearing: the Three-Fold Cord

---

[130] Note this is not 'perfect, sinless, never-missing-the mark obedience', but the purposing of the heart to obey.

8 – The Root of Worship and Fruit of Giving

Let us look more at the intimate relationship between serving, obeying, and fearing. A negative example can be clearly seen in King Saul's disobedience to the command of God. Notice the cause and effect. "And Saul said unto Samuel, I have sinned: for I have transgressed the commandment of the LORD, and thy words: <u>because I feared the people</u>, and <u>obeyed their voice</u>." 1Sam 15:24 Because Saul feared the people, he obeyed their voice. Because he did not fear God, he disobeyed God's voice. What we fear is what we will serve and obey! "And I will give thee … into the hand *of them* whose face thou fearest" (Jer 22:25). Know a person's fears, and you will know both what has mastered them and what they will serve. So it is written that a servant shall fear his master (Mal 1:6). We are called to "<u>serve the LORD with fear</u>, and rejoice with trembling." Ps 2:11 And to "<u>serve God acceptably with</u> reverence and <u>godly fear</u>" (Heb 12:28). If you fear God, he will be your master "and him only shalt thou serve."[131]

The relationship between serving and fearing is true for all our fears. If we fear man, we will serve man's desires and purposes, rather than God's. This is the snare of the fear of man. Paul did not fear man, therefore he did not seek to please man. This is what enabled him to be the servant of Christ: "for if I yet pleased men, I should not be the servant of Christ." Gal 1:10

> **WARNING**: Though we are not to fear man, we must fear the calling that God places in men of authority. Thus, we *are* called to fear those who are sent by God, for they are not acting on their own accord in their calling, but as his representatives, *if* they be true servants of God. Thus, we see when true servants of God were sent, they were in turn received with fear, and obedience was the result (2Co 7:15).

An Obedient Spirit
We must seek peace and pursue it (Ps 34:14b)

The following in scripture are all closely linked together with the fear of God and are often mentioned together:

1. following/walking after the Lord,
2. keeping his commandments,
3. obeying his voice/word,
4. serving him, and
5. cleaving unto him.

Thus, one after another they are commanded us of God. "Ye shall <u>walk after</u> the LORD your God, and <u>fear him</u>, and <u>keep his commandments</u>, and <u>obey his voice</u>, and ye shall <u>serve him</u>, and <u>cleave unto him</u>." Dt 13:4 It is impossible to maintain a humble, teachable, and correctable spirit without also purposing

---

[131] We're commanded to serve God exclusively in our life: Mt 4:10, Lk 4:8, 1Sam 12:24.

to have an <u>obedient</u> spirit. God is looking for children who will be obedient. "As <u>obedient</u> children, not fashioning yourselves according to the former lusts in your ignorance" (1Pe 1:14). The goal or fruit that God is looking for from learning the fear of the LORD is obedience. At its root the true fear of God *is* obeying the LORD from the heart. Over and over again the scripture shows us that to obey God's commands *is* to fear him.

> Now these *are* the commandments, the statutes, and the judgments, which the LORD your God commanded to teach you, <u>that ye might do *them*</u> in the land whither ye go to possess it: <u>That thou mightest fear the LORD thy God</u>, to keep all his statutes and his commandments, which I command thee, thou, and thy son, and thy son's son, all the days of thy life; and that thy days may be prolonged. Dt 6:1-2
>
> Therefore thou shalt <u>keep the commandments</u> of the LORD thy God, to walk in his ways, and to fear him. Dt 8:6
>
> And it shall be with him, and he shall read therein all the days of his life: that he may <u>learn to fear the LORD his God</u>, to keep all the words of this law and these statutes, to do them Dt 17:19
>
> Wherefore now let the fear of the LORD be upon you; <u>take heed and do *it*</u> 2Ch 19:7

Notice in both Deuteronomy 6:2 and 17:19 that the fear of the LORD is defined as keeping God's statutes and commandments and doing them. We must fear the LORD in order to keep his law, his statutes, and his commandments. Obedience is the proper fruit of the fear of the LORD, because the fear of the LORD *is* obedience.[132] The fear of the LORD will change how we do things. Jehoshaphat gave commandments to the priests to fulfill their office with the fear of the LORD. "And he charged them, saying, <u>Thus shall ye do in the fear of the LORD</u>, faithfully, and with a perfect heart." 2Ch 19:9 What we do as servants of the Lord is to be done in the fear of the LORD. Nehemiah as the servant of the LORD records for us that his actions were carved and shaped by his fear of God: "yea, even their servants bare rule over the people: but so did not I, <u>because of the fear of God</u>." Neh 5:15

> When we can pick and choose what parts of God's word we want to do, then the fear of God is truly missing.

God is looking for a complete obedience. Many times our obedience is not done in the fear of God. Our lack of his fear is often evidenced by our partial obedience. When we can pick and choose what parts of God's word we want to do, then the fear of God is truly missing. As John Bevere in his book <u>The Fear

---

[132] Thus, we repeatedly have the command to do so in the fear of the Lord: Lev 19:14,32, 25:17,36,43.

of the Lord says, "In God's eyes, partial or selective obedience is the same as rebellion to his authority. It is the evidence of a lack of the fear of God!"[133]

The Subjection of our Soul
*"Wherefore ye must needs be subject,
not only for wrath, but also for conscience sake." Rom 13:5*

To be ready always to give an answer, we must start by sanctifying the Lord in our heart. He must be set apart and acknowledged to be the *supreme* in authority. This is why our conscience **must** answer to the Lord as the authority that we are subject to. Our subjection to authority, especially the Lord's, is for conscience's sake. "Wherefore ye must needs be subject, not only for wrath, but also for conscience sake." Rom 13:5 When we lose or willingly walk away from our "professed subjection unto the gospel of Christ" (2Co 9:13), then an evil conscience grows within, and spiritually we begin to die. The writer of Hebrews asks those who should have been teachers by now, "shall we not much rather be in subjection unto the Father of spirits, and live?" Heb 12:9 Rebellion to God brings death, but submission to the Author of life brings life.

We must continually return to the Lordship of his authority and allow his Word and the Holy Spirit to rule over our life. We must submit ourselves to the Father's will, even as Jesus did. This only will maintain both a good conscience and the true fear of God. The door of God's counseling room is always open, but so few avail themselves of the consolation that is in Christ, his perfect wisdom, his comfort of love, his peace that passes understanding, his fellowship of the Spirit, his abundant bowels and mercies, and what is the exceeding greatness of his power to us-ward who believe (Php 2:1, Eph 1:19).

If we desire the office of the bishop, if we desire 'to be *inspected* and to have *oversight*' taken to our life by men of God who will help us be made aware of what we are not seeing, then the Bible says we desire a good work to be done in our life. This is not merely a good work, it is a '*beautiful* work, which is both *valuable* and *virtuous*'.[134] So many flee such oversight to their spiritual life, when this is the very reason God gave us the overseers of elders: through the maturity and the gifts and callings that are in them to help us see what we do not see. This is why the office of the bishop resides in elders, mature men of God.

> 'Bishop' is the word *episkope* (G1984) which comes from the Greek roots *epi* (G1909) which means 'over' and the word *skope* or *skopos* (G4649) from which we get our English word "scope" (i.e. 'to be able to see in detail'). The role of the bishop is to 'scope out' or over-

---

[133] John Bevere, The Fear of God (Charisma House, Lake Mary, Florida, 1997), p. 154.

[134] This is the meaning of the Greek word *kalos* (G2570) translated as 'good' (1Tim 3:1).

Where is the Fear of GOD? Losing the Treasure of the Lord

see with insight what is taking place in the realm of the spirit in our life and to warn us of danger.

Why do we forsake this valuable gifting of the body? We are simply unwilling to bow before his Lordship and the authority that we know he requires us to be subject unto in those he has set over us.[135] This pride (i.e. of thinking we are sufficient in ourselves) and this fear of authority are many times why we do not come to the throne of mercy to obtain help in time of need (Heb 4:16). Either we do not realize we need to come, or we do not want to come, or worst of all, we are in a place where there is no one to come to, because no one is taking true spiritual oversight as elders through the office of the bishop. So often our own fears keep us from coming near to authority, and hence the very good that God would bless us with is kept from us by our human fears. We so need the fear of God today to drive away such hurtful fears and establish in their place godly fear. Such godly fear will cause us to draw nigh to authority with a humble heart, so that we may receive the wisdom God puts in his servants.

> **WARNING**: There is a godly fear of authority that should cause us to run **to** authority and not **from** it. Only in drawing nigh to authority (Jam 4:8) can transgression be resolved, disorder be discovered, God's order be reset, the wisdom from above be received, and proper spiritual oversight be taken.

The Fear of the LORD: Our Guide

Let's give an analogy to understand the work of the fear of God in the life of the believer. The fear of the LORD acts as a handrail that guides us along the narrow and tribulation-filled way in our walk with Jesus. Consider walking along a narrow path on the side of a steep canyon, or walking up to the edge of an observation deck atop one of the world's tallest skyscrapers, or driving 60 miles per hour down a country road with oncoming traffic, or climbing an open metal staircase as it ascends seemingly toward heaven to reach the top of a domed building. If there is no railing to mark the edge and to hold onto, no divider or line to mark the lane which you are to be in versus which the oncoming traffic is to be in, then your natural instinct is to fear and to withdraw. It is difficult to put away fear in these situations for good reason. The wisdom of knowing the consequences of a misstep brings about a caution, a dread that is intended to keep us from carelessness or foolishness.

---

[135] The elders are those that are to rule in the house of God (1Tim 5:17, 3:4-5), to whom we are called to obey and to follow their faith (Heb 13:17,7, 24). They function as bishops and shepherds who are to willingly take the oversight and feed the flock (1Pe 5:1-2). Their 'rule' is not the ruling over that the Gentiles do, but it is 'to *stand before*, i.e. (in rank) to *preside*, or (by implication) to *practise*: be over'.

8 – The Root of Worship and Fruit of Giving

Yet simply add a white dotted line down the center of that unmarked country road and every driver breathes easier, even though only passing inches from each other. In fact, with the addition of that insignificant paint that couldn't stop an insect, the cars are able to safely pass each other only inches apart without anxiety. Have you ever wondered, how can something that provides no physical protection (such as a line) provide any safety? For the simple fact that each driver now knows their place.

Submission to order keeps us safe. Each driver knows what the Bible calls "the bounds of their habitation" (Ac 17:26). This is the power of the bounds of our habitation and staying within them. Each driver knows if they stay on their side of the line they are safe. Without a railing atop a 100+ story building, what normal person would go within 4 feet of the edge? Each inch in that case is terrifying to the sane person. Yet add a solid wall or secure fence and people will not only casually walk right up to the very edge, but they will lean on it and enjoy the view. Such is the fear of God. It is the railing that keeps us safe and secure in the grace of God. Grace provides the stunning liberty to go anywhere and the awesome vision that is set before us, but the fear of God is both the steering wheel of a good conscience and the railing of warning to keep us from going too far and killing ourselves. Grace is the road to salvation and the stairway to heaven, but fear is what keeps us safely on them both.

> the fear of God is both the steering wheel of a good conscience and the railing of warning to keep us from going too far and killing ourselves. Grace is the road to salvation and the stairway to heaven, but fear is what keeps us safely on them both.

The fear of God keeps and protects us from danger and from carelessness. The fear of God restricts our freedom to within God's predefined limits by restraining waywardness, yet it does so in a way that brings about *more* freedom than we could otherwise have! In the fear of God we have healthy borders which help remove our fears and bring peace, all because we know we are in the right place. A man may live for a while without the fear of God, but he lives in danger every moment – the danger of becoming careless. During a great storm with strong, gusty winds the man without the fear of God has no sanctuary, no certain dwelling place. So it is written, "Sanctify the LORD of hosts himself; and *let* him *be* your fear, and *let* him *be* your dread. And he shall be for a sanctuary" (Isa 8:13-14). Yes, the fear of God actually brings peace and safety!

Rejoicing in the Fear of God
"Serve the LORD with fear, and rejoice with trembling." Ps 2:11

Where is the Fear of GOD? Losing the Treasure of the Lord

In serving the Lord with the fear of God, several fruits that please God will be borne in our life. Of these, one of the most special and sought after by the LORD is the spirit of worship and praise that comes from the heart that fears him. God is seeking those who will worship him in spirit and in truth, and he finds what he is looking for in us when the fear of God is active in our life.

Do not think that fearing God produces a sour, unexpressive spirit? Nothing could be further from the truth. We naturally think fear will result in cowering and hiding, for this is the result of guilty fear. But the fear of God removes guilt by making a good conscience with God. Thus, it drives one not *away* from God, but *to* him. In speaking of how God will deal with the mighty man, who boasts himself in his mischief and who loves evil and lying, David says,

> The righteous also shall see, <u>and fear, and shall laugh</u> at him: Lo, *this is* the man *that* made not God his strength; but trusted in the abundance of his riches, *and* strengthened himself in his wickedness.
>
> But I *am* like a green olive tree in the house of God: I trust in the mercy of God for ever and ever. I will praise thee for ever, because thou hast done *it*: and I will wait on thy name; for *it is* good before thy saints. Ps 52:6-9

Notice the surprising response of the righteous. They will see the judgment of God against the boastful man and will fear God, and then they will <u>laugh</u> at the empty boastings of that wicked man "who made not God his strength." The good conscience of those who fear God produces not timidity, but boldness. It additionally produces renewed confidence in their commitments to God and to his house. So David says, "I trust in the mercy of God for ever and ever." The end result is a heart of worship, resulting in praise. Those "that fear him, both small and great" are to praise God (Rev 19:5). David says, "But as for me, I will come *into* thy house in the multitude of thy mercy: *and* <u>in thy fear will I worship</u>" (Ps 5:7). Let us investigate what is it to worship God in his fear.

Psalm 34 is the greatest passage on the fear of God.[136] Yet at the same time, in it we see the most exultant spirit of praise and worship. This whole psalm is dedicated to teaching God's children the fear of God, yet how does it open? "I will <u>bless</u> the LORD at all times: his <u>praise</u> *shall* continually *be* in my mouth. My soul shall make her <u>boast</u> in the LORD: the humble shall hear *thereof*, and <u>be glad</u>." Ps 34:1-2 David's heart was overwhelmed with thanksgiving and joy for God's great deliverance. As a result, his heart exploded into praise and adoration of the LORD. This event in David's life, when he was brought before Abimelech king of the Philistines and miraculously delivered, was when David's fear of the LORD was restored. As David saw afresh the great blessing of the

---

[136] It is *the* psalm that teaches us the fear of God. Hence, it references it directly three times (Ps 34:7,9,11).

fear of the LORD, he therefore desired to teach all of us how to fear God and how to recapture it if we have lost it.

> **WARNING**: Christianity always tries to skip steps with the Lord, but we cannot skip steps in the kingdom of God. Christianity goes from altar calls to faith, right to salvation, but the way of the kingdom of God is from the preaching of the word of God to repentance and faith unto salvation. Repentance is always either altered from what it is or skipped. Similarly, Christianity goes from believing in Christ as their Saviour right into being a servant and from that into leadership, but the way of the kingdom is being born again by making Jesus Lord of our life, and then coming into discipleship to learn God's ways, so that we will know how to serve God according to his ways. Leadership only comes as God calls, not as men desire. Lordship and discipleship are completely skipped. So it is with praise and worship. Christianity goes from forgiveness to thanksgiving and praise without ever passing through the fear of God. Yet fearing the LORD, as David shows, should be our first response to his abundant and unmerited provision of mercies.

In David's life it was repeatedly the multitude of God's mercies that brought about firstly the fear of God and secondly a spirit of worship. So David says elsewhere, "If thou, LORD, shouldest mark iniquities, O Lord, who shall stand? But *there is* forgiveness with thee, that thou mayest be feared." Ps 130:3-4 Without God's forgiveness we could not fear him. Isn't this amazing! So many teachers with their natural understanding and thinking teach we should *not* fear God because of the covenant of grace, by which we have the forgiveness of sins. But David exclaims exactly the opposite. It is *because* God forgives, that we ought to fear him.

The true fear of God is thus rooted in the goodness of God in choosing to forgive us. Such fear will always produce overflowing thankfulness and a heart of worship and service. This is why the fear of God cannot be put away by the establishment of the new covenant and the overflowing of God's forgiveness towards man in Christ. The new covenant, in fact, will establish the fear of the Lord in men's heart in utter gratitude of God's great goodness. So it was prophesied, "Afterward shall the children of Israel return, and seek the LORD their God, and David their king; and shall fear the LORD and his goodness in the latter days." Hos 3:5 We ought to be a living spiritual fulfillment of that promise, friend.

The Test of Worship
"in thy fear will I worship" Ps 5:7

The fear of the LORD will lead us to worship the LORD in greater intimacy and depth of openness. In learning how to give unto the LORD through his fear, we will find his ultimate desire is for the very depth of our heart to be given to him. As we have seen already, he must begin first with what our heart is set on – especially our possessions and resources. Next, he will require our time. So we find the fear of the LORD will teach us how to give and then how to give of ourselves in humble, faithful service. The more the fear of the LORD teaches us how to worship our God, the narrower the way of our life becomes, for he demands more and more of us as his obedient sons and daughters. Ultimately, our Master requires the essence of our heart – our hopes, desires, and dreams. Before we look at brokenness, first let us look at how our worship will be tested by God himself, just as it was with Abraham.

If we truly fear God, then we will worship him, both outwardly and inwardly. We will first look at our worship which is outwardly. After that we will look at that worship which is inward and which results from the brokenness that God will lead us into. Our outward worship ought to be freely and openly given without hindrance, for the man that fears God has nothing to fear from man. He cares nothing for man's acceptance or rejection. Thus, the fear of the LORD in this respect can be measured by the depth and breadth of our worship – especially in the presence of others. Such outward worship must be freely forthcoming from us if we truly fear God. We will not be reticent to bow down before God or sing songs from our heart to him, regardless of whether others are watching or not. If we cannot worship with the freedom that is contained in the pages of scripture, then we are still bound up in the traditions of men, in religion, and in looking at ourselves.

Rather, we are to be caught up in the Spirit of God with a heart that has been prepared and rent asunder by his fear. The spontaneity of our worship resulting from our fear of him will be like a flowing fountain. "The fear of the LORD *is* a fountain of life, to depart from the snares of death." Pr 14:27 One of the most insidious snares of death that we must be delivered from is the snare of a religious spirit, a spirit which cannot freely worship its Creator. A religious spirit truly brings death, but the fear of the LORD will cause us to turn away from its 'noose'.

The Fear of the LORD Births New Songs

One amazing way that the fear of God enables us to escape a religious spirit is by the singing of new songs. The Bible reveals that new songs are birthed in our heart by his fear. Thus, no new songs, no fear of God. Let us investigate this. Nine times in the scripture it speaks of singing a new song unto the LORD, yet many believers will have nothing to do with them. All the earth is invited to sing a new song unto him. "O sing unto the LORD a new song: sing unto the

LORD, <u>all the earth</u>." Ps 96:1 We are specifically to sing these new songs, which are his praise, "in the congregation of the saints" (Ps 149:1).[137]

> **WARNING**: Do not misunderstand. We are *never* to be defiant or rebellious and to sing out our new song in the midst of the service if that is not permitted or according to the due order of a house of God, for all things must "be done decently and in order." 1Co 14:40 No, that would bring confusion and would be violating authority. We cannot take things into our own hands to *force* them to happen. The real questions are: (1) "Are you <u>willing</u> and <u>eager</u> to sing new songs when God puts them into your heart?" For we are called to be willing and obedient (Isa 1:19). (2) "Why is your congregation *not* free to sing new songs, when scripture shows it should be a part of our praise unto God?" Are they holding fast to the word of God only, or have the traditions of men made the word of God of none effect?

David says that God will put a new song into our mouth and that when we sing, it will cause others to fear. "And he hath put a new song in my mouth, *even* praise unto our God: many shall see *it*, and fear, and shall trust in the LORD." Ps 40:3 Thus, such songs must truly be birthed *out* of a heart of fearing God, for only the fear of God will beget the fear of God! Remember, every seed bears fruit after its own kind. Only the fear of God in us will birth it in others.

Why would new songs birth fear in others? Because songs that truly come from the heart of God will always magnify God's power, might, and glory. Man's songs ultimately glorify man (which is the problem with much 'Christian' music), but God's songs will glorify God. We have seen God desires to see the fear of God in our hearts, even more than Satan wants to remove it. Hence, the songs of the LORD bring us for that moment into the presence of God and his holiness, and it is the holiness of God that inspires us to fear him. The fear of God will birth new songs within us. So we must ask, "Are we singing the new songs he puts in our mouth through the fear of God? Or are new songs not being put in our mouth because we lack the source, the fear of God?"

The Lifting up of our Heads and Hands in Worship

God is indeed still testing us to see who or what we fear. Can we not lift our heads and our hands before him in public worship, adoration, and thanksgiving according to the scriptures? Can we not openly praise him and acknowledge our amens? For this is what we see in scripture when God was moving among his people:

---

[137] The New Testament declares this is 'the church'. Compare Heb 2:12 with its original quote Ps 22:22. Notice that 'congregation' is made equivalent to 'church'.

> Ezra blessed the LORD, the great God. And all the people answered, Amen, Amen, with lifting up their hands: & they bowed their heads, & worshipped the LORD with *their* faces to the ground. Neh 8:6

Throughout scripture we are exhorted, "Lift up your hands *in* the sanctuary, and bless the LORD." Ps 134:2 Paul commands men everywhere to pray "lifting up holy hands" (1Tim 2:8). In America, people pray almost exclusively with heads bowed down and eyes closed, yet this is not the only way the godly were to pray. Prayer was often with eyes open and heads lifted up unto heaven, from which cometh our help. "My voice shalt thou hear in the morning, O LORD; in the morning will I direct *my prayer* unto thee, and will look up." Ps 5:3 Jesus himself is seen praying with eyes open and looking up unto heaven (Mk 6:41). If there are any people who should pray with eyes open and heads lifted up to heaven, it is us of the new covenant. As it was spoken by Jesus himself, "look up, and lift up your heads; for your redemption draweth nigh." Lk 21:28 How often do those who call upon the name of Christ pray with their bodies bowed down to lay outstretched before him? Yet Muslims, who do not even know the true Jesus or the Father God, pray in such a manner regularly. And the scriptures reprove us for this. The Bible repeatedly shows those who bow down their body before God in true humility and worship.

WARNING: Praying with our eyes open looking to heaven, praising God with our hands raised, and worshipping God outstretched on the ground are only *expressions* of our intimate communion with the LORD. They cannot be made into formulae, which we do at set times during each "worship" service. This is what dead religions do (i.e. stand up, sit down, kneel, bow, rise, etc.). If they are practiced and repeated as part of a program, then they are dead, and there is no life in them. Why? For there is no *life* in the form.[138] The life is in the expressing of our heart toward God. The form must express our heart.

Introducing these new forms is good only as far as breaking the molds of religious tradition. The real problem is cultural norms will often cast into concrete a religious form of what prayer is – such as the bowing of our head and the closing of our eyes – and we begin to think that this is particularly humble prayer! Consider the absurdity of this in the natural. We would never think of trying to use just one tool to fix every problem, nor would we try to use one word or even one sentence to communicate all we need to say. But, when it comes to prayer, we restrict ourselves to only one of the many ways God has given us, because its 'look'. Let us fear God and avoid the snares of religiosity.

---

[138] We are not alive because we have a body. We are alive because we have a spirit. So James says, "For as the body without the spirit is dead, so faith without works is dead also." Jam 2:26 Our worship and our prayer are dead unless (1) our spirit is alive through the new birth and (2) our spirit is actively involved, by listening and responding to God's Spirit, the Spirit of life (Rom 8:2,10, Rev 11:11).

8 – The Root of Worship and Fruit of Giving

Praising Him in the Dance

We could speak of many other areas where a lack of true worship is seen and that demonstrate the absence of the fear of God, but let us deal with just one more, as a particularly pertinent example. The Bible declares that we are to praise him in the dance (Ps 149:3, 150:4). So we see "David danced before the LORD with all his might" (2Sam 6:14). How did David do this? By leaping and dancing before the LORD (v16). If we cannot openly dance before the LORD, then it is evidence that we are bound up by our fear of man, of what others may think, rather than being caught up in the fear of our God. The Bible says there is a time to dance (Ecc 3:4). Do you know the time to dance unto God? Is dancing only for worldly pleasure? Or should there be a time to dance before God in this life to bring *him* pleasure? Yes, but not for those who are bound up by the snares of religion.

Isn't it amazing, David and Michal were a loving husband and wife UNTIL he danced before the LORD! "But as then he that was born after the flesh [i.e. in our case, Michal] persecuted him *that was born* after the Spirit [i.e. in our case, David], <u>even so *it is* now</u>." Gal 4:29 The fruit of David's fear of God, which was born of the Spirit, and the essence of his worship before God, was his dancing before the LORD. This singular event, his dancing publicly before God, became the very thing that caused her to despise her own husband (2Sam 6:16), speak evilly and disrespectfully of him as a king (v20)! These actions revealed the complete lack of the fear of God in her own heart! David's fear of God manifested in his dancing openly before the LORD in the presence of all his people. Yet this same act was what *exposed* his wife's lack of fearing God.

David was able to fully express his heart of worship toward the LORD without being concerned what others thought, because of this one thing: his fear of God. It is the fear of God that sets a person free from the fear of man. Michal would not dance before the LORD. She was too concerned with what even the least slave would think. She looked to "the eyes of the handmaids of his servants" (v20), but not to the eyes of the Lord GOD Almighty, of what he thought about this. Truly, so many peoples' eyes today are on what those around them might see, rather than on pleasing God.[139] The fear of God completely changes the focus of our eyes. We no longer are focused on what others will think about what we do for the LORD, rather, our primary concern is what will the LORD think.

Why Will We Not Dance Joyfully Before Our King and Deliverer?

---

[139] It is this hypocrisy, which children growing up in Christian households see, that often causes such teenagers to take the opposite extreme. Thus, they do *whatever* pleases themselves, with no thought of what God will think, because this is what they have been taught by example through the lack of the fear of God.

Let us look closer at why would Michal not dance? Why did she despise David in her heart for what he did before the LORD? Why did she judge him and belittle his act of joyful worship? Because of this one thing, she had no fear of God. So when we see no spiritual dancing or spiritual songs coming from the saints in the house of God, when we see it limited only to some private home cell groups and not in the corporate setting, when we see it forbidden and reproved as Michal did, then we know there is no fear of God in that place.

People will dance at weddings and joyous occasions. They will dance in exultation when their soldiers come home successful in battle. But why will so many of God's people not dance before him today, in anticipation of that great wedding feast that is to come? Why will we not dance together in the house of God for his great victory, which he has already won for us? "He hath done marvellous things: his right hand, and his holy arm, hath gotten him the victory." Ps 98:1 Why do we not dance for joy when one sinner who was lost is found – like the rejoicing that takes place in heaven (Lk 15:5-10)? Was there not music *and* dancing when the lost son returned home (Lk 15:23-25)? Is this not a picture of the heavenly Father's house (i.e. of the house of God)?

Truly today, we *owe* God his victory dances; we have **robbed** God in this. We have a greater victory than any earthly general has ever won. "For whatsoever is born of God overcometh the world: and this is the victory that overcometh the world, *even* our faith." 1Jn 5:4 Earthly generals have overcome armies and nations, but through the captain of the LORD of hosts, we have overcome the world. "But thanks *be* to God, which giveth us the victory through our Lord Jesus Christ." 1Co 15:57 If we have such victories as these, then why do we *not* have the joyful dancing which is their proper fruit? Is the problem so few are willing to dance before their God a problem of giving?

The Essence of Worship: Giving

"Give unto the LORD the glory due unto his name;
worship the LORD in the beauty of holiness." Ps 29:2

It is impossible to worship in truth without giving, for the heart of worship is the heart of giving. So it is established that God's people are to worship him in their giving. "And now, behold, I have brought the firstfruits of the land, which thou, O LORD, hast given me. And thou shalt set it before the LORD thy God, and worship before the LORD thy God" (Dt 26:10). In worship we are to give unto the LORD. We are to give both of what we have and of our selves. This is why we bring our offerings to the Lord, but we also bring our selves. When we give with a right heart what he desires, then we give glory to the LORD. We give the firstfruits of the increase of our goods, but we also give our hearts as the altar where his feet may freely tread.

8 – The Root of Worship and Fruit of Giving

Giving Glory to God

While we are here, let us spend a moment to show the difference between giving God glory and worshipping him, for we are called to do both. We think 'to give God glory' is only to worship him, for we think the glory he is looking for *is* our worship. Certainly, to give God glory *is* to worship him, but it is to worship him in spirit and in truth. This goes far beyond musical worship. The real glory he is looking for is our willing obedience, offered up from a thankful and sacrificial heart, because of his mercies. "I beseech you therefore, brethren, by the <u>mercies of God</u>, that ye present **your bodies** a living sacrifice, holy, <u>acceptable unto God</u>, *which is* your reasonable service [i.e. *worship*]." Rom 12:1

From the beginning, 'to give God the glory' was to obey God and to confess the truth. The first time we ever see the phrase "give, I pray thee, glory to the LORD God" (Jos 7:19), it is an exhortation from Joshua to Achan to acknowledge the *truth* about what he had done. This goes hand in hand with what Jeremiah shows us, which is that to "give glory to the LORD your God" is to humble yourself and to hear what the LORD has to say.

> <u>Hear ye</u>, and <u>give ear</u>; <u>be not proud</u>: for the LORD hath spoken. <u>Give glory</u> to the LORD your God, before he cause darkness, and before your feet stumble upon the dark mountains, and, while ye look for light, he turn it into the shadow of death, *and* make *it* gross darkness. Jer 13:15-16

O that we would give him the glory he is looking for today, the glory of truth and obedience! How shallow is the glory we often give him compared to what he is due. We may give him songs and shouts of joy, but he is looking for us not to be proud and to hear what he has to say to us. These are the sacrifices of praise he is looking for.

As it was in Jesus' day so it still is today. Ten lepers left Jesus' presence. Ten lepers were healed on the way according to his word. Ten lepers rejoiced in being healed and gave their glory to God by the lifting of their voices to him. Yet only one returned and truly gave glory to God. "And Jesus answering said, Were there not ten cleansed? but where *are* the nine? There are not found that <u>returned to give glory to God</u>, save this stranger." Lk 17:18 According to Jesus, glory to God was *not* given by the nine who lifted their voices to God, but only by the one. Why? Because the one returned (speaking of repentance) in thanksgiving to bow before the Lord (speaking of coming under Jesus' lordship). This is the essence of repentance: to return to God. And this is the glory he is looking for: returning to him and acknowledging his authority in our life.

Many give glory to God in their praises, but because they lack the fear of God, their hearts are far from him. They do not return to thank the Lord their supplier with their life bowed before his feet, ready to receive his instructions. All our sorrow and asking of forgiveness is to no avail ultimately, if we have not returned to the Lord to give him the liberty to instruct and oversee our life. "For ye were as sheep going astray; but are now <u>returned</u> unto the Shepherd and Bishop of your souls." 1Pe 2:25 We must return not only to the Shepherd who will lead us, but also to the Bishop who will correct us and take oversight to our life. If we are still the one making the decisions and setting the direction of our life, then repentance toward God has not taken place, and we are still languishing spiritually. This is the preeminent focal point: Jesus must be Lord *in* and *of* our heart. The fear of God is what prepares our heart and mind for our control to die and his lordship to arise in us.

Glory and True Worship

The fear of the LORD indeed paves the way for true worship to be given to God Almighty. This cry is heard both in Psalms and in Revelation, so that the heights of praise here on earth as well as in heaven echo with the fear of the LORD producing the praises of God.

> <u>Ye that fear the LORD</u>, <u>praise him</u>; all ye the seed of Jacob, <u>glorify him</u>; <u>and fear him</u>, all ye the seed of Israel. My praise *shall be* of thee in the great congregation: I will pay my vows before them <u>that fear him</u>. Ps 22:23,25

> <u>Fear God, and give glory to him</u>; for the hour of his judgment is come: <u>and worship him</u> that made heaven, and earth, and the sea, and the fountains of waters. Rev 14:7

> Who shall not <u>fear thee</u>, O Lord, <u>and glorify thy name</u>? for *thou* only *art* holy: for all nations shall come and worship before thee; for thy judgments are made manifest. Rev 15:4

WARNING: Praise and worship by God's divine right belong to God and God only. Today, in the last days, praise and worship have been merchandized, subsidized, mass produced, secularized, and prostituted. There was a day when the great music of the age was made for the praise of God, and secular artists tried to emulate their quality and depth of meaning by copying what the great composers had created.

Now it is reversed. So many Christian artists, instead of coming out from among the world and being separate (as God commands), have idolized and admired the ungodly music of the world. Hence, they *purposely* and *boastfully* emulate what unsaved worldly men and women do. They believe copying what the world does is to their *credit* when from God's perspective it is to their *shame*.

Hear the heart of David, in contrast, who will have nothing to do with those who hate God. "I will set no wicked thing before mine eyes: I **hate** the work of them that turn aside; <u>it shall not cleave to me</u>." Ps 101:3 Interestingly enough, this word in Hebrew for 'hate' means 'to hate personally'. Rather than

8 – The Root of Worship and Fruit of Giving

loving the music of this world, we ought to personally hate the work of those who turn away from God, as far as it concerns ever being desired and admired in our heart. We may acknowledge that something is skillfully done by those of the world, but let us never desire it in our heart or allow our heart to envy the works of the children of wrath (Ps 37:1). Rather, let us dedicate our own hearts to excellence for the sake of our God.[140]

Instead of the saved pointing the lost to the Lord GOD and being led by the Holy Ghost (as God meant it to be), 'Christian' musicians are trying to entice people using Satan's methods and being unknowingly led by the spirit of this world! The praise and worship that is bought and sold, no longer serve as pure offerings unto God. If you truly listen to the lyrics of so much 'Christian music' today, you will not hear the glorification and exaltation of God Almighty and the demotion and humiliation of man, you will instead hear the reverse. You will hear the exaltation of the artists[141] and the demotion of Almighty God. The Lord is made to become our servant, instead of us being his servant.[142]

The Source of Worship: Does it Arise from the Fear of God?

We are called regularly to examine ourselves to see if we are still in the faith (i.e. walking according to the truth of the word of God).[143] Examine your own experiences and think back with the following Biblical tests to see how authentic, according to the pattern of the word of God, are the praise and worship you have been experiencing.

1. How often listening to modern 'Christian music' have you been brought to the place where according to Psalm 5:7 **in fear** you have worshipped the Lord?

2. When is the last time in a worship service or in a Christian concert you have, according to Psalm 2:11, **'rejoiced with trembling'**? [Probably never!]

3. How often watching 'Christian TV' or listening to 'Christian radio' have you experienced according to Exodus 15:11 'him that is **fearful *in* praises**'?

---

[140] Sadly, it is because of the "prosperity of the wicked" that such envy arises (Ps 73:3), which truly shows that our eyes have been taken off of the greater spiritual reward that is set before us for being faithful to the Lord.

[141] This is evidenced by how self-centered (instead of God-centered), need-oriented ("give me", "I want"), pleasure-seeking, and experience-focused (rather than truth-focused) songs there are. God and his greatness are no longer the focus. Performers and their desires and feelings and flamboyant talents now take center stage.

[142] Yes, the Lord did come as a servant and did serve us as an example for how we should live, but he is not our servant, he is our King! As Jesus himself said, "Ye call me Master and Lord: and ye say well; for so I am." Jn 13:13

[143] We are called to examine ourselves: Ps 26:2, 1Co 9:3, 11:28, 2Co 13:5.

> **WARNING**: Understand, none of these tests have to do with the fear of condemnation because of sin! None of these have to do with the fear of judgment because of a guilty conscience and secret sin. None of these have to do with the fear of losing our salvation because of falling in the same sin again and again. No, these are the true fear of God that result from encountering the living God who is "glorious in holiness and fearful *in* praises".

Why are 'worshipping God in fear' and 'rejoicing before him with trembling' so lacking in our experience? Why do they seem so foreign and strange to us, to almost be thought out of place, like ancient anachronisms? Because the fear of God has been surgically removed from our midsts. It has been subtly stolen by a deceptive thief who knows his true enemy. The LORD who is "glorious in holiness, [*and*] fearful *in* praises" has been skillfully and deliberately removed from our music, our worship, and our hearts by the adversary of our souls, Satan. Christian music has been so twisted from truly being a sacrifice of praise given to the Holy One for his pleasure, not ours! Hence, it is no longer *for* him or *unto* him, for whom it is due. Rather, it has become for *our* enjoyment and entertainment – that which it was never created for!

This is, of course, why Christian music sells so much, is it not? In years past, the main thing sold in Christian bookstores was Bibles and books explaining and teaching on the Bible. Now, the greatest section of nearly every Christian bookstore is devoted and given over to music – some music of which I am sure the Spirit of God will on that day reveal was not Christian music at all, but demonically inspired and sacrificed unto.

The Fruit of Worship: A Giving Spirit

"Vow, and pay unto the LORD your God: let all that be round about him bring presents unto him that ought to be feared." Ps 76:11

True worship cannot be separated from sacrificial giving. We see that the fear of the LORD produces worship, and all worship involves the act of giving. So we should expect also to see an intimate intertwining between the fear of the LORD and giving. In deed, the fruit or offspring of the fear of the LORD is giving. We see this in the sailors who feared God after throwing Jonah overboard and seeing the sea cease from its roaring. "Then the men feared the LORD exceedingly, and offered a sacrifice unto the LORD, and made vows." Jnh 1:16

Once the fear of God was restored in Jonah's heart and he stopped running from God, he immediately also brought forth the sacrifice of thanksgiving and the paying of vows to God. "But I will sacrifice unto thee with the voice of thanksgiving; I will pay *that* that I have vowed. Salvation *is* of the LORD." Jnh 2:9 Notice how the first fruit of worship is a sacrificial spirit of giving, and the

8 – The Root of Worship and Fruit of Giving

second is the making of vows to serve God. "My praise *shall be* of thee in the great congregation: I will <u>pay my vows</u> before them that fear him." Ps 22:25

The fear of the LORD leads to praising him and glorifying him, which in turn brings forth the paying of our vows before his people. This was the same process God desired to have birthed into the Exodus people. "But the LORD, who brought you up out of the land of Egypt with great power and a stretched out arm, him shall ye <u>fear</u>, and him shall ye <u>worship</u>, and to him shall ye <u>do sacrifice</u>." 2K 17:36 This is why covetousness is the enemy of the fear of God, and a sure sign that the fear of God is absent.[144] Our pure and willing worship, and the fear of God that they stem from, are so important to God that he shared with those who were about to enter God's promised land, how to maintain the fear of the LORD in their hearts. How? By faithfully giving unto the LORD.

> Thou shalt <u>truly tithe all the increase</u> of thy seed, that the field bringeth forth year by year. And thou shalt eat before the LORD thy God, in the place which he shall choose to place his name there, the tithe of thy corn, of thy wine, and of thine oil, and the firstlings of thy herds and of thy flocks; <u>that thou mayest learn to fear the LORD thy God always</u>. Dt 14:22-23

Where Shall We Give? A Place which He shall Choose

Deuteronomy 14:22-23 speaks much to us today, concerning both our worship and our fear of God. God desires us to commune with him in the house of God as we give our selves to him. Verse 23 shows us three ways that we will learn the fear of God. These are simple things, but at the very root of producing real change in our heart.

1. by being joined to the local house of God in committing our heart there,
2. through eating [i.e. getting our sustenance] before the LORD,[145] and
3. by the commitment of faithfully giving of our resources there.

Notice first there is a place of worship "which he shall choose". We must allow God to lead us to a house of God where he has put his name (i.e. his *honor*, *authority*, and *character*). It is the place of his choosing, not ours. So many seek a church which they like, based on their own criteria, but God says it is *his* prerogative to choose, not ours. That way when God begins to deal with our stubbornness or disobedience or character, and we no longer like or enjoy the place we are in, we will remain because we know **God** has chosen it for us.

---

[144] Covetousness and the other enemies of the fear of God are discussed in the chapter entitled "Warning Signs of Losing God's Fear".

[145] This is both in fellowshipping with the saints and with the LORD around spiritual and natural food.

Without this, we will never be able to be rooted, grounded, and planted in a local house of God to grow up and mature through trials and correction.

> **WARNING**: Many look for a large church believing that because it is quickly growing it must be 'alive'. But consider, since God likens the church to a body, the *fastest* growing and multiplying cells are **never** the healthiest. We have a special name for such rapidly multiplying cells. They are called cancer. Many times the 'fastest growing' and largest churches have given rise to the most cancerous doctrines that have flooded Christianity. Does the person diagnosed with cancer boast in it, that is, that their cancer is killing them faster than anyone else? Or do they seek at all costs to rid themselves of the cancer? Maybe some large church pastors should truly reconsider their boasting of being the 'fastest growing' church in their region! Remember, if the growth were *truly* of the Lord, and not of men, no man would be able to boast of what they have done.

God will also test our heart concerning whether we regularly give of our substance to the work of the Lord – especially when we are being corrected! We must learn to give unto the Lord's work, as giving unto God and not men. Tithing is our vow to God to entrust our life and livelihood to his care and provision (Gen 28:20), and we are called to fulfill our vows. "Vow, and pay unto the LORD your God: let all that be round about him bring presents unto him that ought to be feared." Ps 76:11 If we fear God we will fulfill our vows to him. "I will pay my vows before them that fear him." Ps 22:25 The men on board the ship with Jonah feared God greatly when they beheld the wonder of his power over the seas. In them we have seen the first fruits of the fear of God in that they "offered a sacrifice unto the LORD, and made vows." Jnh 1:16 So we have seen, giving teaches us how to continue in the fear of God (Dt 14:22-23).

The Heart of Fear, A Heart to Give

"Blessed is the man that feareth the LORD, ...
he is gracious, and full of compassion, and righteous. ...
[he] sheweth favour, and lendeth" Ps 112:1,4-5

Giving is so intimately associated with the fear of the LORD, that God established the tithe not for Himself or for his need, but for our need to learn how to fear him. As we learn to give of our tithe unto God and to fellowship with him in our giving, we learn to fear the LORD always. We see an extended description of the man that fears God in Psalm 112, and at its very center it shows his giving character. This psalm begins, "Praise ye the LORD. Blessed *is* the man *that* feareth the LORD, *that* delighteth greatly in his commandments." Ps 112:1 The psalm continues by describing what will happen to such a man, i.e. how he will be blessed (vv2-4a). Then it looks at his character (v4b): "*he is* gracious, and full of compassion, and righteous." Now in verse 5 we see for the first time

8 – The Root of Worship and Fruit of Giving

what this man will do. Out of all things that could be mentioned the first, and therefore the foremost in priority, that God wants to set before our eyes it is the following:

> A good man sheweth favour, & lendeth: he will guide his affairs with discretion. He hath dispersed, he hath given to the poor Ps 112:5,9

The man that fears God will be one who shows favor to others and who gives to the poor and needy. We have already seen he will be one who gives to God, and now the circle is complete, he will also give to those in need. The fear of the LORD produces a giving heart all the way around. It is impossible to keep the fear of God in our heart without learning how to give unto Jehovah-jireh, the LORD our supplier. Covetousness in fact always involves hiding. When we keep for ourselves what we know in our heart belongs to another, we begin to live a secretive life of hiding from both God and man. By being obedient to God's command to tithe on the firstfruits of our increase, we are learning one of the ways how to fear God.

WARNING: Giving by itself does not produce the fear of God, as Cain, Nadab & Abihu, and Ananias & Sapphira, all so tragically demonstrate. It is *how* we give that determines the result. Our giving, even though designed to teach us the fear of God, must itself be done with a desire to fear God. We must honor God in our giving with fear.

Cain gave to God, but it was unacceptable for it was not given in the fear of God. Cain merely gave <u>of the fruit</u>, but Abel brought <u>the firstlings</u>, meaning he gave the first fruits (Gen 4:3-4). How can we know that the fear of God was lacking in Cain's offering, but present in Abel's? By their actions of course, but also by the requirements of the word of God. Hear what is written: "Be not wise in thine own eyes: <u>fear the LORD</u>, and depart from evil. <u>Honour the LORD</u> with thy substance, and <u>with the firstfruits</u> of all thine increase" (Pr 3:7,9).

Nadab and Abihu brought their gifts before God, but neither were they received; for among other things, they had not "put difference between holy and unholy, and between unclean and clean" (Lev 10:10). They clearly lacked the fear of God for "the fear of the LORD *is* the beginning of wisdom: and the knowledge of the holy *is* understanding." Pr 9:10 The result was they died. Ananias and Sapphira also offered their gift unto God. It similarly cost them their life for they, as well, lacked the fear of God by lying to God (Ac 5:4).

Giving refocuses our attention on the one we are giving to, rather than on our selves. This is why giving unto others brings care and love, and giving unto the LORD leads to worship. The fear of God thus teaches us how not to be covetous. By hearing his Word, by responding to give of our belongings back unto the LORD, and fellowshipping with him in the bringing of our tithe to him, we will learn to fear him. Giving is a holy thing unto God, and we must not dishonour him in it. This is why giving should teach us to fear him, but it depends on *how* we come before him in our giving.

The Test of Our Giving: How We Give

Our giving unto God is to have nothing to do with men or what they do. It is rooted in the awesome greatness of God, who is worthy to be feared. The reason why God commanded his people to give of the firstfruits of their substance to his servants was that they would learn to fear the LORD God always (Dt 14:23). Our continued giving to the LORD causes us, both in times of blessing and in times of lack, to keep our fear of God. When we are blessed or 'full' it is easy to forget the LORD and to deny him. When we are in poverty or 'empty' it is easy to be tempted to unbelief and to steal (Pr 30:8-9).

The fear of God, the worship of God, and the giving of gifts and sacrifices unto him are all closely related. "But the LORD, who brought you up out of the land of Egypt with great power and a stretched out arm, him shall ye <u>fear</u>, and him shall ye <u>worship</u>, and to him shall ye <u>do sacrifice</u>." 2K 17:36 Our heart must begin to find its life no longer in the world but in the kingdom of God, around his people and supporting his work. When we learn to fellowship in giving to God for the increase and expanse of his work, our heart will learn how to fear him. We have seen how God states that all who truly know him and submit to him will both fear him and glorify his name (Rev 14:7, 15:4).

So we see the same way we are to learn to fear God is the same way we are to give him glory. Notice in this next scripture that we give glory to God by (1) coming before him, (2) worshipping him, and (3) bringing an offering. This is what it is to fear God and to give him glory.

> Give unto the LORD, ye kindreds of the people, give unto the LORD glory and strength. Give unto the LORD the glory *due* unto his name: [3] bring an offering, and [1] come before him: [2] worship the LORD in the beauty of holiness. Fear before him … 1Ch 16:28-30

His name is glorified not by merely singing the praises of his greatness, but rather by the manifold worship that comes from our changed lives. The fear of God is to produce change in our life and that change will reflect a life of worship, of bowing down to his authority, willingly serving him, and faithfully obeying him. The change in our life of being conformed to the glorious image of his Son is what glorifies his name.

Conclusions on the Root of Worship & the Fruit of Giving

We have looked at the intimate marriage of obedience and fear, and how neither is complete without the other. God is not satisfied with obedience that is done without his fear. And fear that does not produce wholehearted obedi-

8 – The Root of Worship and Fruit of Giving

ence is weak and incomplete. For the fear of the LORD to be growing in us we need to add to it wholehearted obedience. Just as it takes the intimacy of a husband and a wife to bring forth the fruit of holy offspring, so it takes the joining of the fear of God and obedience to produce life in the realm of the spirit.

When the fear of God is mixed with obedience it produces the safe haven or 'home' of faithfulness. Just like the good home that results from a man and woman living together in covenant, so the spiritual life that springs up in our heart from the faithful joining of fear and obedience enables the fruit or offspring from that spiritual joining to grow up and mature safely within our heart.

The spiritual life that springs from the faithfulness of the fear of God will manifest in true worship and in giving God glory. The glory that God has always desired is our returning in repentance unto him and bowing our life at his feet to come under his authority. Like the one leper who returned and fell at Jesus' feet, so we should give glory to the LORD through the fear of God. The fear of God will greatly affect how we give unto the LORD, and so we shall see how greatly the fear of God will be put to the test in our life.

Chapter 9. The Way of Brokenness and God's Fear
The Narrow Way of the Kingdom

"Better is little with the fear of the LORD than great treasure and trouble therewith." Pr 15:16

If we truly fear God, then we will worship him, both outwardly and inwardly. We have looked already at our worship which is outwardly. Now let us look at that worship which is inward and which results from the brokenness that God will lead us into. Brokenness cannot but lead us to the altar of worship, where we pour out our very will and submit to God's will. There is no greater worship than this, that a man lay down his life for his King.

9 – The Way of Brokenness and God's Fear

Looking at our Inward Worship and the Fear of God

As we continue to walk with the LORD in the fear of God, he desires to increase the depth of our worship. We need to be set free in our outward worship, but even more we need to be set free in our inward worship of the LORD. So, like Abraham (the father of faith), God will bring his children into the place where their own heart and what they most treasure must be sacrificed on the altar of worship. Only this allows the preciousness of the life, which has begun to grow under his tender hand, to be released back unto him. To bring forth this precious fruit of God's fear, many times the vessel must be broken. This can best be seen by an example in Jesus' life.

There was a woman who came to Jesus who had "an alabaster box of ointment of spikenard very precious" (Mk 14:3). She had saved this precious vessel of a costly ointment, but to release it the vessel needed to be broken, and so, "she brake the box, and poured *it* on his head." So it is with those who serve God in the fear of the LORD. A precious gift lies within the alabaster box of their heart, but their heart must be broken and poured out upon the Master. When we fear God and walk before him, the path he will always leads us to is the way of brokenness. This is the narrow way of the kingdom, which Jesus promised to all who would become his disciples and follow in his footsteps.

The Narrow Way of Brokenness
"And whosoever shall fall on this stone shall be broken" Mt 21:44

In the "bless me" doctrines of modern Christianity, the purpose of brokenness for the saint of God has no place. It has been abandoned for an 'easier' gospel where the saint is never to fear and never to be in lack. So many wonderful blessings are associated with fearing God, yet we find the condition of those who fear God all too often to be one, not of blissful immunity to the troubles of life, but the total opposite. Those who fear God greatly are often in great straits and sorrowful troubles. Hear the cry of the woman who came unto Elisha. She was the wife of a disciple of Elisha, a son of the prophets. Her husband was a godly man being trained in the ways of God. He also had a servant's heart to minister unto Elisha. He also feared the LORD, yet what was left for his dear wife when he died? The creditor was coming to take her two sons to be slaves!

> Now there cried a certain woman of the wives of the sons of the prophets unto Elisha, saying, Thy servant my husband is dead; and thou knowest that <u>thy servant did fear the LORD</u>: and the creditor is come to take unto him my two sons to be bondmen. 2K 4:1

The more we love God, the quicker we are brought to the way of brokenness. God cannot use, nor be close in intimate fellowship with, whom he cannot break. It is only in breaking his vessels that the preciousness of what he has put within us will be released. No brokenness, no outpouring. Jesus himself expects each of us to follow him in this narrow way of brokenness, for he himself was broken for us, and he is the way. Jesus promised, if we trust in him and lay our life down, we *will* be broken. "And whosoever shall fall on this stone shall be broken" (Mt 21:44). We must be willing to fall upon this stone.

We all wish that broken-heartedness and contrition in spirit could come solely through a heart of worship and our response to the gentle conviction of the Spirit. But so often the free outpouring of our worship toward the LORD is stopped up, whether by tradition, by the fear of man, or by the many masks of pride. When we study the great men of God recorded in the scriptures we see, though worship is always involved, brokenness did not come through praise and worship only. God uses both indirect and direct means. He uses troubles and afflictions to break our heart.

David now brings us in our understanding of God's fear to the way of brokenness. Thus, when David is ready to teach us God's fear, he speaks of being broken hearted and contrite in spirit and being in many afflictions and troubles.

> *The righteous* cry, and the LORD heareth, and delivereth them out of all their troubles. The LORD *is* nigh unto them that are of a broken heart; and saveth such as be of a contrite spirit. Many are the afflictions of the righteous: but the LORD delivereth him out of them all. Ps 34:17-19

The word of God speaks much of brokenness, but the words of men are often all too silent on such things. Psalm 38 is wholly dedicated to teaching us about the brokenness that results both from our enemies as well as from God's anger. The importance of brokenness to David is evidenced in that he writes Psalm 38 specifically to commemorate his sufferings and afflictions. Thus, it is entitled. "A Psalm of David, to bring to remembrance. O LORD, rebuke me not in thy wrath: neither chasten me in thy hot displeasure." Ps 38:1 We must never forget the chastenings of the Lord which bring us to brokenness.

The Crushing Loneliness of Brokenness

The beauty of brokenness, as revealed in the center of this psalm, is that brokenness breaks our pride, stubbornness, and strength. David says, "I am feeble and sore broken" (Ps 38:8). So we often see brokenness side by side with a contrite or *crushed* spirit (Ps 34:18, 51:17). Part of this breaking process is the isolation of suffering alone. When we are going through true brokenness, we will always feel very much alone. God will ensure it, so that our eyes are only upon him. So the psalmist records,

> I am forgotten as a dead man out of mind: I am like a broken vessel. Ps 31:12

9 – The Way of Brokenness and God's Fear

> I looked on *my* right hand, and beheld, but *there was* <u>no man that would know me</u>: refuge failed me; <u>no man cared for my soul</u>.
>
> I cried unto thee, O LORD: I said, Thou *art* my refuge *and* my portion in the land of the living. Ps 142:4-5

This is a time when no one can help us, not our family, nor our friends, nor a lover – in terms of taking away our pain and bringing lasting comfort. So it was with Jesus, so it must be with us. Repeatedly the scripture shows that he was alone in his life, even though surrounded by his disciples and the multitudes continually.[146] When God is dealing with us by breaking us, we will turn to everyone we know to find help and comfort, but the Lord of our heart will ensure that all others are far away and that all their help is no help at all. They may give it repeatedly, but it flows through our hands like water. We cannot hold on to it. Though we yearn for their comfort and compassion, we will not find it. As David testifies of this time, "My lovers and my friends stand aloof from my sore; and my kinsmen stand afar off." Ps 38:11

> **<u>WARNING</u>**: We often think this is because those around us are insensitive and uncaring, but it is more often because God has dried up their wells of mercy toward us, so they have nothing that they can give us that will satisfy (even though they may try). "But know that the LORD hath set apart him that is godly <u>for himself</u>: the LORD will hear when I call unto him." Ps 4:3

Frustration and anger, resentment and bitterness are great temptations during this time, which if we give place to, will frustrate the grace of God and the Spirit of God and abort God's purpose. No good fruit can come if it be defiled by bitterness. This is why we so need the fear of the LORD to keep our heart in this critical time. Brokenness with the fear of the LORD causes our eyes to look to the hand of our Master and *away* from all other sources of comfort or help (Ps 123:1-3). In our sufferings our eyes must be fixed upon his word.[147] We must wait for him and him alone, for he only is our rock and our strong refuge. So David in Psalm 38 after having spoken that he is "sore broken", immediately says, "I have roared by reason of the disquietness of my heart. Lord, <u>all my desire *is* before thee</u>; and my groaning is not hid from thee." Ps 38:8-9

The Precious Fruits of Brokenness

One of the many fruits of brokenness is the intimacy we have with the Lord and the ensuing ability to hear God's voice more clearly. "The LORD *is* nigh unto them that are of a broken heart" (Ps 34:18). Removed are the blockages of

---

[146] Repeatedly the gospels speak of Jesus being alone (7x): Mt 14:23, 6:47, Lk 9:18,36, Jn 6:15, 8:9, 16:32.

[147] See among many other scriptures: Ps 119:82,123,147-148.

pride, hardness of heart, stubbornness, distractedness, and only seeing it from our perspective. Where we could not hear or see in certain areas before, now there is the way of the LORD set before us. That which was hidden, which we could not perceive, is now opened unto us because our heart has been made soft and pliable.

This is one of the reasons why God so delights in brokenness. Before brokenness we are hard of hearing, but after it our eyes and ears are opened. So David declares his inability to hear what God was saying prior to being broken. "But I, as a deaf *man*, heard not; and *I was* as a dumb man *that* openeth not his mouth. Thus I was as a man that heareth not, and in whose mouth *are* no reproofs." Ps 38:13-14 He could not receive reproof. He could not hear what others were saying to him in correction, nor could he answer.

Once brokenness comes, the reproofs that we have received and learned will be in our mouth. This is part of the healing God does for those who are broken in heart (Ps 147:3). We now like David in Psalm 34 are ready to teach others what we have fallen short in, but are now set free from. This is the sacrifice God is looking for – the brokenness that can acknowledge when and why we have missed God. So often we would sacrifice unto God our labor, our giving up of our possessions or our blessings, but the true sacrifice that God is looking for is the sacrifice of a broken spirit, that is, of allowing God to have his way. "The sacrifices of God *are* a broken spirit: a broken and a contrite heart, O God, thou wilt not despise." Ps 51:17

> Through brokenness, God turns salvation into sanctification and waywardness into faithfulness,
> all through the unlikely agent of *emptiness*.

Through brokenness, God turns salvation into sanctification and waywardness into faithfulness, all through the unlikely agent of *emptiness*. Brokenness is the nexus of the hourglass. It is the place of being completely emptied out. There is nothing we can hold onto while we are being broken. Brokenness will bring us to the end of our strength. It will take us from the realm of our limited strength to the treasure house of his abundant power that is ready to work within us, but which is constrained by our smallness of heart. I know many in their walk with God are now wandering, alienated from God's purpose and direction in their life, all because they have fled from and refused the brokenness that God was trying to bring them into.

Why We Must Not Flee Brokenness

We are often found resisting this work of God. The most common natural response is to run from the place of brokenness that God himself has set before

9 – The Way of Brokenness and God's Fear

us. So Jonah ran from the altar of doing God's will. Jonah despised and hated those of Nineveh and was loathe to serve them because of what they had done to the Israelites. He did not want to see them blessed and to escape God's judgments. What is so significant about the example of Jonah is that he, like all of us, <u>knew</u> God would do surgery on his own heart there. This is why we always run from God when we naturally consider brokenness, because we *know* what he is planning to do, and we fear it more than we fear him!

> But it displeased Jonah exceedingly, and he was very angry. And he prayed unto the LORD, and said, I pray thee, O LORD, <u>*was not this my saying, when I was yet in my country*</u>? Therefore I fled before unto Tarshish: for **I knew** that thou *art* a gracious God, and merciful, slow to anger, and of great kindness, and repentest thee of the evil. Jnh 4:1-2

The place of brokenness is the very place that many, many precious, beloved children of God turn back from following him, never to return. We will suffer the loss of all things through brokenness. Desire alone cannot enable us to endure to the end of this process. We must know and be assured this is the narrow way. God does not have another way. This is the great need of our day: to have the requirements of discipleship written on our heart, so that we know what we *must* do to continue following the Lord. No one can suffer the humiliation of the cross in their life and press on to know him, suffering the loss of all things through brokenness, if they have not come to learn and embrace the requirements of discipleship.

Without proper preparation of knowing what God *must* tear from our lives in order to truly save our soul, we will completely misunderstand his mercy and refuse his authority. The goodness of God is to lead us to repentance (Rom 2:4) – not to strengthen our selfish ways. If we are not properly prepared for the loss of all things, then our heart will become set on its ways and will then become divided. When our heart is divided, we will receive nothing of the Lord, as the apostle warns us (Jam 1:6-8).

How we fight to keep from this very place that God is trying to bring us to. So often in my own life, I have prayed for strength, when in truth Jesus was trying to make me strong by bringing me to a place of abject weakness. Those of the church of Philadelphia (the only church not rebuked by the Lord) only had "a little strength" (Rev 3:8). We inadvertently think God takes pleasure in the mighty and the strong, yet the scriptures repeatedly have shown the opposite to be true. God takes pleasure in the weak things, that he might confound the mighty (1Co 1:27). "He delighteth not in the strength of the horse: he taketh not pleasure in the legs of a man. The LORD taketh pleasure <u>in them that fear him</u>, in those that hope in his mercy." Ps 147:10-11 This is why the fear of God will bring us to a place of weakness through brokenness.

Where is the Fear of GOD? Losing the Treasure of the Lord

If we do not pass through brokenness, we remain settled in our lees, content with our life, unchanged, and still impure in many areas of heart. There were a people called the Moabites in the Bible. Their namesake, Moab, means 'what father' or 'no father'. They speak of the Christian who refuses to submit to correction and when things get hard they hit the road to find another place more to their liking. Their feet love to wander, and they do not refrain their feet. Though they go from place to place, they remain unchanged because they are unwilling to be broken and poured out. Hence, God does not accept them (Jer 14:10, 48:11-12).

> Moab hath been <u>at ease</u> from his youth, and he hath <u>settled on his lees</u>, and hath <u>not been emptied</u> from vessel to vessel, neither hath he gone into captivity: therefore his <u>taste remained in him</u>, and his <u>scent is not changed</u>. Therefore, behold, the days come, saith the LORD, that I will send unto him wanderers, that shall <u>cause him to wander</u>, and shall empty his vessels, and break their bottles. Jer 48:11-12

Why are they not changed? Because when correction or discipline or confrontation occurs, they wander and roam instead of being rooted, grounded, and planted in a house of God where proper oversight can be taken to their life by spiritual parents. They refuse to endure the corrections of the LORD which come through earthly, imperfect vessels. The root of the issue, which God is trying to touch, they will not allow him to.

> **WARNING**: As a minister of the gospel I have repeatedly seen that when a child of God begins to serve their Lord in any capacity, that their Master will now begin to empty them. As he empties them he will also bring in his instruction and correction – and that through earthly overseers. This now becomes the test of their heart. Will they be emptied of their selfishness *and* their way of doing things? This is a difficult time for any. How can we be cured of presumption and thinking that our way is the right way without the fear of the LORD working in us to receive correction?

It is only the fear of the LORD that keeps us from presumptuous sins. So it is written, "And all the people shall hear, and fear, and <u>do no more presumptuously</u>." Dt 17:13 What was the presumption here? The presumption of going one's own way and not hearkening to spiritual oversight through godly counsel. Though the child of God has a heavenly Father, will we come to know him by allowing him to bring correction? The Bible says we *only* know him, IF we receive correction, otherwise we are bastards (Heb 12). Remember, a bastard is an illegitimate child who has a father, they just don't know who he is. Moab did not know his father, for he never received correction from him as his father. Thus, Moab ever wandered in his life, going from place to place but never being emptied.

9 – The Way of Brokenness and God's Fear

The Emptying Process

This is why the emptying process that God initiates through service and confirms it with correction is so indispensable in the life of any saint that would mature. Without being emptied our taste remains in us, rather than the taste of the goodness of the Lord. Without being poured out as a drink offering (Php 2:17-18, Eph 5:2), our scent does not change. When we are settled on our lees (i.e. our dregs), instead of bringing forth the sweet aroma of the sacrifice of the fruit of our lips (Heb 13:15), our mouth is still an open sepulcher, full of grumbling, complaining, arguing, and death.

When we are not emptied and poured out, as was our Master (Isa 53:12), then wanderers will be sent unto us, to whom (when we listen) will make us wander and depart from the place of correction. This will be exactly what our heart wants to hear at that time. But we must be emptied from vessel to vessel by serving others in order to remove the bitterness and dregs that still abide in us. This is how God would get our eyes off of ourselves. Our life as born again Christians must be poured out into the lives of others. We were born to serve and to bring life to others. "And there was given him dominion, and glory, and a kingdom, that all people, nations, and languages, <u>should serve him</u>" (Dan 7:14a). As God said to the sons of Noah after he delivered them from this evil world, so he says to us, "Be fruitful, and multiply, and replenish the earth." Gen 9:1 We are to bring life where there is no life.

So many Christians go from conference to seminar to retreat looking for life, refreshment, and rest. Yet according to the Bible, if we are truly born again we already have life, refreshment, and rest in Jesus. We are not to *seek* these things, but rather to give them away! Through the love of Christ we are to "be filled with all the fulness of God." Eph 3:19 When we go from place to place seeking fulfillment, it only proves that the Moabite spirit is working in us. The Moabite spirit wanders from place to place, never content or complete in the Lord. There can be no satisfying of our life in wandering. "So two *or* three cities wandered unto one city, to drink water; but <u>they were not satisfied</u>: yet have ye not returned unto me, saith the LORD." Am 4:8 We must cease our wandering and return to the LORD to find our true satisfaction and refreshment (Col 2:10).

The Brokenness that Results from Sin

Now brokenness can also come as the result of our sin. Sin produces death, pain, suffering, destruction, separation, and lack. This we dare not willingly enter into. But God in his incredible redemption with which he redeemed us is able to turn the effects of sin into something beneficial. Once we understand sin from God's perspective and are convicted of our sin, then God is able to actually use sin (i.e. our missing of the mark) in our life to remove pride.

Should we sin? God forbid. Sin comes with its own tragic and painful penalty. Because of his iniquities (v4) and his foolishness (v5), David cried out, "I am feeble and <u>sore broken</u>" (Ps 38:8). It is written, "Ephraim *is* oppressed *and* <u>broken in judgment</u>, because he willingly walked after [i.e. away from] the commandment." Hos 5:11 Worldly and fleshly living will also cause our life to be broken. Solomon lets us know that because of intemperance brokenness comes into our life like a city that has been attacked and left in shambles (Pr 25:28). If anyone builds his life on the earth or on earthly principles, he shall be 'utterly broken down', because that is the nature of the earth (Isa 24:19).

Now all of these things take place because of the loss of the fear of God, because we no longer fear the word of our God. When the word is no longer our life, no longer the voice of God to us, then it becomes only a bunch of commandments. If that is how we hear it, then we will "go, and fall backward, and be broken, and snared, and taken." Isa 28:13 If you do not "sanctify the LORD of hosts himself; and *let* him *be* your fear, and *let* him *be* your dread" (Isa 8:13), then you also "shall stumble, and fall, and be broken, and be snared, and be taken" (v15). This is part of the testimony that needs to be bound up as a law and sealed among the Lord's disciples (v16).

But once we miss the mark, should we not learn all we can from our error of sinning? Yes. Through godly repentance and the brokenness of our heart over seeing our sin from his perspective, God is able to reveal the power of his grace. He can reestablish in our heart the authority and wisdom of the truth of his scriptures. He can refocus our eyesight on his strength and power, rather than our own abilities. If we will acknowledge and turn from our sin, God is able to teach us many beautiful things even through our sins and failures.

This is the power of his redemption – it not only brings the forgiveness of sins (Col 1:14), but also the riches of his grace (Eph 1:7). The redeeming of our failures are some of our greatest lessons of the power of God's grace and the great need for humility. But sin *only* works to our advantage through the mercy of God AFTER the fear of God is reestablished. If we lose this safeguard, then God cannot use sin in our life, because of the deception of pride and the hardness of heart that occurs as a result of sin. The marks of sin are then not able to be removed. Thus, we see the incredible importance of the fear of God in the restoration process.

The Banner of Brokenness

Thou hast made the earth to tremble;
> <u>thou hast broken it</u>: heal the breaches thereof; for it shaketh.

Thou hast shewed thy people <u>hard things</u>:
> thou hast made us to drink the wine of astonishment.

Thou hast given a banner to them that fear thee,
> that it may be displayed because of the truth. Selah.

9 – The Way of Brokenness and God's Fear

> That thy beloved may be delivered;
> save *with* thy right hand, and hear me. Ps 60:2-5

The way of brokenness is the narrow way of the kingdom of God. We must enter it with tribulation, enduring the pressure of being conformed to his image. The greatest pressure is in the nexus of the hour glass where our life is being squeezed out and his is being pressed in. The least amount of freedom is in the nexus of the hour glass, for it is the straitness (i.e. the narrowness) of his will in direct opposition to ours. It is the place where there are only two choices: ours and the one that God is setting before us. We cannot turn to the right or to the left. We either go forward to be broken, or we turn back, wounded and hurt, but still unbroken. Our comfort and hope in going through brokenness is this:

1. that the Lord has gone before us   (Isa 53:5-11)
2. that the Lord will be near to us   (Psalm 34:18)
3. that the Lord will be glorified in us   (Rom 8:17-18)

The Way that He Shall Choose

We are certain, if we follow Christ, to encounter many tests and trials. These are to discover and unveil the imperfections that are in us and to fix our eyes on the hope that is set before us and away from the desires of this world. His testings will lead us to examination and to brokenness, and brokenness is God's surgeon's knife to make us whole. Once we allow brokenness to do its secret humbling work, we are now ready in a deeper way to be taught and led. If we fear the LORD, we must recognize that he must teach us in the way which "he shall choose." Our choice in what we would do for the Lord or for ourselves must come to an end. "There is a way which seemeth right unto a man, but the end thereof *are* the ways of death." Pr 14:12 The word of God and his will must have the preeminence (Col 1:18). Thus, the fear of the LORD will bring us immediately under his authority and his will for our life.

There is the way of man, but there is also the way of God. So we see, "What man *is* he that feareth the LORD? him shall he teach in the way *that* he shall choose." Ps 25:12 These are the two choices always set before us: the tree of the knowledge of good and evil (i.e. *our* way) versus the tree of life (i.e. *God's* way). When God's fear is working in us, he will teach us his chosen way. He will not leave us to decide what he has already chosen. It was not for Jesus to choose his life, his ministry, or his friends. Neither if we will follow in the footsteps of our Lord is it our choice to choose what shall be our life, our ministry, or our friends. It is only our choice on whether we will willingly follow his commands and his leading. Jesus' prayer in the garden of Gethsemane did not involve any substitutionary plans come up in the mind of Jesus and offered unto the Father as alternatives. No, the Lord's only struggles were, first, determining the will of God, and second, committing himself to do it.

Where is the Fear of GOD? Losing the Treasure of the Lord

The LORD will order the steps of any man that begins to follow him, for God is a God of order. God will establish our steps and cause us to stand uprightly for he is the Architect of our life, the author and finisher of our faith. We are his workmanship and as soon as he is given complete authority (through our willingness to submit to his plan), then he begins with determination and purpose to reshape and refashion our life in the image of his dear Son. "The steps of a *good* man are <u>ordered</u> by the LORD: and he delighteth in his way." Ps 37:23 So often we look at this verse and think that God is saying God delights in the way of the good man – that is far from what is being said. Yes, God may have some delight in the man whose steps are ordered, but only if the man's ordering is in accordance with God's set order.

God is far more delighted in the one whom he can command and know that it will be done as commanded. God was so delighted in Abraham because he feared God (Gen 22:12) and in that fear would do whatever God asked – no matter how costly the sacrifice! What God delights, primarily in, is the perfectness of his way. Thus, God greatly rejoices when our steps are ordered according to his perfect way. Then, his will is being done on earth as it is in heaven, and his kingdom (which he delights to give, Lk 12:32) is manifest in earth (Lk 11:2). God does not delight in any man's steps just because the man is 'good' for none of us is good, no, not one (Rom 3:10). God only is good (Mk 10:17), and only he can make our steps good in his sight.

Remember, God delights in HIS way. So David prays, "Order my steps in <u>thy word</u>: and let not any iniquity [i.e. any *vanity* (of doing things my way)] have dominion over me." Ps 119:133 This is why God orders our steps and has *before ordained* the good works which we are to walk in (Eph 2:10). He has already determined the way chosen for us, for he knows what is best for us. May we pray as David prayed, "cause me to know the way <u>wherein I should walk</u>; for I lift up my soul unto thee." Ps 143:8 Once the seat of our will, our soul, is lifted up to him, *then* we may follow in his way. As Jesus let Peter know, we cannot follow Jesus now, if we are unwilling to lay our life (or more technically our soul) down (Jn 13:36-38).[148]

The Test of Service

"Now therefore fear the LORD, and serve him in sincerity and in truth: and put away the gods which your fathers served on the other side of the flood, and in Egypt; and serve ye the LORD." Jos 24:14

What a perfect time to now talk about our service of God. Immediately our soul cries out, "I can't possibly serve God when I am broken and hurting!" But that is exactly when God calls us to serve him – when we feel like we have

---

[148] In the Greek, the word 'life' here is *psuche* (G5590), the very word for 'soul'.

nothing to give. God says, "my strength is made perfect in weakness." How can you ever know his perfect strength if you are unwilling to be made weak. And what must our response be?

> Most gladly therefore will I rather glory in my infirmities, that the power of Christ may rest upon me. Therefore I take pleasure in infirmities, in reproaches, in necessities, in persecutions, in distresses for Christ's sake: for when I am weak, then am I strong. 2Co 12:9-10

We started this chapter looking at the brokenness that God will bring into our life that he may prove our worship genuine. We have already looked briefly at how the fear of the LORD should restore our heart to serve.[149] Let us now look at the 'worship' of our service and how we are to serve God with fear and rejoice before him with trembling (Ps 2:11).

Many times the command to fear the LORD is immediately followed by the command to serve him wholeheartedly. If we have no heart to serve God in sincerity and in truth, then we have lost the fear of God in our life – that is for sure. Now any pure hearted servant of God knows the depth of weariness that comes upon the beleaguered warrior committed to doing the will of God. We all may feel like quitting and giving up, especially after the criticisms of carnal Christians, the destructions caused by undiscipled souls, and the rebellions of the self-conceited. But we are not serving men, we are serving our Master. We did not call ourselves, nor place our selves in ministry.

> And no man taketh this honour unto himself [i.e. *to serve God*], but he that is called of God, as *was* Aaron. So also Christ glorified not himself to be made an high priest Heb 5:4-5

We are all priests before our God and Father (Rev 1:6), and he chooses as he sees fit to place us in roles of ministry. Therefore it is not in our power nor our authority to remove ourselves or to decide when to stop. We were called by our commanding officer. We do not sign up with 'conditions'. We 'sign up' *unconditionally*, because he is Lord. We cannot stop serving the one who called us without walking away from him. This is the hard truth, and one that cannot be swallowed by those who walk away, but scripture is perfectly clear on this matter. "For the gifts and calling of God *are* without repentance." Rom 11:29 Paul was completely dedicated to finishing the ministry, because it was God who gave it him to do. It meant more to him than his own life. Paul said in the very promise of suffering that was continually prophesied before him,

> But none of these things move me, neither count I my life dear unto myself, so that I might <u>finish</u> my course with joy, and <u>the ministry, which I have received of the Lord Jesus</u>, to testify the gospel of the grace of God. Ac 20:24

---

[149] Refer to the chapter entitled "The Root of Worship and Fruit of Giving" in the section 'The Marriage of Fear & Obedience: Producing a True Heart of Service'.

Where is the Fear of GOD? Losing the Treasure of the Lord

Paul had to exhort others to follow this same calling to fulfill their ministry that they had received in the Lord. He wrote, "And say to Archippus, Take heed to the ministry which <u>thou hast received in the Lord</u>, that thou fulfil it." Col 4:17 If we have received a ministry in the Lord, then we **must** fulfill it. If we are called of God to serve him, then we cannot "un-call" ourselves from his service – no matter how much we suffer in his service. When we stop serving God because of our suffering, then we have put away our fear of the One who called us, and we have forgotten our calling to suffer for his name's sake. Many times it was in the enduring of suffering and continuing to faithfully serve that God was greatly glorified. Consider Joseph in Egypt, David in the cave, Daniel in Babylon, and many others. Have we forgotten our Lord's first words to him who would become that great servant Paul? "For I will shew him how <u>great things</u> he must suffer for my name's sake." Ac 9:16 God, in fact, must show all of us how great things we must suffer for his name's sake.

> When we stop serving God because of our suffering, then we have put away our fear of the One who called us, & we have forgotten our calling to suffer for his name's sake.

If we will truly fear God in the wicked and evil generation we live in, then we, like all the godly before us, will suffer in the service of our God. It must be so: "Yea, and all that will live godly in Christ Jesus shall suffer persecution." 2Tim 3:12 If they did so to the Master, they will do so to those who follow him. As he promised, "If the world hate you, ye know that *it hated* me before it hated you." Jn 15:18 To live for God is to serve him, and to serve him is to be hated, despised, and persecuted in this world – often by God's own people.

A Servant's Heart
"I thy servant fear the LORD from my youth." 1K 18:12

Once our heart is enlarged through the fear of God, service becomes our desire. So we have seen with the woman that fears the LORD. "She ... worketh willingly with her hands." Pr 31:13 In this way you can measure modern day ministers of the gospel. If they lack a servant's heart, then you know the fear of God needs to be put within them, for the telltale sign of God's fear is the servant's heart. Many of the prophets and apostles of the scriptures were called servants of God,[150] and we ourselves all ought to have the heart of a servant, for it God's highest calling. "As free, and not using *your* liberty for a cloke of maliciousness, but as the servants of God." 1Pe 2:16

---

[150] Most notably, Moses (1Ch 6:49, 2Ch 24:9, Neh 10:29, Dan 9:11, Rev 15:3), Paul (Tit 1:1), and James (Jam 1:1), but so many others as well.

9 – The Way of Brokenness and God's Fear

Many leaders do not have a true servant's heart, or if they do, they do not serve according to God's pattern. Discipleship is the missing foundation of the church. Discipleship will both show us what God expects and will break our will so that we do things as God commands and not as we desire or will. So many go from salvation as a new believer right into servanthood in an area of ministry, but this is not the pattern of the word of God. We must first be discipled, so that we may know how to serve the way God wants us to and not according to our own heart.

In discipleship, we are humbled and broken through instruction and correction so that when we do serve, we serve without the prideful boasting and self-serving flamboyance of so many that are in the limelight of Christianity today. We so need to come under the Lord's correction that can come only through discipleship and submission to authority. True discipleship brings true discipline in our life, not only the self-discipline of temperance, which is needed, but also the discipline of our soul through correction. Men may go through their Bible Colleges today and learn the ways and doctrines of men, but where are they learning to receive correction at the hand of the Lord? Where are they learning as the original disciples to receive correction through men of God without grumbling, complaining, or rebuking it? All the original disciples learned repeatedly how to be correctable.[151]

This is our great problem today. We have "ministers" who know much, but cannot receive correction because they have undisciplined souls. There are many who know much of ruling, but nothing of true servanthood. Consider Peter, who though older in the faith and greater in calling than Paul (being one of the original twelve),[152] yet received Paul's very public rebuke and exposure of his hypocrisy (Gal 2:11-21). Where are the servants of God today who can receive correction through the word of God that comes through other servants of God? Where are the true ministers that when their hypocritical ways are exposed by the writings or letters of another servant of God (as Paul did in the letter of Galatians itself) they will not be offended, but will repent and actually *praise* God that truth is going forth, and people are being set free from error?

---

[151] An enlightening study for the reader is to see in the gospels not only how many times Jesus corrected his disciples, but also to see the severity at times of his rebukes to them. Yet we never see the disciples rebuking Jesus for correcting them! It is clear they understood this was part of their discipleship that they needed.

[152] Paul's apostleship was in no way inferior to Peter's. Paul says, "For I suppose I was not a whit behind the very chiefest apostles." 2Co 11:5 Yet there still remained something special about being "one of the twelve" (*not* in terms of Paul's authority with the Corinthians or the other churches that he had a seal of apostleship upon). Paul freely acknowledged he was *not* of the twelve. "For we dare not make ourselves of the number, or compare ourselves with some that commend themselves: but they measuring themselves by themselves, and comparing themselves among themselves, are not wise." 2Co 10:12

Where is the Fear of GOD? Losing the Treasure of the Lord

Serving in the Fear of God

We see many examples of servants who had the fear of God:

- Obadiah: "I thy servant fear the LORD from my youth." 1K 18:12
- A wife of the prophets: "Thy servant did fear the LORD" 2K 4:1
- Nehemiah and those with him: "O LORD, I beseech thee, let now thine ear be attentive to the prayer of thy servant, and to the prayer of thy servants, who desire to fear thy name" Neh 1:11

Notice how true servants *desire* to fear God's name. The heart of the servant of God will be *pleased* with fearing God's name, for it is in their heart. In fact, the very introduction of Job is as a servant who fears God and departs from evil. "And the LORD said unto Satan, Hast thou considered my servant Job, that *there is* none like him in the earth, a perfect and an upright man, one that feareth God, and escheweth evil?" Job 1:8 (also 2:3)

God expects that if we are servants and he truly is our master,[153] that we ought to fear him. So he says that a servant ought to honor his master by fearing him (Mal 1:6). There is no honor rendered unto God as our Lord if we do not fear him. Even in the New Testament the command is given unto servants to serve with fear and trembling, and it is to be done unto Christ, not unto man (Eph 6:5, Col 3:22). Look at how many times the fear of God precedes the command to serve him.

> Ye shall walk after the LORD your God, and **fear him**, and keep his commandments, and obey his voice, and ye shall serve him, and cleave unto him. Dt 13:4

> Thou shalt **fear the LORD** thy God, and serve him, and shalt swear by his name. Dt 6:13

> Thou shalt **fear the LORD** thy God; him shalt thou serve, and to him shalt thou cleave, and swear by his name. Dt 10:20

> Now therefore **fear the LORD**, and serve him in sincerity and in truth: and put away the gods which your fathers served on the other side of the flood, and in Egypt; and serve ye the LORD. Jos 24:14

> And now, Israel, what doth the LORD thy God require of thee, but to **fear the LORD** thy God, to walk in all his ways, and to love him, and to serve the LORD thy God with all thy heart and with all thy soul, Dt 10:12

> If ye will **fear the LORD**, and serve him, and obey his voice .... Only **fear the LORD**, and serve him in truth with all your heart 1Sam 12:14,24

---

[153] As Jesus said to his disciples of himself, "Ye call me Master and Lord: and ye say well; for so I am." Jn 13:13

9 – The Way of Brokenness and God's Fear

In contrast to what men teach, the grace of God should not remove our fear of God, it should establish it. "Wherefore we receiving a kingdom which cannot be moved, let us have grace, whereby we may serve God acceptably with reverence and godly **fear**" (Heb 12:28). True and acceptable service unto God can only flow out of a heart that fears God. If we lose our fear of God, our desire to serve him will continually wane until we only serve on our terms. Let us not think that serving God and having the fear of God are nice "additions", "medals", or "achievements" to our walk with God, as some imply. No! They are requirements which he demands of us.

> what doth the LORD thy God require of thee, but to **fear** the LORD thy God, to walk in all his ways, and to love him, and to **serve** the LORD thy God with all thy heart & with all thy soul Dt 10:12

The fear of God is what not only keeps our heart pure but also our service. It is easy to serve for selfish reasons. It is all too easy to fall into the snare of serving to get, whether it be internal reward (such as feeling good about our self or the reward of approval from others), or whether it be external reward (such as position, influence, and a means to achieve power). But if our service is built off of the fear of the LORD, then we will indeed "serve him in sincerity and in truth", and we will "serve him in truth with all [our] heart." 1Sam 12:14,24 Our rejoicing in our service should be who we are serving, the greatness and graciousness of the one to whom we freely offer ourselves. Hear Paul's witness in the midst of a great storm, "God, whose I am, and whom I serve" (Ac 27:23). Paul defined his life by whom he belonged to and whom he served. So we would do well to define who we are in the same terms, rather than by the world's standards of our possessions, accomplishments, titles, and following.

The driving force behind true service ought to be God's fear. Many times people serve out of thanksgiving, out of love, and because it is the right thing to do. These noble motives, as precious as they are, cannot sustain us or properly prepare us for serving our heavenly Master, if his fear is lacking. The fear of God must precede and be the foundation of our service of God. God's fear is to produce in us a heart to love him and serve him. So we are to "serve the LORD with fear, and rejoice with trembling." Ps 2:11 In the eyes of man there are many acceptable and worthy services that can be rendered unto God. Men may be moved by great self-sacrifice, but if there is no true fear of God, all such sacrifices are worthless and unacceptable to his holy eye.[154] This is why the fear of God was a requirement on those who would be chosen out to serve:

> The God of Israel said, the Rock of Israel spake to me, He that ruleth over men *must be* just, ruling in the fear of God. 2Sam 23:3

---

[154] To understand more why no service is acceptable to the LORD without the fear of God, refer to the section entitled 'The Salt of the Covenant: The Fear of the LORD' in the chapter entitled "The Door of Mercy to All Those who Fear the LORD" in the book Finding the Treasure of the Lord.

> Moreover thou shalt provide out of all the people able men, <u>such as fear God</u>, men of truth, hating covetousness; and place *such* over them, *to be* rulers of thousands, *and* rulers of hundreds, rulers of fifties, and rulers of tens Ex 18:21

The fear of God is *not* a sign of imperfection or immaturity as some men would think, but on the contrary is a sign of spiritual maturity that indicates a man is *prepared* to serve the Lord. And if some think this is only an old covenant mandate, think again. It is in the New, in the context of that glorious kingdom of God that we are receiving as part of being born again, that we are exhorted to serve God <u>acceptably</u> with godly fear (Heb 12:28).

For Conscience Sake: Serving the Living God

"For this is thankworthy, if a man for conscience toward God endure grief, suffering wrongfully." 1Pe 2:19

There is a service we must render unto the Lord that he expects of us in order to maintain a pure conscience. The rendering of that service as unto the Lord and not as unto man must be done in the fear of God. But to serve the Master with a good conscience in the fear of God will require suffering on our behalf. "For this *is* thankworthy, if a man <u>for conscience toward God</u> endure grief, suffering wrongfully." 1Pe 2:19 Find a person who has no continual and humble service of the Lord, <u>especially</u> if it be because he has suffered wrongfully at the hands of men, then you know you have found a person who does not have a good conscience toward God, and they have lost their fear of him.

This is the word of God. We are never to forsake our ministry (Col 4:17) or our calling (Rom 11:29) – no matter what others may do to us. Paul exhorts us in this regard repeatedly, not only by doctrine, but also by his own example. Sufferings and laborings should not move us, nor cause us to stop running the race of faith. We must finish what he has called us to do. "Insomuch that we desired Titus, that as he had begun, so he would also <u>finish</u> in you the same grace also." 2Co 8:6 Think of all the sufferings that were set before Paul.

> the Holy Ghost witnesseth in every city, saying that <u>bonds and afflictions abide me</u>. But none of these things move me, neither count I my life dear unto myself, so that I might finish my course with joy, and the ministry, which I have received of the Lord Jesus, to testify the gospel of the grace of God. Ac 20:24

Yet none of these sufferings moved Paul from finishing his ministry with joy! This is the legacy of grace that has been left us of all the apostles. They rejoiced in their calling that they were counted worthy to suffer for his name (Ac 5:41). They did not flee the sufferings, nor forsake their ministry, though they like Jesus repeatedly encountered the contradiction or gainsaying of sinners against themselves. We would do well to "consider him that endured such contradiction of sinners against himself, lest ye be wearied and faint in your minds."

Heb 12:3 "For unto you it is given in the behalf of Christ, not only to believe on him, but also to suffer for his sake" (Php 1:29). Why is it so important to finish our ministry? Because it is not *our* ministry, it is the Lord's. We have received the stewardship of fulfilling it from the Lord. No man gave it to us, and therefore we must *answer to him* for its completion.

Growing Weary of Well-Doing
"But ye, brethren, be not weary in well doing." 2Th 3:13

We might well ask ourselves, "Why, when we are serving God, do we oftentimes get to a place where we feel like we are losing our love for God, especially when what we are doing, we are trying to do because we love him?" It is not an uncommon fight for the servant of God to go through – this kind of discouragement and weariness in well-doing. So Paul must exhort the saints in their tribulations, "But ye, brethren, be not weary in well doing." 2Th 3:13

Herein lies the key as to why we lose the fear of God many times, even when we are trying to serve him: because we grow weary of well doing and our heart becomes divided between serving two masters, the Lord and our own desires. Losing our heart to serve is a sign that we are falling away from our first love – for to love the Lord *is* to desire to serve him. Such is the revelation of the scripture. When one is in the place of discouragement and feels as if they cannot go on, they need the comfort and understanding of their fellow soldiers, but that comfort cannot take the form of what we usually desire in such a state.

We desire to hear that it's alright to quit, but this is not the message of our Lord. Jesus calls us to come to him and to find rest, but what is that rest? Is it ceasing from laboring for his heavenly Father? No. Listen, "Come unto me, all *ye* that labour and are heavy laden, and I will give you rest. Take my yoke upon you, and learn of me; for I am meek and lowly in heart: and ye shall find rest unto your souls." Mt 11:28-29 The rest for our souls is actually found in taking up Jesus' yoke upon us, in doing his will. This was Jesus' yoke: to serve the Lord his God with all his heart, mind, soul, and strength.

Remember, Jesus did not come to be served, but to serve, and to give his life a ransom for many (Mt 20:28). Jesus did not have many friends who comforted and exhorted him to continue and to finish his labors for his heavenly Father. In fact, nearly all his friends and even his family many times stood in the way of him serving, and discouraged him from being so zealous. Only the woman who anointed him for his burial was sensitive to the requirement of his heavenly Father, that Jesus must be put to death (Mt 26:10-13).

Jesus had two immovable rocks to lean on and find rest. The first was the power of the Holy Ghost who strengthens us with might in the inner man (Eph 3:16). The second was the comfort of the scriptures. The scriptures assure us that God's plans are for our good, no matter how much we must suffer or endure to have them fulfilled. The comfort and exhortation of the scriptures is born for such times. Both the Spirit and the Word will bring us to a place of brokenness. Many times we draw back from this and flee from it. A heart that is trying to protect itself from being broken is a divided heart. And a divided heart will keep us from both the kind of brokenness Jesus wants us to experience and from the fear of God that he walked in. This is the danger of a divided heart, and why when David wanted to 'walk in God's truth' he prayed, "unite my heart to fear thy name." Ps 86:11

A heart united in doing the will of God will bring us to the beauty of brokenness where we are more malleable and open to what God would speak and tell us. Yet, the overwhelming response to instruction and correction at such times of weariness is often turning away and not listening. Often this leads to bitterness, anger, and resentment. This indeed shows that, through weakness, our soul and our desire for control over our own life has unfortunately grown stronger, rather than weaker as God has intended. God does not want us to be in control of our life – that is his divine right of rule as Lord of our heart. "But sanctify the Lord God in your hearts" (1Pe 3:15). The response of bitterness, anger, and resentment, or even of frustration to instruction and correction should witness to us that our heart has indeed grown farther from the Lord through our trials, rather than closer, and that it is time to return to him.

So often when we come to the place of weariness and discouragement, we think we can "lay down" the ministry that we have received in the Lord, and yet truly believe in our heart that we are not forsaking the Lord. Yet Paul tells Archippus (and us) that this is not so. "And say to Archippus, Take heed to the ministry which thou hast received in the Lord, that thou fulfil it." Col 4:17 Though bonds and afflictions awaited Paul in every city, he kept to his course of serving the Lord. Paul himself speaks to other servants of God of this, "But none of these things move me, neither count I my life dear unto myself, so that I might finish my course with joy, and the ministry, which I have received of the Lord Jesus" (Ac 20:24). When we lose our heart for serving where he has placed us, we are turning away from him and beginning to turn to things that cannot help us and cannot give us the rest or strength we desire.

> Your words have been stout against me, saith the LORD. Yet ye say, What have we spoken *so much* against thee? Ye have said, It is vain to serve God: and what profit *is it* that we have kept his ordinance, and that we have walked mournfully before the LORD of hosts? Mal 3:13-14

The prophets of old linked losing our heart to serve with turning away from the Lord in our heart. When we turn our heart away from serving the Lord with all our heart, then in one way or another we will begin to go after something else that God says is but vanity.

9 – The Way of Brokenness and God's Fear

> And Samuel said unto the people, ... yet turn not aside from following the LORD, but serve the LORD with all your heart; And turn ye not aside: for *then should ye go* after vain *things,* which cannot profit nor deliver; for they *are* vain. 1Sam 12:20-21

We were created to serve God and for all eternity that will be our calling. When time is over and eternity begun "there shall be no more curse: but the throne of God and of the Lamb shall be in it; and his servants shall serve him" (Rev 22:3). God prepares us for our eternal call to faithfulness, by testing our faithfulness in serving him here.

The loss of our heart to willingly serve the Lord is more dangerous than any of us know. God's answer to Jeremiah's complaint in his weariness of serving God was not one of comfort but, as shocking as it may seem, one of rebuke. "If thou hast run with the footmen, and they have <u>wearied thee</u>, then how canst thou contend with horses? and *if* in the land of peace, *wherein* thou trustedst, *they wearied thee,* then how wilt thou do in the swelling of Jordan?" Jer 12:5 God challenges us when we are wearied and feeling like quitting by asking, "How do we ever think we will go on to do what he has prepared for us next, if we want to give up now?" Do we not know that we have even greater battles and challenges that are ahead for us?! "Yea, and all that will live godly in Christ Jesus shall suffer persecution." 2Tim 3:12

If we falter when we are wearied, it can mean years of defeat. God must bring us back to the place where it is our joy to serve him. If we lose our joy in serving our Lord, then we have lost sight of who we are serving. We have forgotten what he has done for us in delivering us, and we must certainly lose our strength (Neh 8:10, Eze 24:25). Remember, it was for this very thing – *not* serving him with joy and with gladness of heart – that God warned his people that they would go into bondage. Either we will serve the LORD "with joyfulness, and with gladness of heart, for the abundance of all *things*" (Dt 28:47), or we will inadvertently begin to serve our enemies.

> Because thou servedst not the LORD thy God with joyfulness, and with gladness of heart, for the abundance of all *things;* <u>Therefore shalt thou serve thine enemies</u> which the LORD shall send against thee, in hunger, and in thirst, and in nakedness, and in want of all *things:* & he shall put a yoke of iron upon thy neck, until he have destroyed thee. Dt 28:47-48

As we go through our struggles and being emptied, God will bring before us others who have need. The Lord tests us to see will we give, even when we think we have nothing to give. "Look not every man on his own things, but every man also on the things of others." Php 2:4 So Elijah tested the woman who had only enough bread and oil for her and her son to eat and then to die.

More Abundant Life

> And Elijah said unto her, Fear not; go *and* do as thou hast said: but make me thereof a little cake <u>first</u>, and bring *it* unto me, and after make for thee and for thy son. 1K 17:13

When we lose our heart of pity for the afflicted (though we do not see it this way), we have forsaken the fear of God. As Job cried out in the midst of his great suffering, "To him that is afflicted pity *should be shewed* from his friend; but he [i.e. *the one who doesn't show pity to his afflicted friend*] forsaketh the fear of the Almighty." Job 6:14 If we do not show pity to one who is afflicted, especially to a friend, then we have forsaken the fear of the Almighty.

The Problem of Unmet Needs

Another problem of serving we all run into is serving with an impure heart – serving to obtain acceptance, recognition, or responsibility (i.e. power). Even though we may not start with any ulterior motives, often our unmet desires in the Lord (due to the lack of intimacy) begin to produce needs in our heart for acceptance, approval, and appreciation. Sadly, this lack of intimacy is often caused by being too busy in our serving, and forgetting our source of strength – our relationship with our King. Whether we recognize these unmet desires or not, these are none other than serving for reward. When this takes root in our heart it is impossible to be faithful to the Lord. The problem is, without the continual purifying fire of God, serving to obtain (just like believing to receive) will always cause self-centered ambition to arise and corrupt our pure service and turn it into covetousness. Our service is to be toward God and God alone. As it is written,

> prepare your hearts unto the LORD, and <u>serve him only</u> 1Sam 7:3
>
> Thou shalt worship the Lord thy God, and <u>him only shalt thou serve</u>. Mt 4:10

Our fear of God must be without duplicity or double-mindedness. We must "in singleness of heart, [*be*] fearing God" (Col 3:22). Amazingly, the word that ends the previous verse in Colossians (v21) is the word 'discouraged' or *disheartened*. In the context of being discouraged, Paul immediately begins to exhort servants not to lose their fear of the Lord, but to maintain a singleness of heart. For, "No man can serve two masters: for either he will hate the one, and love the other; or else he will hold to the one, and despise the other." Mt 6:24 Our service toward God must be in the fear of God, or else soon it will degrade either into thanklessness and bitterness or into self-righteousness, pride, and serving one's own interests.

We soon discover it is impossible to serve God with a purity of heart the way he asks of us without the fear of God. For it is the fear of God that must continue to burn away the chaff that resides in all of our hearts, and which surfaces under pressure and lack. The fear of God, as a fire, must burn within our

9 – The Way of Brokenness and God's Fear

hearts to cleanse away all uncleanness and to keep our hearts stedfast on the vision and purpose of God.

Is this not why we often start well, but all too often do not finish well, especially in purposing to do good and live honestly? Because we become wearied in mind, and we faint in heart (Heb 12:3)! We forget Jesus and his sufferings for us. We forget that great and inestimable debt that has been cancelled for us because of what he endured, and instead we look at and magnify that truly insignificant (in comparison) suffering that we are all called to endure. We allow the burdens of this life to eclipse the glories that are to be revealed in us through these very sufferings.

> And if children, then heirs; heirs of God, and joint-heirs with Christ; if so be that we suffer with *him,* that we may be also glorified together. For I reckon that the sufferings of this present time <u>are not worthy</u> <u>*to be compared*</u> with the glory which shall be revealed in us. Rom 8:17-18

We so often refuse to see any value, any redemptive purpose, in suffering. This is a direct result of the hedonism of the last days. So many times we forget to "follow after, if that [we] may apprehend that for which also [we are] apprehended of Christ Jesus." Php 3:12 And we forget to reach forth unto those things which are set before us (Php 3:13). If we would keep our eye on the prize of being conformed to Jesus' image *through* the pressures that we must assuredly go through, we would, like Paul, be able 'to *take an inventory* and to *estimate*' that the sufferings of this life are not '*deserving, comparable* or even *suitable*' to be considered in light of the glory of the holy temple God is building in us.

> Is this not why we often start well, but all too often do not finish well, especially in purposing to do good and live honestly? Because we become wearied in mind, and we faint in heart (Heb 12:3)!

The vision and hope of being glorified together with him will change our response to suffering. Instead of being beaten down by our struggles, we will actually grow stronger and our hope more stedfast, knowing we are being counted worthy to suffer for the Lord's name. We will like Paul be those "Who now <u>rejoice</u> in [our] sufferings for you, and fill up that which is behind of the afflictions of Christ in [our] flesh for his body's sake, which is the church" (Col 1:24). We will no longer be bound up with our own selfishness, but will be looking for how we can be a blessing to the body of Christ in our suffering! We will no longer think it strange concerning the fiery trial which is come to try us. We will instead "<u>rejoice</u>, inasmuch as [we] are partakers of Christ's sufferings; that, when his glory shall be revealed, [we] may be <u>glad</u> also with <u>exceeding joy</u>." 1Pe 4:12-13 What a transformation the eternal view makes in us.

If we are reproached for the name of Christ, we are to consider ourselves happy because we know "the spirit of glory and of God resteth upon [us]: ... on your part he is glorified." 1Pe 4:14 Repeatedly in scripture, we see the pattern: the Father's glory is revealed through our sufferings, especially when we continue in obedience to his will. This frees us of so many things. No longer do we accuse others and excuse ourselves. No longer do we look primarily at our pain and suffering. These pressures and afflictions, if we will lay hold of the purpose of God, will transform us so that our care is for others, more than ourselves. Our goal will no longer be to look good or to appear right. It will be that God might be glorified in all things, even if it is in our being evil spoken of. No longer do we need to justify our actions or explain them.

How can we come to this point of being able to continue in our service of God while we are suffering? How can we cease from trying to justify ourselves before those who falsely accuse us? "But sanctify the Lord God in your hearts: and *be* ready always to *give* an answer to every man that asketh you a reason of the hope that is in you with meekness and fear" (1Pe 3:15). Often we are all too ready to give an answer to our accusers – no one has to tell us to do that! We are very ready to give an answer to justify what we have done, for this is the very nature of man, to always have an excuse. But this is **not** what this verse is exhorting us to do. Notice, we are called to be ready to give an answer for our hope, not for our righteousness or for our innocence that we so often try to defend. And what is our hope? Our hope is the Lord Jesus Christ and others in his presence at his coming (1Tim 1:1; 1Th 2:19, 2Co 1:7).

Preparing for Brokenness: Enduring the Hard Things
"Thou therefore endure hardness, as a good soldier of Jesus Christ." 2Tim 2:3

We shall be tried by many fiery trials as we serve God. These are in order to bring forth his praise, honor, and glory (1Pe 1:7), but they will come through brokenness. Peter exhorts us not to think it strange that we will go through such trials "as though some strange thing happened to [us]" (1Pe 4:12). Only these fiery trials can reveal in us his glory, as we become partakers of his sufferings (v13). We must be broken and smelted so that he can mold us and shape us as he sees fit. Only in this way can we be conformed into the image of his Son (Rom 8:29).

Is it any wonder then, that though we all are predestinated to be conformed to the image of his Son, yet so many turn back from God's predestinated plan? Many will not endure the narrow way of brokenness and the hardships and sufferings that attend it. Paul had to exhort Timothy, his son in the faith, to "endure hardness, as a good soldier of Jesus Christ." 2Tim 2:3 So many *do consider* suffering for Christ a strange or *alien* thing, so that they will not long endure it. Yet we are called to be a broken people sent to a broken world. God has broken

9 – The Way of Brokenness and God's Fear

this world by his curse on sin, so that some in their pain would reach out for the living God and would find him (Ac 17:27).

Let us examine this banner of brokenness mentioned in Psalm 60 a little closer, for it speaks of the banner that God has given to them that fear God. Notice how God has removed the security of the earth. He has "made the earth to tremble" (v2). God ensures that those who live in the world will experience its brokenness for he has "broken it". "For we know that the whole creation groaneth and travaileth in pain together until now." Rom 8:22 This is, as Paul says, the bondage of corruption (Rom 8:21) that puts a heavy weight on the lost, so that as slaves of sin, they might cry out for deliverance. At the same time, the heart of God desires to "heal the breaches thereof" (Ps 60:2), for creation is ready to fall, "for it shaketh". But he cannot bring forth his healing without showing his people "hard things" and making them 'drink of the wine of astonishment' (v3), that is, the wine of *trembling*.

What are these hard things which cause his own people to be astonished? That he is the Judge of all the earth, but especially of his own people! These are the hard things for us to hear, especially in our generation of pleasure and self-seeking. As Jesus warned religious Saul, so this generation must also be warned, "*it is* hard for thee to kick against the pricks." Ac 9:5 Indeed, God must show us all how much we must suffer for his name's sake. These are the judgments of the LORD, which, when we come to know and believe, we are made drunk with trembling. Is this not the banner of the LORD which he has given to us? Is this not the fear of the LORD that he wants displayed "because of the truth"?

Yes, the fear of the LORD *is* the banner of truth. It is the banner of truth because his fear causes us to live in accordance with the truth and to have the truth in our inward parts. The fear of God keeps truth joined to our heart. Without it, truth will easily be put away. But with it, we can maintain a good conscience. The fear of the LORD will not only deliver God's beloved, but will also deliver all those that hear the heralders of the fear of the LORD. This was Paul's promise to Timothy. "Take heed unto thyself, and unto the doctrine; continue in them: for in doing this thou shalt both save thyself, and them that hear thee." 1Tim 4:16

Chapter 10. The Testings of the Fear of the LORD
The Cost of Possessing God's Great Treasure

The Afflictions, Provings, and
Testings of the Fear of God

*"for God is come to <u>prove you</u>, and that his fear
may be before your faces, that ye sin not." Ex 20:20*

Many are the afflictions of the righteous (Ps 34:18-19). Thus, we find the righteous often crying out to God for deliverance. This is equally true, David warns us, of those who fear him. "He will fulfil the desire of them that fear him: he also will hear their cry, and will save them." Ps 145:19 Though we may have the precious treasure of the fear of the LORD, we will still need our cries to be heard and to be delivered from sore troubles. Not only brokenness is in store for the saint that pursues the fear of God, but also many trials and afflictions.

There are blessings also that are coming for those who fear God, yet every blessing comes with its own series of tests. Testings always precede God's blessings and every blessing is also a test. All we have to do is look at Abraham's life

10 – The Testings of the Fear of the LORD

to prove this to ourselves.[155] Abraham waited long for the blessing of his son. That wait was a great test. But even when the blessing of the promised seed, his beloved son, came it was in itself also Abraham's greatest test. After Abraham proved his fear of God by being willing to sacrifice his well-loved son of promise (Gen 22:12), now other blessings of Abraham's life were released. Thus, those who fear God will be tested in many things.

Table 10-1   Testings of the Fear of the LORD

The Test of: [156]

1. Our Giving
2. Our Worship
3. Our Serving
4. Our Word Life
5. Our Reliance on
6. Our Prayer Life
7. Our Suffering for Truth

God desires to know if we truly believe that "little with the fear of the LORD" is better than great treasure without the fear of the LORD (Pr 15:16). God would know, how much are we willing to sacrifice for the *treasure* of the fear of the LORD? We shall see, we must pay dearly to obtain and keep this precious treasure. The LORD will always find out, why we are following him? Is it for the blessing of what we desire? Is it for someone else? It is for ourselves? Is it for another's glory? It is for our glory, OR is it for his glory? We are nearly always offended when someone questions the sincerity of our intentions or our promises, but God often requires such.

The LORD *must* prove the sincerity of our love (2Co 8:8) to ensure self-centeredness or selfishness is not part of our guiding desire. One little fly in the ointment spoils the whole for God. When God gave the sweet waters to those in the Exodus, "there he proved them" (Ex 15:25). With blessing came testing. When God gave them manna in the wilderness, there he proved them. "Who fed thee in the wilderness with manna, which thy fathers knew not, that he might humble thee, and <u>that he might prove thee</u>, to do thee good at thy latter end" (Dt 8:16). The LORD even put his people to the test on *how* they gathered the blessing (i.e., whether they gathered it with covetousness or in trust).

---

[155] Or even the lives of Joseph, Moses, David, Daniel, or a host of other witnesses.

[156] The first three tests were all discussed in the previous chapter. The remaining tests are covered in this chapter.

> Behold, I will rain bread from heaven for you; and the people shall go out and gather <u>a certain rate every day</u>, <u>that I may prove them</u>, whether they will walk in my law, or no. Ex 16:4

The Test of the Word of God
"Hear the word of the LORD, ye that <u>tremble</u> at his word" Isa 66:5

How do we respond to the authority of what God has already spoken? Ultimately every test will come back to this, for the word of God *is* the issue of life. This is what Satan immediately comes to steal out of our hearts: the word of God (Mk 4:15). Thus, the fear of God is most tellingly revealed by our response to God's word. We will either fear the word of the LORD and act upon it, or we will not fearfully regard it, and we will therefore ignore it. Will we allow his word to direct our way, even when it is contrary to what we would normally do? This is the test of the fear of the LORD.

> **He that feared the word of the LORD** among the servants of Pharaoh
> made his servants and his cattle flee into the houses:
> **And he that regarded not the word of the LORD**
> left his servants and his cattle in the field. Ex 9:20-21

Those who did not fear the word of the LORD, their servants and cattle were destroyed by God. Those who feared the word of the LORD were blessed in their fear. Their servants and cattle were spared because they acted upon what they heard. This is the fruit of the fear of the LORD: obedience to God's word. (Is this not a true foreshadowing of the last days and the judgments which are to come, when so many will not fear God and repent?) Think on this. These were people that had *just* encountered the LORD and who knew <u>nothing</u> of his teachings or commandments, except that when this God spoke it came to pass. When they heard another judgment was coming, they responded immediately to the word that was spoken by fearing the word of the LORD. How we have lost this heart in Christianity!

**When we do not fear God,
we do not take the word of God to heart.**

When we do not fear God, we do not take the word of God to heart.[157] Our actions, God shows us, are the direct result of our response to his word. The fear of God will shape and change our actions. When we fear God in truth we will tremble at his word[158] – no matter who the vessel that brings it. Our response to the word of the LORD will show the presence or absence of God's

---

[157] The word 'regarded' in Exodus 9:21 means 'to take to heart'.
[158] Examples of trembling at his word: Ezr 9:4, Isa 66:2,5, Dan 10:11.

10 – The Testings of the Fear of the LORD

fear. This is why the receiving of godly rebuke and correction by the word of God is so often joined with the fear of God in the scriptures.

> For that they hated knowledge, and did not choose <u>the fear of the LORD</u>: They would none of my counsel: <u>they despised all my reproof</u>. Pr 1:29-30
>
> The ear that <u>heareth the reproof</u> of life abideth among the wise. He that refuseth instruction despiseth his own soul: but <u>he that heareth reproof</u> getteth understanding. <u>The fear of the LORD</u> *is* the instruction of wisdom; and before honour *is* humility. Pr 15:31-33
>
> <u>Whoso despiseth the word</u> shall be destroyed: but he that <u>feareth the commandment</u> shall be rewarded. Pr 13:13

The fear of God will cause us to stop and *not* do what we might otherwise feel free to do without giving it a second thought. So we see with Nehemiah the servant of God: "so did not I, <u>because</u> of the fear of God." Neh 5:15 The word of God brings forth warnings, reprovings, corrections, chastisements, and finally judgment if we do not heed it. Thus, we are directly tested by the word of God. If we do not receive the warnings, then come reprovings. If we do not receive the reprovings, then come corrections. If we do not receive the corrections, then come chastisements. And if we do not receive the chastisements, finally comes judgment.

Notice how God rebukes and then chastens (Rev 3:19). God does not chasten first, and then rebuke. His rebuke always precedes his chastening, so that he gives time and opportunity for us to repent and to learn the importance of hearing his voice. Thus, David is rebuked for his sin with Bathsheba *before* he is chastened. So also Nebuchadnezzar is warned of his pride before he is judged. God desires to develop in each of us an ear to hear his voice. Thus, he will always warn us beforehand. This is to awaken the fear of God in us.

Should our hearts be any less obedient and responsive than those servants of Pharaoh who feared the word of the LORD? They barely knew of the LORD, but we have the record of his testimony and of his very person. For us who have come to know God through his Son and in whom the Spirit of His Son dwells, should we not fear God's word even more? Does the word of our God cause us to tremble? Does it give birth to immediate obedience? Do we fear God because of his mighty judgments that we read of? Or have we lost the sensitivity of heart that those who met God had?

David proclaimed in his beautiful psalm of praise for God's word, "My flesh trembleth for fear of thee; and I am afraid of thy judgments." Ps 119:120 Do we tremble at his word? Do we fear the commandment that *precedes* his judgment (Pr 13:13)? Daniel was such a man, that though he knew the love of his God, he still trembled at his word. "O Daniel, a man <u>greatly beloved</u>, understand the words that I speak unto thee, and stand upright: for unto thee am I now sent. And when he had spoken this word unto me, I <u>stood trembling</u>."

Dan 10:11 Or are we those to whom God will not look and who shall be ashamed because we do not tremble at his word?

> but to this *man* will I look, *even* to *him that is* poor and of a contrite spirit, and <u>trembleth at my word</u>. Hear the word of the LORD, ye that <u>tremble at his word</u>; your brethren that hated you, that cast you out for my name's sake, said, Let the LORD be glorified: but he shall appear to your joy, and they shall be ashamed. Isa 66:2,5

The Test of Reliance: Walking Not in the Counsel of Men
The power of God versus the impotency of men's doctrines and philosophies.

The fear of God, or the absence thereof, can be proven by where we will go for counsel. Do we run to the word of God and seek counsel from its divine wisdom? If we go to the world for counsel, if we listen to man's wisdom, to psychology, and to the dictates of science or man's research rather than the word of God, or if we give ear to those who are rebellious or unfaithful in their walk with the Lord, or if we listen to the carnal, unthankful, or unforgiving, then we have no fear of God. The fear of God will deliver us from the snares of death and drive us to seek out godly counsel from men of God who will guide us into only one thing: "What saith the scriptures?"

We must not walk in the counsel of the ungodly, or stand in the way of sinners, or sit in the seat of the scornful, for all our ways will begin to wither (Ps 1). We must not seek after Egypt, for "they are of the world: therefore speak they of the world, and the world heareth them." 1Jn 4:5 If we hear the world and rely on their counsel, then it reveals that we are of the world and our life is still rooted in this world! Jesus' sheep will hear his word (Jn 10:3,8,27), but the children of this world will hear the wisdom of this world. This is the sign of a backslidden heart: that we do not seek out God for his counsel. So God says of his own backslidden people, "For they *are* a nation <u>void of counsel</u>, neither *is there any* understanding in them." Dt 32:28

Remember, the same "spirit ... of the fear of the LORD" is also "the spirit of counsel" (Isa 11:2). The fruit of the fear of the LORD is to always be led back to the Holy Spirit's counsel and NOT the counsel of man, neither of our own mind, our own will, or the counsel or will of the world. The fear of the LORD will be put to the test in all of us on where we seek out and receive counsel from. Let us be cautious here. Many are subtly embracing evil today. Isaiah descriptively spoke of such a day when God's own people would rebel against him and not take counsel of him.

> Now go, write it before them in a table, and note it in a book, <u>that it may be for the time to come</u> for ever and ever: That this *is* a rebellious people, lying children, <u>children *that* will not hear</u> the law of the LORD: Which say to the seers, See not; and to the prophets, Prophesy not unto us right things, speak unto us smooth things, prophesy de-

ceits: Get you out of the way, turn aside out of the path, cause the Holy One of Israel to cease from before us. Isa 30:8-11

This is a picture of the apostate church where they have no ear to hear God's counsel, but they *do* take counsel from Egypt (i.e. the wisdom of the world). They do not seek God for his ways, but they strengthen themselves in the shadow of Egypt (i.e. they find strength in the world's comforts and protection). God says these things will be to their shame and confusion (vv1-3). Yet, God's people refused to be corrected and brought back into the fold of the Shepherd and Bishop of their souls (1Pe 2:25). Remember, Jesus cannot continue to be our Shepherd who leads us to the quiet, green pastures, if we refuse to allow him to also be the bishop, the *superintendent,* or overseer of our soul to bring counsel and correction.

Many a man of God fell into disfavor with God for walking in the counsel of those whose hearts were not with the LORD. Jehoshaphat joined himself with godless Ahab and paid dearly for it. His works were destroyed by God (2Ch 20:36-37), and he almost lost his life because of hearkening to Ahab's plans, rather than the counsel from a true prophet of God (2Ch 18). So serious is this issue that Paul warned Timothy that not all who call on the Lord, call on him out of a pure heart (2Tim 2:22).

The Test of Being Persecuted for the Truth

"Hear the word of the LORD, ye that tremble at his word; your brethren that hated you, that cast you out for my name's sake, said, Let the LORD be glorified" Isa 66:5

The fear of the LORD goes before us as a banner that is displayed. We have seen: "Thou hast given a banner to them that fear thee, that it may be displayed because of the truth. Selah." Ps 60:4 When one stops trying to please men, and only concerns himself with pleasing God through the fear of him, then this banner of truth cannot be hid. When the fear of God lays hold of our hearts we cannot but speak when things are contrary to the way our King has established them. To not do so is to betray him.

This banner of truth will be despised and rejected by all who will not receive the truth and who choose to live in deception. "For every one that doeth evil hateth the light, neither cometh to the light, lest his deeds should be reproved." Jn 3:20 As a result, persecution for the sake of serving the truth is unavoidable. Anyone who takes a stand on truth because he fears God *will* be slandered, ridiculed, mocked, and persecuted.

Consider this, Jesus was the servant of God (Mt 12:18). Why, then, was he hated? He was hated for this reason: because in the fear of God he spoke the truth – not abstract truth, not theoretical truth, but pointed, convicting truth – truth that exposed the darkness of men's hearts. Jesus spoke the truth that brought life by exposing lies, hypocrisy, deception, and sin so that people might be freed from darkness. "If I had not come and spoken unto them, they had not had sin: but now they have no cloke for their sin." Jn 15:22 Jesus' truth removes the clokes of deception and lies that men try to hide behind. The banner of the fear of the LORD will always expose sin – in us and in others.

The problem is that men love darkness rather than light because their deeds are evil (Jn 3:19), and they love their own way of thinking more than the word of God. Hence, they do not tremble at his word, as we see true saints doing (Isa 66:2,5, Ezr 10:3). This is why Jesus, because of the truth he spoke, was sure to be crucified – both then and now. This is also why the apostles faced death at the hands of those who hated the truth that brings conviction.

> **WARNING**: Even such a small thing as this – believing the truth about the fear of God – will offend many. As long as you agree with man's ideas that the fear of God has been eliminated by the love of God and that any fear of God today is really only an awe or a reverence of him, and not *really* a fear, then all is well. But stand on the word of God that the fear of God is what it says it is, a true fear, a literal 'phobia', which is to cause us to tremble before him and to be afraid of his power, might, and glory, *then* you will face mocking, scourging, and every form of ridicule and resistance.

This is the stranglehold of men's views and opinions, which cannot hear the word for what it says. This should prove to us, by the amount of resistance to the truth, how much Satan hates the true fear of God, and why he works so hard in men's thoughts to conjure up imitations, counterfeits, false reasonings, and excuses on why we should not *really* fear God. Thus, they make God's word of none effect by their traditions, precepts, and reasonings (Mt 15:6).

We will pay a painful price for walking in the true fear of God. So Isaiah said: "Hear the word of the LORD, ye that tremble at his word; **your brethren that hated you, that cast you out** for my name's sake, said, Let the LORD be glorified" (Isa 66:5). Those who would receive the truth of God, who tremble at his word in fearing him, they will most certainly be mocked and hated of their own brethren. It was no different of old, and it shall be even more so as we approach the end of the age. As Noah, a preacher of righteousness who was moved with godly fear, was mocked for preaching the truth of God's judgment, so have all the prophets who warned of judgment to come, from Enoch, to Isaiah, to Jeremiah, to Ezekiel, and so many others that we do not have time to consider here. Any man who holds fast to the fear of the LORD will begin to understand the judgments of God (as we have seen).[159] It is this understanding and knowledge of the truth that he will be persecuted for.

---

[159] See the chapter entitled "God's Judgment, A Cause for Fear" in the book Finding the Treasure of the Lord.

10 – The Testings of the Fear of the LORD

As long as one remains silent, concerning the judgment of God against compromise and wickedness, everything is fine. But the moment one speaks of them, he must surely face the most disparaging contradiction of sinners against his soul. Those who have little or no fear of God will hardly permit you to speak of judgments at all! What is most amazing is that most of this '*disputing*, gainsaying, and strife' will come from those who claim to be God's children, for, as the scripture accurately prophesies, when you truly fear God they will "cast you out for my name's sake" and yet say, "Let the LORD be glorified."

Jesus echoed this same rejection, "men shall hate you, and when they shall separate you *from their company,* and shall reproach *you,* and cast out your name as evil, for the Son of man's sake." Lk 6:22 "They shall put you out of the synagogues: yea, the time cometh, that whosoever killeth you will think that he doeth God service." Jn 16:2 Thus, he who fears the Lord will in the very name of the Lord be mocked! I have seen it time and time again. Whenever one stands on truth and lives in good conscience before God and man, with a heart just to serve others, they will be besmirched and despised by their own Christian brethren, especially by those who don't want to live in true holiness! And they will withdraw from fellowshipping with them. This is the test of the fear of God. Will we compromise the truth to save these 'friendships', or will we as Paul suffer the loss of all things for the sake of "the word of the truth of the gospel"? Are we willing to be hated of our own brethren, natural and spiritual, and to be cast out for his name's sake? The fear of the LORD will tell.

A Trusting Spirit: the Instruction of His Deliverances

At the same time we are undergoing persecution for the sake of standing for the truth, God will also be dealing with our soul and our character. How will we respond to the persecution we must endure? Will we grumble, complain, and grow angry and frustrated with those who misuse us? Or will the fear of God keep us meek and humble, trusting in the LORD's deliverance and vindication, not our own. This is all part of the test of the fear of the LORD.

God has promised he will astonish us as his people and will show us 'hard, *severe,* and grievous' things (Ps 60:3). God is both gentle and harsh with his servants. "And in that day thou shalt say, O LORD, I will praise thee: though thou wast angry with me, thine anger is turned away, and thou comfortedst me." Isa 12:1 He is strong in rebuke and uncompromising in holiness. But if our heart is softened through brokenness as God desires, then brokenness will lead us to a trusting spirit. This is why the way of brokenness is so vital to growing in the fear of God. A trusting spirit will strengthen us through the wilderness of brokenness. Then we will cry out to him and him alone who can help us. Thus, God's judgments and his mercies work together to cause us to fear him. "If thou, LORD, shouldest mark iniquities, O Lord, who shall stand? But *there is* forgiveness with thee, that thou mayest be feared." Ps 130:3-4

It is in the midst of the fiery trials that we are most at danger of coming under God's displeasure and judgment, for there he will see what is in the depth of our heart. In the furnace of affliction, God is looking for a faith that is more precious than fine gold. This is why we must cry out unto the LORD knowing he hears and delivers (Ps 34:15-21). We must put our unwavering trust in him who alone redeems us (Ps 34:22). And we must fear God enough not to accuse him or to think evil of him.

Whenever we undergo trials, afflictions, troubles, persecutions, chastenings, or even judgments, it is our heart and what we really believe about the LORD that is being put on trial. When God's people during the Exodus were put to the test of affliction and faced lack, their distrust and evil surmising of God's purposes immediately surfaced. So they challenged God: "And wherefore hath the LORD brought us unto this land, to fall by the sword, that our wives and our children should be a prey? were it not better for us to return into Egypt?" Nu 14:3 At every lack the people grumbled and complained. God was angry with them for this and his response was to give them what they truly believed. They believed God had brought them out of Egypt to perish, so God gave them up to perishing. What they accused God of is how he judged them. "Say unto them, *As truly as* I live, saith the LORD, as ye have spoken in mine ears, so will I do to you" (Nu 14:28).

> **WARNING**: Do we think the LORD will be any less disapproving of our murmuring in the new covenant, when we have received so much better promises (Heb 8:6) and so much better hope (Heb 7:19)? Whenever those around Jesus murmured, he immediately confronted it and rebuked it.[160] So we are warned by all the Old Testament examples. "Neither murmur ye, as some of them also murmured, and were destroyed of the destroyer." 1Co 10:10

God's afflictions bring us face to face with what we really believe about authority. If in our hearts we believe the LORD is harsh and unjust, when his affliction and judgment hits our life our misjudgments of him will come to the top. So we have the record of all those in Revelation in the last days that will fall under the judgment of God for their wicked deeds and their idolatries. Instead of being like the thief on the cross who repented and who knew that God's judgment of his life was just, they will not repent of the works of their hands (Rev 9:20-21), but will instead blaspheme the name of God (Rev 16:9,11). Their condemnation, then, will be doubly justified.

---

[160] Jesus repeatedly rebuked the scribes and Pharisees when they murmured. We see this when they murmured against his disciples (Lk 5:29-32) and when they murmured against him (Lk 15:1-4, 19:5-27). Jesus rebuked the multitude for murmuring (Jn 6:41-44), and even his own disciples for this (in the eating of his flesh, Jn 6:61-63, and when the precious ointment was poured out upon him, Mk 14:3-9).

10 – The Testings of the Fear of the LORD

God's deliverances firmly fixed before our eyes are what will secure his fear forever in us. So Samuel exhorted the people, "Only fear the LORD, and serve him in truth with all your heart: for **consider how great *things* he hath done for you.**" 1Sam 12:24 We all too often forget the works of the LORD, when they were given to us as a memorial and a heritage. This why God exhorts us not to forget what we have experienced of his great workings. "Only take heed to thyself, and keep thy soul diligently, lest thou forget the things which thine eyes have seen, and lest they depart from thy heart **all the days of thy life**" (Dt 4:9). If we would but consider what great things he has done for us, then the fear of the LORD would stay fresh in our hearts, along with a thankfulness to serve him with all our heart. Remember, no one could have done what the LORD has done to save us, forgive us, deliver us, wash us, cleanse us, and sanctify us. The deliverances of God are to be fixed in our memories.

> There is no king saved by the multitude of an host: a mighty man is not delivered by much strength. An horse *is* a vain thing for safety: neither shall he deliver *any* by his great strength. Behold, the eye of the LORD *is* **upon them that fear him**, upon them that hope in his mercy; To deliver their soul from death, and to keep them alive in famine. Ps 33:16-19

God's deliverances are to be memorials, engraven testimonies in our heart, so that we will not forget the works of the LORD. His deliverances are to produce thankfulness and sincere and truthful service of him who has snatched us from the fire. His deliverances ought to drive out idolatry from our hearts so that we worship only him. Most of all they should instruct us in the fear of God, for we know that it was his grace and mercy which delivered us and not our own works. All of this can be seen in Joshua's exhortation to the people to fear the LORD as he reminds them of God's great, mighty, and repeated deliverances (Jos 24:8-14). And what was his conclusion?

> **Now therefore fear the LORD**, and serve him in sincerity and in truth: and put away the gods which your fathers served on the other side of the flood, and in Egypt; and serve ye the LORD. Jos 24:14

The Test of How We Pray

"He will fulfil the desire of them that fear him:
he also will hear their cry, and will save them." Ps 145:19

The depth of our fear of God will not only be seen in our response to his word, but will also be revealed in how we approach God in prayer. Do we come with a list of demands? Are we frustrated when our prayers seem to go unanswered? Do we complain or murmur, rather than thanking God for his mercies and rejoicing in his salvation? Do we become impatient with God when he does not act according to our time table or our desires? Are we angry with God when things turn out the opposite of how we've believed and prayed? So often we think God will answer our prayer because we have asked it of him. We think our prayers are 'holy' because we have offered them with sincerity. But only what he makes and creates is holy. This is why we must pray his will, not our own. The keys to answered prayer are his will and our submission to that will, but in what we do and in what we pray for.

> If I regard iniquity in my heart, the Lord will <u>not</u> hear *me* Ps 66:18
>
> And this is the confidence that we have <u>in him</u>, that, if we ask any thing <u>according to his will</u>, he heareth us: And if we know that he hear us, whatsoever we ask, we know that we have the petitions that we desired of him. 1Jn 5:15

The true fear of the LORD will produce an effective and consistent prayer life. Thus, we see in the scriptures prayer issuing forth from those who fear God. "He will fulfil the desire of them that fear him: <u>he also will hear their cry</u>, and will save them." Ps 145:19 Let us fear God as we approach him in prayer. God will hear us when we fear him, because our heart is set on doing his will. The promise of answered prayer is the particular possession, the sure heritage of those who fear him. "For thou, O God, hast <u>heard my vows</u>: thou hast given *me* the heritage of those that fear thy name." Ps 61:5 There is a special inheritance for all those who fear God in truth.

> Consider this, Jesus was *not* heard in that he was a son!
> He was heard in that he feared his heavenly Father.

On what basis do we believe God should answer our prayers – that we are sons and daughters of God? This is what we are taught, that God hears us because we are his children. Meditate on this amazing point, though Jesus was the only begotten son of the Father *and* without sin, even he did not demand, nor expect God to answer his cries only because he was a son!

> Who in the days of his flesh, when he had offered up prayers and supplications with strong crying and tears unto him that was able to save him from death, and <u>was heard in that he feared</u> Heb 5:7

> **WARNING**: Neither let us think that Jesus was heard because of "his strong crying and tears", as some by their excessive *volume* in prayer so evidently believe. It is right to mock the foolishness that "God more readily hears our prayer when we pray with strong crying and tears." Elisha so mocked those who prayed to Baal.[161] Jesus himself let his disciples know that the hypocrites pray this way because they do not truly come before God in their prayers (Mt 6:5-8).

---

[161] "Elijah mocked them, and said, <u>Cry aloud</u>: for he *is* a god; either he is talking, or he is pursuing, or he is in a journey, *or* peradventure he sleepeth, and must be awaked." 1K

10 – The Testings of the Fear of the LORD

> The scripture is clear, he "was heard in that he feared [God]". I have seen many a man who with strong crying and tears prayed and prayed, but to no avail. Remember the warning of Esau: "For <u>ye know</u> how that afterward, when he would have inherited the blessing, he was <u>rejected</u>: for he found no place of repentance, though he sought it carefully <u>with tears</u>." Heb 12:17 Tears do not move God. The fear of God in our hearts moves God.

Consider this, Jesus was *not* heard in that he was a son! He was heard in that he feared his heavenly Father. Prayer cannot fulfill its complete potential without the fear of God. I pray this is as stunning for you, as it was for me when I first saw this in the scriptures.

Prayer is Restrained without the Fear of God

The fear of God is so integral to a healthy prayer life that without it our prayer life will lack intensity and consistency. Christians often complain of a weak prayer life, not knowing it is because of the lack of the fear of God in them. God's fear will cause our prayer life to be stirred up and brought into the realm of the holy. Without the fear of God our prayer life will naturally wane and become dull and lifeless. So Eliphaz warns Job that the casting off or the *frustrating* of the fear of God will cause prayer to be restrained, held back before God. "Yea, thou castest off fear, and <u>restrainest prayer</u> before God." Job 15:4

Why is prayer restrained when we lack God's fear? *First*, prayer is restrained because we do not approach God correctly. When we lack the fear that is due him, we come as the arrogant hypocrite who trusts in his own righteousness (Lk 18:9). We come as the man invited to the wedding feast who did not clothe himself in a wedding garment (Mt 22:11-14). We come unprepared before our holy King.

So often we come with a casual attitude as sons of God by faith in Christ Jesus, thinking we are heard because we are sons or because we have the name of Jesus to use. We come presuming we have some authority in coming before the great King of kings, which has not in fact been given unto us. There is only one way to come before the great King and that is humbly in the fear of God. Such is the meaning of the parable of the Pharisee and the Publican. Jesus warned us not to trust in ourselves that we are righteous, especially when we pray, for this is how the Pharisee "prayed thus with himself". The publican stood afar off and did not consider himself worthy even to be heard.[162]

18:27 But it is not so with our God, "Behold, he that keepeth Israel shall neither slumber nor sleep." Ps 121:4 The true and living God does not need to be awakened.

[162] This is a far cry from the Christians' "king's kids" mentality.

Where is the Fear of GOD? Losing the Treasure of the Lord

Let us remember, it is the *right* of kings to be feared, so our God as king must be feared. And it was the publican who was heard and who was justified, because he abased himself in the presence of the King (Lk 18:13-14). Fear belongs to God, and we dare not come before him without it. Even so says the scripture, "Who would not fear thee, O King of nations? for to thee <u>doth it appertain</u>" (Jer 10:7). "My son, fear thou the Lord and the king" (Pr 24:21).

Secondly, prayer is restrained because God will not hear us when we do not fear him. He heard his own son, *not* because he was his son, but because his son feared him. That is a profound truth that we need to lay hold of. Yes, the cries of the newborn are always heard by their father, to take care of their need, but the crying of the adolescent or the youth, as one grows up, are deliberately *not* always heard! Thus, Jesus himself was *not* heard through his own name or because he was a son, but through his fear of the living God! Now we may comprehend why God promises to hear the cry of those who fear him (Ps 145:19).

As we grow, our relationship with our father must change. Now things are no longer based on our desires or the way we would see our needs fulfilled, but the answering of our prayer is based on his great will and wisdom. He "worketh all things after the counsel of his own will" according to his own purpose (Eph 1:11). He works in us "both to will and to do <u>of *his* good pleasure</u>." Php 2:13 It was those servants in Nehemiah's day which feared the name of God who prayed for divine favor before the king. They prayed that deliverance would be granted to God's people to build Jerusalem. But they did not pray for this based on being God's covenant children, for they had all seen what God had done to *his* covenant children in judging them for their continued stubbornness and rebellion! Rather, their cry unto God was rooted in their being servants of God who had a desire to fear God's name (Neh 1:11).

Thirdly, prayer is restrained before God because we ourselves, without the fear of God, will cease to pray. Without the fear of God we will lose much of our fervency in prayer and our strength to endure in prayer. It is impossible to keep watch for long without fear. This is because watching (from our perspective) seems to produce little – so we quickly become bored or tired of it and fall asleep. It is the fear of God that places the LORD firmly before our face. His glory and fear is then what becomes our motivation, our strength to persevere.

When we, through the fear of God, see him by faith who is invisible, we, like Moses, will *endure*. Moses "endured, as seeing him who is invisible." Heb 11:27 This is what the fear of God produces: **endurance**. So we see Noah, because of his fear of God, endured for 120 years to complete what God had asked of him in building the ark. We need more of that today!

Now to endurance must be added watchfulness. Once Nehemiah began the work of building, he <u>continued</u> in prayer unto God, but now he had to add watching. "Nevertheless we made our prayer unto our God, and <u>set a watch</u>

10 – The Testings of the Fear of the LORD

against them day and night, because of them." Neh 4:9 Nehemiah's enemies were natural, but ours are spiritual. How much *more* ought we to pray and watch.

Let us have the fear of God in our prayers, and remember that he does nothing outside of his sovereign will. As we begin to truly fear God it will transform our heart, our mind, our thoughts, and even our prayer life. We will no longer pray as we once did, focused on our will and what we want. We will experience a powerful intimacy in prayer and a new direction. Instead of self-directed prayers, God will show us the way he shall choose (Ps 25:12). The fear of God is the missing foundation of how we are to approach God in prayer, and it is the very door by which prayer is heard and answered. Those who fear God have the assurance that God will hear them when they pray because they fear him (Ps 145:19).

The fear of God will also mark the *depth* of our prayer life. How often do we turn to the Lord for guidance and counsel? The fear of God will drive us to seek him always. Cornelius was unsaved, yet he was "A devout *man,* and one that <u>feared God</u> with all his house, which gave much alms to the people, and <u>prayed to God alway</u>." Ac 10:2 If this marked one who was not even saved yet, but had the fear of God working in him to draw him to salvation, **how much more** ought it to be in those who are saved and are working out their salvation *with* fear and trembling?!

> The fear of God is the missing foundation of how
> we are to approach God in prayer, and it is
> the very door by which prayer is heard and answered.

Let this be a great encouragement to the saint that fears God. Let this propel them in their prayer life, even as it did our Lord. We find Jesus praying all the time during his earthly ministry. Hebrews tells us, "Who in the days of his flesh ... offered up prayers and supplications with strong crying and tears unto him that was able to save him from death" (Heb 5:7). Even now Jesus "ever liveth to make intercession" for us (Heb 7:25).

Jesus had a great assurance in prayer to his heavenly Father. "Jesus lifted up *his* eyes, and said, Father, I thank thee that thou hast heard me. And <u>I knew that thou hearest me always</u>" (Jn 11:41-42). Why did Jesus know that his heavenly Father would always hear him? Because he feared God and knew the Word. "He will fulfil the desire of them that fear him: he also will hear their cry, and will save them." Ps 145:19 If we really knew we were heard by God, I expect we would all pray much, much more. The testimony of the early church regarding prayer is profound. The way of the early church was marked by prayer, and they were those who were "walking in the fear of the Lord" (Ac 9:31).

Inheriting the Promise

"Let us therefore <u>fear</u>, lest, a promise being left us of entering into his rest, any of you should seem to come short of it." Heb 4:1

The fear of the LORD will enable us to enter into his covenants and to walk in them. Thus, it will enable God to fulfill his good plan and purpose for our life. A covenant is a solemn, binding promise between two parties. In each covenant God has made with man he has set conditions under which they may function and operate. Covenants are like working machines. When they are put to use within the guidelines of proper operation they function flawlessly. But when they are abused, neglected, or otherwise operated improperly, they cannot function as they were intended, and they end up broken. This is why we have record of each of the covenants God made with man being broken.[163]

All of God's covenants and promises are spoken in faith that we will fulfill our part of the covenant. So it was with many of the Jews who had the promises and the covenants (Rom 9:4-5). Many times they did not receive the inheritance of what God had promised them because of their hardness of heart. "For what if some did not believe? shall their unbelief make <u>the faith of God</u> without effect?" Rom 3:3 Most Christians today are taught a sloppy, irreverent attitude toward God's promises.

> **WARNING**: This has come to a head in the covetous doctrine of the "faith" movement: 'name it & claim it', 'nab it & grab it', 'imagine it & you can have it'. They speak of the power of the tongue, rather than the power of God. They speak of *your* "creative" ability, rather than God's redemptive plan to recreate you in holiness and true righteousness. They take indiscriminately and without shame from eastern mysticism and methods of visualization, when God condemns such idolatrous mixture. "Thus saith the LORD, <u>Learn not</u> the way of the heathen" (Jer 10:2).

The Bible says it is through faith and patience that we inherit the promises of God. "That ye be not slothful, but followers of them who through faith and patience inherit the promises. And so, after [Abraham] had patiently endured, he obtained the promise." Heb 6:12,15 Because of the fruit of patience working in the fear of the LORD, we see a principle in the scripture that those who feared God often were blessed in their old age.[164]

So what does this have to do with the fear of God? How does the fear of God relate to patience? It is the fear of God that produces the stability, faithful-

---

[163] See 'Covenant Breaking' in the appendix entitled "Definition of Some Biblical Terms" for more information on covenants and why they are by definition conditional.

[164] Like Abraham (Gen 24:1) and Joshua (Jos 23:1-2,14).

10 – The Testings of the Fear of the LORD

ness, and patience that allows the LORD to do his work in us so that we are ready and prepared to receive the promise. As we have seen already, the fear of God is the pedestal,[165] the securing member, that God would have our faith rest upon and be stabilized by, for the fear of God trembles at his word and his word is the very source of true faith.

It was the fear of God that brought such a love for God's word that David wrote the longest psalm of all to proclaim the value of God's word. Every verse of Psalm 119 speaks of God's word, his law, statutes, commandments, precepts, and testimonies. It was in this heart that David sought God so that (1) he would go in the way of those commandments, that (2) his heart would be turned toward the promises of God's testimonies and (3) away from covetousness, and finally that (4) his eyes would be turned away from beholding vanity (i.e. moral *evil* or *idolatry*). Thus, it is the fear of God that kept David in the way. And it is on the basis of devotion to the fear of God that David prays for God to establish and fulfill the word which he had spoken to him. David expected to be heard, like Jesus, because he feared God.

> [1] Make me to go in the path of thy commandments; for therein do I delight. [2] Incline my heart unto thy testimonies, and [3] not to covetousness. [4] Turn away mine eyes from beholding vanity; *and* quicken thou me in thy way. Stablish thy word unto thy servant, who *is devoted to thy fear*. Ps 119:35-38

Consider this, fellow soldier. God has made promises and covenants, which he has given to you, but he can and will only establish these in your life as you become devoted to his fear. As you remain dedicated to God in faithfulness through the fear of God, as you are well-stricken in age, you will be blessed in all things by seeing them come to pass. So "in your patience possess ye your souls" (Lk 21:19). Let us not come short of entering into his promises because we lack the foundation of the fear of God or the patience that issues from it. Let us not faint in the time of testing, for then is our strength small (Pr 24:10). As it is written, "Let us therefore fear" (Heb 4:1).

---

[165] See the chapter entitled "Understanding the New Covenant of Grace & Fear" in the book <u>Finding the Treasure of the Lord</u>.

Chapter 11. Warning Signs of Losing God's Fear
Hearing the Foghorns of Apostasy

"By faith Noah, being <u>warned</u> of God of things not seen as yet, moved with <u>fear</u>" Heb 11:7

We have seen that the fear of God has many counterfeits and substitutes, that either replace the fear of God altogether or rob it of any power to change our life according to the desires of our heavenly Father. We have seen that the fear of God is not merely an awe or reverence of God, but is much deeper and more life changing. The fear of God has not only many imposters but also many enemies. Among these enemies, which we have looked at, are pride,[166] covetousness,[167] the fear of man,[168] and an evil conscience,[169] which manifests in

---

[166] Several examples of how pride causes the fear of God to cease were seen in sections named 'The Dangers of Pride' in the chapter "Why We Forsake the Fear of the LORD".

[167] Covetousness drives out the fear of God in the section 'The Dangers of Blessings' in the chapter "Why We Forsake the Fear of the LORD", and the fear of God drives out covetousness in the section 'A Selfless, Sacrificial Heart' in the chapter "Toward a More Godly, Faithful, and Perfect Heart".

[168] The fear of man drives out the true fear of God in the section 'The Dangers of Losing God's Purpose' in the chapter "Why We Forsake the Fear of the LORD", and the fear of God drives out the fear of man in the section 'The Proper Fear of Authority' in the chapter "Broken Fellowship from the Loss of God's Fear".

dishonesty. The fear of God cannot coexist with pride or with fearing man or with covetousness or with shading the truth. These enemies of the fear of God are why our modern version of Christianity is killing us spiritually. We are taught that we are 'somebody' and that God's desire for us is to be healthy, wealthy, and in the 'front of the line'. We are taught to take part of the truth, the part that benefit us, and ignore the rest. These four enemies of the fear of God are all subtly being taught within the church today as acceptable, when in fact, they are things that God hates. We will also look at following our dreams.

Let us look closer at these enemies which destroy the true fear of God. Their appearance in our heart will be the early warning signs of losing God's fear. We have seen that the fear of the LORD enables us to depart from the snares of death (Pr 14:27). Therefore, the enemies of the fear of the LORD, if we are properly warned of them, will act like buoys that warn us of the shallow waters, which will shipwreck our faith on the shoals of an evil conscience. The enemies of the fear of God should thus become the foghorns of apostasy – warnings that we are departing in our heart from the living God and apostatizing from truth.

Table 11-1   Signs of Losing the Fear of God

The Warning of:
1. Dishonesty (and the Fear of Man)
2. Covetousness (which is Idolatry)
3. Taking Advantage of Others
4. Following Our Dreams
5. Pride of Our Heart

The Warning of Dishonesty

"Moreover thou shalt provide out of all the people able men, such as fear God, <u>men of truth</u>, hating covetousness" Ex 18:21

Dishonesty is the first sign of falling away from the fear of the LORD. The primary work of the fear of the LORD is to keep a good conscience by walking openly without guile, without deception, before God. This is why we see that the first fruit of the fear of the LORD over and over again *is* truth. Notice how sincerity and truth follow from the fear of the LORD in these verses. "Now therefore fear the Lord, and serve him <u>in sincerity and in truth</u>" (Jos 24:14). "Only fear the Lord, and serve him <u>in truth</u> with all your heart" (1Sam 12:24).

---

[169] Evil and the true fear of the Lord cannot coexist is seen in the section 'Departing from Iniquity' in the chapter "Holiness, Righteouness, & Faithfulness to God".

This is as God has planned it. God gives a *banner* to those who fear him, which is openly displayed in the life of those who walk in the fear of God. It flies high and free in the wind of the Spirit for others to behold. God desires it to be a rallying point for other soldiers of the LORD to gather around.[170] But what is this banner, and why does God want it displayed? It is none other than the banner of truth. "Thou hast given a banner to them that fear thee, that it may be displayed <u>because of the truth</u>. Selah." Ps 60:4

We have already looked at this banner as the banner of brokenness. Here we call it also the banner of truth, not because it is a different banner, but because it is upon the truth that we are broken. Jesus said, "And whosoever shall fall on this stone shall be broken" (Mt 21:44). This stone, upon which we are broken, is none other than the stumbling stone of truth, which is Jesus. Jesus said, "I am ... the truth" (Jn 14:6). We also call it the banner of truth because, once we undergo brokenness, truth is now exalted. It becomes our banner. This banner of truth is costly truth, for because of brokenness and persecution it costs us much to carry it. It is the banner of truth because it is for truth's sake that God wants it displayed in each of our lives. As Psalm 60:4 says, this is something truly to stop and think about.

Guile and the Warning to Leadership

Are not our lives and the hypocrisy of our actions as Christians who claim that we know truth and walk in truth compromised when truth is not displayed in our actions and words? Yes. In fact, are we not the greater hypocrites when we claim to be God's possession headed toward heaven, yet we still live for earthly rewards and use natural, carnal means to attain them? and that our church leaders and television spokesmen are the worst offenders in this manner? Yes and yes. Let us get the fear of the LORD back into our hearts, and we will see that we are again growing in wisdom and in favor with both God and men – not the favor from compromising the truth, but the favor of respect from those who see we truly do fear God.

Is it any wonder that truth has perished as a banner in the church, when it is not the first concern of those who are in positions to stand for truth? Men will shade the truth and mix it with the philosophies of the world, speaking what most benefits them and keeps the people in control. Men of God are tempted repeatedly on this issue of guile, whether they will allow something to appear one way, when it in fact is another. When men willingly allow people to believe something contrary to what it is in reality, then they cannot be walking in the fear of God, but in the craftiness of their own thinking.

---

[170] It is because this banner is lacking in so many leaders that the flock is scattered (no, not in numbers, but in purpose, desires, heart, and true spiritual unity).

11 – Warning Signs of Losing God's Fear

> Come, ye children, hearken unto me: I will teach you the fear of the LORD. What man *is he that* desireth life, *and* loveth *many* days, that he may see good? Keep thy tongue from evil, and thy lips from speaking guile. Ps 34:11-13

WARNING: As churches grow larger through the use of worldly techniques, the church must at the same time grow shallower and more naturally minded. When we follow and use the ways of the world, we become like the world. People have a naïve perspective thinking that the mega-churches are clearly unified as evidenced by their size and continual growth in numbers. Yet from God's perspective they are a mixed multitude (Ex 12:38), for though they believe that they believe the same thing, in fact, they each have their own way. Without sound doctrine[171] and being brought into the narrow way of the kingdom of God, we will never learn according to the scriptures how to "all speak the same thing, and *that* there be no divisions among you; but *that* ye be perfectly joined together in the same mind and in the same judgment." 1Co 1:10

Maybe we have forgotten what guile is. We may hate lying, yet never realize that guile is working in us. 'Guile' means 'to decoy or to trick'. A decoy is something that appears to be one way when in reality it is another. Remember what a decoy does. It removes alarm, distracts, and makes others feel comfortable. This warning might be easier to write off or ignore, if the very issue of keeping our lips from speaking guile were not repeated for us in the New Testament as well. Peter quotes Psalm 34:12-13, "For he that will love life, and see good days, let him refrain his tongue from evil, and his lips that they speak no guile" (1Pe 3:10). Earlier he also stated that we must lay aside all guile (1Pe 2:1).

Our most noteworthy example of speaking without guile is Nathanael who openly spoke his mind, even if it offended others. Thus, we see the one who fears God is "*He that* sweareth to *his own* hurt, and changeth not." Ps 15:4 Our story cannot change because of situations, if we are fearing God. But if our story is changing when siturations change, then we are practicing guile. Nathanael did not speak in a way which spared a person's feelings, but he spoke openly what he knew to be true. So Jesus commends him for this.[172]

> And Nathanael said unto him, Can there any good thing come out of Nazareth? Philip saith unto him, Come and see. Jesus saw Nathanael

---

[171] Without sound doctrine we may appear to have unity, but there are hidden divisions among us which cause us to be of different judgments and differing minds. We cannot in truth faithfully follow the Lord Jesus for the purpose of getting our needs and desires met. The multitudes have always followed Jesus for his wonders and fame (Mt 4:23-25, Mk 3:7-8, Jn 6:2) and for his provision of blessings (Jn 6:24-26). But as soon as his word comes with conviction and rebuke, it cannot be received, and they will walk away.

[172] This was not spoken sarcastically or insincerely. Nathanael, by his response, clearly took this as a compliment.

coming to him, and saith of him, Behold an Israelite indeed, <u>in whom is no guile</u>! Jn 1:46-47

Men speak today of using the wisdom of God when they do not openly speak what is the truth. In reality, they are speaking with guile. They are willingly deceiving. It is lying against the truth to allow people to believe contrary to reality. In that area, we must confess the fear of God has been put aside. Often, it is for this simple reason, because place has been given to fearing what the people think or to how they may respond. This is what we see with King Saul. Truth for him was relative to the greater goal of what he was trying to accomplish. For him, the ends justified the means – implicitly. But the truth is not relative, it is absolute. So Jesus could say with certainty, "I **am** ... the truth" (Jn 14:6). Why did Saul sin in disobeying the voice of the LORD before the people and so lose his anointing? "And Saul said unto Samuel, I have sinned: for I have transgressed the commandment of the LORD, and thy words: <u>because I feared the people</u>, and obeyed their voice." 1Sam 15:24 As evidenced not only by King Saul's life, but also by the repeated testimony of history, this is a great temptation for those in positions of leadership.

Who Are We Afraid of?

If we allow others to believe contrary to reality, then we cannot say we are leading them in truth, nor can we say we have laid aside all guile. Leaders are called by God to hold men to the truth. Let no one condemn another in this manner, or think evil of a leader. We are all tempted to conceal the truth. But let us examine ourselves to see if we be in the faith in this area, and let us press on to truth through the fear of the LORD. Let the fear of God keep our heart purged from the compromise of shading truth. "By mercy and truth iniquity is purged: and by the fear of the LORD *men* depart from evil." Pr 16:6 When we fear the people, especially as leaders, or fear what they may do, then we are not fearing the LORD, nor are we departing from iniquity. Listen to Isaiah's rebuke,

> And **of whom** hast thou been afraid or feared, that <u>thou hast lied</u>, and <u>hast not remembered me</u>, nor laid *it* to thy heart? have not I held my peace even of old, and thou fearest me not? Isa 57:11

Isaiah's rebuke has much to say to us about both the price and the process of dishonesty. Notice the direct correlation between being afraid of people and forgetting God, and then lying. Note that this is the direct result of not fearing God. But notice also that when this happens, we don't lay it to our heart. This is the deception of dishonesty. Once we follow this path because of our fear of man we do not give thought to what we have done! Our fear of men is what often causes us to enter into the cycle of dishonesty:

11 – Warning Signs of Losing God's Fear

<u>The Cycle of Dishonesty</u>
1. we lie because we fear men,
2. then we don't remember God,
3. nor do we do lay it to our heart,[173]
4. then we lose our fear of the LORD.

We have seen that the fear of man drives out the fear of God. Now we can see how this is done. For the very first work of the fear of man is to move us to lie. Lying is thus the first step in beginning to not fear God. When we lie, we are not remembering the Lord. As a result, he does not remember us – for a time. Let me explain. When God observes us fearing men, rather than him, and lying to either get what we want or to avoid what we don't want, then he will often hold his peace and be silent. He wants to see if conviction will work in our heart. If we will be honest with our selves and with him. His silence in these times can be deafening, and it is intended to cause us to humble ourselves and to fear him. We must know, *sometimes* when heaven is silent, something *is* wrong. So we see, silence was Saul's reward. "And Samuel came no more to see Saul until the day of his death" (1Sam 15:35). Sadly, this did not prick Saul's heart to repentance.

Who are we afraid of? Whom do we fear, when we lie against what we know to be true? When we are not completely honest, it is because we fear people more than the LORD. The very thing that King Saul feared is the same thing that so many large church senior pastors fear: <u>the people leaving</u>. Saul's first sin was at Gilgal. God was trying to circumcise Saul's heart here, for that is the very first thing God did with the Israelites when he brought them into the land of Canaan. God had every male circumcised at Gilgal, before their enemies (Jos 5:2-9). This was the place where God "rolled away the reproach of Egypt [i.e. the world] from off you" (v9).

> When we are not completely honest, it is because
> we fear people more than the LORD.

But Saul feared losing the people too much. It was all he could see: "the people were scattered from him" (1Sam 13:8b). God's voice through the prophet could not longer be heard. This is what began his departure from the fear of God. Instead of in patience possessing his soul, instead he forsook waiting. "He [*had*] tarried seven days, according to the set time that Samuel had appointed: but Samuel came not to Gilgal" (1Sam 13:8a). He couldn't wait a minute longer once he saw the people leaving. Now Saul made up his own sacrifice in order to impress the people, keep them entertained, and keep them from

---

[173] That is, we do not take it seriously.

leaving (1Sam 13:9-10). This is a very grievous sin in our generation, for it is taking place all the time: the entertaining of God's people!

For this Saul was reproved, and his kingdom was not established (1Sam 13:11-14). Why would Saul *substitute* for what God had commanded? Why would he pretend to do what he *knew* he could not do in truth? Because he feared losing the people! Just before this the Bible says, "the people were scattered from him." 1Sam 13:8 Saul feared this, tragically, more than he feared God, and he knew it, for when he was confronted by Samuel, we hear his pathetic answer: "And Samuel said, What hast thou done? And Saul said, Because I saw that the people were scattered <u>from me</u>" (1Sam 13:11).

Is this not what men with large ministries and much fame fear most, exactly what King Saul feared? This requirement for being men of truth and speaking without guile is so important that it was <u>the first</u> qualification checked for leadership to see if men truly feared God. So we read when God instructed Moses to pick men for the role of judges, he was to pick men "such as fear God, men of truth, hating covetousness" (Ex 18:21). We will know if a man fears God first and foremost by whether he is a man of truth.

We know that God picked Levi and his family to be spiritual overseers leading the people as priests of the LORD. But why was this covenant given to Levi and to his seed? The covenant of life and peace was with him, the Bible says, because of the fear wherewith he feared the LORD of hosts and was afraid before his name. But what was the result of the fear that he had toward the LORD? "The <u>law of truth</u> was in his mouth, and iniquity was not found in his lips" (Mal 2:5-6). The fear of the LORD of hosts will cause truth to be in our mouth, and our lips to be far from lying or shading the truth. Let us forsake the fear of man and its lying ways; but hold fast to the fear of God so that we may hold the banner of truth high.

The Warning of Covetousness

"Moreover thou shalt provide out of all the people able men, such as fear God, men of truth, <u>hating covetousness</u>" Ex 18:21

The next characteristic of men who fear God, after being men of truth, is that they are "hating covetousness". This means that men who fear God have a continual hatred of covetousness. They do not just hate it, rather they are hating it – it is an ongoing attitude of their heart, not a passing anger. Covetousness is the most self-serving of the enemies of the fear of God. Often we do not see how covetousness prevents the fear of the LORD from developing, but it does in a subtle and destructive way. When God gave the requirements to pick out judges who would help Moses in the work of providing sound counsel for the people of God, he was instructed to pick "able men, such as fear God, men of truth, hating covetousness" (Ex 18:21). Only four requirements, two describing

11 – Warning Signs of Losing God's Fear

what kind of men they were (i.e. men of ability and men of truth), and the other two describing their actions (i.e. such as fear God and hate covetousness).

A man may have ability, but have no fear of God; and without the fear of God, he cannot be a man of truth. Without being a man of truth, he will never hate covetousness. But a man may like the truth, but still love money. That is where the danger comes in. Let us now look at the pitfall of greed. The fear of God will make a man content, satisfied with what he has in the LORD. With it we abide satisfied. "The fear of the LORD *tendeth* to life: and *he that hath it* shall abide satisfied" (Pr 19:23). Without it, we will hunger for something to fill our emptiness. We have all the treasure we could ever desire in the reward of the fear of the LORD. [174]

Without the fear of the Lord (and the reward which comes by it), we will often unknowingly be seeking something else in our life; some undefinable more that we must have to be satisfied. Remember what is recorded for us, "The fear of the LORD *tendeth* to life: and *he that hath it* shall abide satisfied." Pr 19:23a Thus, the man who has not the fear of God cannot abide or continue satisfied in his life. He will always be looking for something else. Thus, the lack of the fear of God so often manifests in covetousness – the desire for other things. This is why the lack of the fear of the LORD will always be evidenced by greed, desiring what others have in order to try to fill our internal emptiness.

A counselor or judge of God's people must have the fear of God if he is to lead God's people. That fear of God will protect him from being ensnared in dishonesty and seeking things for himself, such as bribery or greed. Thus, covetousness and dishonesty prevent the fear of God from developing in our heart. In order to secure the fear of God we must repent of these first. Let us be convinced that it is better by far to only have a little, yet have the fear of the LORD, than to desire or even to have great riches. "Better *is* little with the fear of the LORD than great treasure and trouble therewith." Pr 15:16 In the eyes of God covetousness *is* trouble, for it is idolatry personified (Eph 5:5, Col. 3:5).

False Preachers who Love Filthy Lucre

We will be put to test not only by whether we are directly covetous, but also by whether we will listen to and receive that which covetous teachers and prophets will proclaim. God warned the people that he would prove them in this area by sending them false prophets (i.e. false proclaimers, falsely inspired teachers and preachers). We are indeed seeing the same deceiving of covetousness taking place today, even as Peter warned us.

---

[174] Here are the foundational scriptures for the reward of fear of the Lord: Isa 33:6, Ps 61:5, 31:19.

> But there were <u>false prophets</u> also among the people, even as there shall be <u>false teachers</u> among you, who privily shall bring in damnable heresies, even denying the Lord that bought them, and bring upon themselves swift destruction. And through <u>covetousness</u> shall they with feigned words <u>make merchandise of you</u> 2Pe 2:1,3

For the young, the infant or the baby, it is pure poison that they must be kept from, but for the adult they know not to partake of pure poison. Hence, it is the mixture of the sweet and the poison that slowly kills more often. Yes, a false prophet's foretellings do not come to pass (Dt 18:22), but God promised to test our devotion to him, not only based on the witness of whether the sign comes to pass, but also on the witness of the truth of the message. Does it agree with what God has already spoken? Listen,

> If there arise among you a prophet, or a dreamer of dreams, and giveth thee a sign or a wonder, <u>And the sign or the wonder come to pass</u>, whereof he spake unto thee, saying, Let us go after other gods, which thou hast not known, and let us serve them; Thou shalt not hearken unto the words of that prophet, or that dreamer of dreams … Dt 13:1-3

Why would God do such a thing? Why would he allow false signs which come to pass to be done? That he might know our heart. Do we really love him with all our heart and soul? Do we follow wonders, or do we follow the word of God? Do we hold fast to miracles, or do we hold fast to the Most High? As he continues in verse 3, "for the LORD your God proveth you, to know whether ye love the LORD your God with all your heart and with all your soul." Dt 13:3

WARNING: We so often think that false prophets always give false prophecies and that we will know them this way. We think, if they do not come to pass, then they are a false prophet, but if they do come to pass they must be a true prophet. But if we understand the tree of the knowledge of good and evil and the essence of how the fall took place, then we would know this is often not the case. The great error of God's people has not been going after what is evil (initially), but going after that which is good or at least appears to be good.

What Do We Fear God for?

Though there are great blessings in fearing the LORD, we cannot, as false preachers and teachers do today, be caught in the spirit of covetousness and think that the fear of God is another means by which we may obtain God's blessings. That will surely be put to the severest test as it was with Job.

> And the LORD said unto Satan, Hast thou considered my servant Job, that *there is* none like him in the earth, a perfect and an upright man, one that feareth God, and escheweth evil? Then Satan answered the LORD, and said, Doth Job <u>fear God for nought</u>? Job 1:8-9

This is what must be discovered in our life by the LORD. Do we fear God for nought, that is, for no reason? Or, as we have seen already, do we fear God for good reason! God must have each of us tested in our fear of him. Do we fear him only for the blessings we get? This even Satan would know.

Why do you fear God? If we fear him only for the blessings, then that is not the fear of God at all! The foundation that must be proved within us is "Do we fear God for *something*, or do we fear God for *nothing*?" Do we fear God because of what we get from him or because of who he is? Do we fear him enough to know that he has the right to freely take away, as well as to freely give? Thus, Job reproves his wife when she is used by the devil to tempt him: **"What**? shall we receive good at the hand of God, and shall we not receive evil?" Job 2:10

Covetousness, Dishonesty, and the Early Church

Dishonesty and covetousness are a deadly combination. It was for the two of these, and the resulting lack of the fear of God that they clearly represent, that Ananias and Sapphira were put to death (Ac 5). And what was the result of God's judgment of them? Did the early church cry out for mercy? No, it restored the fear of God back to the church, which they had lost. Today, churches seek to swell their ranks by using every possible worldly marketing scheme. Where is their fear of God? The result is the truth is compromised and the Bible is minimized and many times even manifestly set aside. Yet the early church did not do so. Rather, they had the fear of God to keep truth in the church. Look at how their growth took place: by *maintaining* truth through God's fear.

> <u>great fear came upon all the church</u>, and upon as many as heard these things. And by the hands of the apostles were many signs and wonders wrought among the people; (and they were all with one accord in Solomon's porch. And of the rest durst no man join himself to them: but the people magnified them. And believers were the more added to the Lord, multitudes both of men and women.) Ac 5:11-14

The fear of the LORD came upon all the church because lying against the Holy Ghost was not tolerated, but exposed and judged. That fear spread even *outside* the church to all that heard these things. Then were "many signs and wonders wrought among the people" and a true unity joined all the saints because of the fear of God *and* the grace of God manifesting through the divine giftings of the Spirit.

This was not a man-made unity of putting aside sound doctrine, as we have everywhere today – people who believe completely different things and who appear to walk together, when God says such a thing is impossible (Am 3:3). No, this unity in the early church was that that comes from God, when all his people see his severity and his goodness, his judgment and his mercy, his fear and his grace. The unity of God comes when God is put in his proper place through the truth, as the God who is to be both feared and loved.

Where is the Fear of GOD? Losing the Treasure of the Lord

> **WARNING**: How did this fear affect those who would come to the church? "And of the rest [i.e. *those who were not of one accord*] durst no man join himself to them: but the people magnified them." People would no longer just come as the *inquisitive* to see something new or to "give it a try". This was the end, the death, of any 'seeker-sensitive' movement that might have tried to get started in the early church! It caused people to stop coming and seeing and being in and out. People did not 'attend' church anymore. They were either one of them or they stayed away because of the fear of God! This is the way God would have it.

The result of God being properly feared by his people is the faithful were magnified in the sight of all the people. When one *did* decide to come, it was because they were ready to come naked and open before God, without guile and without hypocrisy. So those who truly believed "were the more added to the Lord, multitudes both of men and women." O that we would get the fear of the Lord in the church again. Those who came to the church now were 'laid before' the Lord in humble obedience.[175] We must return to the Biblical pattern. Seeker sensitive methods will only produce shallow, self-seeking, and undisciplined church attenders – those who will come and go as they please. We must forsake the quick rewards of carnal marketing schemes, which will never produce true believers who are laid at the feet of the Master to become followers.

The Warning of Taking Advantage of Others

> And I will come near to you to judgment; and I will be a swift witness against the sorcerers, and against the adulterers, and against false swearers, and against those that oppress the hireling in *his* wages, the widow, and the fatherless, and that turn aside the stranger *from his right*, and fear not me, saith the LORD of hosts. Mal 3:5

God has the right to judge, and contrary to what too many men say today, God does judge his own people. God judges whether we truly have the fear of God by our actions. So we read 5 times these warnings in the book of Leviticus.

[1] Thou shalt not curse the deaf, nor put a stumblingblock before the blind, but shalt fear thy God: I *am* the LORD. Lev 19:14

[2] Thou shalt rise up before the hoary head, and honour the face of the old man, and fear thy God: I *am* the LORD. Lev 19:32

[3] Ye shall not therefore oppress one another; but thou shalt fear thy God: for I *am* the LORD your God. Lev 25:17

[4] Take thou no usury of him, or increase: but fear thy God; that thy brother may live with thee. Lev 25:36

[5] Thou shalt not rule over him with rigour; but shalt fear thy God. Lev 25:43

---

[175] This word 'added' in Acts 5:14 means 'laid before'.

11 – Warning Signs of Losing God's Fear

Those who curse the deaf or trip up the blind have no fear of God. Those who dishonour the aged have no fear of God. Those who oppress others and take advantage of the weak and make unjust gain from others in need have no fear of God. Those who bear harsh rule over othes have no fear of God. Notice that after several of these warnings not to live this way, God places his signature warning: "I *am* the LORD (your God)". Thus, it is God's authority, it is who he is, that should cause us to fear him and to show mercy and to walk humbly before our God. God also states in Malachi 3:5 that he knows whether we have the fear of God or not, specifically by how we treat people. Let us look at what Malachi lists as those that do not fear the LORD:

Table 11-2   Those who Lack the Fear of God

OPEN LACK OF GOD'S FEAR	WALKING IN DARKNESS
1. sorcerers	– Thou shalt have no other gods before me, Ex 20:3
2. adulterers	– Thou shalt not commit adultery, Ex 20:14
3. false swearers	– Thou shalt not bear false witness, Ex 20:16
CONCEALED LACK OF FEAR	TAKING ADVANTAGE OF THE WEAK/NEEDY
4. oppress the hireling	– Thou shalt not kill, Ex 20:13
5. oppress the widow	– Thou shalt not steal, Ex 20:15
6. oppress the fatherless	– Honour thy father, Ex 20:12
7. turn aside the stranger *from his right*	– Thou shalt not covet, Ex 20:17

It is obvious that anyone involved in sorcery has no fear of God, for this is an abomination to God (Dt 18:10-14). It is obvious also anyone involved in adultery has no fear of God, for this is a violation of the very trust that represents our marriage symbolically to the Lord. False swearers, false witnesses, those who assure you they are telling you the truth but are knowingly lying, all of these also clearly have no fear of God, as we have seen. These first three we are not at all surprised, for the scripture is clear that all sorcerers, adulterers, and liars will be cast into the lake of fire to burn forever (Rev 21:8, 1Co 6:9-10).

But God goes beyond these and lists four more! In Malachi 3:5 God shows we have no fear of him, if we (1) oppress the hireling in his wages, or if we (2) oppress the widow or (3) the fatherless *for any reason*, or if we (4) turn aside the stranger from what is rightfully due him. To steal, or be covetous, or to take advantage of another, especially the vulnerable, is to have no fear of God. Those who have not pity for the poor and the hurting or who have no thought of the need of others have no fear of God. A lack of compassion for the poor and needy is the initial evidence of the much larger problem of selfishness – the worship of one's own self (my needs, my wants, my plans, my way of doing things). Jude speaks of those who feed themselves **without fear** in the midst of the feasts of charity of the church. They do not think of the needs of others who greatly need the charity (i.e. the help) of the church. They only look to what they can get. They are clouds *without water*, they promise much, but give nothing. They are fruits trees which boast of their fruit, but they have no fruit to give to others. Thus, he speaks of their greediness and their looking for reward.

> Woe unto them! for they have gone in the way of Cain, and ran greedily after the error of Balaam for reward, and perished in the gainsaying of Core. These are spots in your feasts of charity, when they feast with you, <u>feeding themselves without fear</u>: clouds *they are* without water, carried about of winds; trees whose fruit withereth, without fruit, twice dead, plucked up by the roots Jude 1:11-12

Notice again the evidences in Malachi 3:5 (listed above) of those that fear not the LORD of hosts, but this time pay close attention to the order. These are given in order from most severe and obvious, to least severe (or just beginning) and least obvious. Most anyone involved in sorcery or witchcraft would be recognized instantly, as one who has no fear of God.[176] After this in severity would be adulterers – those who commit adultery or 'figuratively *apostasize*' from the LORD and think nothing of it. Thirdly, would be false swearers, and those in the last group would be those who take advantage of others. In other words, the very first sign we would expect to see of one who is losing their fear of God would be their oppressing of the hireling in their wages, or oppressing the widow or the fatherless, or turning aside the stranger from their right! These four states are then four steps toward the increasing loss of the fear of God.

The judgment of God against Amalek was that "he feared not God" because when he met the Israelites on their exodus he "smote the hindmost of thee, *even* <u>all *that were* feeble</u> behind thee, when thou *wast* faint and weary" (Dt 25:18). Thus, "the LORD hath sworn *that* the LORD *will have* war with Amalek from generation to generation." Ex 17:16 God truly hates the heart of Amalek, for it is the heart that takes advantage of the weak. This is evidenced by God's promise that those of Amalek would perish for ever (Nu 24:20).

The one time God reveals his name as Jehovah-nissi (i.e. the LORD our **banner**) it is in connection with judging the works of Amalek (Ex 17:14-16)! Thus, the banner of the fear of the LORD is the banner of truth and mercy, which defends the poor. This banner of defending the poor and the weak is so obvious to man's conscience that even the repentant thief on the cross knew when the other thief mocked Christ on the cross, saying, "If thou be Christ, save thyself and us" (Lk 23:39) that this certainly was the evidence of having no fear of God. For the repentant thief rebukes him saying, "Dost not thou fear God, seeing thou art in the same condemnation? And we indeed justly; for we receive the due reward of our deeds: but this man hath done nothing amiss." Lk 23:40-41

---

[176] See 'Sorcery in the Church' in the appendix entitled "Definition of Some Biblical Terms".

11 – Warning Signs of Losing God's Fear

Why is taking advantage of others the first evidence of a lack of fear? Because to fear God is first to realize that we are nothing compared to God Almighty, and second, that no one is any greater or any lesser than any other in God's eyes. All men are but dust. Thus, the eternal companion of the fear of the LORD is humility. You may not easily see some men's pride (for this can be hidden for a long while by a religious man), but you will always see his selfishness manifested first in his treatment of the disadvantaged, the poor, and the needy. This is because a man will easily take advantage of others when he considers himself better than them. When we see ourselves different from others, privileged and better, then we have fallen into the pride of Lucifer.

> **WARNING**: Note this pattern in Mal 3:5. This first step of oppressing the disadvantaged will always lead to becoming a false swearer. The end result of this path is always to become one or the other, either a sorcerer or an adulterer, whether physically or spiritually. Why will oppressing others lead to false swearing? Because oppression must always justify itself. Oppression is in fact defrauding others, and always works through deceitful actions in order to obtain what it wants. It should be easy to see how defrauding others ultimately always leads to either sorcery (trying to control others) or adultery (trying to use others).

Of course, one may not do any of these, and yet still have no fear of God. The mere fact that these are the particular ones God mentions, shows us that they are the very ones that Satan wants to implant in us, if we do have the fear of God. These are the pathway our adversary the devil has planned to ensnare our feet in order to extract the fear of God from us. Oppressing the poor and needy is of great consequence, for it is the very first step in losing the fear of God. Think on this. This is the *one thing* the pillars of the church of Jerusalem (i.e. James, Peter, and John) wanted to ensure in Paul's ministry to the Gentiles: that he "should remember the poor".[177] Paul as a pillar of the churches of the Gentiles likewise says, "the same which I also was forward to do." Gal 2:10

This hypocrisy of appearing to be justified in robbing others of mercy and common respect, even the unregenerate see through. Thus, the thief on the cross, whom the Bible calls a malefactor (i.e. a *wrong-doer*, a *criminal*). Though he was a criminal, when the repentant thief saw Jesus' response of forgiveness versus the mocking condemnation of the people, the leaders, and the soldiers and then the mocking of the other thief, then even he knew that the other mocking

---

[177] This concern from 'the apostles to the circumcision' and the corresponding response from Paul, 'the apostle to the Gentiles', clearly reveals the heart of true apostles. When men would focus on the external signs of an apostle, "in signs, and wonders, and mighty deeds" (2Co 12:12), few recognize the heart and calling of an apostle in relationship to people. Their heart is to care for the needs of people, and in particularly, to take care of the poor.

thief had no fear of God. "But the other answering rebuked him, saying, Dost not thou fear God, seeing thou art in the same condemnation?" Lk 23:40

The Warning of Following Our Dreams
"For in the multitude of dreams and many words there are also divers vanities: but fear thou God." Ecc 5:7

Let us look at a subtle form of deception which often causes us to lose our fear of God. God clearly and evidently uses dreams among the saved,[178] but even the lost[179] are guided by God at times through dreams. But few dreams, in fact, are truly of God. Notice how Ecc 5:7 says, "For in the **multitude** of dreams ... *there are* also *divers* vanities" (Ecc 5:7). This clearly witnesses that *many* dreams are but vanities (i.e. they are meaningless and to no purpose). This Hebrew word translated 'vanities' means 'emptiness; figurative *transitory* and *unsatisfactory*'. Many dreams according to the word of God have no lasting value and no ability to satisfy our heart. Is this not why we have the expression 'chasing dreams' to express one who is pursuing an illusion?

The fear of God is our protection against the multitude of dreams which may mislead us into so many diverse kinds of vanities. This Solomon knew from his own experiences and why he warned us. "For in the multitude of dreams and many words *there are* also *divers* vanities: but fear thou God." Ecc 5:7 Thus, when a dream is brought to us, whether ours or another's we must hold fast to the fear of God. We must fear God *before* laying hold of a dream and taking it as truth. In the light of so many dreams and words which we may hear even from others, we must remember, "but fear thou God."

We see much in the scripture of false dreams and visions. So a dream may come from the desires of our own heart (Jer 23:25-26, 29:8) and "a dream cometh through the multitude of business" (Ecc 5:3) – that is, being too busy with too many concerns and being overly tired in mind. We may dream also because of being hungry or thirsty (Isa 29:8) or because of substance abuse, whether alcohol or drugs. And Satan himself may seduce us with dreams.

God's answer to the multitude of man's dreams and to the many words (which man uses to interpret for himself those dreams) is to fear God so that

---

[178] Examples of dreams from God to his people: Jacob (Gen 28:12, 31:10-13), Joseph (Gen 37:5-10, 42:9), the prophets (Nu 12:6, Jer 23:25-32), Saul (1Sam 28:6,15), Solomon (1K 3:5-15), Job (7:14), Daniel (Ch. 7), NT Joseph (Mt 1:20; 2:12-13,19,22), Paul (Ac 16:9, 18:9, 27:23), and those filled with the Holy Ghost (Joel 2:28, Ac 2:17).

[179] Examples of dreams from God to the lost: Abimelech (Gen 20:3-8), Laban (Gen 31:24), Pharaoh's butler & baker (Gen 40:5-22), Pharaoh himself (Gen 41:1-36), the Midianites (Jdg 7:13-15), Nebuchadnezzar (Dan 2 & 4), the wise men from the east (Mt 2:12), and Pilate's wife (Mt 27:19).

we may depart from vanity. Keep this forefront in your thoughts when meditating on a dream. Our dreams and our interpretations of those dreams will always lead us to diverse vanities that only produce *emptiness*. There is deep, lasting satisfaction in the fear of the LORD (Pr 19:23), but outside of it is only transitory and unsatisfactory emptiness. Only by laying aside our desires and wants, can we hope to see dreams from an unprejudiced perspective. This is even more important to do when the dream is in fact from God. Then, more than at any other time, we must be assured we have the Spirit's interpretation and the Spirit's direction on what to do with the dream and not our own.

> **WARNING**: When a saint has a dream that he believes is from God, it is important to have it be confirmed by other mature men of God who speak truth. It is often dangerous for it to only be witnessed by one's own spirit. Once we are born again, normally we can rely on our spirit to be witnessed by the Holy Spirit, but in this case because of the deceitfulness of our own heart (Jer 17:9) and the ability to collude (so that we are both the receiver and the manipulator and even the generator of the promise) is so great, it is simply prudent to seek wise counsel. So it is twice recorded (Pr 11:14, 24:6), "in the multitude of counsellors *there is* safety."

Why are dreams such a problem, especially if God himself chooses to speak through them (Ac 2:17, Nu 12:6)? First, because not all dreams are from God as we have seen. Many of them according to the word do not come from God. But even those which do come from God may be a very real problem. How can that be? Because a dream plays right into our will and our desire. If men can take the scripture and turn it to their own means, certainly our soul can do the same with a dream which only we have received. In following a dream it is easy to now forget other things, to forsake what has already been asked of us to do, and thereby to abandon our submission to authority. Thus, dreams may appeal directly to our pride, for now we have a hidden knowledge that we believe sets us above others. So dreams can be very dangerous to our spiritual well-being.

> **WARNING**: For anyone involved in taking oversight spiritually to people's lives, it is too often the case that God's own lambs are taken captive by false visions of their own heart and deceptive dreams of their own mind. Dreams may come many different ways,[180] and the deceptiveness of our own heart is beyond what any of us know. People must be warned then to be very careful and cautious in too easily giving heed to dreams or to put their trust in them.

---

[180] God may bring dreams as in the two previous footnotes, but so may Satan, for he counterfeits every good thing which God does. As we saw already in the table 'The

Where is the Fear of GOD? Losing the Treasure of the Lord

Dreams, if they come from God, should reflect, of course his character, but also his goal and his methods. God will not author nor condone a dream in which compromise or disobedience is encouraged. Yet so often dreams that are not from God, whether from our own desires or planted there by demonic forces, lead us away from righteousness and into compromise. Such dreams "tend to embolden men to hope for good in a way disagreeing with the word of God."[181] Scripture shows us God has several goals or purposes in giving dreams, which we need to look at. Let us look at the ones that concern the fear of God. God gives dreams to inspire men to fear him, to warn them of danger, and to comfort and strengthen them in their afflictions and trials that are awaiting them.

The faithful record we have of true dreams from God is that they moved people in the fear of God to *obey him*. This is God's primary purpose in giving people dreams: to fear God. The result of Jacob's dream was that the fear of God came upon him (Gen 28:12,17). Abimelech was warned in a dream not to touch Sarai "for the woman which thou hast taken; she *is* a man's wife" (Gen 20:3). The result was that he feared God, repented, and obeyed. Let this be the fruit of any dream that we would heed. Let us fear God.

Often dreams are for *warning*, for this is the first work of the fear of God, which is to warn us of the way which we should not go. Laban the Syrian was warned in a dream not to argue with Jacob (Gen 31:24). Joseph in the New was warned in a dream of wicked men that would try to kill the baby Jesus (Mt 1:20; 2:12-13,19,22). The wise men from the east were similarly warned of Herod's intentions (Mt 2:12). Pilate's wife was warned in a dream to have nothing to do with the murder of Jesus (Mt 27:19). In summary, dreams from God should *increase* the fear of God in us by warning us to obey his word and to prepare.

> **WARNING**: There is yet another danger to dreams, even when they do come from God, and it is the interpretation of the dream. Any mixture of God's purpose and means with our own can only be disastrous, for now we will pursue the part of our own making as if it were of God – this is but another form of idolatry, which will always end in shame and disappointment (Ps 97:7). I have observed both in my own life and in other dear saints in great straits who have received the revelation of God's encouragement and exhortation only to see the dream misread and misapplied.

Remember, if God's response to the multitude of dreams is "but fear thou God", then a true dream with a true interpretation will always produce this fruit: the fear of God (along with its tell-tale characteristic: submission to authority).

Counterfeiting of What is Real' in the chapter entitled "Cheap Imitations and Artificial Substitutes".

[181] Bunyan, p. 127.

If the interpretation of a dream produces a lessening of the fear of the LORD or a lessening of being able to hear authority so that we are hearing or obeying the word of God less, then *know* it is either a false dream, a false interpretation, or both! Remember, this does not mean we should ignore dreams, but only that, just as the scripture warns us, let us have the fear of God concerning them.

Dreams are also for *comfort* (Joel 2:28, Ac 2:17). Such comfort is the rest or blessing of what God will do in the future. God knows the sufferings, disappointments, and trials that await us just around the corner or even down the road. So he will speak to us hope beforehand so that we do not despair. So we see often these dreams are tested to the utmost by extreme suffering, such as Joseph's dream of ruling (Gen 37+). Because such dreams of comfort are tested, often they come with God's exhortations to prepare, such as Pharaoh's dream of the years of plenty and of famine (Gen 41), and Paul's visions of the night that he received promising protection (Ac 18:9-11, Ac 27:22-26).

Dreams May Become Idolatry

Those who pay attention to their dreams more than to the word of God will soon find themselves defiling their own flesh, despising and speaking evil of rulers and authorities. For so it is written, "Likewise also these *filthy* dreamers defile the flesh, despise dominion, and speak evil of dignities." Jude 1:8 This is unavoidable if we are a dreamer. It is the predetermined course of following our own dreams, or even the interpretations thereof, which lead to idolatry. First, we will give place to our flesh and indulge our own will. Next, we will despise any authority over us who tries to bring correction or even warning. Lastly, we will speak evil of those in authority who don't fully support our dream. Thus, the following of dreams can easily lead into rebellion and idolatry.

Understand, idolatry completely removes us from being under any authority. Idolatry is a defilement and always causes us to be defiled so that Jude's words are very prophetic. Dreamers will always defile their own flesh and will become filthy, because their own will now gets exalted. This is the destruction of those who lose the fear of God by following their own dreams, they can no longer hear the warning even that comes from authorities, which are set over them to watch over them and protect them (Heb 13:17). When a person loses the fear of God, they lose their ability to hear correction, and they rush headlong toward destruction. Paul describes them thusly:

> For men shall be lovers of their own selves, covetous, boasters, proud, blasphemers, disobedient to parents, unthankful, unholy, Without natural affection, trucebreakers, false accusers, incontinent, fierce, despisers of those that are good, Traitors, heady, highminded, lovers of pleasures more than lovers of God; 2Tim 3:2-4

Notice how these people who have departed from God are *first* lovers of their own selves. Then comes covetousness – the desire to have and take what belongs to others. Then comes boasting of one's abilities and conquests, followed by blasphemies against God, and disobedience to authorities. They lose thankfulness, holiness, true love and even human kindness. They break covenant and betray the Lord. They falsely accuse others, with fierceness, and despise those that are good. They have no self-restraint or self-control, but feed on whatever their eye desires, so they love their pleasures more than they love God. Notice also they are heady. The word 'heady' most often people associate with pride which may be its source, but actually it has more to do with being rash. The Greek word means *falling forward*, i.e. *headlong*. This is the end of all who lose the fear of God, they will fall headlong into the snares that are laid for their feet. They are missing the fear of the LORD which enables us to escape the snares of death (Pr 14:27).

The Warning of Pride: Forgetting Who We Are
"But the other answering rebuked him, saying, Dost not thou fear God, seeing thou art in the same condemnation?" Lk 23:40

Pride is the most deadly of these enemies, although many times it is the hardest for people to see, both in themselves and in others. If you've been taught or have believed that "You're somebody in the Lord", search the scriptures, friend. The greatest servants of God in the Bible knew they were <u>nothing</u> and that God was everything. They knew that they deserved nothing from God, so they pled for mercy and grace; they didn't demand what was coming to them.

> **WARNING**: There are teachers that actually teach we should demand the things we want from God, nay, more that we should command him. Thus, they make the Almighty God our slave, when we are called everywhere in scripture to be his slaves! God forbid that we should treat God so disrespectfully and dishonorably. He has every right to command us, for we are in eternal debt to him, but he is in no debt to us. We have no right to command him – ever!

Many times Paul warns the Corinthians of spiritual pride. In the great chapter on love, Paul states that no matter how wonderful the things he does are, yet "he **is** nothing" and has **done** nothing worthy of merit (1Co 13:1-3). He must bring to their remembrance, "Who then is Paul, and who *is* Apollos, but ministers by whom ye believed, even as the Lord gave to every man?" 1Co 3:5 Remember, a 'minister' was not a position of honor and respect and power as people think today. This word 'minister' means 'one who *runs* errands; an *attendant* or *waiter*'. Paul and Apollos, far from being some great ones, were mere vessels, servants, table-waiters, errand-runners, messengers.

Paul had a great calling, but Paul was not great, and he knew that, for he says, "But we have this treasure in earthen vessels, that the excellency of the power may be of God, <u>and not of us</u>." 2Co 4:7 We have 'great men of God' today who in God's eyes are nothing. "Not that we are sufficient of ourselves to think <u>any thing as of ourselves</u>; but our sufficiency *is* of God; Who also hath made us able ministers [i.e. one who *runs* errands; an *attendant* or *waiter*] of the new testament" (2Co 3:5-6).

Pride is the direct antagonist of the fear of the LORD. It works to undermine the true fear of God in every way. Remember what the fear of God is. According to Proverbs 8:13 it *is* to hate evil. And what is this evil that is to be hated? This same verse immediately calls out pride and then arrogancy! Pride and arrogancy can strike all of us in the most hidden and unexpected ways. We expect these to be only the problem of the successful, rich, powerful, or skilled. We expect it not to be in those whom many would consider failures, but pride and arrogancy afflict us all and only the fear of the LORD will drive it from us.

Look at the repentant thief on the cross. Initially, both thieves mocked Jesus (Mt 27:44). But when the other 'malefactor' railed on Jesus saying, "If thou be Christ, save thyself and us" (Lk 23:39), then everything changed. The other thief now repents and rebukes the mocking thief, saying, "Dost not thou fear God, seeing thou art in the same condemnation?" Lk 23:40 This is why pride and arrogancy so often get the upper hand in our hearts, because we forget where we have come from. We forget, apart from the grace of God, who we are and what we have done (1Co 15:10). Thus it is written, "Such is the way of an adulterous woman; she eateth, and wipeth her mouth, and saith, I have done no wickedness." Pr 30:20 We forget, like the unrepentant malefactor on the cross, that we are all under the same condemnation of death because of our sin. How can any of us boast over another?

When we forget that we are but sinners, all under "the same condemnation" because of sin, then we will have no fear of God. When we arise in our hearts like Pharaoh or the Egyptians and think that we are better than other people, we will not fear God. Speaking of Pharaoh it is written, "But as for thee and thy servants, I know that ye will not yet fear the LORD God." Ex 9:30

> **WARNING**: This process of self-exaltation happens all the time to churches that begin to get a handle on the truth. Because they are not rooted in brokenness, the truth, which they begin to learn, actually kills them spiritually through pride! They begin to think they are the only ones. "Thy wisdom and thy knowledge, it hath <u>perverted thee</u>; and thou hast said in thine heart, I *am,* and none else beside me." Isa 47:10 They forget who they are and where they were taken from, and instead of holding fast to their first mission of reaching the lost, taking care of the poor, and discipling God's people, instead they follow the subtle self-exaltation of the fallen angels, and they begin to do their own works.

As Jesus' bride, let us always have the covering of humility. "For this cause ought the woman to have power [i.e. *authority*] on *her* head because of the angels." 1Co 11:10 When we are wise in our own eyes, we are not fearing the LORD (Pr 3:7). To quote from Matthew Henry's Commentary on Proverbs 3:7-12, "There is not a greater enemy to the fear of the Lord in the heart, than self-conceit of our own wisdom." If we allow sin's sinfulness to be known in our own heart and God's continued forgiveness of our wickedness, such will crush our pride, it will wipe away the dust of our self-deception, it will birth humility and lowliness of mind, and will again pave the way back to the fear of God.

> "There is not a greater enemy to the fear of the Lord in the heart, than self-conceit of our own wisdom."

Remember, God's promise. If we will meditate daily in the scriptures so that we learn to fear the LORD and to do his commandments, our heart will be kept from being lifted up above our brethren (Dt 17:15-20 & Rev 1:5-6). Put away the fear of God and you will forever be subject to the domination of pride and arrogancy which God hates. Follow after the fear of the LORD in obedience, then the pride that lies in all of our hearts will be kept in continual subjection by being exposed to the light of truth.

Staying Clear of the Reefs
"he that feareth God shall come forth of them all." Ecc 7:18

In 2Timothy 3:2-4 we saw many snares that would come in the last days. These should sound very familiar to us, for they are the very same snares we have been considering, which signal the loss of the fear of God in us: selfishness, covetousness, pride, rejecting authority, loss of holiness through defilements, and taking advantage of others. Thus, what Paul is describing there are the very results of losing the fear of God. This is the spirit of disobedience that is working in the world, the tragedy of our day – that there is no fear of God before our eyes. We can depart from these errors, as we have seen, only through the fear of God. The fear of God is the key to departing from evil and escaping the snare of the last days that will come upon all the world. As Jesus said,

> And take heed to yourselves, lest at any time your hearts be overcharged with surfeiting,[182] and drunkenness, and cares of this life, and so that day come upon you unawares. For <u>as a snare shall it come</u> on all them that dwell on the face of the whole earth. Lk 21:34-35

These signs are snares which are coming upon all who "dwell on the face of the whole earth". This word 'snare' menas 'a *trap* (as *fastened* by a noose or

---

[182] Surfeiting in the Greek means 'a *headache* (as a *seizure* of pain) from drunkenness', that is, from over-indulging or excessive pleasure seeking. It is '(by implication) *debauchery* (by analogy *gluttony*)'.

notch); figurative a *trick* or *stratagem (temptation)*'. These traps are set for all of us. These temptations and tricks will come to all of us in these last days. Are we prepared for them through the fear of God? Or will we be caught unawares?

We are living in the last days and people's hearts everywhere are being *burdened* with headaches and worries from seeking after their own desires and trying to save their own life and possessions. The cares of this life are overwhelming many hearts so that their focus is only here and now. "What shall we eat? or, What shall we drink? or, Wherewithal shall we be clothed?" Mt 6:31 Eternity and standing before the Almighty God, as a result, have long been forgotten. Satan is working diligently to remove the fear of God from before our eyes. But it must be recaptured by a faithful remnant if they would escape these snares.

Let not the great and terrible day of the LORD catch any of us unawares, so that it comes *unexpectedly* or *suddenly*. Let us prepare for his coming through the fear of the LORD, so that that day comes with great expectation to us, as unto a prepared and chaste virgin, "as his wife [*who*] hath made herself ready." Rev 19:7 How does a bride make herself ready for her groom? First, by putting away her own selfish desires and putting on the all-encompassing desire to please her bridegroom. O that we would truly prepare for his coming by seeking to please him and not ourselves.

The preparation of the heart for his coming must be done through the fear of the LORD. There is no acceptable service of waiting upon him that he can receive without being salted with this grace of the fear of God. Remember, one of the beautiful fruits of the fear of God we have seen was the selflessness that it creates within us. This will keep us from being lovers of our own selves and from the covetousness it naturally leads to. The fear of God will produce a true care and affection for the need of others.

The fear of the LORD will also keep us from being boasters and being proud, because the fear of the LORD *is* to hate evil, of which the first and foremost evil is pride and arrogancy (Pr 8:13). God's fear will also keep us from being blasphemers. You say how could God's people ever be blasphemers? God says we are a blasphemer when we ignore or despise his word and when we reject or despise authorities (1Tim 6:1)![183] Thus, the fear of the LORD will lead us into true holiness and will create a heart within us to keep covenant.[184] When God's fear is working in us we will not bear false witness or be false accusers. Thus, the fear of God is the answer to each of these marks of apostasy that will be so prevalent in the last days (2Tim 3:2-4).

---

[183] This is why we spent time looking at how to properly fear authority, how to receive men of God, and the necessity of receiving correction.

[184] The fear of God leads to both the revelation of God's covenant (Ps 25:14, 111:5) and the keeping of it (Jer 32:40, Mal 2:5).

Where is the Fear of GOD? Losing the Treasure of the Lord

> The fear of God enables us to love God more than anything else, and it is why we need the spirit of the fear of the LORD so desperately today as the spirit of the last days falls upon and overtakes so many.

But more than what the fear of the LORD keeps us from, it is what it brings us into – that is its greatest work in us. The holiness, that only it can produce, is of great value in the eyes of God, for he has always been seeking a holy seed (Ezr 9:2, Mal 2:15). The fear of the LORD will cause us to stay satisfied and to be content in our life. "The fear of the LORD *tendeth* to life: and *he that hath it* shall abide satisfied" (Pr 19:23). This produces great continence or *self-control*.

We have seen how the fear of God produces a faithful spirit, and a patient spirit, so that we may avoid being heady (i.e. rash) and so that we bear much fruit. It will also produce a humble spirit, for the fear of the LORD makes us aware of whom we must stand before. The fear of God enables us to love God more than anything else, and it is why we need the spirit of the fear of the LORD so desperately today as the spirit of the last days falls upon and overtakes so many.

> those that fear him are men of truth, men of singleness of heart, perfect, upright, humble, holy men. Wherefore, reader, examine, and again I say, examine, and lay the word and thy heart together before thou concludest that thou fearest God.[185]

Be not as those of Jeremiah's day, of which we spiritually are surely in today, and do not put off your quest both to recapture and to treasure the fear of God in your life. If you have it, then seek to increase and purify it. "Therefore love it, nourish it, exercise it, use all means to cause it to increase and grow in thy heart".[186] Seek to establish it and beautify it, and let it be the banner of truth that is put on display in your life in order to woo others also into this highest of all duties unto God. If you have it not, then seek it with all your heart today, before it is too late and your heart is hardened beyond conviction (Isa 63:17). Do not say as those of Jeremiah's sad generation that were given over to destruction: "Neither say they in their heart, Let us now fear the LORD our God" (Jer 5:24). You must say and act upon it, "Let us **now** fear the LORD our God" and "O LORD ... unite my heart to fear thy name." Ps 86:11

---

[185] Bunyan, p. 129.
[186] Bunyan, p. 136.

Appendix I.   Definition of Some Biblical Terms

The kingdom of God will always turn the world upside side (Ac 17:6). It must, because God's ways are not our ways and God's thoughts are not our thoughts (Isa 55:8) – even after we are born again as illustrated by the Corinthians to whom Paul says, "And I, brethren, could not speak unto you as unto spiritual, but as unto carnal, *even* as unto babes in Christ." 1Co 3:1 This is why in Jesus' first recorded teaching in Matthew chapters 5, 6, and 7, over and over again he must distinguish between what they had heard that was contrary to the truth[187] from what he was telling them.[188] The spirit of the Pharisees that Jesus was dealing with in no way has diminished in the earth but has in fact increased. Therefore, the same must be done today before we can properly understand the kingdom of God. Hence, the following terms must be defined according to God's word and not man's usage.

1. Bishops & Pastors: Understanding the Office & Function

You have heard it said, "My name is Pastor Bill" and "I am Bishop Jones", but I tell you no man of humility will ever allow you to call him by a title, for there are no titles in the kingdom of God. This is not the place to fully explain this, but a deep enough explanation is needed to put things in proper perspective in order to see why the present use of the terms Bishop & Pastor as titles so displeases our Father in heaven. Just because the words 'bishop' and 'pastor' occur in scripture men think they can justify their actions for calling themselves these, but no man in the scripture ever called himself by one of these titles.

A bishop is none other than an elder exercising his office of oversight and correction unto the saints. Similarly, the pastor or shepherd was never meant to be a title, but is rather an elder fulfilling his calling to feed the flock of God. Men say it is pastors who feed the flock, yet the scripture says it is elders who labor in the word and in doctrine (1Tim 5:17). God says it is elders who are to feed the flock, and that they function as shepherds. Men say bishops are over the churches and preside over multiple congregations, when the scripture shows it was the apostles that took oversight to the churches, and elders took oversight to the local flock (1Pe 5:1-2). God says bishops are in the local church and are none other than elders, for elders have been given the oversight to the souls of the saints.

These things are evidenced in Acts 20:28 when Paul calls for the elders (not the pastors) of the church of Ephesus and tells them that the Holy Ghost has made them overseers to feed the flock. In this we see the two main functions of

---

[187] "Ye have heard that is was said": Mt 5:21,27,31,33,38,43.

[188] "But I say unto you": Mt 5:18,20,22,26,28,32,34,39,44; 6:2,5,16,25,29.

I – Definition of Some Biblical Terms

elders: to oversee and to feed. 'Overseers' is the Greek word *episkopos* (G1985) which is the word used everywhere for bishop/bishops.[189] Thus, the elder is the bishop. There is no separate position, only a specific function of the elder. The overseer's function is to take the oversight [*episkopeo* (G1983)]. This latter word is used by Peter in his exhortation of elders to take the oversight of the flock of God. "Feed the flock of God which is among you, <u>taking the oversight</u> *thereof*" 1Pe 5:2 Note here again elders, of whom Peter was one (v1), were to take oversight (i.e. to bishop) and to feed (i.e. to shepherd) the flock.

Also, in verses 3 & 4, Peter goes on to mention that the elders are to be examples to the flock and not lords over them, remembering that their reward will come from the chief Shepherd. Why is the Lord mentioned as the "chief Shepherd" in this specific context of elders and nowhere else? Because the elders *are* the shepherds over the flock, but they have a chief Shepherd to report to. This is another serious problem with the church. There are no chief shepherds or "senior pastors" as men would call them in the church! We already have a chief or senior shepherd, the Lord Jesus Christ – and he doesn't need any competition or substitutes. Each man of God who follows Jesus is to be a man of no reputation, and unlike the Lord who has now been exalted and has a name which is above every name, we ought not to have any title, for he only should be exalted in our midst.

In conclusion, remember Paul never laid hands on pastors, only on elders, ordaining them in each church (Ac 14:23). This is why there is not a single man called a bishop or a pastor in the entire New Testament. No such men were ever ordained in the church of Jesus Christ. The only leadership in the local church is elders. In the epistles where it refers to bishops (Php 1:1, 1Tim 3:1-2, Tit 1:7) it is clear these are the elders. The first two references always put bishops functioning in conjunction with deacons in the local church (i.e. the bishops are seen laboring in the office of the elders). Notice in Titus 1:5 it specifically refers to the ordination of elders, and thus it leads naturally right into their qualifications as bishops (i.e. as overseers).

The focal point is, though a man fulfills a *function* of a shepherd and a bishop, we should never use these terms as a title before their name or in place of their name, for that only produces pride and self-exaltation. It is a lifting up of men in the sight of people, when God would have only Jesus exalted. In the kingdom of God, no man has a title. Remember, you may be a plumber, but your name is not Plumber Bob. Let us stop calling men Pastor and their name, for it grieves the heart of God. Even Job *knew* not to give flattering titles to men, lest God be angry with him. "Let me not, I pray you, accept any man's person, <u>neither let me give flattering titles unto man</u>. For I **know** not to give

---

[189] The verses where bishop(s) is used: Php 1:1, 1Tim 3:2, Tit 1:7, 1Pe 2:25.

flattering titles; *in so doing* my maker would soon take me away." Job 32:21-22 Now you know not to do it also.

Bishop Ministry: The Need for Correction

The primary role of bishop ministry, the second calling and functioning of elders, is to take oversight through correction and exhortation. Scripture reveals that bishop ministry is primarily to the soul of an individual, whereas shepherd ministry is primarily to the spirit of an individual to feed them and to lead them into quiet resting places. The function of bishop ministry should not surprise us, nor be grievous to our soul, for the word of God itself is filled with correction.

God's people today are often oblivious that a full ¾'s of the purpose of the word of God is dedicated to correcting us when we are out of the way! Hear what Paul says to Timothy, "All scripture *is* given by inspiration of God, and *is* profitable for doctrine [i.e. *instruction*], for reproof [i.e. *conviction*], for correction [i.e. a *straightening up again*, i.e. (figurative) *reformation*], for instruction [i.e. *training*; by implication disciplinary *correction*] in righteousness" (2Tim 3:16). One quarter of the purpose of the word of God is for our instruction (i.e., it is profitable for pure doctrine). The other ¾'s of the word of God is to bring us back to him through conviction, correction, and chastisement when we err from truth. Thank God that the true God loves us so much he will bring correction to us and not just let us continue on in the destruction of our own ways. "As many as I love, I rebuke and chasten: be zealous therefore, and repent." Rev 3:19

Some mega-churches openly confess "sin is not on our menu". Therefore we ought to know by the scriptures then that the true God is not on their menu either, for the first thing God always does is to talk to his people about their sin. Reread Jesus' first recorded teaching (Matthew chapters 5, 6, & 7). It is all about defining the full depth of the sinfulness of sin. Reread Paul's words to the Christians in Rome in Romans chapter 3. It is all about revealing the depth of the sinful nature that is in man.[190] "If we say that we have no sin, we deceive ourselves, and the truth is not in us." 1Jn 1:8 Thus, when pastors do not regularly talk about sin, then we know sin is not being reproved, rebuked, corrected, or exposed there. Hence, the word of God clearly is not properly being ministered and ¾'s of the word of God is being discarded for ulterior motives or for the sake of pleasing the people by not offending their soul through correction. Thus, the precious ministyr of the true bishop has been forsaken. This is the apostate church prophesied in Isaiah 30.

Development of Elders in the New Testament

---

[190] When you read Romans 3, Paul is not talking only about the lost. He is talking about all of mankind, lost and saved, so that we will never forget what is truly in our flesh.

I – Definition of Some Biblical Terms

Many mistakenly think elders did not function in the Jerusalem church until they are specifically mentioned first in Acts 11:30. But this would be a very naïve misunderstanding of life in the early church. We must remember that God ordained eldership rule not in the new covenant but in the old covenant. God has ordained by his word that elders are the builders of the house of God, which was known even from the very beginning of Acts (Ac 4:8,11). Every Jew only understood the gathering of God's people in the light of seasoned elders who oversaw the people of God, for this is what they knew throughout the Old Testament scriptures. Nowhere do we see this discarded in the New. In fact, as soon as Gentile churches were formed from disciples, immediately men were laid hands upon and ordained with prayer and fasting to be elders (Ac 14:23).

We have proof the apostles functioned as elders also by their letters. Peter declares, in addition to being an apostle, that he was also an elder (1Pe 5:1). Similarly, John declares he was an elder (2Jn 1:1, 3Jn 1:1). Paul and Barnabas must have functioned as elders in Antioch before they were sent out as apostles. Thus, the apostles in Jerusalem before they were released to travel as apostles must have functioned as elders during that time. During this time they are busy discipling and raising up faithful men to be elders who would watch over the Jerusalem church so that the apostles could fulfill their calling to be sent out. Hence, we see the apostles not only teaching the saints at Jerusalem as shepherds,[191] but also bringing forth bishop ministry.[192]

Lastly, we see the apostles of Jerusalem were specifically functioning as elders prior to their sending out because of what must be filled in Judas' vacancy. Let us review again this principle. Remember, elders have both a pastorate and a bishoprick, for so Paul exhorts the elders of Ephesus. They were 'made overseers' and were to "take heed therefore … to all the flock" to "feed the church of God" (Ac 20:28). Peter gives the same instructions to elders when he tells them to "feed the flock of God which is among you, taking the oversight *thereof*" (1Pe 5:2). In both cases the word 'feed' is the Greek word *poimaino* (G4165), which means 'to *tend* as a shepherd'. 'Overseer' in Acts 20:28 is the Greek word *episkopos* (G1985), which is the word for 'bishop'. Similarly, 'taking oversight' in 1Pe 5:2 is the Greek word *episkopeo* (G1983), which is the verb form of bishop (i.e., 'to bishop'). Thus, elders function as shepherds and as bishops.

---

[191] The apostles clearly functioned as shepherds before being sent out as apostles: Ac 2:40-42, 4:2, 5:21,25.

[192] Bishop ministry covers a broad spectrum, but we see this ministry continually fulfilled by the apostles while they are in Jerusalem functioning as elders. We see this in exposing Judas' sin (Ac 1:25), the correction of the mockers (2:13-36), the judgment brought to Ananias & Sapphira (5:1-11), the ending of the murmuring of the Grecian Jews through the selecting of deacons (6:1-7), the discipline of Simon's wrong motives (8:18-24), and even the *misdirected* oversight when Peter was reproved for going into Cornelius' home (11:2-3).

Consider now what Peter is saying when he stands up in Acts chapter 1 and declares, "Let [Judas'] habitation be desolate, and let no man dwell therein: and his <u>bishoprick</u> let another take. That he may take part of this <u>ministry</u> and <u>apostleship</u>, from which Judas by transgression fell" (Ac 1:20,25). Judas' vacated office is described as a 'bishoprick'. But notice also that Judas had both a ministry *and* an apostleship to fulfill. His ministry was his bishoprick as an elder. His apostleship was his ordaining as an apostle. In light of all that we know about elders functioning as bishops until they are sent forth, and the apostles having to function as elders until non-apostolic elders could be raised up in Jerusalem, Peter is declaring that the apostles did have an eldership role of oversight or bishoping to fulfill in Jerusalem.

The Functioning of the Government of God

When matters of great doctrinal substance needed to be decided in the early church, it was *not* a denominational board or a synod that met, but it was the apostles and elders. Read Acts 15 again, for it is our only recorded "church council", and thus it is the only pattern left for us. See who decided the issue. It was not the congregation; it was not voted on by majority consent; a deacon board didn't make the decision, nor did elected representatives, nor do we see any mention of evangelists, teachers, or even pastors.

It was apostles and elders (Ac 15:2), apostles and elders (Ac 15:4,6), apostles and elders (Ac 15:22, 16:4).[193] Their decision was witnessed by the moving of the Holy Ghost, but was decided solely based on the testimony of the word of God (Ac 15:15-18). This is the government of God. O how we have strayed from the pattern of the purity of the word of God and substituted men's methods and structures in place of what God has established. We must get back to the word of God. A man-made "church" structure which is contrary to the pattern revealed in the scripture can never perfect the saints to do the work of the ministry, nor can they properly prepare the saints for the coming of the Lord.

Most Christians have no idea that Jesus' first work in coming to this earth was not redemption, but the establishing of his government and rule in the earth. The great burden that weighed on Jesus' shoulders was the establishing of the government of God. And he wants that governing, or rule of God, to increase without end.

> For unto us a child is born, unto us a son is given: and <u>the government shall be upon his shoulder</u>: .... Of the increase of *his* govern-

---

[193] No wonder we are in such a mess doctrinally in the church today. We could not even have such a council if we tried, for we have neither apostles functioning in and over the churches as humble, broken, holy men, nor do we have true teaching and shepherding elders according to the scriptures who also perform the bishoping role of bringing correction and oversight to the saints.

I – Definition of Some Biblical Terms

ment and peace *there shall be* no end, upon the throne of David, and upon his kingdom, to order it, and to establish it with judgment and with justice from henceforth even for ever. The zeal of the LORD of hosts will perform this. Isa 9:6-7

To order and to establish his government (i.e. his rule) on this earth would take the zeal of the LORD of Hosts to perform. This is why Jesus was zealous to establish the kingdom of God in the earth. The rule and reign of the kingdom of God is resisted more than anything else by religious men and by the devil. Why? Because religious men and the god of this world (i.e. Satan), whom they unwittingly serve, each have their own kingdoms and their own power and authority, and they will not lay it down before a servant of God who comes proclaiming the authority of the word of God. This is why we must get back to the authority of the word of God and the preeminence of Jesus Christ.

2. Covenant Breaking

> But the mercy of the LORD *is* from everlasting to everlasting <u>upon them that fear him</u>, and his righteousness unto children's children; <u>To such as keep his covenant</u>, and to those that remember his commandments to do them. Ps 103:17-18

Men speak of unconditional covenants, but there are in truth no such things. The very idea of an unconditional covenant violates the principle of how covenants are established. A covenant is always a solemn, binding agreement between two or more parties. Both parties in any covenant are always involved. Every covenant in scripture was and is conditional upon both parties' solemn respect for the covenant.[194] The thing that is forgotten about covenants is that they always require something of *each* party. If this were not the case, then it would just be a promise or a pledge, but it would *not* be a covenant.

This is why broken covenants are illustrated throughout the scripture. The covenant of God's presence was broken (Lev 26:9,15, Dt 31:16,20), the everlasting covenant was broken (Isa 24:5), the covenant of the fathers was broken (Jer 11:10), the covenant of the sabbath was broken (Nu 15:32-36). Even in the New Testament we see "covenantbreakers" – those who once knew God in covenant, but who hold the truth now in unrighteousness (Rom 1:31,21,18) who have departed from the faith (1Tim 4:1). God knew his covenants would be broken. God even *prepared* for them to be broken by making laws on how to handle when covenants were broken. He did this for instance with the covenant of circumcision (Gen 17:14) and also the covenant of the sabbath, not to mention the covenant of marriage (Dt 24:1,3).

---

[194] Webster's New Universal Unabridged Dictionary, Deluxe Second Edition, Dorset, & Baber, 1979, p.420, gives the following primary definition for 'covenant': a binding and solemn agreement by two or more persons, parties, etc. <u>to do</u> or <u>keep from doing</u> <u>some specified thing</u>.

> God is NOT man's slave. If man rejects the covenant and doesn't respond to God's correction through the hardness of his heart, God is under no compulsion to continue to honor the *illusion* of a covenant which we have already broken!

God promised never to break his covenant with us (Jdg 2:1, Ps 89:34), but it is we who break covenant with him. Thus, he only breaks covenant with us *after* we have broken it with him (Ps 89:39, Isa 33:8, Zec 11:10), and are unwilling to make it right through repentance. God is NOT man's slave. If man rejects the covenant and doesn't respond to God's correction through the hardness of his heart, God is under no compulsion to continue to honor the *illusion* of a covenant which we have already broken! "For thus saith the Lord GOD; I will even deal with thee as thou hast done, which hast despised the oath in breaking the covenant." Eze 16:59

> **WARNING**: Many have wondered what is and is not the unpardonable sin. The refusal to repent *is* the unpardonable sin. It is the one thing that God cannot forgive, and for which we are **not** to pray for forgiveness. This is the "sin unto death" (1Jn 5:16-17), for without repentance no man can escape the judgment of condemnation. We are to pray earnestly for people to come to repentance, but we cannot pray for God to forgive them if they will not repent, for he will not. "**IF** [*through repentance*] we confess our sins, he is faithful and just to forgive us *our* sins, and to cleanse us from all unrighteousness." 1Jn 1:9

Understand the conditions of God's covenants with man. *Every time* God speaks of keeping covenant with us, it is always in the context of our keeping covenant with him through obedience, repentance, and loving him with all our heart.

> Know therefore that the LORD thy God, he *is* God, the faithful God, which keepeth covenant and mercy with them that <u>love him and keep his commandments</u> to a thousand generations Dt 7:9

> <u>if ye hearken to these judgments</u>, and <u>keep</u>, and <u>do them</u>, that the LORD thy God shall keep unto thee the covenant and the mercy which he sware unto thy fathers Dt 7:12

> O LORD God of Israel, *there is* no God like thee in the heaven, nor in the earth; which keepest covenant, and *shewest* mercy unto thy servants, <u>that walk before thee with all their hearts</u> 2Ch 6:14

> O LORD God of heaven, the great and terrible God, that keepeth covenant and mercy for <u>them that love him and observe his commandments</u> Neh 1:5

I – Definition of Some Biblical Terms

> O Lord, the great and dreadful God, keeping the covenant and mercy <u>to them that love him</u>, and <u>to them that keep his commandments</u> Dan 9:4

Everlasting Covenants which were Broken by God

The covenant of David was an everlasting covenant, "a covenant of salt" (2Ch 13:5), that he should always have a son to reign upon his throne (Jer 33:21). Though God ultimately fulfilled this spiritually in Christ, yet naturally it was clearly broken and set aside by man's disobedience with the last king of Judah, Zedekiah (Eze 17:15-19). Thus, it lay broken for over 400 years, and unfulfilled in many a man's lifetime.

How did God finally fulfill his covenant? It was not until he could find a humble and obedient man and woman, Joseph and Mary, who would obey God implicitly and who believed by faith, that God could restore that which was broken. (But such a thing did not come without cost to both of them.) So we see Joseph was a just man (Mt 1:19) who repeatedly obeyed the dreams which God gave him,[195] and Mary was a woman of God who believed the word of the Lord which was brought to her (Lk 1:38-39) and was filled with thanksgiving for his mercies (Lk 1:46-55), who meditated on the word of the Lord (Lk 2:19), and persevered unto the end, being there at the cross.[196]

We can also look at the covenant of marriage (Pr 2:17) which is a life-long covenant, not to be put asunder by man, yet God himself made provision for its dissolution under certain conditions (Dt 24:1-3, Mt 5:31-32). Shockingly to many, but God even divorced his own people when they were so exceedingly sinful and hardhearted (Isa 50:1, Jer 3:8)! Thus, for hardness of heart God put his own bride away (Mt 19:8).[197] Let us now look at two examples of those who were profane. These were men who had holy callings on their lives to fulfill, but who 'crossed over the threshold' of God's will and walked out of the door of God's kingdom, leaving the holy things of God behind, for their own desires .

The Warning of Esau, a Profane Son

> Looking diligently lest any man fail of the grace of God; lest any root of bitterness springing up trouble *you*, and thereby many be defiled; Lest there *be* any fornicator, or profane person, as Esau, who for one morsel of meat sold his birthright. Heb 12:15-16

---

[195] Joseph faithfully obeyed the warnings of the Lord: Mt 1:20,24, 2:13-14, 2:19,21, 2:22.

[196] Mary, the mother of Jesus, at the cross: Jn 19:25, Mt 27:56, Mk 15:40, Lk 24:10.

[197] Scripturally it is always the male who has the authority to put away or divorce the female (not vice versa). Notice 1Co 7:12-13, "let **him** not put **her** away" versus "let **her** not leave **him**".

Esau and Jacob were both blessed by Isaac (Heb 11:20). Although Esau was a son who was loved of his father more than Jacob (Gen 25:28), yet he ultimately was cut out and removed from the covenant of God's promise which was by faith unto Abraham and Isaac and Jacob. Why did this happen? Esau did not follow after peace and holiness, but rather followed after the desires of his flesh. He became a cunning hunter of the field (which represents the world). Esau, in modern terms, was an accomplished businessman who knew how to play the world to get what he wanted.

But the New Testament calls Esau a profane man. This word 'profane' in the Greek means '*crossing the door-way* or the *threshold*, to be *heathenish* or *wicked*'. He crossed out of the door of his covenant with God, and forsook God's covenant blessings for natural pleasures and rewards. For one morsel of meat, for a bowl of beans, Esau sold his entire birthright (Gen 25:31). This shows how much he valued his own desires and the pleasing of his flesh and how little he valued his natural and spiritual inheritances that were laid up for him. The scripture says in doing this he *despised* his birthright (Gen 25:34). On top of this, he despised the wisdom of his father and mother in marriage, choosing not one, but two Hittite (i.e. Canaanite) women (Gen 26:34) "which were a grief of mind unto Isaac and to Rebekah." Gen 26:35

Like many carnal Christians today, Esau did not pursue holiness. Neither did he follow after peace. After his brother Jacob deceived him, he refused to forgive him and *purposed* to kill him (Gen 27:41). Thus, in this also, he despised what he had, for the blessing which he had received from his father was to *serve* his younger brother (Gen 27:40). Man does not look at it this way, but Esau's blessing was actually greater than his brother's! Jesus showed us the call to serve others is the highest calling in the kingdom of God! *Again*, Esau missed out on the blessing of what God had for him, because Esau despised the wisdom of both his natural and his spiritual father. God kept trying to bless Esau, but Esau was too profane, too naturally minded, too given to the things of this earth.

Esau's growing disrespect and rebellion against his father only increased through the unforgiveness and bitterness that were working in his heart. Esau observed when his father blessed his brother Jacob by sending him to Laban for a wife "and that as he blessed him he gave him a charge, saying, Thou shalt not take a wife of the daughters of Canaan" (Gen 28:6). What was Esau's response? Deliberate spite arose in Esau toward his father.

> And Esau <u>seeing</u> that the daughters of Canaan <u>pleased not</u> Isaac his father; Then went Esau unto Ishmael, and took unto the wives which he had Mahalath the daughter of Ishmael Abraham's son, the sister of Nebajoth, to be his wife. Gen 28:8-9

Esau, by his actions and by his heart, despised his father and, as a result, God himself. Esau, because of the chastening he had received, could no longer respect authority. (How much he is like the Christian today who refuses to be

I – Definition of Some Biblical Terms

corrected.) It was for all these things, which God saw beforehand, that God hated Esau. Remember also this, these things are **not** under the Law. The Law did not come until Moses. So these events are BEFORE the Law. As it is written, God "preached before the gospel unto Abraham" (Gal 3:8). So these things are representative of the gospel and the covenant of grace!

Think on this. Esau was a son. Esau was greatly loved by his father and grew up in his father's house. Esau received blessings from his father (Heb 11:20). Esau had an inheritance and a birthright, but he forsook all of these and despised all of these things. He despised his inheritance, his birthright, his brother, his mother, and even his father. Thus, he was rejected by his own brother, his own father, and by God himself! And Esau is given forth to us in the new covenant to take warning that we not "fail of the grace of God". How do we fail of the grace of God today? by going the way of Esau, in bitterness, being intimate with the world, despising authority, and profaneness.

The Warning of Eli and his Profane Sons

> Wherefore the LORD God of Israel saith, I said indeed *that* thy house, and the house of thy father, should walk before me for ever: but now the LORD saith, Be it far from me; for them that honour me I will honour, and they that despise me shall be lightly esteemed. 1Sam 2:30

We must take warning also from Eli and his sons. As God has made an 'unbreakable covenant' with us, so he made it with Eli also. Eli, as well, did not respond to God's warnings. God warned him correct his own sons and instead he ended up honoring his sons above God (1Sam 3:29). This proved spiritually fatal for him, as he lost everything! So God *can* break even his everlasting, eternal covenants if we do not honor him. God is no respecter of persons. If he broke his eternal covenant with Eli because Eli honored his sons above God, do we think God will look aside when we honor ourselves and our selfish wants above him? Impossible. By his immutable character he is bound to break his eternal covenant with us also. Do you see now why the fear of God must be recaptured in our heart? This is why the writer of Hebrews continues,

> See that ye refuse not him that speaketh. For if they escaped not who refused him that spake on earth, much more *shall not* we *escape*, if we turn away from him that *speaketh* from heaven Heb 12:25

> We by no means earn our blessings, but we *are* required to walk consistent with what we have received freely by faith.

Can we see how much the precepts of men teaching grace unbounded are actually teaching a doctrine that produces lawlessness in the hearts of men? We by no means earn our blessings, but we *are* required to walk consistent with what we have received freely by faith. And if we do not, then God is free to call *us* the liar for how we have betrayed our confession of faith. This is why Paul declares in Romans chapter 3,

> For what if some did not believe [*later*]? shall their unbelief make the faith of God without effect? God forbid: yea, let God be true, but every man a liar; as it is written, That thou mightest be justified in thy sayings, and mightest overcome when thou art judged. Rom 3:3-4

Remember, Paul was speaking of those "to whom *pertaineth* the adoption, and the glory, and the covenants, and the giving of the law, and the service *of God,* and the promises" (Rom 9:4). We also, as those in Christ, have received the adoption, the glory, the covenants, the giving of the law,[198] the service of God, and the promises, for these were taken from natural Israel and given to another nation (i.e. to spiritual Israel, those who are in Christ), as Jesus himself prophesied (Mt 21:43-45). In Christ, we have received the spiritual fulfillment of all that was promised to the people of God, for we are the people of God by faith – IF we come out and are separate from the world (2Co 6:18-7:1).

> That at that time ye were without Christ, being aliens from the commonwealth of Israel, and strangers from the covenants of promise, having no hope, and without God in the world: But now in Christ Jesus ye who sometimes were far off are made nigh by the blood of Christ. Now therefore ye are no more strangers and foreigners, but fellow citizens with the saints, and of the household of God   Eph 2:12-13,19

Receiving the Grace of God in Vain

Paul's words in Rom 3:3-4 could well apply to Christianity today. "For what if some did not believe [*later*]?" They certainly believed in God, that is not the issue of unbelief here. What they did not believe in was the word of correction that came through those servants God had sent unto them! They no longer submitted to the word of correction. Such is sadly the case many times today. And what will God do in these cases? Will he honor his covenant of grace even though the grace of God has been received in vain (2Co 6:1) – meaning no fruit of holiness has come forth? Will he honor those who have done despite unto the Spirit of grace? No, he will not honor them who dishonor him!

---

[198] We have received 'the giving of the law' in several aspects. *First,* we received it on the road to salvation, for the law of judgment was our schoolmaster *to bring us* unto Christ (Gal 3:24-25). *Second,* we received it in the law of liberty by which, through the revelation of the scriptures, we come to know what manner of men we are and through confession and repentance we are set free (Jam 1:22-25, 2:8-12). *Third,* we received it as the law of the LORD, the very Word of God, by which we know truth and grow up (Ps 19:7-8, 1Pe 2:2) and which we delight in and serve (Ro 7:22,25, 8:7). *Fourth,* we received it in the law of Christ (Gal 6:2) so that we love the brethren by bearing their burdens.

I – Definition of Some Biblical Terms

> Of how much sorer punishment, suppose ye, shall he be thought worthy, who hath trodden under foot the Son of God, and hath counted the blood of the covenant, wherewith he was sanctified, an unholy thing, and hath done despite unto the Spirit of grace? Heb 10:29

> <u>Be it far from me</u>; for them that honour me I will honour, and they that despise me shall be lightly esteemed. 1Sam 2:30

How do we receive the grace of God in vain? How do we insult the Spirit of grace? By not *approving* ourselves as ministers of Christ, by the enduring of afflictions and temptations. The grace of God is received in vain when we walk after the flesh and not after the Spirit. When we manifest the works of the flesh, we grieve the holy Spirit of God (Eph 4:30), for he was given so that we might have the power to crucify the flesh, not give place to it. Jesus himself crucified his own flesh by the power of the Spirit. Christ "through the eternal Spirit offered himself without spot to God" (Heb 9:14). This is how we approve ourselves unto God: by living *and* walking in the Spirit and crucifying our flesh.

Let the New Testament warning to covenantbreakers suffice to alert us that all covenants with God are conditional upon our "keeping covenant" with him and never losing a heart of repentance. Let us not receive the covenant of grace and truth in vain. As it is written, "All the paths of the LORD *are* mercy and truth unto <u>such as keep his covenant</u> and his testimonies." Ps 25:10

3. <u>Predestinated to be Conformed</u>

Many times Romans 9:11-13 is misinterpreted so that people believe God arbitrarily hated Esau, but loved Jacob. They will quote the previous verse, "For *the children* being not yet born, neither having done any good or evil, that the purpose of God according to election might stand, not of works, but of him that calleth" (Rom 9:11). But, if this meant that God hated Esau based on God's own choice, having nothing to do with Esau's works, this would contradict great portions of the scripture, not to mention that God is everywhere said to be a respecter of no persons.[199] God is "not willing that any should perish" (2Pe 3:9). "For God so loved the world, that he gave his only begotten Son, that whosoever believeth in him should not perish, but have everlasting life." Jn 3:16

No, God's election stands not in that he has arbitrarily loved Jacob and hated Esau. He has loved them based on their heart and the fruit of their ways that he *foresaw*. If "a prudent man foreseeth the evil" and takes appropriate action (Pr 22:3, 27:12), certainly God also foresees and acts accordingly. Because God knows what shall be, therefore he loves or hates because of who he knows that person in the depth of their heart to be. He loved Jacob because he knew

---

[199] God repeatedly lets us know he is no respecter of persons: 2Sam 14:14, 2Ch 19:7, Ac 10:34, Rom 2:11, Eph 6:9, Col 3:25, Jam 2:1,9, 1Pe 1:17.

Jacob loved him. As it is written of the Lord (for he *is* wisdom), "I love them that love me." Pr 8:17a So God hated Esau because Esau hated and despised him. Thus, "whom he did foreknow, he also did predestinate" (Rom 8:29). God's election and predestination stands in this: that it is his sovereign choice to choose who will serve who (the older or the younger). Thus, the verse immediately following the one concerned with God's election says, "It was said unto her, The elder shall serve the younger." Rom 9:12 This was confirmed also in Isaac's blessing of Esau, "thou ... shalt serve thy brother" (Gen 27:40).[200]

A final proof of this is the very first time we see recorded that God hated Esau (which is in Malachi 1:2-3). Because this is the first time it is mentioned, therefore it is the foundational verse which will show us why God hated Esau. There the context of why God loved Jacob, but hated Esau is found in verse 6. Esau had not honored either his natural father or his spiritual father, and this is why God hated him even in the womb, for God knew beforehand the kind of man Esau was.

> A son honoureth *his* father, and a servant his master: if then I *be* a father, where *is* mine honour? and if I *be* a master, where *is* my fear? saith the LORD of hosts unto you, O priests, that despise my name. And ye say, Wherein have we despised thy name? Mal 1:6

4. Sorcery in the Church

The first time we see sorcery mentioned in the scripture it is in Egypt. Pharaoh had his wise men and sorcerers, whom the Bible also calls magicians. It records for us that they mimicked by their enchantments the miracles of God, which Moses the servant of God had done (Ex 7:11). Is it possible that the very same thing is being done also today, especially with the worldliness of the church (since the world is represented scripturally by Egypt)? Are enchantments being done today to deceive God's people and keep them from the true fear of God? Consider, what the result was of the enchantments of the sorcerers? Pharaoh and the people did not hearken to the words of the true servant of God, so that they had no fear of God (Ex 7:13).

Many of God's people do not recognize and see how much that is being done in the name of Christ today is in fact witchcraft and sorcery. Large parts of God's flock are being seduced by those who make themselves out to be some great one, who are in fact no different than Simon Magus. Listen to what the scripture says of this "great one":

> But there was a certain man, called Simon, which beforetime in the same city used <u>sorcery</u>, and <u>bewitched the people</u> of Samaria, <u>giving out that himself was some great one</u>: To whom they all gave heed,

---

[200] Remember, this was not a cursing, but a blessing. See the previous definition of Covenant Breaking in the sub-section entitled 'The Warning of Esau, a Profane Son'.

I – Definition of Some Biblical Terms

from the least to the greatest, saying, <u>This man is the great power of God</u>. And to him they had regard, because that of long time <u>he had bewitched them with sorceries</u>. Ac 8:9-11

Many big popular ministers today 'give out that themselves are some great one', and they are bewitching God's people with sorceries. The word 'bewitched' in the Greek (existemi, G1839) means 'to *astound*'. People are so astounded by what "men of God" do that even the people proclaim the person's greatness, saying they have the great power or the anointing of God. I have been to third world nations and seen the overflow of this sorcery in their countries as they mimic what American and European Christianity produces. Poster after poster proclaims this man or woman with great titles before their names, their pictures, and the glorification of their great power (i.e. their anointing). Compare this with Paul's humble words,

> Who then is Paul, and who *is* Apollos, but ministers [i.e. *servants*] by whom ye believed, even as the Lord gave to every man? So then neither is he that planteth <u>any thing</u>, neither he that watereth; but God that giveth the increase. 1Co 3:5,7

WARNING: In Samaria we see the persistent attempt of sorceries and the desire to mimic the true gifts of God trying again to infiltrate the true church. Here we see it comes in, as it often does, through a new believer who has not yet been discipled, but who is immediately ready in his own heart of zeal to be before the people in a position of *honor*. Notice Simon Magus himself also became saved (Ac 8:13), yet even after he was saved, he still tried to buy or purchase the gifts which the apostles were given by God (vv18-19). Why did Simon Magus desire to buy such power or ability? Because he had lost his previous influence, but still wanted to maintain that position of power!

How can we know this was in his heart? Because of the judgment against him by the apostle. Peter calls his desire 'wickedness', saying, "For I perceive that thou art in the gall of bitterness, and *in* the bond of iniquity." Ac 8:23 Why does Peter say "the gall of bitterness"? Because Simon Magus had lost his position, place, ministry, and influence among the people and when he saw that the apostles had this, he wanted it for himself. Thus, it was *envy* that was working in his heart. Too many big name leaders in Christianity have this same spirit of envy working in them. Thus, they are always competing with one another. Remember, envy's cure is the fear of God (Pr 23:17). Because so many leaders have no true fear of God, envy is working in them.

When God's people get their eyes on a man and begin to think he is some great one, it is because of sorceries that are deceitfully being done. Remember, demonic forces are involved with sorcery and those who practice them or are involved with them will by no means inherit the kingdom of God (Rev 22:15, 21:8). Few ever come out of the influence of being under such sorceries (Rev

9:21). Remember also the effect of those who do sorceries, it keeps those who watch and behold from hearing and believing the true words of God. Such people are never brought to repentance by the preaching of the kingdom of God that brings in God's authority and displaces man's authority.

Behold how sorcery has always tried to get into the midst of God's people: such was the case in Egypt during Moses' day, such was the case in Samaria in Philip's day, and such also was the case in Paul's day.

> And when they had gone through the isle unto Paphos, they found a certain <u>sorcerer</u>, a false prophet, a Jew, whose name *was* Bar-jesus: Which was with the deputy of the country, Sergius Paulus, a prudent man; who called for Barnabas and Saul, and desired to hear the word of God. But Elymas the <u>sorcerer</u> (for so is his name by interpretation) withstood them, **seeking to turn away the deputy from the faith**. Ac 13:6-8

Keeping Sorcery Out of God's Church: the Need for Apostolic Authority

When people are under the spell of witchcraft only the preaching of the kingdom of God can break them free from it. Thus, we see the Samaritans were bewitched *until* Philip came preaching the kingdom of God (where no man is exalted) and they repented. When the power of the kingdom of God is manifested through apostles (or those who have been under apostolic tutorage) who live and suffer for God, sorcery is removed from God's people. The only way sorcery can be kept out of the church is with the authority of God. This is why we see in each of the cases where sorcery was attempting to infiltrate God's people the work of an apostle was used by God to confront it and judge it. Thus, we see Moses and Aaron (who were types and shadows of the apostolate), Peter and John, and Paul and Barnabas all confronted the sorcerer spirit.

It is amazing how each of these pairs of men who were working as men sent by God to deliver God's people encountered sorcerers who attempted to prevent people from being set free. First, we see Moses and Aaron must confront the sorceries of the Egyptian magicians, which the Bible calls "wise men and sorcerers" (Ex 7:11). Next we see Peter and John, who knowing the kingdom of God had come to Samaria instantly knew sorcery would try to raise its ugly head. "Now when the apostles which were at Jerusalem heard that Samaria had received the word of God, they sent unto them Peter and John." Ac 8:14 This is of course exactly what happened with Simon the sorcerer who comes to believe (Ac 8:9-24). Next we see Barnabas and Saul. Not coincidentally it is on their *first* apostolic journey that they encounter resistance from Elymas the false prophet on the isle of Cyprus in Paphos. Scripture states that this "sorcerer" withstood them (Ac 13:6-12). Thus, a clear pattern exists in the scripture that the preaching of the kingdom of God by apostles always exposes sorcery. This is seen another time in Paul's life.

I – Definition of Some Biblical Terms

> And the evil spirit answered and said, Jesus I know, and Paul I know; but who are ye? And this was known to all the Jews and Greeks also dwelling at Ephesus; and <u>fear fell on them all</u>, and the name of the Lord Jesus was magnified. And many that believed came, and confessed, and shewed their deeds. Many of them also which used curious arts brought their books together, and burned them before all *men:* and they counted the price of them, and found it fifty thousand *pieces* of silver. So mightily grew the word of God and prevailed. Ac 19:15,17-20

Is it any wonder, that the result of such things was again the rebirthing of the fear of God, "fear fell on them all, and the name of the Lord Jesus was magnified" (v17)? We should not think these are in any way isolated events as the church was trying to get established, only for that first agae. No, for so it is written as a warning to Timothy that he must also surely face the same such sorcerers, "Jannes and Jambres withstood Moses, <u>so do these</u>" (2Tim 3:8).

5. <u>Politics & the Christian</u>

Jesus said, "And blessed is *he,* whosoever shall not be offended in me." Mt 11:6 Why did Jesus say this of all people to a very sincere, earnest, and faithful man of God, a great prophet, John the Baptist, and to his disciples? This seems such a strange and stunning comment to make. Jesus encouraged the disciples of John, and thereby John the Baptist himself, not to be offended by the truth and the power by which he spoke. This is because Jesus did not fit people's molds or their expectations, then, even as it is today.

Let us understand one thing well. Jesus did not come to set up a natural kingdom or to take over the governments of this world. The kingdom of God cannot be hijacked and used for political reform without leaving Christ behind. This even the apostles of the Lord were very confused about. "When they therefore were come together, they asked of him, saying, Lord, <u>wilt thou at this time</u> restore again the kingdom to Israel?" Ac 1:6 But it was not the time, neither is now the time. That must wait for Jesus' return as King of kings.

So Jesus did not come for political means and this offended John, as it offends many Christians today who are involved in attempting to use politics to try to bring about God's purposes – but this is not God's way, nor his purpose under the new covenant. This is why you will never see a man of God in the new covenant who used politics to try to change the laws or to reform people. This can only produce hypocrisy. Salvation and godliness through the new birth and through maturing in the truth of the word of God is our goal, not external conformance or laws of holiness.

It is the wrong realm that many of God's people are preoccupied with. Political Christians are bound up in a natural world and a natural way of thinking, while God is forever exhorting his people to be a spiritual people with a spiritual way of thinking. We are called to be "an holy nation" (1Pe 2:9), whose politics is not in this world. Paul had to warn even his beloved Philippians, "For <u>our conversation is in heaven</u>; from whence also we look for the Saviour, the Lord Jesus Christ" (Php 3:20).

> This word 'conversation' is *politeuma* (G4175), from which we get our English word 'political' or 'politics'. It means 'a *community*, i.e. (abstract) *citizenship* (figurative)'. It comes from the word *politeuomai* (G4176) which means 'to *behave* as a citizen'.

Note again what Philippians 3:20 says: our *citizenship* is in heaven. Our politics are not in this earth. Those who are preoccupied with earthly politics are naturally minded, not spiritually minded. Therefore they approach things naturally and not from God's heart. Such people are the zealots of Jesus' day who would bring political and governmental reform, even by force if necessary, but Jesus could not work with such. He had to *retrain* them through discipleship (just like he must do with everyone who has their *own* ideas).

Thus, Simon Zelotes, the zealot,[201] was an apostle who had to change and begin to follow Jesus. Simon Zelotes, before meeting Jesus, was a man who once sought for Jewish political independence. Now that he was an apostle all that had to be <u>left behind</u>. He had a higher calling, a greater independence and a better liberty to seek for those who were oppressed! Why was his name left as Simon Zelotes? To show that Christ Jesus changes everything from the natural into the spiritual. Now Simon the zealot would be a zealot for the kingdom of God and not the kingdoms of men. Do you think Simon when back to political reform and forsook his apostleship? Hardly. Now he labored to build a spiritual kingdom within men, by reforming men's hearts, not their laws or governments.

What man of God in the scriptures ever put himself forward for political purposes? What man of God every 'ran for office'? Certainly not Joseph – God did that. It was not sought out by Joseph or even desired. Certainly not Daniel – God did that. It was not sought out by Daniel or even desired. How then can a man of God seek to be elected, when we are called to seek those things <u>which are above</u>? How can we seek to change things by earthly means through politics, when we are called to be dead to this world?

> If ye then be risen with Christ, seek those things which are <u>above</u>, where Christ sitteth on the right hand of God. Set your affection on things <u>above, not on things on the earth</u>. For ye are dead, and your life is hid with Christ in God. Col 3:1-3

If a man becomes born again in office, then let him fulfill his office faithfully as a Daniel and as a Joseph or even as one of the Centurions who came to faith in the Lord Jesus, but no man should *seek* the office. For the greatest work

---

[201] Zelotes is a Greek word which means 'a *Zealot*, i.e. (special) *partisan* for Jewish political independence'.

I – Definition of Some Biblical Terms

that any of us can do and to which we are all called to do, the greatest influence a man can have is to win the lost and disciple them in the things of God. Think on this friend. Any man who fulfills Jesus' command to win the lost and to disciple them to obey the scriptures has more influence in changing his world, than any political leader anywhere, at any time.

> Any man who fulfills Jesus' command to win the lost and to disciple them to obey the scriptures has more influence in changing his world, than any political leader

Let us follow Jesus. He is our pattern. Remember what Jesus said to the highest political leader in all of Israel. He did not talk to Pilate about injustice – not even his own. He did not speak to him about mercy for the Jews. He did not speak to him about unrighteous laws, as so many Christians are consumed with today. No! He only spoke about eternal truth (Jn 18:37) to try to prick the man's heart to repentance in order to find that one needful thing: salvation. Hear Jesus' words.

> Jesus answered, My kingdom is not of this world: if my kingdom were of this world, then would my servants fight, that I should not be delivered to the Jews: but now is my kingdom not from hence. Jn 18:36

When Paul got his chance to speak to Felix the governor, what did he speak to him about? Political reform, better laws, more rights? No, "he reasoned of righteousness, temperance, and judgment to come" (Ac 24:25). When the soldiers came to John the Baptist asking what they should do, did he tell them to try to institute legal or military reform? No. "And the soldiers likewise demanded of him, saying, And what shall we do? And he said unto them, Do violence to no man, neither accuse *any* falsely; and be content with your wages." Lk 3:14

So why do Christians in America fight for the laws to be changed? Why do they fight for Jesus? Because, as Jesus said, they are in the **wrong** kingdom! If they were "not of this world" as he said, then they would not fight for him. But because they are of this world, therefore they do fight for him. Let us get back to the right kingdom, saints, the kingdom of God. Let us stop fighting for Jesus, and instead fight the good fight of faith to manifest in our own life holiness, righteousness, godliness, and the fear of God, and that we may lead others into the same life of truth. That will change our world more than we know! That is God's only method for revival – people turning to the Lord through the word of God, not through political laws.

Appendix II. The Fear of God and Unbelievers

For the Purpose of Salvation

God uses the fear of the LORD, not only in believers, as this book series has focused on, but also in unbelievers. Let us look briefly at that work that God does in the lost through the fear of God. The fear of God is to draw all men unto the Lord so that their hearts may be dealt with – that is its purpose. God wants to use the fear of God in unbelievers' hearts to work repentance unto salvation. This is why the lost need to see the fear of God working deeply in the life of true believers, so that it might be a witness and a conviction to them. The fear of God in a true disciple is a powerful weapon of righteousness, which God's Spirit uses to take captive those in captivity.

> **WARNING**: Be cautious saint, never contradict the work of the Spirit by sparing another's soul in order to try to woo their soul by mercy, grace, or some sort of man-focused ooey-gooey "I love you, you love me". Such things were never brought forth by true men of God in the scriptures, nor was an idea of unconditional acceptance as is preached today. God has never taught the "come as you are" attitude in regards to approaching him. He has always called men to repentance, to change their ways. May you not be deceived by the false methods of man's evangelism methods in use today. The times of such ignorance (i.e. of man's devices), God now commands "all men every where to repent" (Ac 17:30). Remember, why Jesus came: "to call sinners to repentance." Mt 9:13

The Work of the Fear of God in the Life of the Unbeliever

> Then Peter opened *his* mouth, and said, Of a truth I perceive that God is no respecter of persons: But in every nation <u>he that feareth him</u>, and worketh righteousness, is accepted with him. Ac 10:34-35

We have the awesome promise (in Acts 10:34-35) that Peter made when preaching to the Gentile unbelievers in Cornelius' house, that God will accept whoever fears him and works righteousness. But this cannot be taken out of context. Peter is by no means saying that unbelievers who fear God and work righteousness are saved and going to heaven. No, for salvation is not by works. What Peter is saying is that though a person is not saved, but fears God and works righteousness, God is pleased with that and accepts their dedication of heart to serve him as best they know, and that God will use this to draw them unto him -- if their fear and desire to please him continues.

This is exactly what God did for Cornelius and his whole family who was taught to fear God and do works of righteousness. It was the fear of God that led Cornelius to obey God and *prepared* him for salvation. How then does God

II – The Fear of God and Unbelievers

'accept' those who fear him, but are still lost? God accepts them by sending men unto them to preach the gospel to them! God accepted Cornelius and his family in terms of *favoring* them (above all other Gentiles) by the fact that God chose them to be the first Gentiles to come to faith in Christ after Pentecost. So, God fulfilled Solomon's prayer that he had prayed so many centuries before.

> Moreover concerning a stranger, that *is* not of thy people Israel, but cometh out of a far country for thy name's sake; (For <u>they shall hear</u> of thy great name, and of thy strong hand, and of thy stretched out arm;) <u>when he shall come and pray</u> toward this house; Hear thou in heaven thy dwelling place, and do according to all that the stranger calleth to thee for: that all people of the earth may know thy name, **to fear thee** 1K 8:41-43

> How then does God 'accept' those who fear him, but are still lost? God accepts them by sending men unto them to preach the gospel to them!

God's pleasure will be manifested toward the lost, even as was done in Cornelius' case, by sending men of God to such people to preach to them the everlasting gospel, by which they may be saved – if they receive the word which is preached. As it is written, "that through his name whosoever believeth in him shall receive remission of sins. While Peter yet spake these words, the Holy Ghost fell on all them <u>which heard the word</u>." Ac 10:43-44

The fear of God in the lives of unbelievers is to bring them to salvation. The fear of God turns them from their own self-destructive ways to humble themselves before his awesome might and power to cry out for forgiveness. Thus, God's fear prepares their heart to meet the living God and to be able to hear the demands of his word with a heart to obey it. In the scripture we see many examples of unbelievers having the fear of God because of the lives of believers and the workings of God in their midst.

The Need for the Fear of God in the Church

The greatest part of why such does not happen today is because there is no fear of God in the church. We can only reproduce after our own kind. The lack of God's fear in believers comes from the lack of sound doctrine "which is according to godliness" (1Tim 6:3). Let's consider an Old Testament example. When the book of the law of the LORD was with those sent out by Jehoshaphat to go throughout all the cities of Judah and teach the people, what was the result? "The fear of the LORD fell upon all the kingdoms of the lands that *were* round about Judah" (2Ch 17:10). O that God's people would get back to the sound doctrine of the scriptures and be delivered from the smooth doctrines and teachings of men.

Where is the Fear of GOD? Losing the Treasure of the Lord

God was able to mightily deliver Jehoshaphat and the people because they believed in the LORD their God so that they would be established, and they believed his prophets so they would prosper (2Ch 20:20). But their faith was not the empty covetous faith we see today. Their faith was established in the fear of God. When God's people have the word of God dwelling richly in them, then they will have an ear to hear the commandment and direction of the LORD and to hear his servants, which he sends unto them. The result of this great victory in Jehoshaphat's day and the rejoicing that ensued was that "the fear of God was on all the kingdoms of *those* countries, when they had heard that the LORD fought against the enemies of Israel." 2Ch 20:29

> **WARNING**: So many are taught that Jehoshaphat's battle was won by their praises, yet the scripture shows that it was because they believed God and his servants. Their praise was only the acknowledgement of their faith. We *cannot* praise our way into victory. Remember, many times God's own people worship him in vain! "This people draweth nigh unto me with their mouth, and honoureth me with *their* lips; but their heart is far from me." Mt 15:8 How can this be? It is because men teach for doctrines the commandments of men (Mt 15:9)! We must first make the choice to believe and trust in the living God. Then, by faith in his promise, we worship God and watch him move. "By faith Jacob ... worshipped" (Heb 11:21). If we worship, yet do not truly believe what God has said and commanded, our worship will always be in vain before God.

When people were around Jesus, and they saw the miracles that were done, often the fear of God was the result. But many of those who received the fear of God in these cases were specifically people who did not know God. For instance, when the man taken with palsy was lowered through the roof and was healed we see this response: "And they were all amazed, and they glorified God, and were filled with fear, saying, We have seen strange things to day." Lk 5:26 The Gadarenes were clearly Gentiles outside God's covenant, unbelievers in heart and raising. After they heard about the destruction of the swine and saw the demoniac delivered and in his right mind, "they were taken with great fear" and pled for Jesus to depart from them (Lk 8:37). When all those who attended the funeral train of the widow of Nain's son saw the resurrection of the young man, a similar response was had.[202]

---

[202] The vast majority of people at a funeral are typically those who do not have a living, vital relationship of obedience to the Lord. Remember, the dead bury the dead (Lk 9:60). Funerals, even if of a believer, are attended by many who are not saved, as evidenced even today.

II – The Fear of God and Unbelievers

That All Might Come to Know They are but Men
"Put them in fear, O LORD: that the nations may know themselves to be but men. Selah." Ps 9:20

The fear of God is used by God not only to directly bring men to salvation, but also indirectly. It does this by humbling them in preparation for salvation. Before salvation can even be considered by the pride of man, a person must be brought to the brink of seeing the smallness, the complete inability to deliver themselves. Thus, the second work of the fear of the LORD is to humble us before him. The fear of the LORD is designed by God to reveal to our proud heart the end of our capabilities and the smallness of our strength.

In this spirit we see David cries out in Psalm 9.[203] We will either see what the Son of God has come to do for us in saving us from what we could not save ourselves from (i.e. from the wrath of God and the consequences of sin). Or we will die by the Son's judgment because his blood is found to be on our hands, and we have rejected his free gift of forgiveness, being unwilling to come under his lordship.

> But his citizens hated him, and sent a message after him, saying, We will not have this *man* to reign over us. ... But those mine enemies, which would not that I should reign over them, bring hither, and slay *them* before me. Lk 19:14,27

So David prays, "Put them in fear, O LORD: *that* the nations may know themselves *to be but* men. Selah." Ps 9:20 Who are these people that God should put in fear? We see three different groups of people addressed in verses 17 & 19.

1. the heathen   (i.e. those who do not know God),
2. those that do wickedly (i.e. those who have put away their conscience),
3. those that forget God (i.e. those who once knew him, but walk away).

Before men can come to the Lord, so often they must first be broken of their self-dependence and self-reliance. This is yet another sign of those who once knew God but are now forsaking him in their heart: self-dependence and self-reliance reassert themselves in their heart. These are those that <u>forget</u> God and lose their fear of God. This is evidenced by the fact that they are no longer aware that they are but mere men. Their own self-importance or selfish desires have eclipsed the greatness of the Mighty God and the supercedence of his will over ours. They no longer "Selah" or 'stop and think about' such evident spiritual truths. We are called to be his servants. He is *not* called to be ours, as so many treat him today.

---

[203] It is of significance that Ps 9 is subtitled "upon Muthlabben", which when translated means "*To die for the son*"!

The Difference in Response to God & to His Gifts Lies in Us

The scripture reveals several responses by unbelievers and believers to the fear of God. We must understand, just because we see different responses, that does not mean the event or stimulus is any different. Two men may undergo the same event, but respond completely differently. One heart may be converted, while another is hardened. This is often more a reflection of the difference between those involved, than what took place.

So it is with the fear of God. Many good authors on the fear of God have classified different types of fear in response to God and shown which ones we ought to have and which ones we ought not to have. So also I, when I first wrote these books did the same, for it is the natural way of explaining the differences. But God began to show through the scriptures concerning the fear of God that **he** is the source of fear – not us!

- He is fearful in sight (Heb 12:21).
- He is terrible in majesty (Job 37:22),
- He is frightening in his works (Ps 66:3,5, 145:6),
- He is both fearful & dreadful in his presence (Dan 9:4).

So we have a *reason* to fear and dread God (Job 13:11,21, Isa 8:13). Jacob declared that even the house of God, the place where God dwells with his people, "How dreadful *is* this place." Gen 28:17 The scripture repeatedly refers to the fear of God as "**his fear**" (Ex 20:20, Job 9:34) and from God's persective as "**my fear**" (Ex 23:27, Jer 2:19, 32:40, Mal 1:6). Thus, though it sound trivially simple: God is the source of the fear of God. So he says, "I will put my fear in their hearts, that they shall not depart from me." Jer 32:40b God's fear is given to men so that they might be drawn to God and not depart from him.

Now we know that because the LORD is the LORD therefore as he says "I change not." Mal 3:6 By the nature of God, he does not change. He is unchangeable (Heb 7:24) and uncorruptible (Rom 1:23, 1Tim 1:17).[204] He does not change and neither do his attributes. So James records of the heavenly Father "with whom is no variableness, neither shadow of turning." Jam 1:17 As he does not change, so his fear does not change.

So I began to see that the fault or difference was not in the type of fear that people received when they encountered God, for God does not change. Neither does the fear of God, which comes from him, change. The only thing that changed to explain the difference of the *response* to the fear of God was the person themselves. It was how they received or responded to the clean and enduring fear of God that made the difference. It has been shown in the previous

---

[204] 1Tim 1:17 uses the word 'immortal' which in the Greek literally is incorruptible.

II – The Fear of God and Unbelievers

book that the fear of God is his gift to us through the Spirit. Therefore, as a gift from God it does not change. "Every good gift and every perfect gift is from above, and cometh down from the Father of lights, <u>with whom is no variableness</u>, neither shadow of turning." Jam 1:17 The gifts of God are after his own nature. God does not change and his gifts do not change, and therefore his fear does not change.

The Examples of God's Grace and God's Word

So it is with God's grace. Two men may both receive the grace of God, but one is changed from his old ways while the other is not. One may frustrate the grace of God in their life (Gal 2:21) or receive it in vain (2Co 6:1) or even turn the it into lasciviousness (Jude 1:4). While another is taught by the same grace of God to deny ungodliness and worldly lusts and to live soberly, righteously, and godly in this present world (Tit 2:11-12, 1Co 15:10). They learn "the true grace of God wherein [they] stand" (1Pe 5:12). That is, they learn to stand against sin through God's grace. Is the fault in the grace of God which they received? Did one receive a *lesser* grace than the other? No, there is no fault in God's grace. The fault is in the heart of man which received the gift. Is this not why God calls the one heart evil (Heb 3:12) and the other good (Lk 8:15)? Yes.

Consider this, there is no fault in the grace of God that is received by men. Yet we see men respond very differently to the grace of God, which has been given them. In the same way there is no fault in the word of God, which men may read from the Bible or hear preached. Yet we see men respond very differently to the knowledge of the truth that is given them. Thus, the fault lies with us – with the soil of our heart, as the parable of the sower of the seed shows (Lk 8:4-18). It lies in how we *respond* to the goodness of God. It is how we *receive* the gift of God. Note, the seed is not sufficient of itself to grow without soil. It must find the good soil to be planted in, so that it can become fruitful. Paul warned the Romans of this, "Or despisest thou the riches of his goodness and forbearance and longsuffering; not knowing that the goodness of God [*should*] leadeth thee to repentance?" Rom 2:4

> God's word, God's grace, and God's fear are all given freely to us to lead us to repentance, but we must cherish them and hold on to them and allow them to do their work on us by laying apart all filthiness and receiving them with meekness

Notice even Jesus had to deal with this responsibility of the heart to respond to God's gifts (in this case, the gift of forgiveness). "Wherefore I say unto thee, Her sins, which are many, are forgiven; for she loved much: but to whom little is forgiven, *the same* loveth little." Lk 7:47 God's word is sufficient for us all. Some will allow it to change them, while others will not. The fault is not in the seed, it is in the soil. God's word, God's grace, and God's fear are all given freely to us to lead us to repentance, but we must cherish and hold on to each, allowing each to do their work on us by laying apart all filthiness and receiving each with meekness (Jam 1:21).

Of course, there *is* a false fear of God. One that does *not* come from God. That we have already talked about at length, so we needn't say more here.[205] That is the one that Isaiah describes, when he says, "Wherefore the Lord said, Forasmuch as this people draw near *me* with their mouth, and with their lips do honour me, but have removed their heart far from me, and their fear toward me is taught by the precept of men." Isa 29:13 This fear is not "his fear"; rather, it has as its source man and not God. Thus, it cannot produce the life of God, for it is not of God. Notice that this false fear of God is taught to men. Instead we will not focus on man's different responses to God's fear.

We shall see several such different responses, but remember it is still the same fear of God that is inspiring each of them. One will have the fear of the LORD that results in his being drawn to God, while another will receive the same fear of God that results in his being driven from God. In this case it is not the fear that makes the difference – even though many have tried to distinguish these. The issue is our *response* to God's fear. Both responses have the identical stimuli: God and his Spirit. The Spirit of God inspires us to fear the Almighty God, and Father of our Lord Jesus Christ. The problem, the fault, the deficiency is not in God, nor in the fear that his Spirit inspires, but in us. Do we allow ourselves to be open and naked before God? Or do we hide from "the eyes of him before whom we have to do" (Heb 4:13)? Or do we find ourselves fighting against God (Ac 5:39)? Let us now look at the different responses to the fear of God.

The Different Responses to God's Fear

	The Response:	The Result
1.	Godly Fear	righteousness & salvation
2.	Passing Fear	hypocrisy & disobedience
3.	Ignorant Fear	false worship & slothfulness
4.	Petrified Fear	inaction & torment
5.	Fleeing Fear	departing from God
6.	Rebelling Fear	fighting against God

---

[205] This was in the chapter entitled "Cheap Imitations and Artificial Substitutes".

II – The Fear of God and Unbelievers

1. That which Works Righteousness & Leads to Salvation

First, there is the right response to the fear of God that opens the door of one's heart to bring salvation and holiness. We will call this godly fear. In this case, the fear of God is able to change the heart and to work righteousness. It is able to awaken the conscience and quicken it. This we have seen already with Cornelius. He feared God with all his house (Ac 10:2). Though this man was not saved, yet the fear of the Lord paved the way in his life to prepare him for salvation and to be able to willingly receive it, when it was brought to him. The same fear of God that worked in him also worked in his whole family. The fear of God in his life produced (Ac 10:2,22):

1. a just/righteous character,[206]
2. a devout or pious character,[207]
3. a similar heart in his whole family,
4. a heart to give "much alms to the people",
5. a commitment to pray to God always,[208]
6. a good report among others,
7. who received warnings.

Though this man may put many true believers to shame (because they have not the fear of God in such measure, though they should), yet he still needed salvation – just as many reverent 'god-fearing' people do today. But because he had a godly response to the fear of God which was given him, he was able to hear the heavenly warning or 'admonishment'. When the commandment came concerning what to do (i.e. how to be saved, Ac 11:14), his heart was quick and ready to obey, for it had been prepared by the fear of God.

The scripture says he <u>immediately</u> sent for Peter. The fear of God properly received opens the door of our heart to hearken diligently and receive the words of men of God (Ac 10:44), especially those who are sent to us. Before Peter had come, Cornelius had gathered many to hear everything that would be commanded of him by God (Ac 10:33). Clearly he set an anticipation in their hearts which explains why they were so eager to hear the words of the apostle. Here are some others who through the fear of the Lord came to salvation:

---

[206] He is called 'a just man' (v22). This word 'just' means '*equitable* (in character or act); by implication *innocent, holy*' and is also translated 'righteous'.

[207] This word 'devout' means '*well-reverent*, i.e. *pious*' and is also translated 'godly'. It was so contagious that it affected those soldiers who waited on him continually (Ac 10:7).

[208] In fact his prayers and alms were so noteable that the angel said they "are come up for a memorial before God." Ac 10:4

a. <u>The Repentant Thief on the cross</u>:
But the other answering rebuked him, saying, <u>Dost not thou fear God</u>, seeing thou art in the same condemnation? Lk 23:40

b. <u>The Centurion at the foot of the cross</u>:
Now when the centurion, and they that were with him, watching Jesus, saw the earthquake, and those things that were done, <u>they feared greatly</u>, saying, Truly this was the Son of God. Mt 27:54

2. <u>The Response of Superstition: Passing Fear</u>

People may fear God when they see his mighty acts of judgment, but their fear fades away over time as remembrance recedes, and especially if no repentance accompanies their instant, but temporary, alarm and fright. Such people miss the salvation that could be theirs – IF only they in the fear of God had turned in repentance to ask, "What must I do?"[209] We can call this *passing* fear, for it is only temporary and momentary in nature. It is not witnessed by any lasting change. It is faddish in nature.

Sadly, as the judgments of God continue to hit America many will "go to church" for a season, but will not in truth change their life through the fear of God. Before long they return to their slumber and their sin. A few will try to "have God", yet still keep their own life. They would have their fire insurance, yet still keep playing with fire (i.e. living riotously according to their pleasures). Many will fear God but continue to serve their own gods. Their fear of God, then, is nothing more than a religious fear. It is *superstition*. Superstition will always cause corruption and mixture.

The commands of the true God, in this case, always get mixed with those of 'other' gods and, thus, forming (to them) a happy eclectic mix, comfortable to their own mindset. This they mistakenly believe will appease 'all the gods'. But the true God is not honored by *any* form of mixture or corruption. He is a holy God that abhors mixture. He calls this keeping of our old ways, this mixing of the things of God with the things of the world, idolatry. The true God is a jealous God, and will have no other gods in our midst. Such people are the same as those who formed the original Samaritans, who "feared the LORD, <u>and</u> served their own gods, <u>after the manner of the nations</u> whom they carried away from thence. Unto this day they do <u>after the former manners</u>" (2K 17:33-34).

God has promised to bring forth judgment when his ways are mixed with those of the world. He has left us all repeated testimonies of his displeasure in

---

[209] This is the recurrent cry of those who found salvation in the book of Acts, "What must I do?": at Pentecost (Ac 2:37), with Saul on the road to Damascus (Ac 9:6), and the Philippian jailer (Ac 16:30). Note also the equivalence of Cornelius being told "what thou oughtest to do" (Ac 10:6) and "words, whereby thou ... shall be saved." Ac 11:14

II – The Fear of God and Unbelievers

this area. So often mankind does not receive correction from God's judgments and amend its ways. Rather, they do as the superstitious Samaritans of old did:

> Howbeit they did not hearken, but they did after <u>their former manner</u>. So these nations feared the LORD, <u>and</u> served their graven images, both their children, & their children's children: as did their fathers, <u>so do they unto this day</u>. 2K 17:40-41

Unbelievers, without God's help, will always live in the world according to the principles of the world, because they are of the world. Thus, their response to tragedies is to try to avoid them in the future. This, without true repentance, always produces superstition. The superstitious response to the fear of God will cause a person when they hear of God's impending judgment to take warning and to have a *form* of obedience or submission, but such is only *temporary* conformance, for it is external. It only exists as long as there are outward reinforced threatenings.

This is best exemplified in Pharaoh. When the terrors of God's judgments in the 10 plagues came upon him, he was brought to fear. He even called to the man of God and pled for mercy, even acknowledging that he had sinned. "And Pharaoh sent, and called for Moses and Aaron, and said unto them, I have sinned this time: the LORD is righteous, and I and my people are wicked." Ex 9:27 But Moses knew his heart. He knew this was not true repentance. So he says he will pray to God and the judgment will be taken away, "but as for thee and thy servants, I **know** that ye will <u>not yet fear the LORD God</u>." Ex 9:30

Once the danger passes the unconverted returns to his hard-heartedness. Even as with Pharaoh of old, so with so many even unto today. When the threats of danger are removed, then they immediately return to their self-directed, self-serving, self-centered ways of life, which is to continue to satisfy and pursue their own wants and desires without any fear of God at all. This is the fear that hits people's heart after every major catastrophe.[210] Those who have such temporary fear may change externals and begin to do what looks right in the sight of men, but the heart is unchanged. They still desire to go their own way and to do what they want. Their life is still in their control, and their 'amendments' are often only attempts to be 'good'.

With superstitious fear people are merely temporarily halted in their tracks by the fear of judgment and the threat of loss. But as the freshness of the fear recedes and the nearness of present judgment seems more and more distant, they return slowly, but surely to their pigsty of an evil conscience and to wallowing in the fouled mud of their desires.

---

[210] This is exactly what took place immediately following the September 11, 2001 World Trade Center bombing. Many flocked to the church for a time and a short season, but they soon fell away. This was repeated again with the Indonesian (or Boxing Day) Tsunami of 2004, December 26.

The scriptures are filled with the examples of those who received temporary warning, reproof, and protection, but who had no lasting change and most likely perished. Because they had no lasting changes, they did not fear God (Ps 55:19).

a. <u>The Servants of Pharaoh</u>:
He that <u>feared the word of the LORD</u> among the servants of Pharaoh made his servants and his cattle flee into the houses Ex 9:20

b. <u>The Workers of Iniquity</u>:
Have all the workers of iniquity no knowledge? who eat up my people *as* they eat bread, and call not upon the LORD. There were <u>they in great fear</u>: for God *is* in the generation of the righteous. Ps 14:4-5

c. <u>The Adversaries of God</u>:
According to *their* deeds, accordingly he will repay, fury to his adversaries, recompence to his enemies; to the islands he will repay recompence. So shall they <u>fear the name of the LORD</u> from the west, and his glory from the rising of the sun. When the enemy shall come in like a flood, the Spirit of the LORD shall lift up a standard against him. Isa 59:18-19

d. <u>The People of the Powerful & Mighty Nations</u>:
Therefore shall the strong people glorify thee, the city of the terrible nations <u>shall fear thee</u>. For thou hast been a strength to the poor, a strength to the needy in his distress, a refuge from the storm, a shadow from the heat, when the blast of the terrible ones *is* as a storm *against* the wall. Isa 25:3-4

And it shall be to me a name of joy, a praise and an honour before all the nations of the earth, which shall hear all the good that I do unto them: and <u>they shall fear and tremble</u> for all the goodness and for all the prosperity that I procure unto it. Jer 33:9

Superstitious Fear in the Church of Jesus Christ

This superstitious response afflicts not only the loast, but even the church of Jesus Christ. This is the fear that must have been what was working in Ananias and Sapphira, for we know that true "fear came upon every soul" at Pentecost (Ac 2:43), and therefore came upon these two as well. So the fear of God may come upon your soul, dear saint, but what is your *response* to that holy fear of God? Does it become in you the exceeding fear of God that cleanses the inside of your cup? Or does it result in you forsaking that for the fear of self-preservation, a superstitious fear, a fear that has at its root how we can be protected, blessed, and provided for. The true fear of God is designed to change us, to bring about in us an abhorring of our own heart and our sinful ways and a fleeing to lay hold upon the hope that is set before us "to be conformed to the image of his Son" (Rom 8:29).

II – The Fear of God and Unbelievers

This superstitious fear is so far less than that which God wants from us. Instead of us having (as many think) too much fear, in this case we actually have too little fear. We have not allowed the full effect of the fear of God to take root in our heart and so produce the appropriate fruit. Remember, the proper fruit of the true fear of God is the serving of God Almighty for his awesome power, might, and judgment. Whereas the fruit of this inferior fear of God is merely the serving of our self. In this case we serve God only as long as it is convenient or seems necessary.

After the judgment of God against Ananias and his wife, we see a renewal of the true fear of God. The Bible says "and <u>great fear</u> came on all them that heard these things." Ac 5:5 And again after the judgment of God against his wife Sapphira, "And <u>great fear</u> came upon all the church, and upon as many as heard these things." Ac 5:11 To truly be preserved from God's wrath we cannot afford such a superstitious fear to be in us that allows us to still be in charge of our life. We must have the fear that puts God in his proper place of authority. Thus, Ananias and Sapphira had too little of the fear of God to preserve them. Like most of the Christian church, there is too little of God's fear.

3. <u>The Response of False Worship: Ignorant Fear</u>

They feared the LORD, **and** <u>served their own gods</u>, after the manner of the nations whom they carried away from thence. So these nations feared the LORD, **and** <u>served their graven images</u>, both their children, and their children's children: as did their fathers, <u>so do they unto this day</u>. 2K 17:33,41

Vast millions today serve God (so they think) in fear, but their worship is in vain for they worship after the traditions and commandments of men. Their worship, like their fear of God, is taught by the precept of man (Isa 29:13). Thus, their service is not unto God, but in essence unto men. What they worship, they worship ignorantly. This is a fear in which the individual may be very committed to weekly worship, to praying, to serving in some manner, and even to daily reading of the scriptures. Year by year passes by, but they do not change. Their dregs remain within them and their scent is not changed (Jer 48:11). Their fear never causes them to be emptied of their own ways.

We see a clear example of this response in the Samaritans. The ancient Samaritans feared God, but still served their own gods. Thus, we are given the commandment to fear the LORD **and** to serve him, for the very reason that people can fear him, yet still not serve him. "Thou shalt fear the LORD thy God, **and** serve him, and shalt swear by his name." Dt 6:13 Remember, the service we are talking about here is not the service that so many Christians offer to God, one in which they are in control and do things as they please. No, true service must be under authority. It must be done in submission to authority according to what he has asked.

Where is the Fear of GOD? Losing the Treasure of the Lord

Ignorant Fear Oftentimes Says, "It won't happen to us"

So even among the Jews there were those who feared God, but did not put away their idols in order to serve the living God in sincerity and truth. Joshua wanted to see the people truly serve the LORD by putting away their idols. "Now therefore fear the LORD, <u>and serve him</u> in sincerity and in truth: and put away the gods which your fathers served on the other side of the flood, and in Egypt; and serve ye the LORD." Jos 24:14 Samuel echoes this same cry years later. "Only fear the LORD, <u>and serve him</u> in truth with all your heart: for consider how great *things* he hath done for you." 1Sam 12:24

Sadly many people believe on the Lord and begin to follow him and yet still hold onto their old gods, their old trusts. They may have been taught faith, but the foundation of repentance was never firmly planted in their heart. Because of ignorance (of the deep need for repentance), they are not cleansed from the old. Instead of turning away from the old, they merely mix in the new. This is what Jacob's family had done and he knew it. Thus, when he went up to Bethel (the house of God) he commanded them to put such false trusts away (Gen 35:3).

> Then Jacob said unto his household, and to all that *were* with him, Put away the strange gods that *are* <u>among you</u>, and be clean, and change your garments: And they gave unto Jacob all the strange gods which *were* in their hand, and *all their* earrings which *were* in their ears; and Jacob hid them under the oak which *was* by Shechem. Gen 35:2,4

The Jews of Jeremiah's day had so corrupted their worship and their fear of God that they were trusting in God's sanctuary, more than God. "Thus saith the LORD of hosts, the God of Israel, Amend your ways and your doings, and I will cause you to dwell in this place. Trust ye not in lying words, saying, The temple of the LORD, The temple of the LORD, The temple of the LORD, are these." Jer 7:3-4 Notice they also had lost their 'baptism of repentance' (i.e. their continual immersion into change), and they were no longer amending their ways. So they were instead trusting in lying words, which could not profit (v8).

John the Baptist had to deal with this same smug self-confidence. "And think not to say within yourselves, We have Abraham to our father: for I say unto you, that God is able of these stones to raise up children unto Abraham." Mt 3:9 Are we any different today who trust in our church in the multitude of its structures or the size of our congregation or the extent or age of our denomination? rather than working out our salvation in fear and trembling (Php 2:12) with a good conscience before both God and men (Ac 23:1, 24:16).

Consider when Israel (namely the 10 northern tribes) went into captivity for forsaking the LORD and giving themselves unto idolatry and every evil act. God says that backsliding Israel committed adultery. But what was the respone of Judah? Did she fear God? Did she repent of her sins when she saw the judgment of God against her sister? No. She continued in her ways. God says, "And

II – The Fear of God and Unbelievers

I saw, when for all the causes whereby backsliding Israel committed adultery I had put her away, and given her a bill of divorce; yet her treacherous sister Judah <u>feared not</u>, but went and played the harlot also." Jer 3:8 Judah had *forgotten* her own wickedness against God (Jer 44:9), and all the judgments that had come against her as a result. She was willingly ignorant. And because she forgot, she put away the fear of God. God says of them of Judah: "They are not humbled even unto this day, <u>neither have they feared</u>, nor walked in my law, nor in my statutes, that I set before you and before your fathers." Jer 44:10

The judgments of God against Judah were designed by him to bring Judah to fear, but she feared not. Similarly, God's judgment of bringing Israel into captivity was also designed by him to bring Judah to fear, but again she feared not. God called this treachery. His judgments *always* bring the fear of God to them whose heart is willing to be turned. Thus, God says of Judah that she was treacherous. She was ready 'to *pillage*'. She cared nothing for the destruction of her sister. She only cared how she might profit from it! Are not these the ones being described by Paul, "Who knowing the judgment of God, that they which commit such things are worthy of death, not only do the same, but have pleasure in them that do them." Ro 1:32

We must allow the judgments of God, especially in these last days, to awaken us to righteousness that we sin not. "Awake to righteousness, and sin not; for some have not the knowledge of God: I speak this to your shame." 1Co 15:34 When Paul says "some have not the knowledge of God", it is clear he says this to believers. What "knowledge of God" can this be, but the knowledge of the fear of God, which so few know today.

Was this response of Judah not similar to the Pharisees and the Sadducees? They cared nothing for truth or for mercy, and they had no genuine fear of God, though they claimed to fear him. They cared only for their kingdoms and their power. Thus, it was no problem to put one to death for the sake of maintaining the status quo. They found it quite "<u>expedient for us</u>, that one man should die for the people, and that the whole nation perish not." Jn 11:50 So let us look at the evil response to the fear of God that the Pharisees and the Sadducees had. Now scripture shows us the former added to what God asked (Mk 7:1-13), while the latter took away (Ac 23:8, Lk 20:27), but neither truly obeyed what God had said.

1. <u>The Pharisees</u>: These put away God's fear by staying busy with so many extra commandments of men and traditions, so that the word of God was made of no effect (Mt 15:3-6). Instead they could take pride in their meticulousness, in their attention to detail (Mt 23:23), believing they were the pure ones. This way they did not have to change their heart, for it was far from him (Mt 15:7-9). This very same spirit is seen even unto today in the outward forms of penance and the manifold traditions that so many religious people hold to.

2. <u>The Sadducees</u>: These put away fhe fear of God by reducing the word of God only to a historical record and excising the cry of the prophets, which are unto every generation. In this way they did not have to have their heart dealt with. The parts of the scripture that they fell short in, they could justify their ignorance of by saying that it had passed away. Thus, they could boast in their exclusivity and hide in their self-confident pride, believing they were the pure ones.

Such ignorant fear is also *ungodly* fear, for it never transforms our hearts to increase in any godliness. So 2K 17:33 & 41 show us such fear produces no good fruit and no godly change. Ungodly fear enables people to fear the LORD, yet still serve their own god – the god of their own making. In so doing, they yet serve graven images, for the image of god that they worship is a false representation, made after the making of man's own hands and thoughts – thus it is in truth a graven image. Such worship and fear have no power to bring forth life. They only produce death, resentment, bitterness, and hardness of heart.

This is the fear that through the new covenant we should be delivered from. "That he would grant unto us, that we being delivered out of the hand of our enemies might serve him without fear" (Lk 1:74). We are not to serve him any longer with an ungodly fear. We are to serve him with a godly fear. "Wherefore we receiving a kingdom which cannot be moved, let us have grace, whereby we may serve God acceptably with reverence and <u>godly</u> fear" (Heb 12:28). Let us serve God acceptably with godly fear.

The Slothful Servant

Sadly, this fear is not limited to the lost. Many compromising believers fear those who serve the Lord in holiness, but not in a way that they want to become like them, but rather that they may hide from them. Those with this ungodly fear lose their heart for the things of God because they do not want to forsake their own desires. We will serve what we love, and if we love something in place of God, then it is an idol and God hates it.

Truth in our conscience, as well as "the word of truth" from the Bible and "the Spirit of truth" from God, form a three-fold cord which binds our sin. But if we refuse to change, and we continue in the hypocrisy of loving what God jealously says we must depart from, then we will always lose our heart toward serving the Lord. Our heart will no longer be given in his service in purity and fervently.[211] We are to be "not slothful in business; fervent in spirit; serving the Lord." Rom 12:11 There must be a fervency in spirit in our service of the Lord, but how can such be, when we are loving something else, more than him?

---

[211] This is the most common "burden" that those who tire of serving complain of. Children of God no longer find joy in serving in the capacity God has chosen for them, because in their heart they begin to pursue some other desire or love.

II – The Fear of God and Unbelievers

The loss of our heart toward serving the LORD is manifested most clearly in the slothful servant. Make no mistake, this was *not* a tare among the wheat – this was one of God's own! He was a servant of the master and was in the vineyard of the master. He was trusted by the master, received a talent from him, and was given a charge by him. Thus, he was believed to be faithful. None of these things apply to the lost. He even feared the master. As he himself said, "For I feared thee" (Lk 19:21). He even *knew* the master by name, and previously had labored faithfully for him, which was why he was given a charge by the master.

The slothful servant was clearly part of God's household of faith, yet he became an "unprofitable servant" who was cast into "outer darkness: [*where*] there shall be weeping and gnashing of teeth." Mt 25:30 Though he feared his Lord, he "digged in the earth, and hid his lord's money" (Mt 25:18)! When the master returned the servant gave it unto him, for he knew enough not to *spend* the talent (i.e. the gift of God) on himself and his own desires. He could not directly steal it. But he *did* spend his time and his heart on what he would, and not on what his Lord had commanded. Thus, by his inaction he still stole from his master. "He also that is slothful in his work is brother to him that is a great waster [i.e. a spoiler]." Pr 18:9

This servant still saw his time and his life as his own, rather than belonging to the master. How many Christians there are like that today! They have forgotten first their profession that Jesus is their Lord and second that they have been bought with a price and they are not their own (1Co 6:19-20). This man's fear made him shrink from service and be a slothful servant. Rather than serve with gladness and expeditiousness as the fear of God moves us, his half-hearted fear caused him to completely misjudge his Lord and **to do nothing** for his Lord.

His fear was half-hearted because it did not possess his whole heart. If he had feared his Lord sufficiently, he would never have spent his time doing his own thing and ignoring his Lord's charge, nor would he have dared to speak such evil of his master, much less think them. He said, "Lord, I <u>knew thee</u> that thou art an hard man, reaping where thou hast not sown, and gathering where thou hast not strawed" (Mt 25:24). When in fact he did NOT know the master rightly. This was part of the problem. That is why we classify this as ignorant fear. He feared the master, but not according to true knowledge. The two other faithful servants who brought increase to the master feared the master also, but in the correct way, according to knowledge.

This is one of the fruits of slothfulness. Slothful, sloppy service will result in sloppy, incomplete knowledge of the Lord. Thus, his 'knowledge' was completely faulty. It was in fact ignorant! Had not the Lord sowed into his servant? Yes, the talent had been given by the Lord himself! O how we misjudge the Lord of glory when we lack the full and complete fear of God. The slothful man perceives fear, but in his fear he does nothing about it. "The slothful *man* saith, *There is* a <u>lion</u> in the way; a <u>lion</u> *is* in the streets." Pr 26:13

Where is the Fear of GOD? Losing the Treasure of the Lord

The faithful man, on the other hand, walks in the fear of God, and changes his ways so that he may fulfill his Lord's commands. Thus we see Hananiah "was a faithful man, and feared God above many." Neh 7:2 Where did his faithfulness come from but from his great fear of God. That is, he received the fear of God in fulness and not in part. The fear of God, correctly received, will cause us to change into his likeness and to follow in his footsteps.

4. The Fear that Leads to Inaction: Frozen Fear

"Selah. Because they have <u>no changes</u>, therefore they fear not God." Ps 55:19

There is another response to God's holy fear and that is to do nothing at all. Often those with this response are gripped by inaction. They end up being frozen, much like the deer that is caught in the mesmerizing gleam of the headlights and cannot move. They fear what is coming, but they find no proper place to flee. The fear of judgment therefore paralyzes them. They continue to trust in what they know (which is the old), rather than allowing the Lord to teach them of himself (i.e. the new). In remaining still and doing nothing, they hope to avoid notice by hiding or blending in. The true fear of God leads to the refuge of a sincere trust in God. But this response of *frozen* fear finds no refuge.

Contrary to what men teach and believe, faith and trust are to work hand in hand with the fear of God. Each ought to produce the other. If the fear of God does not produce faith and trust, it is because either our response to the fear of God is incorrect or because we do not fear God enough. Remember, the right fear of God produces the knowledge and revelation of God! We are to come to know who God is through his fear. This is why those who have feared him most, knew him best.

Though the deer is stunned by the lights of an oncoming car, it is because the deer neither knows the source of the light and because it does not fear the source of the light *enough* to flee to safety. Both ignorance and the lack of sufficient fear combine to bring the beast into grave often fatal danger. If it was assured by knowledge (through the observation of other deer) that death or at least great harm was imminent, it would take action immediately. Though we think the deer is terrified, by its actions the deer is actually not terrified enough!

So it is for us. We may see the light of God's glory and that he is coming in judgment, but we do not fear his judgment enough, or we would immediately begin to change and to forsake many ways and thoughts in our life. So David wrote, "Selah [i.e. stop and think about it]. Because they have <u>no changes</u>, therefore they fear not God." Ps 55:19 So we see, because God is among his people (2Co 6:16) that some will be frozen by the fear of God. Rather than draw near to see what the LORD is doing, some will draw back desiring to have nothing to do with those who walk in God's presence. So it is written, "they journeyed: and the terror of God was upon the cities that *were* round about them, and they did not pursue after the sons of Jacob." Gen 35:5

Fear that hath Torment

Thus, this ungodly fear is by its very nature *tormenting*. It both lives in torment and it in turn seeks to torment others. It is the fear that the demons know, and thus we can call it a *demonic* fear. James says of them, "the devils also believe [that there is one God], and tremble." Jam 2:19 Notice that this fear incorporates faith, it believes in the one God, but it refuses to depart from iniquity. Listen to what the demons said when Jesus encountered them. They cried out, "art thou come hither to torment us before the time?" Mt 8:29 They recognized Jesus' authority as the Son of God and acknowledged "the most high God", yet they still refused to repent. Yes, they might seek his mercy, but only so that they might go and continue to do their will! "What have I to do with thee, Jesus, thou Son of the most high God? I adjure [*or*, beseech] thee by God, that thou torment me not." Mk 5:7 [Lk 8:28]

This is the fear that the demons would continually try to inflict upon God's disobedient children, so that they might make them ineffective in any service of God. Demons know they have a day of torment coming, and thus in frustration they try to torment others and so cause men not to repent, not to turn from their wicked ways, but to continue in the same way. It was the work of demonic forces which caused many in Jesus' own day to be taken with 'torments' (Mt 4:24, 8:6). This same spirit can work in God's children who are refusing to obey God's word. Thus, disobedient Saul tormented David, but David refused to become like him. On the other hand, when the servant who was forgiven his great debt did not show mercy likewise to another who owed him a small debt, he was turned over "to the tormentors" (Mt 18:34). Thus, Christians today who do not forgive others their sins are often the most tormented people on earth. And such people cannot but torment others, much like Saul did to David.

This is the fear that John speaks about, that perfect love (which is based on knowing another person) will cast out. "There is no [*we could say, tormenting*] fear in love; but perfect love casteth out [*tormenting*] fear: because [*ungodly*] fear hath torment. He that feareth [*in this way*][212] is not made perfect in love." 1Jn 4:18 This frozen or tormenting fear is seen even in Revelation when the judgment of Babylon finally arrives. Then the merchants will be "standing afar off for the fear of her torment" (Rev 18:10,15). Notice that it may be accompanied by cries of despair ("Alas, alas") and by "weeping and wailing", but for all this, repen-

---

[212] Of course, I have added the clarifying comments in brackets, lest we misunderstand what John is saying, as some would misinterpret him. Many claim this verse means that there is no fear of God in the new covenant. This cannot be, for John himself in his book Revelation testifies of the necessity to fear God (Rev 11:18, 14:7, 15:4, 19:5).

tance still is not found. No change occurs. These will be those 'fearful' who "shall have their part in the lake which burneth with fire and brimstone: which is the second death." Rev 21:8

5. The Response of Departing from God: Fleeing Fear

We see others who through the fear of God fled from the LORD. This is the *flight* response. This flight respone was the very thing that God wanted to put upon Israel's enemies – IF Israel would only walk in the fear of God. "I will send my fear before thee, and will destroy all the people to whom thou shalt come, and I will make all thine enemies turn their backs unto thee." Ex 23:27 This fear would cause the unsaved to "tremble, and be in anguish because of thee." Dt 2:25 But this response was not seen only in Israel's enemies, it is also seen in those who make themselves the enemies of God.

When this response lays hold of a heart they will refuse to submit to God, and thus, wll not stay around to allow authority to deal with them and bring correction. The fear that causes men to flee will be that which is specially seen in the last days judgment (Isa 2:2), for on that day no one will fight against him because of his manifested glory! He will come then to judge the idolater, the mean man and the proud man, as well as all those who've turned aside from following him (v8-17).

> Enter into the rock, and hide thee in the dust, <u>for fear of the LORD</u>, and for the glory of his majesty. And they shall go into the holes of the rocks, and into the caves of the earth, <u>for fear of the LORD</u>, and for the glory of his majesty, when he ariseth to shake terribly the earth. Isa 2:10

The flight response causes people to turn aside from following the LORD. Samuel the prophet also deals with the fear of fleeing from God when giving his warning to the people:

> And Samuel said unto the people, **Fear not**: ye have done all this wickedness: <u>yet turn not aside from following the LORD</u>, but serve the LORD with all your heart; <u>And turn ye not aside</u>: for *then should ye go* after vain *things*, which cannot profit nor deliver; for they *are* vain. ... **Only fear the LORD**, and **serve him in truth** with all your heart: for consider how great *things* he hath done for you. 1Sam 12:20-21,24

The true fear of God will convict us and motivate us to depart from iniquity and to turn *back* to serve the LORD with all our heart, which is why after instructing the people to not fear, Samuel immediately exhorts them to fear God. Submission to God's fear causes us to turn toward him, but fleeing against his fear causes us to turn aside from him and to try to hide our wickedness from him. When we love darkness rather than light, the fear of God will always cause us to flee from him in order to hold on to what we love more. When we are caught in this, we will come under the conviction of sin and compromise, but we will not come clean. We will not maintain a good conscience. Instead, we will hide just like Adam and Eve did in the garden (Gen 3:6-10). This will be very prevalent in the last days, even as Paul had to deal with (1Tim 1:19).

This same fear gripped the Israelites when they saw the presence of God atop the mount of God. They could not endure to hear God speak to them anymore (Heb 12:20). Thus they pleaded with Moses, "Speak thou with us, and we will hear: but let not God speak with us, lest we die." Ex 20:19 When in fact the record shows they would not listen to Moses either! So, "the people stood afar off" (v21). They refused to draw near. This was why they quickly fell away into idolatry. Notice Moses rebukes this fear and implores them to have the true fear of God instead, which will keep them from sinning (Ex 20:20).

We may be convicted to uncomfortableness and even to trembling, but like the demons, though they have such great fear, they will not let go of their way in order to both fear *and* serve the Lord. This group is similar to those who are paralyzed with fear, for both groups refuse to draw near. One is like the deer that freezes when danger is near, while the other immediately runs like the rabbit in panic trying to escape, not knowing or caring where it flees to. Neither group will come to the source of conviction to be healed and set free from disobedience. But both groups will perish as a result. The former immediately by the oncoming danger, while the latter will perish by and by when they rush head long into a snare and are now caught by 'the hunter' (of souls).

6. The Response of Fighting God: Rebelling Fear

Lastly we consider the *fight* response or what we might call *wicked* fear. In this case those who rebel against God because of their fear of him will turn against him and try to fight against him and his servants. They will turn and fight for what they want. Instead of the rebellion being covert (i.e. by fleeing and hiding), this response is manifested in overt rebellion (i.e. by fighting against what we fear).

To the undiscerning, this may not seem like fear at all (from the outside), for in fact the person may seem outwardly very bold and self-assured. But inwardly they are a coward. They are just like King Saul of old who feared losing control and therefore outwardly seemed to be in complete control. These are those who fear God (of a sort), but their hardened heart drives them to hate God and his people, and in turn to fight against them. Remember how when Saul met David, who truly feared God. At first Saul loved and respected him (and vice versa). But in time because of jealousy, Saul fought against David and hated him, trying with all his might to kill David! *Jealousy* is often one of the fruits of this evil response to the fear of God.

Where is the Fear of GOD? Losing the Treasure of the Lord

We also see this response displayed for us with the Philistines, coincidentally, when God had decided to abandon his people because of their lack of fear and reverence for the holy things of God. This occurred through the compromise of Eli and the wickedness and hypocrisy of his two sons, Hophni and Phinehas. As a result, the ark of the covenant, which was the presence of God amongst God's people, was lost to them. Notice how because the Philistines were afraid, they fought even harder against Israel.

> And when the Philistines heard the noise of the shout, they said, What *meaneth* the noise of this great shout in the camp of the Hebrews? And they understood that the ark of the LORD was come into the camp. And the Philistines were <u>afraid</u>, for they said, God is come into the camp.
>
> And they said, Woe unto us! for there hath not been such a thing heretofore. Woe unto us! who shall deliver us out of the hand of these mighty Gods? these *are* the Gods that smote the Egyptians with all the plagues in the wilderness.
>
> Be strong, and quit yourselves like men, O ye Philistines, that ye be not servants unto the Hebrews, as they have been to you: quit yourselves like men, and **fight**. And the Philistines **fought**, and Israel was smitten, ... 1Sam 4:6-10

The Israelites continually battled this 'fight' response also during their Exodus. It plagued them both externally and interally. It is easiest to understand how the enemies of Israel might have this response, so we will look at that first. Externally it was most evidently seen in Amalek who met them by the way. When he saw that they were faint and weary, he "smote the hindmost of thee, *even all that* were feeble" (Dt 25:17-18). Why did he do this? because "he feared not God." So, those who do evil to God's people and who oppress them do not fear God. What is God's judgment of them?

> And the LORD said unto Moses, Write this for a memorial in a book, and rehearse it in the ears of Joshua: for I will <u>utterly put out the remembrance of Amalek from under heaven</u>. And Moses built an altar, and called the name of it Jehovah-nissi: For he said, Because the LORD hath sworn that the LORD will have war with Amalek from generation to generation. Ex 17:14-16

It cannot be coincidental that we have looked at the banner of the fear of the LORD, which is also the banner of truth, and that we see when God cursed Amalek because he did not fear God at the same time God revealed his name as 'Jehovah-nissi' (i.e., the LORD our banner). The LORD wants every generation to know him as the defender of the poor and the weak, especially of those who fear him. But that those who oppress his people without fear, they will be found fighting against God himself, and they will be destroyed.

II – The Fear of God and Unbelievers

Let us now look at how this 'fight' response affected them internally. Often it arose from their frustrations and fears as they passed through the furnace of afflictions, which was to try them and purge them. When the evil report was given about the land being filled with giants, the people wept and cried all night. Then they murmured against Moses and accused God of trying to kill them (Nu 14:1-3). What was their next step, but to make their own captain and return to where they had come from (v4). This Joshua and Caleb vehemently rebuked and called this what it was: *rebellion* against the LORD. They reveal that the root of this response was fearing the people of the land (v9). Thus, the fear of man often is the root in this evil response, causing those who once walked in faith now to falsely accuse both God and his servants.

Do not think this is just an old covenant problem, for Stephen in rebuking the hard-hearted religious people of his day brings this very incident to their mind. He shares that this problem afflicted the "church in the wilderness" under Moses (Ac 7:38-39). He implies that it is still a problem in the 'church in the kingdom' under Jesus, and that this was the heart that they were operating under. Thus, he rebukes them for being stiffnecked and uncircumcised in heart (v51), just like the Exodus believers.

Conclusions on the Fear of God and Unbelievers

The fear of God is a powerful tool in the lives of God's people to affect the lost and to prepare them for salvation. Whenever God's people returned to the LORD in wholehearted repentance and learned the word of God, the result was that their neighbors, the unsaved who looked on, came to the knowledge of the fear of God. We have seen that the fear of God not only leads the lost to salvation, but it also prepares the heart for salvation. ???

We also looked at the gift of the fear of God and how God gives the same gift to all – believers and unbelievers alike. But the response to the fear of God is as varied as the heart of those it comes to. Some will cherish it and allow it to do a good work in them to bring them to salvation. Others despise it or hide from it and are actually driven from God by the very gift which he gives to them to bring them to him! We saw the following bad responses to the fear of God: superstition, ignorant worship, paralysis, hiding, and rebellion. So many, not understanding this, have tried to classify these different responses as if they were different kinds of the fear of God, when the real issue is how we receive the one true gift of God's fear. When God reproved the early church for not having enough of the fear of God, his judgment caused great fear to come upon all the church. Though they all had God's fear, for it had come upon every soul (Ac 2:43), yet they needed much more of his fear working in their hearts. Let us grow in this grace of the fear of God, so that God is properly feared.

Appendix III. The Scriptures on Fearing God

Complete List of Scriptures on the Fear of God[213]

The following is a comprehensive list of all scriptures directly related to the fear of God. They are grouped loosely by phrase. Only part of the verse is shown. Bold indicates presence of the fear of God, while underline indicates its lack.

A. Fear of God/Fear of the LORD [exact phrases]: 38x

Gen 20:11 And Abraham said, Because I thought, Surely the <u>fear of God</u> *is* not in this place; and they will

1Sa 11:7 And the **fear of the LORD** fell on the people, and they came out with one consent.

2Sa 23:3 the Rock of Israel spake to me, He that ruleth over men *must be* just, ruling in the **fear of God**.

2Ch 14:14 And they smote all the cities round about Gerar; for the **fear of the LORD** came upon them:

2Ch 17:10 And the **fear of the LORD** fell upon all the kingdoms of the lands that *were* round about Judah,

2Ch 19:7 Wherefore now let the **fear of the LORD** be upon you; take heed and do *it*: for *there is* no iniquity

2Ch 19:9 Thus shall ye do in the **fear of the LORD**, faithfully, & with a perfect heart.

2Ch 20:29 And the **fear of God** was on all the kingdoms of *those* countries, when they had heard that

Neh 5:15 yea, even their servants bare rule over the people: but so did not I, because of the **fear of God**.

Job 28:28 Behold, the **fear of the Lord**, that *is* wisdom; and to depart from evil *is*

Ps 19:9 The **fear of the LORD** *is* clean, enduring for ever: the judgments of the LORD *are* true *and*

Ps 34:11 Come, ye children, hearken unto me: I will teach you the **fear of the LORD**.

Ps 36:1 The transgression of the wicked saith within my heart, *that there is* no <u>fear of God</u> before his eyes.

Ps 111:10 The **fear of the LORD** *is* the beginning of wisdom: a good understanding have all they that

Pr 1:7 The **fear of the LORD** *is* the beginning of knowledge: *but* fools despise wisdom and instruction.

Pr 1:29 For that they hated knowledge, and did not choose the <u>fear of the LORD</u>:

Pr 2:5 Then shalt thou understand the **fear of the LORD**, and find the knowledge of God.

Pr 8:13 The **fear of the LORD** *is* to hate evil: pride, and arrogancy, and the evil way,

Pr 9:10 The **fear of the LORD** *is* the beginning of wisdom: and the knowledge of the holy *is* understanding.

---

[213] A summary list of the most important scriptures relating to the fear of God is in the appendix entitled 'The Scriptures on Fearing God' in the book <u>Finding the Treasure of the Lord</u>.

III – The Scriptures on Fearing God

Pr 10:27 The **fear of the LORD** prolongeth days: but the years of the wicked shall be shortened.
Pr 14:26 In the **fear of the LORD** *is* strong confidence: and his children shall have a place of refuge.
Pr 14:27 The **fear of the LORD** *is* a fountain of life, to depart from the snares of death.
Pr 15:16 Better *is* little with the **fear of the LORD** than great treasure and trouble therewith.
Pr 15:33 The **fear of the LORD** *is* the instruction of wisdom; and before honour *is* humility.
Pr 16:6 By mercy and truth iniquity is purged: and by the **fear of the LORD** *men* depart from evil.
Pr 19:23 The **fear of the LORD** *tendeth* to life: and *he that hath it* shall abide satisfied;
Pr 22:4 By humility *and* the **fear of the LORD** *are* riches, and honour, and life.
Pr 23:17 Let not thine heart envy sinners: but *be thou* in the **fear of the LORD** all the day long.
Isa 2:10 Enter into the rock, and hide thee in the dust, for **fear of the LORD**, and for the glory of his majesty.
Isa 2:19 the holes of the rocks, and into the caves of the earth, for **fear of the LORD**, and for the glory of his
Isa 2:21 the clefts of the rocks, and into the tops of the ragged rocks, for **fear of the LORD**, and for the glory
Isa 11:2 And the spirit of the LORD shall rest upon him, … the spirit of knowledge and of the **fear of the LORD**;
Isa 11:3 And shall make him of quick understanding in the **fear of the LORD**: and he shall not judge after …
Isa 33:6 shall be the stability of thy times, *and* strength of salvation: the **fear of the LORD** *is* his treasure.

Ac 9:31 and were edified; and walking in the **fear of the Lord**, and in the comfort of the Holy Ghost,
Rom 3:18 There is no fear of God before their eyes.
2Co 7:1 let us cleanse ourselves from all filthiness of the flesh and spirit, perfecting holiness in the **fear of God**.
Eph 5:21 Submitting yourselves one to another in the **fear of God**.

B. Fear* God/Fear* the LORD/Fear thy God [exact phrases]: 75x

Gen 22:12 for now I know that thou **fearest God**, seeing thou hast not withheld thy son, thine only *son* from me.
Gen 42:18 And Joseph said unto them the third day, This do, and live; *for* I **fear God**:
Ex 1:17 But the midwives **feared God**, and did not as the king of Egypt commanded them, but saved the
Ex 1:21 And it came to pass, because the midwives **feared God**, that he made them houses.
Ex 9:30 But as for thee and thy servants, I know that ye will not yet fear the LORD God.
Ex 14:31 the people **feared the LORD**, & believed the LORD, & his servant Moses.

Where is the Fear of GOD? Losing the Treasure of the Lord

Ex 18:21	thou shalt provide out of all the people able men, such as **fear God**, men of truth, hating covetousness;
Lev 19:14	Thou shalt not curse the deaf, nor put a stumblingblock before the blind, but shalt **fear thy God**:
Lev 19:32	Thou shalt rise up before the hoary head, and honour the face of the old man, and **fear thy God**:
Lev 25:17	Ye shall not therefore oppress one another; but thou shalt **fear thy God**: for I *am* the LORD your **God**.
Lev 25:36	Take thou no usury of him, or increase: but **fear thy God**; that **thy** brother may live with thee.
Lev 25:43	Thou shalt not rule over him with rigour; but shalt **fear thy God**.
Dt 6:2	That thou mightest **fear the LORD** thy God, to keep all his statutes and his commandments,
Dt 6:13	Thou shalt **fear the LORD** thy God, & serve him, & shalt swear by his name
Dt 6:24	And the LORD commanded us to do all these statutes, to **fear the LORD** our God, for our good always
Dt 10:12	And now, Israel, what doth the LORD thy God require of thee, but to **fear the LORD** thy God, to walk
Dt 10:20	Thou shalt **fear the LORD** thy God; him shalt thou serve, and to him shalt thou cleave, and swear by his name.
Dt 14:23	the tithe … that thou mayest learn to **fear the LORD** thy God always.
Dt 17:19	and he shall read therein all the days of his life: that he may learn to **fear the LORD** his God
Dt 31:12	Gather … that they may hear, and that they may learn, and **fear the LORD** your God, and observe to do
Dt 31:13	And *that* their children, which have not known *any thing,* may hear, and learn to **fear the LORD**
Jos 4:24	might know the hand of the LORD, that it *is* mighty: that ye might **fear the LORD** your God for ever.
Jos 22:25	ye have no part in the LORD: so shall your children make our children cease from <u>fearing the LORD</u>.
Jos 24:14	Now therefore **fear the LORD**, and serve him in sincerity and in truth: and put away the gods which
1Sa 12:14	If ye will **fear the LORD**, and serve him, and obey his voice, and not rebel against the command
1Sa 12:18	and the LORD sent thunder and rain that day: and all the people greatly **feared the LORD** and Samuel.
1Sa 12:24	Only **fear the LORD**, and serve him in truth with all your heart: for consider how great *things* he hath done for you.
1K 18:3	Now Obadiah **feared the LORD** greatly:
1K 18:12	he shall slay me: but I thy servant **fear the LORD** from my youth.
2K 4:1	Thy servant my husband is dead; and thou knowest that thy servant did **fear the LORD**:
2K 17:28	from Samaria came and dwelt in Bethel, and taught them how they should **fear the LORD**.
2K 17:32	So they **feared the LORD**, and made unto themselves of the lowest of them priests of the high places,
2K 17:33	They **feared the LORD**, and served their own gods, after the manner of the nations

III – The Scriptures on Fearing God

2K 17:41	So these nations **feared the LORD**, and served their graven images, both their children, and
Neh 7:2	he *was* a faithful man, and **feared God** above many.
Job 1:1	name *was* Job; and that man was perfect and upright, and one that **feared God**, and eschewed evil.
Job 1:8	none like him in the earth, a perfect and an upright man, one that **feareth God**, and escheweth evil?
Job 1:9	Then Satan answered the LORD, and said, Doth Job **fear God** for nought?
Job 2:3	none like him in the earth, a perfect and an upright man, one that **feareth God**, and escheweth evil?
Ps 15:4	In whose eyes a vile person is contemned; but he honoureth them that **fear the LORD**.
Ps 22:23	Ye that **fear the LORD**, praise him; all ye the seed of Jacob, glorify him; and **fear him**,
Ps 25:12	What man *is* he that **feareth the LORD**? him shall he teach in the way *that* he shall choose.
Ps 33:8	Let all the earth **fear the LORD**: let all the inhabitants of the world stand in awe of him.
Ps 34:9	O **fear the LORD**, ye his saints: for *there is* no want to them that fear him.
Ps 66:16	Come *and* hear, all ye that **fear God**, and I will declare what he hath done for my soul.
Ps 112:1	Blessed *is* the man *that* **feareth the LORD**, *that* delighteth greatly in his commandments.
Ps 115:11	Ye that **fear the LORD**, trust in the LORD: he *is* their help and their shield.
Ps 115:13	He will bless them that **fear the LORD**, *both* small and great.
Ps 118:4	Let them now that **fear the LORD** say, that his mercy *endureth* for ever.
Ps 128:1	Blessed *is* every one that **feareth the LORD**; that walketh in his ways.
Ps 128:4	Behold, that thus shall the man be blessed that **feareth the LORD**.
Ps 135:20	Bless the LORD, O house of Levi: ye that **fear the LORD**, bless the LORD.
Pr 3:7	Be not wise in thine own eyes: **fear the LORD**, and depart from evil.
Pr 14:2	He that walketh in his uprightness **feareth the LORD**: but *he that is* perverse in his ways
Pr 31:30	Favour *is* deceitful, and beauty *is* vain: *but* a woman *that* **feareth the LORD**, she shall be praised.
Ecc 7:18	yea, also from this withdraw not thine hand: for he that **feareth God** shall come forth of them all.
Ecc 8:12	yet surely I know that it shall be well with them that **fear God**, which **fear** before him:
Ecc 12:13	Let us hear the conclusion of the whole matter: **Fear God**, and keep his commandments:
Isa 50:10	Who *is* among you that **feareth the LORD**, that obeyeth the voice of his servant, that walketh *in*
Jer 5:24	Neither say they in their heart, Let us now **fear the LORD** our God, that giveth rain, both the former
Jer 26:19	did he not **fear the LORD**, and besought the LORD, and the LORD repented him of the evil which
Hos 3:5	return, and seek the LORD their God, and David their king; and shall **fear the LORD** and his goodness

More Abundant Life

Where is the Fear of GOD? Losing the Treasure of the Lord

Jnh 1:9	I *am* an Hebrew; and I **fear the LORD**, the God of heaven, which hath made the sea and the dry *land*.
Jnh 1:16	Then the men **feared the LORD** exceedingly, and offered a sacrifice unto the LORD, and made vows.
Mal 3:16	Then they that **feared the LORD** spake often one to another: and the LORD hearkened, and heard *it,*
Mal 3:16	remembrance was written before him for them that **feared the LORD**, and that thought upon his name.
Lk 23:40	answering rebuked him, saying, Dost not thou <u>fear God</u>, seeing thou art in the same condemnation?
Ac 10:2	A devout *man,* and one that **feared God** with all his house, which gave much alms to the people,
Ac 10:22	Cornelius the centurion, a just man, and one that **feareth God**, and of good report
Ac 13:16	Then Paul stood up, and beckoning with *his* hand said, Men of Israel, and ye that **fear God,**
Ac 13:26	whosoever among you **feareth God**, to you is the word of this salvation sent.
Col 3:22	Servants, obey ...; not with eyeservice, as menpleasers; but in singleness of heart, **fearing God**:
1Pe 2:17	Honour all *men.* Love the brotherhood. **Fear God**. Honour the king.
Rev 14:7	Saying with a loud voice, **Fear God**, and give glory to him; for the hour of his judgment is come:

C. The Fear of God/the Fear of the LORD [general references]: 147x

Gen 31:42	Except the God of my father, the God of Abraham, and the **fear** of Isaac,
Gen 31:53	And Jacob sware by the **fear** of his father Isaac.
Ex 9:20	He that **feared** the word of the LORD among the servants of Pharaoh made his servants and his cattle
Ex 20:20	Fear not: for God is come to prove you, and that **his fear** may be before your faces, that ye sin not.
Ex 23:27	I will send **my fear** before thee, and will destroy all the people to whom thou shalt come,
Dt 4:10	Gather me the people together, and I will make them hear my words, that they may learn to **fear me**
Dt 5:29	O that there were such an heart in them, that they would **fear me**, and keep all my commandments always
Dt 8:6	Therefore thou shalt keep the commandments of the LORD thy God, to walk in his ways, and to **fear him.**
Dt 13:4	Ye shall walk after the LORD your God, and **fear him**, and keep his commandments, and obey his voice
Dt 25:18	*even* all *that were* feeble behind thee, when thou *wast* faint and weary; and he <u>feared not</u> God.
Dt 28:58	written in this book, that thou mayest **fear** this glorious and **fearful** name, THE LORD THY GOD;

III – The Scriptures on Fearing God

1K 8:40	That they may **fear thee** all the days that they live in the land which thou gavest unto our fathers.
1K 8:43	that all people of the earth may know thy name, to **fear thee**, as *do* thy people Israel;
2K 17:25	And *so* it was at the beginning of their dwelling there, *that* they <u>feared not</u> the LORD: therefore
2K 17:34	Unto this day they do after the former manners: they <u>fear not</u> the LORD, neither do they after
2K 17:36	him shall ye **fear**, and him shall ye worship, and to him shall ye do sacrifice.
2K 17:38	And the covenant that I have made with you ye shall not forget; neither shall ye <u>fear other</u> gods.
2K 17:39	But the LORD your God ye shall **fear**; and he shall deliver you out of the hand of all your enemies.
1Ch 16:25	For great *is* the LORD, and greatly to be praised: he also *is* to be **feared** above all gods.
1Ch 16:30	**Fear** before him, all the earth: the world also shall be stable, that it be not moved.
2Ch 6:31	That they may **fear** thee, to walk in thy ways, so long as they live in the land which thou gavest
2Ch 6:33	that all people of the earth may know thy name, and **fear** thee, as *doth* thy people Israel,
2Ch 20:3	And Jehoshaphat **feared**, and set himself to seek the LORD, and proclaimed a fast throughout all Judah.
Neh 1:11	be attentive to the prayer of thy servant, and to the prayer of thy servants, who desire to **fear** thy name:
Neh 5:9	ought ye not to walk in the **fear** of our God because of the reproach of the heathen our enemies?
Job 6:14	To him that is afflicted pity *should be shewed* from his friend; but he <u>forsaketh the fear</u> of the Almighty.
Job 9:34	Let him take his rod away from me, and let not his <u>fear</u> terrify me:
Job 9:35	*Then* would I speak, and <u>not fear</u> him; but *it is* not so with me.
Job 25:2	Dominion and **fear** *are* with him, he maketh peace in his high places.
Job 37:24	Men do therefore **fear** him: he respecteth not any *that are* wise of heart.
Ps 2:11	Serve the LORD with **fear**, and rejoice with trembling.
Ps 5:7	*into* thy house in the multitude of thy mercy: *and* in thy **fear** will I worship toward thy holy temple.
Ps 9:20	Put them in **fear**, O LORD: *that* the nations may know themselves *to be but* men. Selah.
Ps 14:5	There were they in **great fear**: for God *is* in the generation of the righteous.
Ps 22:25	My praise *shall be* of thee in the great congregation: I will pay my vows before them that **fear him**.
Ps 25:14	The secret of the LORD *is* with them that **fear him**; and he will shew them his covenant.
Ps 31:19	*Oh* how great *is* thy goodness, which thou hast laid up for them that **fear thee**;
Ps 33:18	Behold, the eye of the LORD *is* upon them that **fear him**, upon them that hope in his mercy;
Ps 34:7	The angel of the LORD encampeth round about them that **fear him**, and delivereth them.

Where is the Fear of GOD? Losing the Treasure of the Lord

Ps 40:3	And he hath put a new song in my mouth, *even* praise unto our God: many shall see *it*, and **fear**,
Ps 52:6	The righteous also shall see, and **fear**, and shall laugh at him:
Ps 60:4	Thou hast given a banner to them that **fear thee**, that it may be displayed because of the truth. Selah.
Ps 61:5	For thou, O God, hast heard my vows: thou hast given *me* the heritage of those that **fear** thy name.
Ps 64:9	And all men shall **fear**, and shall declare the work of God; for they shall wisely consider of his doing.
Ps 67:7	God shall bless us; and all the ends of the earth shall **fear him**.
Ps 72:5	They shall **fear thee** as long as the sun and moon endure, throughout all generations.
Ps 76:7	Thou, *even* thou, *art* to be **feared**: and who may stand in thy sight when once thou art angry?
Ps 76:8	Thou didst cause judgment to be heard from heaven; the earth **feared**, and was still,
Ps 76:11	let all that be round about him bring presents unto him that ought to be **feared**.
Ps 85:9	Surely his salvation *is* nigh them that **fear him**; that glory may dwell in our land.
Ps 86:11	Teach me thy way, O LORD; I will walk in thy truth: unite my heart to **fear** thy name.
Ps 89:7	God is greatly to be **feared** in the assembly of the saints, and to be had in reverence of all
Ps 90:11	Who knoweth the power of thine anger? even according to **thy fear**, *so is* thy wrath.
Ps 96:4	the LORD *is* great, and greatly to be praised: he *is* to be **feared** above all gods
Ps 96:9	O worship the LORD in the beauty of holiness: **fear** before him, all the earth
Ps 102:15	So the heathen shall **fear** the name of the LORD, and all the kings of the earth thy glory.
Ps 103:11	For as the heaven is high above the earth, *so* great is his mercy toward them that **fear him**.
Ps 103:13	Like as a father pitieth *his* children, *so* the LORD pitieth them that **fear him**.
Ps 103:17	But the mercy of the LORD *is* from everlasting to everlasting upon them that **fear him**
Ps 111:5	He hath given meat unto them that **fear him**: he will ever be mindful of his covenant.
Ps 119:38	Stablish thy word unto thy servant, who *is devoted* to **thy fear**.
Ps 119:63	I *am* a companion of all *them* that **fear thee** & of them that keep thy precepts
Ps 119:74	They that **fear thee** will be glad when they see me; because I have hoped in thy word.
Ps 119:79	Let those that **fear thee** turn unto me, and those that have known thy testimonies.
Ps 119:120	My flesh trembleth for fear of thee; and I am **afraid** of thy judgments.
Ps 130:4	But *there is* forgiveness with thee, that thou mayest be **feared**.
Ps 145:19	He will fulfil the desire of them that **fear him**: he also will hear their cry, and will save them.
Ps 147:11	The LORD taketh pleasure in them that **fear him**, in those that hope in his mercy.

III – The Scriptures on Fearing God

Pr 13:13	despiseth the word shall be destroyed: but he that **feareth** the commandment shall be rewarded.
Pr 14:16	A wise *man* **feareth**, and departeth from evil: but the fool rageth, and is confident.
Pr 24:21	My son, **fear** thou the LORD and the king: *and* meddle not with them that are given to change:
Pr 28:14	Happy *is* the man that **feareth** alway: but he that hardeneth his heart shall fall into mischief.
Ecc 3:14	nothing can be put to it, nor any thing taken from it: and God doeth *it*, that *men* should **fear** before him.
Ecc 5:7	For in the multitude of dreams and many words *there are* also *divers* vanities: but **fear** thou God.
Ecc 8:13	neither shall he prolong *his* days, *which are* as a shadow; because he <u>feareth not</u> before God.
Isa 19:16	and it shall be **afraid** and **fear** because of the shaking of the hand of the LORD of hosts,
Isa 25:3	Therefore shall the strong people glorify thee, the city of the terrible nations shall **fear** thee.
Isa 29:13	but have removed their heart far from me, and their <u>fear</u> toward me is taught by the precept of men:
Isa 29:23	they shall sanctify my name, and sanctify the Holy One of Jacob, and shall **fear** the God of Israel.
Isa 33:14	The sinners in Zion are **afraid**; fearfulness hath surprised the hypocrites. Who among us shall dwell
Isa 41:5	The isles saw *it*, and **feared**; the ends of the earth were **afraid**, drew near, and came.
Isa 57:11	And of whom hast thou been <u>afraid or feared</u>, that thou hast lied, and thou <u>fearest me not</u>?
Isa 59:19	So shall they **fear** the name of the LORD from the west, and his glory from the rising of the sun.
Isa 60:5	Then thou shalt see, and flow together, and thine heart shall **fear**, and be enlarged; because ...
Isa 63:17	O LORD, why hast thou made us to err from thy ways, *and* hardened our heart from <u>thy fear</u>?
Jer 2:19	know therefore and see that *it is* an evil *thing* and bitter, ... that <u>my fear</u> *is* not in thee, saith the LORD
Jer 3:8	yet her treacherous sister Judah <u>feared not</u>, but went & played the harlot also
Jer 5:22	<u>Fear</u> ye not me? saith the LORD: will ye not <u>tremble</u> at my presence, which have placed the sand
Jer 10:7	Who would <u>not fear</u> thee, O King of nations? for to thee doth it appertain:
Jer 32:39	And I will give them one heart, and one way, that they may **fear** me for ever, for the good of them,
Jer 32:40	to do them good; but I will put my **fear** in their hearts, that they shall not depart from me.
Jer 33:9	hear all the good that I do unto them: and they shall **fear** and **tremble** for all the goodness and
Jer 44:10	They are not humbled *even* unto this day, neither have they <u>feared</u>, nor walked in my law,

Where is the Fear of GOD? Losing the Treasure of the Lord

Dan 6:26	That in every dominion of my kingdom men **tremble** and **fear** before the God of Daniel:
Hos 10:3	We have no king, because we <u>feared not</u> the LORD; what then should a king do to us?
Am 3:8	The lion hath roared, who will not **fear**? the Lord GOD hath spoken, who can but prophesy?
Mic 7:17	they shall be **afraid** of the LORD our God, and shall **fear** because of thee.
Zep 3:7	I said, Surely thou wilt **fear me**, thou wilt receive instruction; so their dwelling should not be cut off,
Hag 1:12	and the people did **fear** before the LORD.
Mal 1:6	and if I *be* a master, where *is* my **fear**? saith the LORD of hosts unto you, O priests, that despise ...
Mal 2:5	My covenant was with him of life and peace; and I gave them to him *for* the **fear** wherewith he **feared me**,
Mal 4:2	But unto you that **fear** my name shall the Sun of righteousness arise with healing in his wings;
Mt 10:28	but rather **fear him** which is able to destroy both soul and body in hell.
Mt 27:54	those things that were done, they **feared greatly**, saying, Truly this was the Son of God.
Mt 28:4	And for **fear of him** the keepers did shake, and became as dead *men*.
Mt 28:8	And they departed quickly from the sepulchre with **fear** and great joy; and did run to bring his disciples word.
Mk 4:41	And they **feared exceedingly**, and said one to another, What manner of man is this, that even the wind and the sea obey him?
Mk 5:33	But the woman **fearing** and **trembling**, knowing what was done in her, came and fell down before him,
Lk 1:50	And his mercy *is* on them that **fear him** from generation to generation.
Lk 5:26	And they were all amazed, and they glorified God, and were filled with **fear**,
Lk 7:16	And there came a **fear** on all: and they glorified God, saying, That a great prophet is risen up among us;
Lk 8:37	the Gadarenes round about besought him to depart from them; for they were taken with **great fear**:
Lk 9:34	While he thus spake, there came a cloud, and overshadowed them: and they **feared** as they entered into
Lk 9:45	and it was hid from them, that they perceived it not: and they **feared** to ask him of that saying.
Lk 12:5a	But I will forewarn you whom ye shall **fear**:
Lk 12:5b	**Fear him**, which after he hath killed hath power to cast
Lk 12:5c	power to cast into hell; yea, I say unto you, **Fear him**.
Lk 18:2	Saying, There was in a city a judge, which <u>feared not God</u>, neither regarded man:
Lk 18:4	afterward he said within himself, Though I <u>fear not God</u>, nor regard man;
Ac 2:43	And **fear** came upon every soul: and many wonders and signs were done by the apostles.
Ac 5:5	And Ananias hearing these words fell down, and gave up the ghost: and **great fear** came on all them
Ac 5:11	And **great fear** came upon all the church, and upon as many as heard these things.

III – The Scriptures on Fearing God

Ac 10:35 But in every nation he that **feareth him**, and worketh righteousness, is accepted with him.
Ac 19:17 And this was known to all the Jews and Greeks also dwelling at Ephesus; and **fear** fell on them all,
Rom 11:20 because of unbelief they were broken off, and thou standest by faith. Be not highminded, but **fear**:
Rom 13:7 to all their dues: tribute to whom tribute *is due;* custom to whom custom; **fear** to whom **fear** [which certainly includes God!];
1Co 2:3 And I was with you in weakness, and in **fear**, and in much **trembling**.
2Co 7:11 *what* clearing of yourselves, yea, *what* indignation, yea, *what* **fear**, yea, *what* vehement desire,
2Co 7:15 whilst he remembereth the obedience of you all, how with **fear** and **trembling** ye received him.
Eph 6:5 Servants, be obedient to them that are *your* masters according to the flesh, with **fear** and trembling,
Php 2:12 but now much more in my absence, work out your own salvation with **fear** and **trembling**.
1Tim 5:20 Them that sin rebuke before all, that others also may **fear**.
Heb 4:1 Let us therefore **fear**, lest, a promise being left *us* of entering into his rest, any of you should seem to come short of it.
Heb 5:7 with strong crying and tears unto him … and was heard in that he **feared**;
Heb 11:7 By faith Noah, being warned of God of things not seen as yet, moved with **fear**, prepared an ark
Heb 12:21 And so terrible was the sight, *that* Moses said, I exceedingly **fear** and quake:
Heb 12:28 let us have grace, whereby we may serve God acceptably with reverence and godly **fear**:
1Pe 1:17 judgeth according to every man's work, pass the time of your sojourning *here* in **fear**:
1Pe 3:2 While they behold your chaste conversation *coupled* with **fear**.
1Pe 3:15 an answer to every man that asketh you a reason of the hope that is in you with meekness and **fear**:
Jude 1:12 These are spots in your feasts of charity, when they feast with you, feeding themselves <u>without fear</u>:
Jude 1:23 And others save with **fear**, pulling *them* out of the fire; hating even the garment spotted by the flesh.
Rev 11:11 they stood upon their feet; and **great fear** fell upon them which saw them.
Rev 11:18 shouldest give reward unto thy servants the prophets, and to the saints, and them that **fear** thy name,
Rev 15:4 Who shall not **fear thee**, O Lord, & glorify thy name? for *thou* only *art* holy:
Rev 19:5 Praise our God, all ye his servants, and ye that **fear him**, both small & great.

D. Afraid of God & Dread of God: 41x+8x = 49x

Gen 3:10 And he said, I heard thy voice in the garden, and I was **afraid**, because I *was* naked; and I hid myself.
Gen 18:15 Then Sarah denied, saying, I laughed not; for she was **afraid**.
Gen 28:17 And he was **afraid**, and said, How **dreadful** *is* this place! this is none other but the house of God,

Where is the Fear of God? Losing the Treasure of the Lord

Ex 3:6	And Moses hid his face; for he was **afraid** to look upon God.
Ex 15:14	The people shall hear, *and* be **afraid**: sorrow shall take hold on the inhabitants of Palestina.
Ex 15:16	**Fear** and **dread** shall fall upon them; by the greatness of thine arm they shall be *as* still as a stone;
Dt 5:5	(I stood between the LORD and you at that time, to shew you the word of the LORD: for ye were **afraid**
Dt 9:19	For I was **afraid** of the anger and hot displeasure, wherewith the LORD was wroth against you
1Sa 4:7	And the Philistines were **afraid**, for they said, God is come into the camp.
2Sa 6:9	And David was **afraid** of the LORD that day, and said, How shall the ark of the LORD come to me?
1Ch 13:12	And David was **afraid** of God that day, saying, How shall I bring the ark of God *home* to me?
1Ch 21:30	could not go before it to enquire of God: for he was **afraid** because of the sword of the angel of the LORD.
Job 13:11	Shall not his excellency make you **afraid**? and his **dread** fall upon you?
Job 13:21	Withdraw thine hand far from me: and let not thy **dread** make me **afraid**.
Job 21:6	Even when I remember I am **afraid**, & **trembling** taketh hold on my flesh.
Job 23:15	Therefore am I troubled at his presence: when I consider, I am **afraid** of him.
Ps 27:1	whom shall I **fear**? the LORD *is* the strength of my life; of whom shall I be **afraid**?
Ps 65:8	They also that dwell in the uttermost parts are **afraid** at thy tokens:
Ps 77:16	The waters saw thee, O God, the waters saw thee; they were **afraid**:
Ps 83:15	So persecute them with thy tempest, and make them **afraid** with thy storm.
Ps 119:120	My flesh trembleth for fear of thee; and I am **afraid** of thy judgments.
Isa 8:13	Sanctify the LORD of hosts himself; and *let* him *be* your **fear**, and *let* him *be* your **dread**.
Isa 13:8	And they shall be **afraid**: pangs and sorrows shall take hold of them; …
Isa 19:16	and it shall be **afraid** and **fear** because of the shaking of the hand of the LORD of hosts
Isa 19:17	mention thereof shall be **afraid** in himself, because of the counsel of the LORD of hosts
Isa 33:14	The sinners in Zion are **afraid**; **fearfulness** hath surprised the hypocrites.
Isa 57:11	And of whom hast thou been **afraid** or **feared**, that thou hast lied, and hast not remembered me
Jer 2:12	Be astonished, O ye heavens, at this, and be horribly **afraid**, be ye very desolate, saith the LORD.
Dan 9:4	I prayed unto the LORD my God, and made my confession, and said, O Lord, the great and **dreadful God**, keeping the covenant and mercy …
Am 3:6	in the city, and the people not be **afraid**? shall there be evil in a city, and the LORD hath not done *it*?
Mic 7:17	they shall be **afraid** of the LORD our God, and shall fear because of thee.
Hab 3:2	O LORD, I have heard thy speech, *and* was **afraid**: O LORD, revive thy work in the midst of the years
Mal 1:14	for I *am* a great King, saith the LORD of hosts, and my name *is* **dreadful** among the heathen.

III – The Scriptures on Fearing God

Mal 2:5	and I gave them to him *for* the **fear** wherewith he **feared** me, and was **afraid** before my name.
Mal 4:5	Behold, I will send you Elijah the prophet before the coming of the great and **dreadful** day of the LORD:
Mt 17:6	And when the disciples heard *it,* they fell on their face, and were sore **afraid**.
Mk 9:6	For he wist not what to say; for they were sore **afraid**.
Mk 9:32	But they understood not that saying, and were **afraid** to ask him.
Mk 10:32	and they were amazed; and as they followed, they were **afraid**.
Mk 16:8	for they **trembled** and were amazed: neither said they any thing to any *man;* for they were **afraid**.
Lk 2:9	the glory of the Lord shone round about them: and they were sore **afraid**.
Lk 8:25	And they being **afraid** wondered, saying one to another, What manner of man is this!
Ac 10:4	And when he looked on him, he was **afraid**, and said, What is it, Lord?
Ac 22:9	And they that were with me saw indeed the light, and were **afraid**; …
Rom 13:3	For rulers are not a terror to good works, but to the evil. Wilt thou then not be **afraid** of the power?
Rom 13:4	if thou do that which is evil, be **afraid**; for he beareth not the sword in vain:

E. Terror of God & Terrible God: 11x+17x = 28x

Dt 4:34	by signs, and by wonders, and by war, and by a mighty hand, and by a stretched out arm, and by great **terrors**
Dt 7:21	the LORD thy God *is* among you, a mighty God and **terrible**.
Dt 10:17	For the LORD your God *is* God of gods, and Lord of lords, a great God, a mighty, and a **terrible**, which regardeth not persons, nor taketh reward:
Dt 34:12	And in all that mighty hand, and in all the great **terror** which Moses shewed in the sight of all Israel.
Neh 1:5	I beseech thee, O LORD God of heaven, the great and **terrible** God, that keepeth covenant and mercy …
Neh 4:14	remember the Lord, *which is* great and **terrible** …
Neh 9:32	Now therefore, our God, the great, the mighty, and the **terrible** God, who keepest covenant and mercy …
Job 6:4	the **terrors** of God do set themselves in array against me.
Job 31:23	For destruction *from* God *was* a **terror** to me, and by reason of his highness I could not endure.
Job 37:22	Fair weather cometh out of the north: with God is **terrible** majesty.
Ps 47:2	For the LORD most high *is* **terrible**; he *is* a great King over all the earth.
Ps 66:3	Say unto God, How **terrible** *art thou in* thy works! through the greatness of thy power shall thine enemies submit themselves unto thee.
Ps 66:5	Come and see the works of God: he *is* **terrible** *in his* doing toward the children of men.
Ps 68:35	O God, *thou art* **terrible** out of thy holy places: the God of Israel *is* he that giveth strength and power unto *his* people. Blessed *be* God.
Ps 76:12	He shall cut off the spirit of princes: *he is* **terrible** to the kings of the earth.
Ps 88:15	I *am* afflicted and ready to die from *my* youth up: *while* I suffer thy **terrors** …
Ps 88:16	Thy fierce wrath goeth over me; thy **terrors** have cut me off.

More Abundant Life

Where is the Fear of GOD? Losing the Treasure of the Lord

Ps 99:3	Let them praise thy great and **terrible** name; *for* it *is* holy.
Isa 10:33	Behold, the Lord, the LORD of hosts, shall lop the bough with **terror**:
Jer 17:17	Be not a **terror** unto me: thou *art* my hope in the day of evil.
Jer 20:11	But the LORD *is* with me as a mighty **terrible** one: therefore my persecutors shall stumble,
Jer 32:21	with signs, and with wonders, and with a strong hand, and with a stretched out arm, and with great **terror**;
Lam 2:22	Thou hast called as in a solemn day my **terrors** round about, so that in the day of the LORD'S anger
Joel 2:11	for the day of the LORD *is* great and very **terrible**; and who can abide it?
Joel 2:31	The sun shall be turned into darkness, and the moon into blood, before the great and the **terrible** day of the LORD come.
Zep 2:11	The LORD *will be* **terrible** unto them:
2Co 5:11	Knowing therefore the **terror** of the Lord, we persuade men; but we are made manifest unto God;
Heb 12:21	And so **terrible** was the sight, *that* Moses said, I exceedingly fear and quake:

F. Trembling before God: 34x

Ezra 9:4	Then were assembled unto me every one that **trembled** at the words of the God of Israel
Ezra 10:3	those that **tremble** at the commandment of our God; and let it be done according to the law.
Ezra 10:9	all the people sat in the street of the house of God, **trembling** because of *this* matter
Job 4:14	Fear came upon me, and **trembling**, which made all my bones to shake.
Job 21:6	Even when I remember I am afraid, and **trembling** taketh hold on my flesh.
Job 37:1	At this also my heart **trembleth**, and is moved out of his place.
Ps 2:11	Serve the LORD with fear, and rejoice with **trembling**.
Ps 97:4	His lightnings enlightened the world: the earth saw, and **trembled**.
Ps 99:1	The LORD reigneth; let the people **tremble**: he sitteth *between* the cherubims; let the earth be moved.
Ps 104:32	He looketh on the earth, and it **trembleth**: he toucheth the hills, and they smoke.
Ps 114:7	**Tremble**, thou earth, at the presence of the Lord, at the presence of the God of Jacob;
Ps 119:120	My flesh **trembleth** for fear of thee; and I am afraid of thy judgments.
Isa 64:2	to make thy name known to thine adversaries, *that* the nations may **tremble** at thy presence!
Isa 66:2	but to this *man* will I look, *even* to *him that is* poor and of a contrite spirit, and **trembleth** at my word.
Isa 66:5	Hear the word of the LORD, ye that **tremble** at his word; your brethren that hated you, that cast you out
Jer 5:22	Fear ye not me? saith the LORD: will ye not **tremble** at my presence
Jer 10:10	he *is* the living God, and an everlasting king: at his wrath the earth shall **tremble**

III – The Scriptures on Fearing God

Jer 33:9 and they shall fear and **tremble** for all the goodness and for all the prosperity that I procure unto it.
Eze 32:10 and they shall **tremble** at *every* moment, every man for his own life, in the day of thy fall.
Dan 6:26 That in every dominion of my kingdom men **tremble** and fear before the God of Daniel
Dan 10:11 And when he had spoken this word unto me, I stood **trembling**.
Joel 2:1 let all the inhabitants of the land **tremble**: for the day of the LORD cometh,
Hab 3:16 When I heard, my belly **trembled**; my lips quivered at the voice: rottenness entered into my bones
Hab 3:16 and I **trembled** in myself, that I might rest in the day of trouble:

Mk 5:33 But the woman fearing and **trembling**, knowing what was done in her, came and fell down before him
Mk 16:8 And they went out quickly, and fled from the sepulchre; for they **trembled** and were amazed:
Lk 8:47 And when the woman saw that she was not hid, she came **trembling**, and falling down before him
Ac 7:32 Then Moses **trembled**, and durst not behold.
Ac 9:6 And he **trembling** and astonished said, Lord, what wilt thou have me to do?
1Co 2:3 And I was with you in weakness, and in fear, and in much **trembling**.
2Co 7:15 whilst he remembereth the obedience of you all, how with fear and **trembling** ye received him.
Eph 6:5 with fear and **trembling**, in singleness of your heart, as unto Christ;
Php 2:12 but now much more in my absence, work out your own salvation with fear and **trembling**.
Jam 2:19 Thou believest that there is one God; thou doest well: the devils also believe, and **tremble**.

Content Index: Finding A Specific Topic

A

Abraham
    blessings, 214

accusing God, 222

afraid of God
    his voice, 47

agreed, 127

antichrists, 16

apostasy, 11
    adultery, 242
    covetousness, 236
    dishonesty, 231
    dreams, 244
    hour of, 14
    pride, 248
    taking advantage, 240
    warnings, 230

apostles
    heart of, 243

authority
    fear of, 137

authority, 268

awe, 161

B

banner of truth, 219, 232

beasts, 15, 99

beginning
    the Word, 19

Bevere, John, 170

Bible
    colleges, 320
    for correction, 256
    keeps us in his fear, 110
    King James, 72
    reading daily, 26

Bible Colleges, 91

bishop, 255
    ministry, 256
    office of, 171

body of Christ
    blessing in suffering, 211

bride of Christ, 249

brokenness
    alone, 192
    banner of, 195
    beauty of, 208
    fleeing, 195
    intimacy, 193
    pressure, 199
    surgeon's knife, 199
    unemptied Moab, 196
    way of, 192

Bunyan, John
    faith/hope may deceive, 57

C

call to return, 18

cancer, 186

children
    substitution, 108
    with father, 132

Christianity
    merchandizing, 54
    mixture, 54
    skips steps, 175

comfort
    false, 132
    follows mourning, 135
    in brokenness, 199
    of love, 133
    of rebuke, 209
    to continue, 207
    too much, 12

coming of the Lord, 47, 58, 109, 258
    prepare, 152, 251

condemnation, 249

conscience
    evil, 76
    good, 76, 321
    guilty, 46
    seared, 77
    work of, 162

correction
    rejected, 30

covenant
    breaking, 259
    working machines, 228

covetousness
    hiding, 187

cycle of
    dishonesty, 234

Content Index: Finding a Specific Topic

D

danger of
  beyond measure of rule, 33
  blessings, 22, 25
  boasting, 32
  idolatry, 31
  lack of oversight, 29
  meddling, 35
  rejecting correction, 30
  ungodly relationships, 27

day of the LORD
  fearful, 58

dead works, 83

decoy, 233

deliverances, not forget, 223

denying the Lord, 124
  right to rule, 78

departing, 159
  from evil, 159, 250

discipleship
  first requirement of, 29
  forsaking all, 158
  Nehemiah, 104
  pattern, 96
  skipped, 175, 203

dreams
  comfort, 247
  deceptive, 244
  defile flesh, 247
  fear God, 246
  idolatry, 246
  warning, 246

E

edified, 132

election, 265

evil
  departing from, 159, 163
  pride, 88

excusing & accusing, 47

F

faith
  family of, 102
  feigned, 76
  movement, 228
  patience, 228

false
  comfort, 133, 136
  peace, 132, 136

false fear of God, 40
  false profession, 64
  false worship, 50
  fear of consequences, 46
  fleeing fear, 290
  frozen fear, 288
  ignorant, 283
  no obedience, 57
  precepts of men, 49
  pride, 42
  rebelling fear, 291
  slothful, 287
  superstitious, 280
  temporary, 280
  tormenting, 289
  ungodly, 286
  zealous hypocrisy, 42

false prophets, 15
  prophesy peace, 325

fear
  of authority, 172
  of his name, 65
  of man, 235
  response to, 276
  superstitious, 79, 281
  temporary, 281
  worship in, 174

fear of God
  choosing, 82
  companions
    faith & hope, 57
    humility, 243
    salvation, 57
  compassion, 102
  devoted to, 106
  end of self-sufficiency, 90
  endurance, 226
  false, 79
  forsaking, 20
  godly, 279
  guide, 172
  hating evil, 163
  healing, 64
  his, 41
  his holiness, 146
  his name, 62, 63
  his presence, 93
  humble us, 275
  in our heart, 83
  maturity, 64
  new songs, 176
  no change, 42
  offends, 220
  paying of vows, 184
  prepares the heart, 206
  protection, 173
  rejoicing in, 174
  removed, 319
  response to the Word, 216
  righteousness, 163, 279

More Abundant Life

rooted in his
    goodness, 175
salvation, 273
Satan hates, 220
seek him, 44
thanksgiving, 184
unbelievers, 184, 272

fellowship
    breaking with
        erring, 156

freedom
    intoxicating, 18
    misunderstood, 96
    restricted, 173
    Satan's, 88

fulfillment, 113

G

G-d, 66

giving
    heart, 186
    how, 187

glory
    given to God, 188
    giving, 181

government of God, 258

grace
    Biblical, 124
    in vain, 264
    understanding, 123

great ones, 266

growing up
    of age, 134

guile, 233

H

habitation
    bounds of, 173

heady, 248

hearing his voice, 325
    fear of God, 87
    growing deafness, 322

heart
    callousness, 87
    divided, 92
    enlarged, 95
    faithful, 106
    friendship, 118
    giving, 186
    hardened, 92
    humble, 90
    idolatry, 31
    integrity, 114
    new, 84
    perfect, 107
    preserved, 104
    pure, 93
    selfless, 101
    servant, 202
    service, 168
    single, 92
    soft, 86
    united, 111
    whole, 113
    willing, 109

holiness
    called to, 144
    demanded by
        adoption, 152
    feared, 147
    practical, 152
    result of fear of
        God, 148

honesty, 114

hour of darkness, 10

house of
    God, 185

hypocrisy, 232

I

infidel, 153

inheriting promises, 228

integrity, 117

J

jealousy, 291

Jeremiah's day
    Babylon, 326
    proud, 181
    provoking God, 131
    spirit of error, 325

Jesus
    bishop of souls, 182
    fighting for, 271
    purity of name, 72

Job
    Eliphaz' folly, 112

judgment
    flee from, 131
    hard things, 221
    our role, 37
    pursue us, 136

K

kingdom of God, 49
    narrow way, 199
    suffer loss, 19

kings & priests, 21

knowing
    by doing, 38

Content Index: Finding a Specific Topic

L

last days, 11, 251

leadership, 236

liberty. *See* freedom

likemindedness, 126

love
 of brethren, 102
 proof of, 102, 215

M

measure of rule, 33

mega-churches, 12, 256

merismos, 116

ministers
 correction, 203
 feared, 147

mixture, 280
 multitude, 233

N

name of the Lord, 70
 intimacy, 69
 suffering for, 73

no fear of God
 Amalek, 242
 covetousness, 185
 lack of holiness, 144
 Michal, 179
 no pity to afflicted, 210
 taking advantage, 240

O

obedience
 incomplete, 109
 marriage with fear, 168
 substitute, 236

offense, 322

once saved, always saved, 125

order
 our steps, 200

oversight, 29, 171, 245, 254, 256, 257

P

paradox, 37
 freedom in serving, 97

peculiar people, 11, 145

pleasing God, 112

politics, 269
 of this world, 133

prayer
 early church, 227

predestinated, 37
 to be conformed, 265

pride, 29, 30, 31, 32, 33
 grip of, 88
 overweening, 43
 self-sufficiency, 172

prophets
 warn, 326

R

redemption, power of, 198

refuge of lies, 137

relationships
 ungodly, 27
 with disobedient, 156

remnant, 131

repentance
 skipped, 175

repentant thief, 243

righteousness
 precedes peace, 327

riotous living, 151

S

sacrifice
 substitute, 48

salvation
 Cornelius, 279

Samarianism, 50

seeker-sensitive movement, 240

self-esteem, 45

self-exaltation, 249

sent forth, 103

serve
 for all eternity, 209
 joyfully, 209

serving
 from heart, 202
 fulfill it, 202
 problems, 210
 unto the Lord, 206

sincerity, 116

snares of death

religious spirit, 176

soberness, 59

sons
  of perdition, 17
  prodigal, 151
  profane, 262, 263

sorcery, 266

soul
  subjection, 171

spirit
  faithful, 165
  filthiness, 152
  good, 159
  new, 84
  obedient, 169
  of disobedience, 250, 325
  of supplanting, 318
  purpose of, 86
  trusting, 221

strait, 80

Strong's, 153

stumbling block, 105

subjection, 171

T

temple, rebuilding, 17

tests
  counsel, 218
  how we pray, 223
  of the word, 216
  persecution, 219
  service, 201
  worship, 176

titles, 254

trembling
  at his word, 217

truth
  dispensational, 320
  in the inmost part, 114, 115

turn it off, 159

U

unto this day, 52

W

way we shall go, 199

weariness
  in mind, 211
  in well-doing, 36

wisdom
  hidden, 50
  of God, 234

worship
  authenticity, 183
  dancing, 179
  for his pleasure, 184
  giving, 180
  holy silence, 45
  ignorant, 50
  lifting hands & head, 177
  merchandized, 182
  place of, 185

Y

Yeshua, 74

The following quotes are from this book concerning the fear of God. They are provided here in summary to help punctuate the importance of God's fear. They are especially useful for rereading on occasion to see if the fear of God is still being treasured in your heart.

Because the fear of the Lord was designed to be in our face, we will see things very differently when we have it. 164

God is looking for more than just obedience! He is looking for the obedience that has the fear of God in it. 109

God's solution to our pride and the spirit of boasting and comparing and judging of others is the fear of God. 88

Great fear of God produces great faithfulness toward God in our service of him. 106

If the beginning of wisdom is the fear of the Lord, then we see that that person who fears not God must be both proud of heart and still filled with their own wisdom, not God's. 88

It is not coincidental that singleness of heart does not exist in the scripture apart from the fear of God, for only the fear of God can make our heart truly single. 84

Jesus was *not* heard in that he was a son! He was heard in that he feared his heavenly Father. 225

Learning the fear of the LORD will be like threading a needle. It will be easy to miss the whole point and end up with nothing, unless there is great care, patience, perseverance, steadiness, and preparation of heart to pursue it. ... 38

Our lack of the fear of God is often evidenced by our partial obedience. When we can pick and choose what parts of God's Word we want to do, then the fear of God is truly missing in us. 170

Our lack of the fear of God is the direct result of putting our desire for comfort, before our need for conviction! 133

The false fear of God and hypocrisy are not only friends they are brethren. 43

The fear of God becomes our lens to stay focused on our Lord and King. 92

The fear of God enables us to love God more than anything else, and it is why we need the spirit of the fear of the LORD so desperately today 252

the fear of God is both the steering wheel of a good conscience and the railing of warning to keep us from going too far and killing ourselves. Grace is the road to salvation and the stairway to heaven, but fear is what keeps us safely on them both. 173

The fear of God is the consciousness of his presence. When we have the fear of God we are astutely aware that the LORD is not only overseeing and watching our actions, but is in fact the inspector and observer of the innermost thoughts of our heart. 93

The fear of God is the missing foundation of how we are to approach God in prayer, and it is the very door by which prayer is heard and answered. 227

The fear of God will never allow us to conceal our sin and not repent. This is the inestimable value of the fear of the Lord, and why it is the salt of the covenant which preserves us. 115

The fear of the LORD is envy's cure. 95

The fear of the LORD must cut away the crust and callousness of our heart and awaken in us a conscience which can be easily pricked. 38

The greater the measure of our fear of God, the greater our ability to hear the voice of the LORD. 327

The true fear of God will cause us to have a soft heart that is sensitive to God's voice, a teachable heart to hearken to his voice, a humble heart that will follow his lead, a correctable heart that is willing to change its direction, and a servant's heart that is desirous to give to the LORD. 87

The true fear of God will cut to a man's heart and expose his evil and selfish desires, giving no place for arrogance and pride to hide. 44

The true understanding of God's grace and forgiveness should not lead to carelessness or smug assurance, as it so often does today. Rather, it should lead to the conviction to fear God continually for what he has done to pay the price for our sin and his rightful demand upon our life to command our obedience. 123

This is the day and hour of deception that we live in. Even those with good hearts who truly love the LORD are being deceived because of the lack of the fear of God in them. 327

This is the message of the fear of the LORD – a removal of our self-sufficiency (i.e. our counsel, wisdom, understanding, and strength) and a dependency on him whom we ought to fear. 90

Those who gain the victory over the beast are those who overcome the world in their life through their fear of God. 147

When pride enters our heart it corrupts the fear of God and turns it into the false fear of God that works in knowledge only, but not in power. 88

Thanksgiving: The Fruit of Our Labors

To produce anything of enduring substance and quality requires great labor, cost, planning, and time. It will involve more than a little uncertainty, knocking and seeking, trying doors, several failures, and of course much faith and patience in order to inherit the blessing of accomplishing the Lord's vision for something. The writing and publishing of this book has been all that and more. I truly expected this work to be in print 5 years before it was. I, myself, have grown through this process and learned many things 'not to do'.

It is with much thanksgiving to God first that he did not give up on me, but continued to instruct, to inspire, and to provoke to finish this work. There were many, many times I was so discouraged with the process, not of writing, but of getting this work published, that I was ready to quit and forget I had ever started such an endeavor. (The joy was truly in the writing of this work and not in the publishing of it.) If anything reflects his glory and his truth in this book, it is to the Lord GOD Almighty and his marvelous Spirit that all praise, honor, and glory are due. Any fault, error, or short-coming is certainly due to me and the limit of the understanding of God's ways to which I have attained. As I am always urging others to do, I myself am continually trying to press on, as it is written, "But grow in grace, and *in* the knowledge of our Lord and Saviour Jesus Christ. To him *be* glory both now and for ever. Amen." 2Pe 3:18

Much of this work was done in secret, in the wee hours of the night, day after day laboring to produce something for God's glory – perfecting, refining, rethinking, rephrasing. Along the way there are always those who as friends and co-workers come alongside at God's set time to fill in the gaps that one person cannot possibly all do. I would thank most of all my wife with whom none of this could have happened. It was her who lent me to the Lord to have the time to do this and who bore the burdens of a home and of children. She has truly shared this vision with me and has, during it, been willing to give up all to glorify the Lord. I thank her from the bottom of my heart. She has the very talents and gifts, which in many areas I lack. She has been a co-laborer at my side, and her excitement for this book has been at times even greater than my own. Thank you wifey!

I would also like to thank New Covenant Christian Center, International. I would not be where I am in the Lord, living for his glory, without all of you. You are my joints and marrow, the very body of Christ to me, and truly you are for his glory! David prays in Psalm 20 that help would be sent him from the sanctuary and he would be strengthened out of Zion (i.e. the congregation of the saints). Truly this has happened many a time in my life through you all. I love you New Covenant. There has never been a body of faithful disciples like you. Stay strong in truth and in righteousness and in the power of his might.

Thanksgiving: The Fruit of Our Labors

Glorify God in your body and in your spirit, for you are the Lord's – you are the apple of his eye! May you come to know how much he truly loves you.

The gratitude in my heart always overflows for Mr. Kim C. Gossett, a true father in the faith, a man like Paul, who has suffered the loss of all things, and has been an example in "doctrine, manner of life, purpose, faith, longsuffering, charity, patience, persecutions, [and] afflictions" (2Tim 3:10-11). Without you as my friend I would still be lost and wandering in the mire of Christianity. It is because of you and your heart to raise and train men of God, that the kingdom was manifest to me so long ago on my first journey to Kenya, Africa, at your side. Thank you for showing me the world through Jesus' eyes! My journeys to the nations with you have been the fulfillment of my heart. Though not involved directly in the book, the meat of what is here, the teaching of righteousness, the call to holiness, the exposing of the doctrines and traditions of men is because of the endless hours of preaching, counsel, and godly exhortation that you continually give out. May the Lord continue to strengthen you and those at your side as you build the kingdom of God one soul at a time.

Many thanks to those of you my friends who diligently took the time to read the book and review it for me and gave me your insights and criticisms. Many were unwilling or too busy, but those who did have my abundant thanks. I am thankful for your love and honesty and your commitment to help, but most of all that you love Jesus in spirit and in truth. Ros, an especial thanks to you. You took on this project as if it were your own. Your labor helped keep this project alive.

Special thanks go to "For His Glory" and all the hours you spent laying the foundation for the book cover. I owe you a debt of love and thanks, Raymund and Michelle. I can't wait until you are doing full-time what you have been called to do 'for his glory'. Magnus, thank you so much for your attention to detail and the great artwork. It has been a true pleasure working with you. You helped in many ways. Dan, you were one of those whom God brings in at the last minute to save the day. Thank you for doing all the layout adjustments and fine tuning. It never could have been printed without you. Last of all I thank Jason, a man of great humility and servitude, without whose help just at the right time, this work would still just be in a computer and not in print.

Chapter photos from Dreamstime and Photos.com
with explicit rights and permissions

Cover art and graphic design by Magnus Andersson
of Innervision Design Inc.

Cover layout and fine-tuning by Dan Snyder

An Epilogue: A Spirit of Supplanting

Often we may desire more of the Spirit, but when we listen to 'anointed' men or women, what we so often get is the spirit of supplanting. Instead of the testimony of the word of God, we often get the testimony of men, their views, interpretations, opinions, experiences, dreams, and even traditions – all of which subtly supplant the word of God.

> 'Supplant' in the scripture is a powerful word which means 'to *swell out or up*; to *seize by the heel*; fig. to *circumvent* (as if *tripping* up the heels); also to *restrain* (as if holding by the heel)'.

When the word of God is supplanted by men's testimonies of their experiences it produces a swelling up of the individual, both in their eyes and in those who hear him. Your attention is focused on what God did in their life. Your eyes are restrained from being fixed on Jesus as they should (Heb 12:2-3), and sadly the power of the word of God is circumvented, rather than released into your life. The supplanting of God's word always causes the hearers to be tripped up and held back in their walk with the Lord, so that growth and forward progress is halted! The awe that should be toward God only is subtly supplanted onto men.

Remember, you are *never* called in your life to build off of what a man says or **even** what he has experienced. So many do that very thing today. They build their life off of the miraculous testimonies of a man, but it is not permitted by God. Even the Jerusalem council to decide the fate of the Gentiles concerning circumcision could not rest on the true Holy Ghost supplied miracles that had taken place through the hands of Paul and Barnabas or even the salvations that had come through Peter. NO, the issue was still not settled for all these true signs and wonders. Only the scripture that was revealed to James finally settles the matter. It was not until these words were spoken that the issue was confirmed: "And to this agree the words of the prophets; <u>as it is written</u>" (Ac 15:15). We can only build our life off of the word of God, for Jesus Christ who is the Word made flesh, is the only foundation upon which we can build (1Co 3:11). We may receive miracles as being done by the Holy Ghost, yet what they mean or what action we should then take, still must wait upon the confirmation of the word, even as we see the early church doing. This is the church's true foundation: the scriptures.

> The fear of God is not some added grace we need to achieve.
> It is an innate grace given to us in the new birth,
> which we must not lose!

If we truly desire the things of the Spirit, then let us desire the first work of the Spirit. Let us earnestly desire that which we need most: "the spirit ... of the fear of the LORD." Isa 11:2 This was the very spirit that anointed Jesus and was upon him in whose footsteps we need to follow. It is the spirit of the fear of the LORD that will truly open up the realm of the Spirit to us, for the Spirit of truth will guide us into all truth (Jn 16:13). He will glorify Jesus, who is the word of God. The true Spirit of God will always lead us to the word so that we may drink and be satisfied. Thus as we have seen, the spirit of the fear of the LORD will bring us into *spiritual* knowledge (Isa 11:2).

The fear of the LORD is the root of knowledge, might, counsel, understanding, and wisdom – all that the saint needs to overcome in this life. When the Comforter comes to take residence in us, he, by his very presence, brings with him the fear of God, because he *is* the spirit of the fear of the LORD. The Spirit of God, therefore, plants or *births* the fear of the LORD in us when he comes to indwell us. God's word now waters and suckles God's fear in us, as we receive it as it is in truth, the word of God and not the word of men (1Th 2:13). We must understand: The fear of God is not some added grace we need to achieve. It is an innate grace given to us in the new birth, which we must not lose!

Those who Extract the Fear of God from our Hearts

As with most everything else in our walk with God, the fear of God must be nurtured and developed for it to grow, but it was initially planted there by the Spirit of life. Woe be to any man therefore that removes from our heart this foundational root! We are warned, "Remove not the ancient landmark, which thy [*fore*]fathers have set." Pr 22:28

Where is the Fear of GOD? Losing the Treasure of the Lord

The problem is many behind pulpits today are NOT truly born again. Remember, becoming born again does NOT take place by merely believing in Jesus. The demons believe and they tremble (Jam 2:19), but they are not saved. We must confess Jesus as Lord of our life (Rom 10:9), that is the doorway of salvation. Of those pastors and teachers who are born again, many have put away the fear of God and few have ever been discipled in kingdom principles, so that in all respects God says they are babes who are "unskilful in the word of righteousness." Heb 5:13 Rare is the man of God today who knows and teaches the kingdom of God from the foundation of the doctrine of Christ. Today men think that a Bible College can train them for ministry. They take pride in what they have learned from men, rather than being humbled by what they have learned from no man, but by the Spirit of God.

One doctrine taught in many seminaries is "dispensational truth". This doctrine has brought about much false doctrine into the Lord's church. God has declared under the old covenant already that "I *am* the LORD, I change not" (Mal 3:6). It would be a great mistake to think that God has changed in the new covenant, for that would make God a liar. No, God has not changed, and how he deals with man has not changed. Truth does not change. It is eternal. Jesus had to deal with dispensationalists his entire ministry, and they always *resisted* the truth he brought forth, because of their narrow way of compartmentalizing the word of God and even God himself. Thus, Jesus rebuked them saying, "Ye do err, not knowing the scriptures, nor the power of God." Mt 22:29

There were several dispensationalists Jesus had to deal with. The main dispensationalists were the Sadducees. They picked and chose what parts of the Bible they would believe. "For the Sadducees say that there is no resurrection, neither angel, nor spirit" (Ac 23:8). The Samaritans were also dispensationalists. They only believed the first five books of the Bible, the Pentateuch.[214]

> **WARNING:** We are filled today with the same Saduceean and Samaritan spirit of dispensationalists: those who will not believe in speaking in tongues, the baptism of the Holy Ghost, in apostles and prophets, in miracles, in God judging his own people, and in the true fear of God, which is in trembling before the Almighty! Be careful that you are not caught up in denying the word of God, by attempting to segregate God's works into separate time periods and putting God into a theogolically convenient box (Mk 10:9).

Bible colleges are a contradiction in terms, for though they call themselves *Bible* colleges, yet it seems they study every book BUT the Bible. "Ministers" are produced by the thousands who in truth know nothing of discipleship for

---

[214] In the same spirit today, many of the modern bible versions use the Samaritan Pentateuch to interpret the Old Testament books of Moses, instead of using the Hebrew manuscripts ordained by God.

An Epilogue: A Spirit of Supplanting

their own life, nor do they have a true understanding of servanthood and its requirements. So how can they "minister" by example when they have never learned to serve? How can they teach "them to <u>observe</u> all things whatsoever I have commanded you" (Mt 28:20), if there is no true example to observe? Yet these are the very first things Jesus taught to those who followed him. We are in a worse situation than that of the writer to the Hebrews, for it cannot even be said today of so many in major ministries,

> For when for the time ye ought to be teachers, ye have need that one <u>teach you again</u> which *be* the first principles of the oracles of God; and are become such as have need of milk, and not of strong meat. Heb 5:12

The Hebrews had at least been taught "the first principles of the oracles of God" at one time. The rebuke that was brought to them was that they had forgotten this foundation. They had to be <u>taught again</u> because they had left this foundation and become "dull of hearing" (Heb 5:11). Such can hardly even be said of so many preachers and teachers today, for they have never been taught these things in the first place, but rather have been filled with the views, opinions, and doctrines of men! The spirit of the Pharisees, the Sadducees, and the Herodians is alive and flourishing in Christianity today. Many have never come to know the narrow way of the kingdom. There are many preachers today who excel in comfort and in smooth words, but God's people are not being raised into spiritual maturity. They are being kept as spiritual babes.

Novocain is being fed to many a young saint and killing their in-born desire for holiness, obedience, and the fear of God. These godly graces are instead being supplanted by pride, covetousness, and hypocrisy. Many today at one time truly had a pure heart and a true faith in God, but because of a lack of sound discipleship and the spiritual principles on how to grow up have left a good conscience and walk with the Lord no more or they walk alone. Paul warns us about these very things: "for they will increase unto more ungodliness" (2Tim 2:16). We end up being taught from teachers who have no true fear of God working in them, either because the spirit of the fear of the LORD does not even dwell in them or because they have forsaken a good conscience and thereby put away the fear of the Lord.

Hymenaeus and Alexander were such men in Paul's day. "Holding faith, and a good conscience; which some having put away concerning faith have made shipwreck: Of whom is Hymenaeus and Alexander" (1Tim 1:19-20). Note, they did not put away faith, for they still taught people about Jesus and to believe in him, and were still ministers of the gospel. They were even convinced they were right! But they took faith and made it run aground and sink because it was not portered and protected by a good conscience. When confronted by correction from Paul through the word of God, they put away a good conscience and would not listen. So is the present state of so many ministers in

Laodicean America. They do not have a good conscience to hear the word of God and be corrected through another servant of God.

> **WARNING**: I have noticed all too often a disturbing trend in older Christians. As one grows in true grace, knowledge, and love,[215] though we should grow in assurance and boldness in the truth, yet we should also grow in a depth of humility and a willingness to be corrected by the word of God. This humility should be ensured because we know that 'what we have' we have received from the Lord, not of ourselves, nor from any man. As Paul wrote, "But we have this treasure in earthen vessels, that the excellency of the power may be <u>of God,</u> and <u>not of us.</u>" 2Co 4:7 Real growth does not come from us. One may plant and another water, but God gives the increase. "So then neither is he that planteth <u>any thing</u>, neither he that watereth; but God that giveth the increase." 1Co 3:7 And no matter how much we grow we are still nothing! We deceive ourselves if we think otherwise. "For if a man think himself to be something, when he is <u>nothing</u>, he deceiveth himself." Gal 6:3

Where are the noble Bereans today who will receive the word with all <u>readiness</u> of mind and search the scriptures daily to see whether those things which they have heard are so (Ac 17:11)? Rare is the older Christian that is able to hear truth from the word of God by another brother, which they have not heard already. Instead of growing softer to the voice of the Lord and being able to hear the word more readily, so often those whom others consider more 'mature' Christians, because of their knowledge, have less of an ear to hear truth than the newborn believer. This is a tragedy of the highest order and shows that so many are *not* growing in the true grace of God which ought to more and more humble us. As Paul warned the Corinthians, "we know that we all have knowledge. Knowledge <u>puffeth up</u>, but charity edifieth." 1Co 8:1 All of this would be kept in check, if only the fear of God was the companion of the grace of God in our heart.

Not Being Offended, But Willing to Offend
"Though all men shall be offended because of thee,
yet will I never be offended." Mt 26:33

Darkness will increase in the last days, yet at the same time knowledge will be increased, and "many shall run to and fro" (Dan 12:4). We live in a time when busyness marks the Christian's life and though we are to be busy about our Father's business, we are never to forget "one thing is needful" (Lk 10:42) – to sit at the feet of Jesus and to hear the instruction of our Lord (v39). In the darkness and wickedness of these last days God's people rarely take time to

---

[215] We're to grow in grace, knowledge, & love: 2Pe 3:18 & Eph 4:15, 1Th 3:12, 2Th 1:3.

consider the glory of the LORD and few today truly have an ear to hear the authority of his word. O, the masses flock to mega-churches seemingly to hear from God but they are not fed the word that brings reformation, correction, and chastisement for true growth in godliness. They are not being fed the pure word of God at all, for they are not being corrected.[216] They are being wooed into a feel-good deception that will ultimately bring them under the judgment of God. "Correction *is* grievous unto him that forsaketh the way: *and* he that hateth reproof shall die." Pr 15:10

Jeremiah lived in such a day as ours where the vast majority of those who called themselves God's people "received no correction" (Jer 2:30):

> *but* they have refused to receive correction: they have made their faces harder than a rock; they have refused to return.[217] Jer 5:3

> But thou shalt say unto them, This *is* a nation that obeyeth not the voice of the LORD their God, nor receiveth correction: truth is perished, and is cut off from their mouth. Jer 7:28

Mega-pastors will not speak the fullness of the truth of God's word, for it is cut off from their mouth. To do so would destroy their kingdom and financially plunge them into ruin. Why can we be so sure that the masses would flee, if the word of truth was ministered in power to bring proper correction? Because Jesus said this is the most common response to the word of God who initially believe.

> And these are they likewise which are sown on stony ground; who, when they have heard the word, immediately receive it <u>with gladness</u>; And have no root in themselves, and so endure but for a time: afterward, when affliction or persecution ariseth <u>for the word's sake</u>, <u>immediately they are offended</u>. Mk 4:16-17

Jesus, as the true servant of God, unlike so many who are leading large ministries, was willing to lose all those that followed him over the issues of truth and obedience to the word of his Father. He purposefully brought offense through his Father's word many times. People were repeatedly offended at Jesus and his words. "And they were <u>offended in him</u>" (Mt 13:57). Even Jesus' disciples were amazed at how willing Jesus was to offend others. "Then came his disciples, and said unto him, Knowest thou that the Pharisees were <u>offended</u>, after they heard this saying?" Mt 15:12 He had to offend even his own disciples. "Then saith Jesus unto them, All ye shall be <u>offended because of me</u> this night" (Mt 26:31/Mk 14:27).

---

[216] In the appendix entitled "Definition of Some Biblical Terms" under the description of 'Bishops & Pastors: Understanding the Office & Function', see the subsection 'Bishop Ministry: The Need for Correction'.

[217] This word 'return' in the Hebrew means 'to *turn* back or away' and carries the Old Testament concept of repentance.

When Jesus truly told his disciples what they needed to do in order to follow him, many were offended. "When Jesus knew in himself that his disciples murmured at it, he said unto them, Doth this <u>offend you</u>?" Jn 6:61 Jesus never shied away from bringing offense. Better to offend people, than to offend God by not openly speaking the truth. If we are to truly follow Jesus, the test is that we must be willing to overlook what we are offended by and allow the truth to cut to our heart. So said Jesus even to John the Baptist, "And blessed is *he*, whosoever shall not be <u>offended in me</u>." Lk 7:23 All will be put to the test in this. Will we be offended and walk away, as those in Jesus' day? "From that *time* many of his disciples went back, and walked no more with him." Jn 6:66

Few indeed will allow themselves to come under God's correction and chastening when it comes through an earthly messenger. Many people will swear they are correctable and that they receive God's instruction, yet when put to the actual test of whether they will submit to God's word or not, they fail. But God defines our sonship by whether we receive correction with a good heart or not. "My son, <u>despise not</u> the chastening of the LORD; <u>neither be weary</u> of his correction: For whom the LORD loveth he correcteth; even as a father the son *in whom* he delighteth." Pr 3:11-12 God, in particularly, proves our obedience and submission by how we respond to the servant of the Lord who brings us the word of correction. This is the unchanging pattern of scripture. This is why the prophets of the Old and the apostles of the New, as messengers of God who brought God's word to His people were beaten, abused, stoned, driven from cities, and killed. Over my years in ministry this is the single greatest proof of whether we are truly God's obedient children or are in fact under our own authority: how well do we receive spiritual correction from men.

Few today want to talk about the sufferings, the persecutions, the afflictions that the true life of following the Lord brings, but Paul did not hesitate to warn the disciples of such things. In fact, it was how he confirmed or *'further supported'* and *reestablished'* their souls. "Confirming the souls of the disciples, *and* exhorting them to continue in the faith, and that <u>we must through much tribulation</u> enter into the kingdom of God." Ac 14:22 Note that Paul supported and reestablished the souls of the disciples not by placating their souls with the blessings of God, but rather with the warnings that we must endure much tribulation, if we are to enter into the kingdom of God and not turn back from it.

Note also that Paul did not say we may or might go through these tribulations, nor that we should go through them, but rather that we **must** go through them. Notice how immediately after exhorting Timothy that if we live godly in Christ Jesus we will certainly suffer persecution, he immediately warns him about those who teach otherwise: those evil men and seducers who being deceived will in turn deceive many. "Yea, and all that will live godly in Christ Jesus shall suffer persecution. But evil men and seducers shall wax worse and worse, deceiving, and being deceived." 2Tim 3:12-13

An Epilogue: A Spirit of Supplanting

Jesus warned his disciples repeatedly to properly prepare their hearts so that they would not be offended and walk away. The true Jesus is not interested in wooing people into a false delusion that the way of the cross is easy and full of blessings. "These things have I spoken unto you, that ye should <u>not be offended</u>." Jn 16:1 What things did Jesus tell his disciples? That we should suffer for his sake! That we would be hated and persecuted, not loved if we followed Jesus in truth and held fast to his name. Why? Because we are NOT of the world or like the world. Lastly, he shared with them that "if they have kept my saying, they will keep yours also." (Jn 15:18-20) The true test of whether people obey and submit to God is not what they say they will do or even how they may appear to submit and obey on their own terms. Jesus told his disciples that they would know if people were really keeping Jesus' sayings if they keep the sayings of discipled men of God who speak the word of God in truth.

The Key to Hearing God's Voice

"The voice of the LORD is upon the waters: the God of glory thundereth: the LORD is upon many waters." Ps 29:3

The Spirit of God rarely speaks to us (except about our sin) unless our heart is set on obedience. Men whose hearts have departed from obedience to the Lord for a long time will hear from the spirit, but not the Holy Spirit. The spirit they will hear from will be the deceiving spirit of error, which is the spirit of disobedience "that **now** worketh in the children of disobedience." Eph 2:2 Such was the case with Hananiah the prophet in Jeremiah's day. This man prophesied great swelling words of blessing and peace, promising liberty (2Pe 2:18-19). Consider this, he spoke these things in the *house* of the LORD to the *people* of the LORD in the *name* of the LORD, yet the LORD had not spoken to him!

Jeremiah lays down the principle of false prophets which we would do well to heed today. It was the **standard** that true prophets do not generally prophesy blessings, but rather warn of judgments. False prophets on the other hand do the opposite. Jeremiah thus states,

> The prophets that have been before me and before thee of old prophesied both against many countries, and against great kingdoms, of war, and of evil, and of pestilence. The prophet which prophesieth of peace, when the word of the prophet shall come to pass, then shall the prophet be known, that the Lord hath truly sent him. Jer 28:8-9

Hananiah contradicted the word which Jeremiah spoke by the Spirit of God saying that <u>his</u> words, not Jeremiah's were truly inspired. Hananiah had his great drama of breaking the yoke that Jeremiah had put around his neck, yet Jeremiah says of this prophet, "Hear now, Hananiah; The LORD hath not sent thee; but thou makest this people <u>to trust in a lie</u>." Jer 28:15 Even though all that Hananiah spoke of was blessing toward God's people, yet Jeremiah states that he actually "taught rebellion against the LORD." Jer 28:16 This will only increase in the last days where "prophets of God" will continue to speak blessings in the name of the LORD in the house of God, yet God has not sent them, and they will make people trust in a lie, rather than in the whole counsel of God's word.

> **WARNING**: So it is today, we have so many false prophets that prophesy of their blessings unto a disobedient and gainsaying people, and God is not pleased. Many like the children of Jeremiah's day are being taken captive by the world (i.e. Babylon) and are serving its king (the King of Babylon). The true prophetic message has always been to warn God's people and to prepare a holy people who obey the living God. Rarely has it been to merely proclaim blessings. Remember, even the prophets in the New Testament are always prophesying of impending judgments, trials, and sorrows![218] This is a far cry from the 'personal prophecies' for 'personal blessings' that we are hearing of today.

We see a similar conflict arise between the two prophets: Micaiah the son of Imlah and Zedekiah the son of Chenaanah. Zedekiah prophesied unto the kings of Israel and Judah, Ahab and Jehoshaphat, great blessing and victory in their upcoming battle. But Micaiah prophesied of great defeat and shame. O how the people of God today will be put to the test by such things! So many would side with Zedekiah, claiming the word of God as their promise: "But thanks *be* to God, which giveth us the victory through our Lord Jesus Christ." 1Co 15:57 Yet it was Micaiah that truly spoke from the LORD. Again, we see the drama from the false prophet, for he made horns to push the enemy back (1K 22:11). But Micaiah explains that the LORD had put a lying spirit in the mouth of all of Ahab's prophets (v23). Again, we see the indignant rebuke from the false prophet toward the true:

> But Zedekiah the son of Chenaanah went near, and smote Micaiah on the cheek, and said, Which way went the Spirit of the LORD from me to speak unto thee? And Micaiah said, Behold, thou shalt see in that day, when thou shalt go into an inner chamber to hide thyself. 1K 22:24-25

Such things ought to bring great warning and soberness to us today. So many want to hear the blessings of the LORD, but have no ear to take warning and to receive correction. The great movements that look like they are of God today are producing subjects of Ahab: those who love to hear the great report of how God will deliver, but who have no ear to hear the word of correction.

---

[218] It cannot be of insignificance, then, that the *only* example of New Testament prophets actually speaking a prophecy are those from Agabus the prophet. We must use him as the normative example of what born again prophets ought to prophesy concerning. We see he prophesies of the great dearth that was to come upon the whole world (Ac 11:27-28) so that the disciples might be prepared. Again, we see him prophesy to Paul of his sufferings that await him in Jerusalem (Ac 21:10-11) so that Paul might be warned. We see an obvious lack of the 'bless-me, bless-me' prophecies of today.

An Epilogue: A Spirit of Supplanting

Sadly, even godly Jehoshaphat could not hear the true word of the LORD that brought correction! That evidences how far his own heart had compromised the truth. This is the day and hour of deception that we live in. Even those with good hearts who truly love the LORD are being deceived because of the lack of the fear of God in them. We must recapture the grace of the fear of the Lord.

The Spirit of God desires greatly to speak to his people, but before he can speak of comfort, peace, and blessing, he must fulfill his first ministry and calling. The Spirit's first calling is to *reprove* the worldliness that is still in us. This worldliness is regarding our sin, regarding our lack of righteousness in following the Lord Jesus, and regarding the judgment which is to come upon the children of disobedience (Jn 16:8-14, Eph 2:2, 5:6, Col 3:6).

Everyone desires to hear of peace and comfort, but the **work** of righteousness *is* peace (Isa 32:17). If we do not hearken to his commandments, we cannot have God's peace (Isa 48:18). Thus, he must lead us into righteousness before he can lead us into peace, for righteousness always precedes true peace. This is why the kingdom of God is first righteousness, second peace, and third joy (Rom 14:17). This is why Paul exhorts Timothy to follow after righteousness, faith, charity, and then peace (2Tim 2:22). Notice the order: first righteousness, then faith, then charity, and lastly peace. Those who seek peace without righteousness, faith, and charity will always end up deceived and in possession of a false peace.

Now the Spirit of God desires to lead us into righteousness, but we must be willing to be led. It is difficult for the Holy Ghost to speak to the rebellious because they are not listening. They have stopped up their ears.

> But they <u>refused to hearken</u>, and pulled away the shoulder, and <u>stopped their ears</u>, that they should not hear. Yea, they made their hearts *as* an adamant stone, lest they should hear the law, and the words which the LORD of hosts hath sent in his spirit by the former prophets: therefore came a great wrath from the LORD of hosts. Zec 7:11-12

God's people truly need to hear the voice of God in the last days. The key then to hearing is the willingness to hear and obey, but this only comes from the fear of God. The greater the measure of our fear of God, the greater will be our ability to hear the voice of the LORD. "What man *is* he that feareth the LORD? <u>him</u> shall he teach in the way *that* he shall choose." Ps 25:12 The fear of God will enable us to continually be taught by the Lord which way he would have us to go. The fear of God is the preserving salt of our heart. First, because the fear of God enables us to depart from iniquity, and second, because it opens our ears to hear which way we should go. Thus, the fear of God is the key to hearing his excellent voice and preparing us for his return. God's fear is so needed in these last days before the coming judgments of our God and King.

*"And I say unto you my friends,
Be not afraid of them that kill the body,
and after that have no more that they can do.
But I will forewarn you whom ye shall fear:* **Fear him**,
*which after he hath killed hath power to cast into hell;
yea, I say unto you,* **Fear him.**" *Lk 12:4-5*

An Epilogue: A Spirit of Supplanting

Resources: Table for the Hungry

If you are looking for more sound Biblical teaching centered around the kingdom of God and not from the doctrines of men, please enjoy these teachings and materials. Proceeds from these resources go to New Covenant World Outreach which feeds the poor, clothes the naked, visits those in prisons & hospitals, and preaches the kingdom of God around the world.

Books/Booklets

Where is the Fear of GOD? Finding the Treasure of the Lord
Where is the Fear of GOD? Losing the Treasure of the Lord
The Gospels in Concert: Putting the 4 Gospels in Divine Order
The Epistles in Concert: Putting Acts & the Epistles in Divine Order
Christianity versus the Kingdom of God
The Growing Process [a chart]

Tape Series

Christianity vs. the Kingdom of God
The Pillars of the New Covenant
Discerning Soul from Spirit
The Healing of the Heart
The Fatherhood of God
Learning to Overcome
Hope Set Before Us
A Place of Refuge
Consider Jesus
Heart Care

Contact

Let us know of your desire or need and we will get back to you as soon as we can. To contact us you may email us at info@MoreAbundantLife.com or feel free to visit us at www.MoreAbundantLife.com to learn more. There you can order the tape series. Find the latest news about how our ministry in Kenya is going by visiting our blog: KingomMinistryInKenya.BlogSpot.com. Mail correspondence is via: More Abundant Life, P.O. Box 24526, San Jose, CA 95154.

www.ingramcontent.com/pod-product-compliance
Lightning Source LLC
Chambersburg PA
CBHW070655100426
42735CB00039B/2000